REGISTER OF MARRIAGES AND BAPTISMS

PERFORMED BY

REV. JOHN CUTHBERTSON

REGISTER OF MARRIAGES AND BAPTISMS

PERFORMED BY

REV. JOHN CUTHBERTSON

COVENANTER MINISTER

1751-1791

WITH

INDEX TO LOCATIONS AND PERSONS VISITED

By

S. HELEN FIELDS

CLEARFIELD

Reprinted for
Clearfield Company by
Genealogical Publishing Co.
Baltimore, Maryland
1996, 1998, 2008

ISBN-13: 978-0-8063-1047-3
ISBN-10: 0-8063-1047-2

Originally published: Washington, D.C., 1934
Reprinted by Genealogical Publishing Company
Baltimore, Maryland, 1983
Library of Congress Catalogue Card Number 83-81655

Made in the United States of America

TABLE OF CONTENTS

	Page
INTRODUCTION	vii–xv
ILLUSTRATIONS	xvii–xxiv

PERSONS VISITED:

Marriages	3–15
Baptisms	19–57
Others	263–284; 285–301

PLACES VISITED:

Index of	61–65
Connecticut	261
Delaware	240–241
Maryland	242–243
Massachusetts	259–260
New Jersey	243–245
New York	246–259
Pennsylvania	69–240

QUOTATIONS	67–261; 285–301

INTRODUCTION

Rev. John Cuthbertson was born near Ayr, Ayrshire, Scotland, April 3, 1718. Reference to his birthday is made by him in his Diary from year to year, the first one on April 3, 1753, as follows:

"Birthday—entering me into the 35th year of life from 1718."

His parents were devout members of the persecuted Church of Scotland; his early instruction was under private tutors; his Theological studies under Rev. John McMillan, who, with Rev. Thomas Nairn, a Ruling Elder, constituted the Reformed Presbytery of Scotland, which was organized in 1743. By this Court he was licensed on May 16, 1745, and ordained at Braehead on May 18, 1747, ministering to the Covenanters in Scotland. Baptisms solemnized by him in 1747 and 1748 are recorded on page 65 of the Register of Rev. John McMillan,(*) as edited by Rev. Henry Paton, M.A., of Scotland.(†) While Moderator of this Presbytery, Doctor Cuthbertson was sent to minister to the scattered Covenanters in Ireland, but because of the earnest entreaties of the Scottish Covenanters in America for an Under Shepherd, he was sent to this country in 1751, the first Reformed Presbyterian Missionary to come to America. Of him, Dr. W. E. McCulloch says:

"Verily John Cuthbertson was one of God's noblemen, a true hero of the cross. He is representative of the heroic home missionaries of that day, expert workmen in the task of empire building, to whom our and all other churches of Christ owe a debt incalculable."

* In Doctor McMillan's Register we note the following Cuthbertsons, some of whom no doubt belong to the immediate family of Rev. John Cuthbertson:

In 1716 (page 19), the baptism of Agnes, born May 27, 1716, to John Cuthbertson in Walston.

In 1720 (page 24), the baptism of Helene, born June 4, 1720, to John Cuthbertson in Dunsyre.

In 1722 (page 26), the baptism of Margaret, March 28, 1722, to John Cuthbertson in Libberton.

In 1724 (page 32), baptized Thomas, April 25, 1724, to John Cuthbertson in Libberton.

At Braehead, December 17, 1743, Alexander Kirkland and Elizabeth Cuthbertson, both in Kilmarnock parish, were married by Rev. John McMillan.

† Index by S. Helen Fields.

From Edinburg, Scotland, Mr. Cuthbertson wrote a letter on February 22, 1745, to his sister Margaret at their home in Greenback, Bunolo. This is reproduced on pages xx and xxii. A History of the Church of Scotland was brought to America with him, and contains his signature on the first page, a facsimile of which will be found on page xxiv. This History was the work of David Calderwood at the appointment of the General Assembly, and is "The True History of the Church of Scotland From the beginning of the Reformation, unto the end of the Reign of King James VI." While on a recent trip to Waynesboro, Franklin County, the writer was shown this ancient book by Mrs. Jacob H. Stoner, in whose possession it now is. It is bound in sheepskin and is 8 by 12 inches. After this trip Mrs. Stoner was going carefully through the volume, page by page, and in it discovered the letter to his sister referred to in the beginning of this paragraph.

A Diary was kept by Doctor Cuthbertson from the date he landed in America in 1751, when thirty-three years of age, up to a short time before his death, which occurred in his seventy-third year. His first entry in the Diary is as follows:

"After being forty-six days, twenty and six-tenth hours at sea from London Derry Loch, landed safely at Newcastle August 5th, 1751, about eight in the forenoon. . . ."

The Diary of Rev. John Cuthbertson is a personal record, containing, in addition to his entries of marriages, baptisms, etc., many expressions of intimate family life, and abbreviations for his own information. From this he no doubt gathered his data for church reports. We find in it the names of the families to whom he ministered, many of them having lived in America from 1720, and earlier; it gives the names of families coming to America with and after him. From his entries, during his ministry he married approximately 600 persons and baptized more than 1800 children. Over 5,000 different families is a conservative estimate of the number mentioned by Mr. Cuthbertson. The book itself is four and one-half inches long by three and one-half inches broad, and a little over an inch thick. It is bound in soft, brown vellum. His handwriting is wonderfully clear and the book well preserved, showing disintegration only where bound to the cover. (See page xvii.)

In tracing its history, information has recently been received from Mrs. Mary D. Sinclair and her sister, Mrs. Florence Donaldson Henderson, of Steubenville, Ohio, that the Diary of Rev. John

Cuthbertson passed into the hands of Mrs. Rebecca Buchanan Junkin, their Grandmother, because of her descent from representative families in his Societies. This was left, it is believed, at one of their homes, where he was thought to have died. Mrs. Junkin suffered a fractured leg in her old age, and while confined to her room made a copy of the Diary, contained in two large volumes. Thereafter, in 1896, Dr. Joseph Buchanan, a cousin of Mrs. Sinclair, thought it wise to place the Diary in the then Allegheny, Pa., Theological Seminary for safe keeping. Dr. Wm. M. Glasgow states in his Church History, published in 1888, that he had the loan of the original Diary from Mrs. Junkin. Revs. A. S. Aiken and J. N. Adair gathered vital statistics from it for their sketch of Rev. John Cuthbertson, published in 1878. Whether these gentlemen also made copies of it is not known, but it would have been difficult for them to have accomplished what they did without doing so.

Mss. copies of the original Diary of Rev. John Cuthbertson are to be found in several places: The earliest one of record is that made by Mrs. Junkin, and now in Steubenville, Ohio. One was made in 1914 by William H. McNaugher, son of the President of the Pittsburgh Theological Seminary (formerly the Allegheny Theological Seminary, and now (1933) the Pittsburgh-Xenia Theological Seminary). A carbon copy of this is retained in the Seminary, as is also a transcription of it by the writer. From these other copies have been made. One is in the Library of the State Historical Society at Harrisburg, Pa., and one, with complete index by the writer, in the Library of the National Society of the Daughters of the American Revolution, Washington, D. C. One was presented to the Library of the Genealogical Society of Pennsylvania, Philadelphia, Pa., by Mr. Albert L. Hood of that city, on September 8, 1914, apparently the original of the copy in the Pittsburgh-Xenia Theological Seminary. A Mr. Nilson, deceased, of Chambersburg, Pa., had copies typed some years ago, and the one at Harrisburg is believed to be from one of his copies.

Interesting medical prescriptions were inserted by Rev. John Cuthbertson in the back of his Diary, several of which are cited here:

"*The famous American Receipt for the Rheumatism.*

"Take of garlic two cloves, of gum ammoniac, one drachm; blend them by bruising together. Make them into two or three bolus's with fair water and swallow one at night and the other in the morning. Drink strong sassafras tea while using these. It vanishes also contraction of the joints."

"100 pounds have been given for this."

"*Ague: to cure.*

"Take a large spoonful of flour brimstone in a gill of mountain wine the moment the fit seizeth. If this cure not, repeat, with fit."

"*Worms: to kill.*

"Take teaspoonful Alum, another of Link powder; grind fine, mix, divide into 3; sweeten, give every other morning. P. E."

The Scottish Covenanters were to be found in the Cumberland Valley region as early as 1720. They settled principally along the Conococheague Creek; the Octoraro; Pequea; Conestoga; Swatara and other streams flowing from the east into the Susquehanna. This valley extends in a southerly direction from Harrisburg, Pa., into Maryland and Virginia. It was the practice of the Covenanters to organize themselves, as in Scotland, into Societies or Correspondences among those living in the same general localities. These met annually or semi-annually as a Presbytery, known as "The General Meeting." Mr. Cuthbertson presided over these meetings, usually held at Middle Octoraro, from 1751 until 1774, when the Reformed Presbytery of America was organized and Revs. Matthew Linn and Alexander Dobbin took over some of his heavy responsibilities.

The principal Society of Rev. John Cuthbertson was at Middle Octoraro, Lancaster County, Pa. At this place he bought a farm from "Josias Kerr" on January 24, 1757 (p. 142), about a year after his marriage to Miss Sally Moore, one of the daughters of Walter Moore, whose home was about fifteen miles from Philadelphia, on the Pennypack Creek. This farm is located about two miles from the stone church in which he often preached. Here he maintained his home during the remainder of his life. It is now owned by Mr. Frank J. Trout, who has lived here with his family for over thirty years. The original stone house, with its twenty-two inch walls, forms the center, an addition having been added on either side. The entrance door contains the original barn-door hinges. The whole place presents a modern appearance, and is most attractive. It is not difficult, however, to picture in one's mind how it must have looked in the early days. We find here also the ancient barn of stone, and peering into its vast interior one can almost hear the voice of Mr. Cuthbertson as he talks to his favorite horses—

Rapha, Courage, Race, Bess, Kennet, Snip, Tib, etc. A picture of the home (page xvii) was taken by Rev. Wm. M. Anderson of Philadelphia, who, with Mrs. Anderson and the writer, made a trip to Middle Octoraro in June, 1930. In this home Mr. Cuthbertson's three children were reared—Sarah, John and Walter. Walter was born June 12, 1769, and died when a little over twenty years of age. He is buried in Middle Octoraro Graveyard. John, born March 21, 1764, became a physician and lived and practiced in West Middletown, Pa., until his death on September 27, 1827, in his 63rd year. Mr. Cuthbertson purchased the farm on which his son John lived, and refers to it in his Diary as his "plantation." Sarah, the only daughter, born May 21, 1762, kept house for her brother, and after the death of Mr. Cuthbertson, the mother made her home with them. Mrs. Cuthbertson, referred to in the Diary as "Sally" and "Y," died on January 10, 1807; Sarah, the daughter, on March 23, 1836, aged 73 yrs. None of Doctor Cuthbertson's children married. His son John, his daughter, and Mrs. Cuthbertson are buried in Lower Buffalo Graveyard, Independence Township, Washington County, Pa., which was erected in 1795. The writer is indebted to Rev. J. Earl Hughes of West Middletown, Pa., for locating the graves for her and taking photographs of them. These are reproduced on page xviii.

Mr. Cuthbertson travelled mostly on horseback, often walking and leading his horse; he sailed, rowed, or walked on the ice over the Susquehanna and other streams. He covered a total distance of more than 70,000 miles during his ministry. Guided apparently by his compass and blazed trees, and depending upon the instinct of his faithful beast, he struggled through the unbroken forests from one meeting place to another, and from one home to another. He encountered deep snows and raging blizzards; scorching sun and heavy rains; he was often cold, sick and hungry, as shown by frequent entries; he braved wild beasts, venomous serpents, cruel Indians; the waters were often dangerously high. Most of his studying was done on these long rides.

When Rev. John Cuthbertson came to America in 1751, he was accompanied by his sister, Janet Cuthbertson Bourns, and her husband, Archibald Bourns, of Lanark, Scotland, with their infant son John. Archibald Bourns settled soon after, near what is now Fairfield, and was then Middletown, Adams County, Pennsylvania, on a farm presented to his sister by her brother. This farm is on the now historic Gettysburg Battlefield. Archibald Bourns was the second brother of William Burness, father of Robert Burns, the beloved Poet of Scotland. Another brother, Thomas, emigrated to America from Scotland, and settled in Mifflin County, Pennsylvania, in 1747. An article under the title, "A Franklin County Cousin of Robert Burns" by C. W. Craemer, Esq., of Waynesboro, Pennsylvania, is included in the volume of "The Kittochtinny Historical Society," 1908–1915. This tells about John Burns, the cannon-maker, son of Archibald and Janet Cuthbertson Bourns, who was born in Scotland in 1747, and gives the names of many of the descendants of John Burns. Only a few of them will be mentioned here. One of John Burns' children, James Burns, the fifth son, married Jean Downey, a descendant of the Dinwiddie family of Scotland, which traces its ancestry back to 1296. "General" James Burns had two children, Rosanna and Jane. Rosanna married William Smith Amberson, a prominent merchant of Waynesboro, Pa. They had five children. The writer was recently at the home of Dr. James Burns Amberson, of Waynesboro, a son, now 87 years of age, and still engaged in medical practice. The only other one of these children living at this time is Mr. Presley Neville Amberson, retired. Doctor Amberson was married to Miss M. K. Good, December 1, 1873. They have six children, all living. The writer met Miss Mary E., William Smith and Jean Downey, while in Waynesboro. She also visited the original John Burns' farm at the foot of the North and South Mountains, three miles from Waynesboro, on the Little Antietam Creek, and saw the site of the original log house, and the spot on which John Burns carried on his trade of sickle-making, and where he made, what is believed to be, the first wrought-iron cannon in America. This was captured in the Battle of Brandywine and taken as a trophy to England. John Burns was in the Battle of Brandywine at the time his cannon was captured. Because of his superior skill as a smith he was sent home to repair gunlocks and make bayonets for use of the Army. He married Esther, daughter of Jeremy Morrow of Adams County, Pa., August 19, 1772 (page 80), and they had seven sons and four daughters. John and Esther Burns are buried in the old Covenanter Graveyard high on a knoll on the Willow Glen farm, where many other members of the Burns' family are resting. John was the Grandfather of one of Ohio's early Governors and one of its counties is named for him.

Samuel Rhea Burns, son of Jeremy, second child of John Burns, the cannon-maker, married Margaret Renfrew, a cousin. One child is living, Mrs. Sallie Coffman, widow of Dr. J. J. Coffman of Scotland, Pa. The writer has been in correspondence with Mrs. Coffman. She and her late husband have done much to keep the family records intact. Mrs. Coffman refers to her son, Rev. D. Rhea Coffman of Long Branch, N. J., formerly of Steubenville, Ohio.

Two other children were born to Archibald and Janet Cuthbertson Bourns in America—Janet and James. Janet became the wife of Nathaniel Mitchell of Washington County, Pa. Mr. Mitchell served throughout the Revolutionary War and was for three years with the armies of General Washington. They are direct ancestors of the writer. Their marriage is recorded by Rev. John Cuthbertson on the upper left-hand page of the open Diary, as pictured on page xvii. They had ten children: James, Margaret, Elizabeth, Francis, Mary, John, Joseph, Thomas, David and Samuel.

The burial place of Nathaniel Mitchell and Janet Burns Mitchell is in the old Covenenter Graveyard at West Alexander, Washington County, Pennsylvania. Of their descendants mention is made of only a few personally known to the writer, or with whom she has had correspondence; namely, Alfred Hatcher Mitchell, Attorney, St. Clairsville, Ohio; Alfred Hewetson Mitchell, of the "Daily News," Martins Ferry, Ohio. In Washington, D. C., Mrs. Mary Fields Craig, widow of W. Franklin Craig; her daughter, Margaret H., a school teacher; and her son, Donald Alexander Craig, Sr., an executive of the U. S. George Washington Bicentennial Commission; Washington newspaper correspondent, and charter member of the National Press Club; his young son and daughter, Donald Alexander, Jr., Radio and Dramatic Editor of the Washington "News," and Elizabeth Adams Craig; Mrs. Caroline Fields Lester, widow of Rev. Wm. H. Lester, D.D., Missionary to Chile, S. A.; and Miss Margaret B. Fields. In Steubenville, Ohio, are Miss Katharine Cunningham and Mrs. Hannah Cunningham Shark (Mrs. Ernie).

James Burns, son of Archibald and Janet Cuthbertson Burns, married Jane Gebby, eventually becoming one of Ohio's pioneers. He owned several acres of land on which Cincinnati now stands.

That the heart of Doctor Cuthbertson was with the Covenanter cause, and that he longed for its firm establishment in America, is evidenced in his letter to his sister's son, John Burns, written only a little over a year before his death in March, 1791.   Copies of this letter were given different members of the family by Doctor John Francis Bourns, a son of Jeremy.   He died December 21, 1899, in Norristown, Pa., aged 90 years.   He is the only member of the family who continued spelling the name Bourns.   A copy of this letter is published here:

"Mr. John Bourns, Antietam.

Very dear Nephew:—I have nothing new to inform you unless of ye death of Mrs. Talbot, my wife's sister, who, after five or six months' sore affliction, departed ys transitory life July 7th, was decently interred on ye 9th.   Old Robert Ramsey also is deceased since.   A new in-comer from Ireland was brought to & lay 10 days in my house, dyed & was buried from it.   The Sovereign Lord is exercising various methods of proceedure in his adorable providence; but above all others, irreligion; practical religion almost laid aside.   What need there is for each of us to press forward in our closet and family devotion.   The rising generation appears to practice as if they did not believe they yr is a God, and that he concerned himself with this world—particularly with his first and noblest creature, man.   Eternal things are laid aside.   This world's perishing things enhance all our cares,—cheating, overreaching, defrauding & every other wickedness abounding.   Our coalescence with ye Seceders, I apprehend, is almost at an end.   Mr. L. can inform you hereof.   Was told that ye Covenanters in ye north of Ireland, at a late meeting of yr Presb'y had appointed a minister to come over here.   Should divine Providence favor this, I expect ye true Covenanting cause might again lift up ye head in ys western world.   I wrote Mr. McMillan at Glasgow ye other week.   I had some thoughts of coming back to see you but I fear inability.   The Doctor proposeth in a few weeks coming back to see you, &c.   Remember me to your spouse, children, Sam & Spouse, with other inquiring friends.

Your sincere well-wisher and friend.

Jno. Cuthbertson."

"Octoraro, Aug. 19, 1789."

Rev. John Cuthbertson died on March 10, 1791, aged 72 years, 11 mos. and 7 days.   He is buried in Middle Octoraro Graveyard, attached to the stone church where he labored until March 20, 1783.   (See page 134.)   The Middle Octoraro Church contains an inscription cut into the stone: "Built in 1754.   Rebuilt by Associate Congregation in 1849."   Photographs of Mr. Cuthbertson's grave, with its cracked and crumbling slab, and the now unused church, were taken for the writer by Rev. Wm. M. Anderson in 1930, and are reproduced on page xviii.   On the slab is the following inscription:

" Here lies the body of the
Rev. John Cuthbertson,
who, after a labour of about forty years in
the ministry of the Gospel among the
diffenting Covenanters in America
departed this life 10th March, 1791,
in the 73rd year of his age."

"Psalm 112 . . . "The Righteous shall be in everlasting remembrance."

This same quotation is on the tombstone of his wife.

Inscriptions are on Mr. Cuthbertson's stone for his son, Walter, and his sister-in-law, Mrs. Elizabeth Talbot, who are buried beside him.

The following published works have been consulted by the writer, as not only these authors but others have had access to the original Diary of Rev. John Cuthbertson and have quoted freely from it:

"A Biographical Sketch of Rev. John Cuthbertson" by Revs. A. S. Aiken and J. N. Adair, 1878.

"History of the Reformed Church in America" by Rev. Wm. M. Glasgow, 1888.

"American Church History Series," Vol. XI, by Rev. James Brown Scouler.

"United Presbyterian Church and Its Work in America" by Rev. W. E. McCulloch.

Various Histories of Adams, Cumberland, Franklin, Lancaster, York and other Pennsylvania Counties, and Maryland County Histories.

To Mr. Erskine Ward of Walden, N. Y., a direct descendant of David Rainey, son of James Rainey, the writer is indebted for a review of the Orange County, N. Y., locations, and additional information in footnotes. Also for photographs of the home of James Rainey, built in 1765 (page xix), two and one-half miles east of Pine Bush, Orange County, where Mr. Ward's mother, grandmother and Great Grandfather, David Rainey, were born. In one end of the building, built for the purpose, services were held until 1793, and here Rev. John Cuthbertson organized the first Covenanter Society in New York. In 1793 the Coldenham-Covenanter Church, five miles west of Newburgh, N. Y., was built. The present building was erected in 1838.

Note: See articles by S. Helen Fields in the "National Genealogical Society Quarterly," Vol. XX, March, 1932, No. 1, and Vol. XXI. March, 1933, No. 1, for names of additional Covenanters.

Photo by S. Helen Fields, Washington, D. C.

Open Diary, Pages 152–153.

Quoting from top of left-hand page: "April 19th (1772).—rode 9 miles to Tract. Baptized Jeremiah son to John Murray and Agnes to Mat. Beggs." April 20th.—"Married Nathaniel Mitchel and Jat. Burns."

Photo by Rev. Wm. M. Anderson, D.D., Philadelphia, Pa.

Home of Rev. John Cuthbertson, Middle Octoraro, Lancaster Co., Pa.

Photo by Rev. J. Earl Hughes, West Middletown, Washington Co., Pa.

Graves of Rev. John Cuthbertson's wife, daughter and son John. (See Introduction, page xi.)

Photo by Rev. Wm. M. Anderson, D.D., Philadelphia, Pa.

Grave of Rev. John Cuthbertson. (See Introduction, page xiv.)

Photo by Rev. Wm. M. Anderson, D.D., Philadelphia, Pa.

Middle Octoraro Church. (See Introduction, page xiv.)

Photo by Mr. Erskine Ward, Walden, N. Y.

Home of James Rainey, built in 1765.   (See Introduction, page xv.)

Photo by Mr. Erskine Ward, Walden, N. Y.

The end of the home of James Rainey, built in 1765, used for services.
(See page xv.)

Facsimile of Letter from John Cuthbertson to his sister Margaret Cuthbertson,
February 22, 1745. (See Postscript, Address, etc., page xxii.)

"Dear Sister,

You now enjoy the blefsful Summer of Life, when all is in its prime, the Affections lively, Memory strong, Body quick & vigorous, so yt all things are now fitted for mutual afsistance in some noble undertaking, and what more honourable & gainful than ye Service of your Creator: O remember this in ye Days of your youth: No tongue, or pen can exprefs the pleasure you shall enjoy in all Duties & Ordinances, private & publick, and in all you put your hand to; shall always have a Friend to cling closer than any Brother: I'm in no doubt about ye maintaining ye form & usual Courfe of Duties.   But, dear Sister, I'm very much afraid you may have lost much of your former fervency & warmth of Love to Him whose blefsed Self you would once rather have enjoyed than many worlds of painted Vainities: O arife & come away! Sit not loitering, Saying he has forgotten to be gracious, he has been angry with me, & so has hid His face from me; What can I then do? What, have you not all ye blefsed offers of Christ yt any have.   Cry unto God, thou art the guide of my youth, lead me therefore in thy blefsed ways & Suffer not my feet to slip from thy Testimonies: Believe it, Christ is well pleased with a returning Child; Make much use of your Bible & never take it in your hand without remembering yt it is ye Word of God, & so ufe it; pray frequently & fervently both for yourself & others; & forget not Zion, in all your Prayers let Zion have a share, So do you remember him who thus writes unto you, & desires always to prefent your Soul's cafe before ye Throne of Grace: With my hearty Respects to Father, Mother, Brethern & yourself, I in haste remain

"Your sincere Welwisher
& Brother
Jo. Cuthbertson.

"Edin:
Feb. 22d
1745

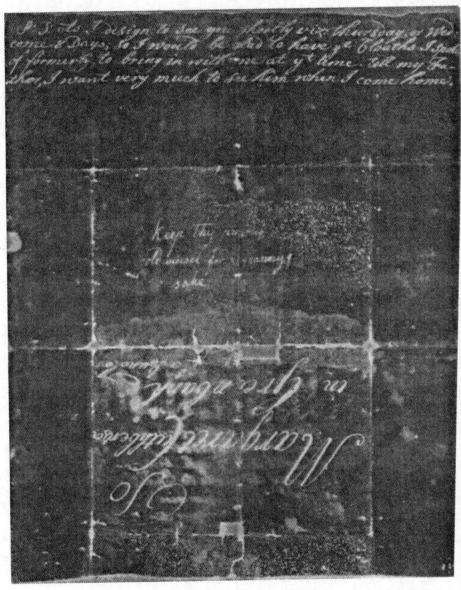

Continuation of letter to his sister Margaret by Rev. John Cuthbertson with address.

"P.S. As I design to see you shortly viz: thursday, or Wed: come 8 Days; So I would be glad to have ye Cloaths I spoke of formerly to bring in with me at yt time. tell my father, I want very much to see him when I come home."

"To
Margaret Cuthbertson
in Greenbank,
Bunolo"

"Keep this precious
old morsel for ye Grannys
sake." *

* (Apparently written in later years on back)

Kindness of Mrs. Jacob H. Stoner, Waynesboro, Pa.

Facsimile signature of Rev. Jo. Cuthbertson on front page of "A True History of
the Church of Scotland," as described on page viii.

PERSONS VISITED

MARRIAGES AND BAPTISMS

(*a*) Under the titles, "Marriages" and "Baptisms," dates are placed in the first column to enable the research worker to refer more readily to Diary quotations on the pages cited.

(*b*) Under "Marriages" the second column is a double index and includes all names in the third column.

MARRIAGES

Date	Name	Married to	Page
Jan. 1, 1765	Aitken, Margaret	Da.(vid) McQuig	157
Jan. 31, 1760	Alexander, Janet	James Scot	148
Dec. 9, 1773	Andrew, Mary	Alexander Kilpatrick	170
May 1, 1770	Andrews, John	Jean Cooper	165
Sept. 21, 1769	" Susanna	Wm. Woods	164
Mar. 27, 1770	Armstrong, Thomas	Jean McCrea	83
Sept. 3/4, 1781	Ayres, Agnes	John McClintock	230
Sept. 7, 1781	" James	Eleanor Davidson	230
Dec. 12, 1758	" Margaret	John Moore	202
Dec. 23/28, 1754	" William	Elizabeth Buchanan	209–210
Apr. 2/3, 1781	Balantine, William	Susanah Marlin	229
Apr. 23, 1765	Barclay, William	Margaret Ramsay	157
Apr. 2, 1770	Begs, Matthew	Martha McKinley	79
Nov. 19, 1761	Bell, Margaret	Gab. Walker	151
Feb. 5, 1770	" Robert	Sally Bell (or Swan)	102
Feb. 5, 1770	"(?)Sally	Robert Bell	102
Oct. 29, 1764	Biggar, Sam	Abigail Wil(son)	214
Apr. 6, 1761	Birney, Jean	James Ramsay	150
Dec. 21, 1758	(Black?), Hew	Mary Black	145
Dec. 21, 1758	Black, Mary	Hew (Black?)	145
July 4, 1758	" Thomas	Margaret McCubray	144
Mar. 18, 1762	Blackburn, Ann	Andrew (McKnaught)	152
Nov. 26, 1751	" Jo(hn)	Ann Logan	242
July 13, 1752	Blakely, Elizabeth	Thomas Jones	119
Sept. 27, 1757	Boyd, Jean	John Robieson	134
Apr. 18, 1763	" Mary	John Brakenridge	75
May 14, 1771	Boyle, Charles	Elizabeth Torbit	80
Apr. 18, 1763	Brakenridge, John	Mary Boyd	75
June 25, 1765	Branan, John	Mary Walker	158
Mar. 23, 1778	Branon, John	May (Dixon ?)	225
Mar. 31, 1758	Branwood, And.	Sarah Gibson	73
May 22, 1753	Brattan, Helen	Wm. Finton	103
Oct. 17, 1780	Broadly, Jean (Negroes)	Newport Walker	178
Feb. 7, 1760	Broedy, James	Elizabeth Girvan	148
May 6, 1762	Brostrer, Joseph	Mary McKnight	152
Dec. 14, 1753	Brown, Ann	Benjamin McCormick	209
Oct. 22, 1753	" Ben	Mary Mitch(el)	95
Mar. 9, 1773	" Benjamin	Agnes Ritchie	123
Jan. 14, 1754	" James	Mary McClellan	139
Jan. 3, 1757	" Janet	John Gebie	185
Apr. 6, 1761	" Janet	T. Scott	150

Date	Name	Married to	Page
Feb. 21, 1788........	Brown, Jean............	James Teenan...........	183
June 18, 1771.......	" John............	Mary Guililand.........	98
Feb. 4, 1779.......	" Margaret.........	Wm. Dunlap............	176
Jan. 25, 1787.......	" Martha..........	James Oliver............	234
Jan. 27, 1761.......	" Math............	Eleanor McCormick......	109
May 2, 1758.......	Brownlie, J............	Jean Ker...............	211
Mar. 22, 1769.......	" James..........	Eliz. Rankin...........	82
Mar. 22, 1769.......	" Margaret.......	James Leiper...........	82
Dec. 23/28, 1754.....	Buchanan, Elizabeth.....	William Ayres......	209-210
Mar. 8/9, 1779......	" Elizabeth......	Richard Easton..........	226
Feb. 26/28, 1753.....	" George........	Jean Paterson........	208-209
Jan. 20/21, 1773......	" Gilbert........	Sarah Walker...........	168
		(Daughter John Walker)	
Oct. 14, 1755........	" Helen........	James Hill..............	190
Jan. 12, 1775........	" Janet........	James Glen.............	170
Apr. 11, 1771........	" Janet (Jat.)....	Archibald Shield........	166
Oct. 3, 1765........	" John.........	Jean (White)............	215
Aug. 17, 1778........	" Margaret.....	Wm. Neaton............	240
Feb. 15, 1776........	" Mary........	John Mitchel...........	172
Apr. 4, 1754........	" Walter.......	Mary Coulter...........	95
Dec. 24, 1762........	" Wal(ter).....	Agnes Toulan...........	110
Apr. 20, 1772........	Burns, Janet (Jat.).......	Nathaniel Mitchel........	70
Aug. 19, 1772........	" John...........	Esther Murray...........	80
Jan. 15, 1760........	" Sister...........	Francis Meredith.........	70
Sept. 25, 1770........	B......., E......	Thomas Mc(Knaughtan)..	113
Jan. 29, 1759........	B......., Ha.....	James Miens.............	108
Oct. 10, 1754........	Ca..., Mary...........	Matthew Ritchie.........	139
Sept. 4/5, 1780.....	Cachy, Sam...........	Eleanor Moor...........	178
May 8/9, 1752......	" Sam...........	Esther Coulter..........	136
Oct. 31, 1768........	Calbreath, Ann.........	T. Kennety.............	162
Oct. 23, 1770........	" Han...........	John Shenan............	166
Feb. 8, 1759........	" Isobel........	John Park...........	145-146
Feb. 8, 1759........	" Jean........	Peter Wilson........	145-146
Apr. 5, 1756........	" Robert.......	Elizabeth Cumin(gs)......	141
June 8, 1761........	" Wm...........	Jean Lowry.............	150
Aug. 20, 1772........	Caldwel, Matth........	Margaret Reid...........	80
May 21, 1753........	*Calhoun, Adam........	Janet Woods............	103
May 17, 1753........	" Jas...........	Sarah Taylor............	106
Mar. 1, 1757........	Cany....., Elizabeth.....	Alexander Young.........	191
Oct. 9, 1753........	Carson, David..........	Sarah Woods............	106
Feb. 13/14, 1775.....	Clark, George...........	Margaret Sinclair........	221
Nov. 17, 1783........	" Margaret.........	James Kennedy..........	232
Mar. 28, 1782........	" Robert.........	Jean Gebby.............	231
Dec. 19, 1775........	" Wm.............	Margaret Rowan.........	98
Mar. 21, 1769........	Cochran, Mary..........	W. Finley..............	129
Jan. 18, 1759........	Colhoun, Eliz............	Henry McCormick.......	108

* See also Colhoun.

Date	Name	Married to	Page
Apr. 20, 1766	*Cooper, Elizabeth	John Stewart	159
May 1, 1770	" Jean	John Andrews	165
Mar. 4, 1766	Coulter, Ag.	John Maeben	158
June 21, 1774	" Agnes	Sam Fegan	170
Dec. 23, 1778	" Agnes	Daniel McReady	175
May 8/9, 1752	" Esther	Sam Cachy	136
Mar. 19, 1754	" Hew	Mary Sloan	95
Apr. 4, 1754	" Mary	Walter Buchanan	95
June 30, 1778	" Nat.	Isobel Dunlap	175
Nov. 14, 1757	" Nath.	Gr. Lough.	143
Mar. 17, 1767	" Nath.	Margaret Stewart	112
May 24/25, 1784	" (?) Nathaniel	Isobel (Park)	181
Mar. 4, 1788	" Nathaniel	Margaret Moor	183
Jan. 5, 1752	Couper, Anna	Phinehas Whiteside	189
Sept. 23, 1751	Crain, Richard	Jean Espie	103
Sept. 26, 1763	Crawford, Eliz.	John Hutchinson	76
Nov. 21, 1758	" John	Margaret Wilson	211
Mar. 14, 1770	Crook, James	Mary Crunk(leton)	117
Nov. 3, 1755	Crooks, Jo	Margaret McClure	72
Mar. 9, 1773	Cross, Martha	Joseph McMurray	123
June 11, 1776	" Wm.	Margaret Ramsay	222
Mar. 14, 1770	Crunk(leton), Mary	James Crook	117
Apr. 5, 1756	Cumin(gs), Elizabeth	Robert Calbreath	141
Feb. 24, 1763	Cumings, George	Margaret Kirkpatrick	153
June 15, 1761	**Cuthry, Wm.	Esther Mc(Millan)	150
June 7, 1756	Dale, Florence	James Paterson	141
Sept. 7, 1781	Davidson, Eleanor	James Ayres	230
Feb. 22, 1759	Dickson, Eleanor	Sam Rob(ieson)	146
Nov. 11, 1773	Dinwoody, Mary	John Wilson	81
Apr. 17, 1770	Dixon, Hannah	Alexander McCulloch	92
Mar. 23, 1778	(") May	John Branon	225
Nov. 23, 1769	" Sarah	James Robieson	164
June 11, 1761	Dougherty, Mary	John McConel	186
July 28, 1757	" Thomas	Mary Robieson	211
Mar. 16, 1752	Dowglas, Isaac	Mary Sloan	92
May 16/17, 1770	Duffield, George	Eliz. McNaughtan	79
Nov. 13, 1764	Duncan, H.	Jean Mitchel	133
Apr. 15, 1788	Dun(can), J.	Widow (Brown?)	236
Apr. 10, 1769	Dun(can), J.	—— Stew.?	217
Apr. 17, 1769	Duncan, Jean	W. Thomson	94
Nov. 24, 1772	" Rebecca	Enos. McDonald	168
June 30, 1778	Dunlap, Isobel	Nat. Coulter	175
Oct. 3, 1759	" Mary	John Kane	197
Feb. 13, 1770	" Rebecca	Joseph Widrow	132
Feb. 4, 1779	" Wm.	Margaret Brown	176

* See Couper also.
** See Guthry also.

Date	Name	Married to	Page
Mar. 8/9, 1779	Easton, Richard	Elizabeth Buchanan	226
Aug. 28, 1752	Estin, Janet	Thoas Paxton	189
Sept. 23, 1751	Espie, Jean	Richard Crain	103
May 16, 1757	" Joseph	Elizabeth McCormick	108
May 27, 1781 (24)	Ewing, Jean	Elijah Forsyth	229
Jan. 7, 1768	(Ewins), Alexander	Frances Ewins	161
Jan. 7, 1768	Ewins, Frances	Alexander (Ewins?)	161
Jan. 15/16, 1787	Farmers, Mary	James Purdy	182
June 21, 1774	Fegan, Sam	Agnes Coulter	170
Mar. 10, 1752	Ferguson, James	Mary McCormick	105
Apr. 24, 1758	Ferrier, And	Jean Marlin	144
Feb. 15, 1757	Finey, Thomas	Susan Stewart	107
June 12, 1770	" Thomas	Margaret Swan	102
June 10, 1765	Finley, James	Margaret Finley	157
June 10, 1765	" Margaret	James Finley	157
Mar. 21, 1769	" W	Mary Cochran	129
May 22, 1753	Finton, Wm	Helen Brattan	103
May 27, 1781 (24)	Forsyth, Elijah	Jean Ewing	229
Mar. 11/12, 1776	(Fulerton ?), Ann	John Woods	195
Feb. 7, 1769	Fulerton, Humphrey	Martha Mi(tchel ?)	193
Jan. 22, 1782	" Jean	Alexander White	179
May 9, 1780	" Margaret	John McFadden	195
Feb. 28, 1760	Fulton, James	Mary Moore	202
Nov. 25/26, 1778	Gebby, Ann	James Long	226
Feb. 9/10, 1789	" James	Janet Gebby	237
	(John Gebby's son)		
Feb. 9/10, 1789	" Janet	James Gebby	237
	(Wm. Gebby's daughter)		
Mar. 28, 1782	" Jean	Robert Clark	231
Apr. 30, 1787	" Mary	Sam Morrison	235
June 11, 1761	" Wm	Ann McMillan	186
Jan. 3, 1757	Gebie, John	Janet Brown	185
Mar. 31, 1758	Gibson, Sarah	And. Branwood	73
Aug. 24, 1762	Giffan, John	Eleanor Heron	90
Apr. 12, 1768	Giffe(n), Eleanor	Robert Hamilton	91
Feb. 7, 1760	Girvan, Elizabeth	James Broedy	148
Jan. 7, 1773	" John	Mary Laughlin	168
May 25, 1761	" Thomas	Mary McNiely	109
Jan. 12, 1775	Glen, James	Janet Buchanan	170
Mar. 4, 1790	" Joseph	Jean Ramsay	237
Dec. 30, 1771	Graham, John	Martha Millar	194
Nov. 25/26, 1765	Grahams, James	Ruth Little	96
Mar. 5/11, 1753	Gray, Finlay	(?)	199
Jan. 3, 1760	" Isobel	Daniel Sinclar	147
Oct.(22), 1765	Greenlie, James	Agnes Guililand	111
Jan. 31, 1764	" W	Mary Thomson	110

Note: For Galbreath. see Calbreath.

Date	Name	Married to	Page
Oct.(22), 1765	Guililand, Agnes	James Greenlie	111
June 18, 1771	" Mary	John Brown	98
Dec. 15, 1762	Guthry, Mary	Th. McClellan	153
Sept. 22, 1755	Hamilton, Margaret	—— Reid	93
Apr. 12, 1768	" Robert	Eleanor Giffe(n)	91
Oct. 17, 1785	Hanna, John	Dorathy Harris	182
Oct. 17, 1785	Harris, Dorathy	John Hanna	182
Nov. 23/24, 1763	Henry, George	Margaret Young	213
Aug. 9, 1759	" James	Sus. McKnaught	147
Apr. 7, 1772	Hen(ry), W.	Marjory Sconler	219
Aug. 24, 1762	Heron, Eleanor	John Giffan	90
Oct. 14, 1755	Hill, James	Helen Buchanan	190
June 17, 1771	Hilton, Mary	And. Nicol	219
Apr. 1, 1761	Holms, Gab. (Helms?)	Mary Moore	133
Dec. 29, 1772	Houston, Martha	George Mitchel	168
Apr. 8, 1765	Howston, James	Isobel Neilson	111
Sept. 26, 1763	Hutchinson, John	Eliz. Craw(ford)	76
Sept. 17, 1764	Jamiesons, Elizabeth	John McCleary	214
Apr. 2, 1753	January, Peter	Debora McMichan	119
May 19, 1772	Johnston, Jean	Wm. Thom(son)	188
Apr. 24, 1781	Jones, Elizabeth	Matthew McClung	195
July 13, 1752	" Thomas	Elizabeth Blakely	119
Oct. 3, 1759	Kane, John	Mary Dunlap	197
Nov. 17, 1783	Kennedy, James	Margaret Clark	232
Feb. 25, 1771	" Thomas	Mary McCallin	97
Aug. 9, 1773	" Thomas	Eliz. Lowry	123
Oct. 31, 1768	Kennety, T.	Ann Calbreath	162
May 11, 1769	Ker, Alexander	Sarah Murray	78
May 2, 1758	" Jean	J. Brownlie	211
Dec. 30, 1756	K(er), Mary	Hew Reynolds	185
Mar. 1, 1757	Kilgore, Charles	Jean McClure	191
Dec. 9, 1773	Kilpatrick, Alexander	Mary Andrew	170
Oct. 14, 1751	" Janet	George McKown	135
Feb. 24, 1763	Kirkpatrick, Margaret	George Cumings	153
Jan. 7, 1773	Laughlin, Mary	John Girvan	168
June 1, 1772	La(w), Janet	Robert Martin	169
Jan. 2, 1777	Law, William	Eliz. Smith	123
Mar. 22, 1769	Leiper, James	Margaret Brownlie	82
Mar. 4, 1760	" Sam	Mary McDr. (McBr.?)	148
May 1, 1764	" Samuel	Sarah McCleary	121
Nov. 25/26, 1765	*Little, Ruth	James Grahams	96
Oct. 17, 1780	" Sam	Elizabeth Spencer	178
Nov. 9, 1768	Lochhart, Mary	John Murray	162–163
June 29, 1762	Lochhead, Margaret	John Ritchie	153
June 1, 1762	" Robert	Martha McKnaught	152
Nov. 26, 1751	Logan, Ann	Jo(hn) Blackburn	242

* See Lyttle also.

Date	Name	Married to	Page
Nov. 25/26, 1778	Long, James	Ann Gebby	226
Nov. 14, 1757	Lough(head), Gr.	Nath. Coulter	143
Dec. 12, 1752	Loughhead, Jas.	Eleanor M(itchel)	94
Jan. 19, 1764	" Joseph	Jean Robieson	155
July 6, 1769	" Martha	Walter Moore	164
May 10, 1768	" Reb.	Sam Nelson	217
Apr. 25, 1765	" William	Sarah Thomson	193
Sept. 3, 1751	Love, Robert	Rachel Sloan	100
Aug. 9, 1773	Lowry, Eliz.	Thomas Kennedy	123
June 8, 1761	" Jean	Wm. Calbreath	150
Aug. 15, 1769	" Mary	John Robertson	78
Oct. 28, 1788	Lyttle, Hanna(h)	James Spier	237
Mar. 24, 1769	McBryar, Esther	And. Reid	97
Feb. 25, 1771	McCallin, Mary	Thomas Kennedy	97
July 22, 1762	McCleary, Andrew	Margaret Mitchel	188
Sept. 17, 1764	" John	Elizabeth Jamiesons	214
May 1, 1764	" Mary	Sam Smith	121
May 1, 1764	" Sarah	Samuel Leiper	121
Jan. 14, 1754	McClellan, Mary	James Brown	139
Dec. 15, 1762	" Th.	Mary Guthry	153
Mar. 21, 1769	McClenachan, Letitia	John Neal	129
Sept. 3/4, 1781	McClintock, John	Agnes Ayres	230
Apr. 24, 1781	McClung, Matthew	Elizabeth Jones	195
Mar. 11, 1752	McClure, Eliz.	Jo(hn) Taylor	105
Mar. 1, 1757	" Jean	Charles Kilgore	191
Nov. 3, 1755	" Margaret	Jo(hn) Crooks	72
June 11, 1761	McConel, John	Mary Dougherty	186
Apr. 2, 1761	McCord, Jos.	E	192
Oct. 31, 1758	" Mary	James Paterson	145
Apr. 17, 1759	" Sarah	John Paterson	146
Apr. 1, 1755	McCormick, Agnes	Peter Peters	106
Dec. 14, 1753	" Benjamin	Ann Brown	209
Jan. 27, 1761	" Eleanor	Math. Brown	109
May 16, 1757	" Elizabeth	Joseph Espie	108
Jan. 18, 1759	" Henry	Eliz. Colhoun	108
Oct. 17, 1752	" Jo(hn)	Mary Strehon	92
May 22, 1764	" Martha	Alexander Robieson	96
Mar. 10, 1752	" Mary	Jas. Ferguson	105
July 28, 1755	" (k) Mary	Wm. Paterson	107
Mar. 27, 1770	McCrea, Jean	Thomas Armstrong	83
July 4, 1758	McCubray, Margaret	Thomas Black	144
Apr. 17, 1770	McCulloch, Alexander	Hannah Dixon	92
Nov. 24, 1772	McDonald, Enos.	Rebecca Duncan	168
Mar. 19, 1761	McDowel, Betty	T. Ramsay	150
Mar. 4, 1760	McDr. (McBr.?), Mary	Sam Leiper	148
May 9, 1780	McFadden, John	Margaret Fulerton	195
Nov. 7, 1760	McG......., Sus(an)	Thomas Montgomery	149

MARRIAGES 9

Date	Name	Married to	Page
Feb. 27, 1770	McGlaughlin, James	Margaret Mitchel	165
Oct. 13, 1775	McKee, Robert	Mary Thomson	258
Apr. 2, 1770	McKinley, Martha	Matthew Begs	79
Feb. 15, 1757	McK. James	Martha Milroy	107
Jan. 10, 1757	McKn. Barb.	John Rob(ieson)	191
June 7, 1760	McKnaught, Agnes	Math. Thorn	109
Jan. 17, 1758	" John	Mary Paterson	143
June 1, 1762	" Martha	Robert Lochhead	152
Aug. 9, 1759	" Sus.	James Henry	147
May 6, 1762	McKnight, Mary	Joseph Brostrer	152
Mar. 18, 1762	McKt. Andrew	Ann Blackburn	152
Sept. 25, 1770	McKt. Thomas	E. B.	113
Oct. 14, 1751	McKown, George	Janet Kilpatrick	135
Apr. 2, 1753	McMichan, Debora	Peter January	119
Oct. 25, 1762	McMiens, And.	Ann Wilson	240
June 11, 1761	McMillan, Ann	Wm. Gebby	186
June 15, 1761	" (?) Esther	Wm. Cuthry	150
Dec. 13, 1764	" Mary	William Marlin	214
Apr. 9, 1778	McMillans, John	Jean Paton	225
Mar. 9, 1773	McMurray, Joseph	Martha Cross	123
Nov. 8, 1753	McMuray, Mary	Robert Scot	185
Dec. 11, 1752	McNair, Alexander	Ann Thorn	104
May 16/17, 1770	McNaughtan, Eliz.	George Duffield	79
May 25, 1761	McNiely, Mary	Thomas Girvan	109
Jan. 1, 1765	McQuig, Da.	Margaret Aitken	157
Dec. 23, 1778	McReady, Daniel	Agnes Coulter	175
Mar. 27, 1771	McWilliams, Wm.	Sarah Nickle	219
Feb. 25/26/27, 1772	McYlahlin, James	Sarah Wilson	123
Mar. 4, 1766	Maeben, John	Ag(nes) Coulter	158
July 1, 1766	Mar..., Susanna	John Marlin	216
Apr. 24, 1758	Marlin, Jean	And. Ferrier	144
July 1, 1766	" John	Susanna Mar.	216
June 28, 1784	" John	Rachel Neilson (or Marlin)	233
Oct. 14, 1765	" Mary	Dan Sinclair	215
June 28, 1784	(Marlin ?), Rachel	John Marlin	233
Apr. 2/3, 1781	Marlin, Susanah	Wm. Balantine	229
Dec. 13, 1764	" William	Mary McMillan	214
Aug. 24, 1773	Marshal, Sam	Mary Murphy	81
Oct. 8, 1770	Martin, John	Agnes Thomson	165
June 1, 1773	" Robert	Janet La(w)	169
Nov. 25, 1767	Mauchlin, Wm.	Martha Reid	216
Oct. 22, 1788	Maughlin, Jean	Robert Wilson	236
May 29, 1787	Mehowl, Sara	Hew Sutherland	183
Jan. 15, 1760	Meredith, Francis	Sister (Janet) Burns	70
Jan. 29, 1759	Miens, James	Ha. B.	108
June 22, 1752	" Martha	And. White	105
Oct. 30, 1775	Millar, Gavin	Susana Rainey	252

Date	Name	Married to	Page
Dec. 30, 1771	Millar, Martha	John Graham	194
Feb. 15, 1757	Milroy, Martha	James McK(naughtan?)	107
May 3, 1763	Mitchel, D.	(?)	133
July 6, 1762	" David	Mary Smith	110
Dec. 12, 1752	M(itchel?), Eleanor	James Loughhead	94
Dec. 29, 1772	Mitchel, George	Martha Houston	168
Feb. 3, 1774	" George	Mary Wilson	123
Aug. 17, 1756	" James	Mary Sloan	141
Dec. 14, 1769	" James	Han(nah) Peterson	164
Aug. 11, 1773	" Janet (Morison?). (?)		98
Nov. 13, 1764	" Jean	H. Duncan	133
May 19, 1772	" Jesse	Ruth Mitchel	188
Feb. 15, 1776	" John	Mary Buchanan	172
July 22, 1762	" Margaret	Andrew McCleary	188
Feb. 27, 1770	" Margaret	James McGlaughlin	165
Feb. 7, 1769	Mi(tchel), Martha	Humphrey Fulerton	193
Oct. 22, 1753	Mitchel, Mary	Ben. Brown	95
Apr. 24, 1770	" Mary	Robert Ramsay	165
Oct. 29, 1765	" Matthew	Mary Richie(son?)	77
Apr. 20, 1772	" Nathaniel	Jat. (Janet) Burns	70
May 19, 1772	" Ruth	Jesse Mitchel	188
Apr. 20, 1773	" Sally	Robert Thomson	169
June 8, 1761	" Thomas	Sarah Scott	150
Oct. 29, 1765	" William	Mary Wilson	77
Nov. 7, 1760	Montgomery, Thomas	Sus. McG.	149
Nov. 3, 1755	Mooney, Jo(hn)	Janet Thomson	72
Dec. 28, 1762	Moore, Agnes (Moor)	Hew Stewart	69
Sept. 4/5, 1780	" Eleanor (")	Sam Cachy	178
Dec. 12, 1758	" John	Margaret Ayres	202
Mar. 4, 1788	" Margaret (")	Nathaniel Coulter	183
Feb. 28, 1760	" Mary	James Fulton	202
Apr. 1, 1761	" Mary	Gab. Holms (Helms?)	133
July 6, 1769	" Walter	Martha Loughhead	164
Aug. 11, 1773	Morison (Mitchel?), Janet. (?)		98
Apr. 30, 1787	Morrison, Sam	Mary Gebby	235
Sept. 17, 1753	Morton, John	Elizabeth Mtear's	120
Feb. 26, 1761	" John	Susan Smith	150
June 4, 1761	" Thomas	Ann Thompson	74
Oct. 24, 1782	Motherel, Agnes	John Reed	180
Sept. 17, 1753	Mtear's, Elizabeth	John Morton	120
Oct. 22, 1767	Muir, James	Reb. Stewart	131
Nov. 19, 1753	" Jean	William Reid	138
Aug. 24, 1773	Murphy, Mary	Sam Marshal	81
Aug. 19, 1772	Murray, Esther	John Burns	80
Aug. 24, 1773	" Jean	Wm. Paterson	81
Nov. 9, 1768	" John	Mary Lochhart	162–163

Date	Name	Married to	Page
Aug. 29, 1768	Murray, Martha	David Parkhill	78
May 11, 1769	" Sarah	Alexander Ker	78
May 18/19, 1767	Navin, John	Martha Swansie	94
Mar. 21, 1769	Neal, John	Letitia McClenachan	129
Aug. 17, 1778	Neaton, Wm.	Margaret Buchanan	240
Apr. 8, 1765	Neilson, Isobel	James Howston	111
June 28, 1784	(" ?) Rachel	John Marlin	233
May 10, 1768	Nelson, Sam	Reb. Loughhead	217
Mar. 27, 1771	Nickle, Sarah	Wm. McWilliams	219
June 17, 1771	Nicol, And.	Mary Hilton	219
Sept. 20, 1757	Niely, Thomas	Margaret Paterson	142
Jan. 25, 1787	Oliver, James	Martha Brown	234
Feb. 8, 1759	Park, John	Isobel Calbreath	145-146
May 24/25, 1784	(Park), Isobel	Nathaniel Cou(lter)	181
Aug. 29, 1768	Parkhill, David	Martha Murray	78
June 7, 1756	Paterson, James	Florence Dale	141
Oct. 31, 1758	" James	Mary McCord	145
Nov. 22, 1773	" Janet	John Paterson	187
Feb. 26/28, 1753	" Jean	George Buch(anan)	208-209
Apr. 17, 1759	" John	Sarah McCord	146
Nov. 22, 1773	" John	Janet Paterson	187
Jan. 2, 1754	" Margaret (Mt.)	William Reynolds	185
Sept. 20, 1757	" Margaret	Thomas Niely	142
Feb. 27, 1770	(" ?) Margaret	Sam Paterson	165
Jan. 17, 1758	" Mary	John McKnaught	143
Mar. 29, 1768	" Ma(ry?)	Elijah Stewart	161
Jan. 12, 1773	" Mary	John Thomson	168
Apr. 10, 1764	" R.	Mary Stewart	110
Feb. 27, 1770	" Sam	Margaret (Paterson?)	165
July 28, 1755	" William	Mary McCormic(k)	107
Aug. 24, 1773	" Wm.	Jean Murray	81
May 4, 1762	Patterson, John	Agnes Scott	152
Aug. 27, 1779	Pattison, Agnes	James Ridgway	228
Mar. 17, 1772	" Elizabeth	Joseph Tait	167
Apr. 9, 1778	Paton, Jean	John McMillans	225
Aug. 28, 1752	Paxton, Thoas.	Janet Estin	189
Aug. 7, 1783	Peck, Magda	Henry Rich	254
Apr. 1, 1755	Peters, Peter	Agnes McCormick	106
Dec. 14, 1769	Peterson, Han.	James Mitchel	164
Jan. 15/16, 1787	Purdy, James	Mary Farmers	182
Nov. 3, 1789	Quin, Jas.	Agnes Weaver	237
Oct. 30, 1775	Rainey, Susana	Gavin Millar	252
Apr. 6, 1761	Ramsay, James	Jean Birney	150
Feb. 26, 1777	" Jas.	Margaret Stuart	92
Mar. 4, 1790	" Jean	Joseph Glen	237
Mar. 13, 1771	" John	Phoebe (Ramsay?)	166
Apr. 23, 1765	" Margaret	William Barclay	157

Date	Name	Married to	Page
June 11, 1776	Ramsay, Margaret	Wm. Cross	222
Mar. 13, 1771	(?) Phoebe	John Ramsay	166
Apr. 24, 1770	Ramsay, Robert	Mary Mitchel	165
Apr. 23, 1778	" Susan	John Reid	225
Mar. 19, 1761	" T.	Betty McDowel	150
Mar. 22, 1769	Rankin, Eliz.	James Brownlie	82
Mar. 27, 1770	" Mary	James Scott	83
Oct. 22, 1764	Redduc(k), John	Mary Reid	193
Oct. 24, 1782	Reed, John	Agnes Motherel	180
Sept. 22, 1755	Reid,	Margaret Hamilton	93
Mar. 24, 1769	" And.	Esther McBryar	97
Apr. 23, 1778	" Jean	James Stewart	225
Apr. 23, 1778	" John	Susan Ramsay	225
Aug. 20, 1772	" Margaret	Matth. Caldwel	80
Feb. 15, 1773	" Margaret	William Walker	91
Nov. 25, 1767	" Martha	Wm. Mauchlin	216
Oct. 22, 1764	" Mary	John Redduc(k)	193
Nov. 19, 1753	" William	Jean Muir	138
Dec. 30, 1756	Reynolds, Hew	Mary K(er)	185
Jan. 2, 1754	" William	Mt. Paterson	185
Aug. 7, 1783	Rich, Henry	Magda Peck	254
Oct. 29, 1765	Richie(son?), Mary	Matthew Mitchel	77
Mar. 9, 1773	Ritchie, Agnes	Benjamin Brown	123
June 29, 1762	" John	Margaret Lochhead	153
Aug. 27, 1779	Ridgway, James	Agnes Patterson	228
Oct. 10, 1754	Ritchie, Matthew	Mary Ca	139
Jan. 10, 1757	Rob. John	Barbara McKn(aughtan)	191
Jan. 17, 1769	" Joseph	Jean Vogan	163
Feb. 22, 1759	" Sam.	Eleanor Dicks(on?)	146
June 18, 1771	Robertson, James	Margaret Young	98
Aug. 15, 1769	" John	Mary Lowry	78
May 22, 1764	Robieson, Alexander	Martha McCormick	96
Nov. 23, 1769	" James	Sarah Dixon	164
Jan. 19, 1764	" Jean	Joseph Loughhead	155
Sept. 27, 1757	" John	Jean Boyd	134
July 28, 1757	" Mary	Thomas Dougherty	211
Jan. 24, 1757	Rodger, Alexander	Margaret S.	191
Apr. 25, 1765	Ross, Jean	Arthur Scott	193
Aug. 14, 1753	" Rebecca	John Walker	138
Dec. 19, 1775	Rowan, Margaret	Wm. Clark	98
Jan. 24, 1757	S. Margaret	Alexander Rodger	191
Mar. 25, 1762	Sconler (Scouler?), Margaret	Wm. Young	212
Apr. 7, 1772	" (Scouler?), Marjory	W. Hen(ry)	219
Jan. 31, 1760	Scot, James	Janet Alexander	148
Nov. 8, 1753	" Robert	Mary McMuray	185

Date	Name	Married to	Page
May 4, 1762	Scott, Agnes	John Patterson	152
Apr. 25, 1765	" Arthur	Jean Ross	193
Mar. 27, 1770	" James	Mary Rankin	83
Feb. 12, 1771	" Mt	A. Spier	113
July 1/2, 1767	" Philip	Elizabeth Wilson	160
June 8, 1761	" Sarah	Thomas Mitchel	150
Apr. 6, 1761	" T.	Janet Brown	150
Oct. 23, 1770	Shenan, John	Han. Calbre(ath)	166
Dec. 15, 1762	" Margaret	John Walace	153
Apr. 11, 1771	Shield, Archibald	Jat. Buchanan	166
Oct. 14, 1765	Sinclair, Dan	Mary Marlin	215
Jan. 3, 1760	" Daniel	Isobel Gray	147
Feb. 13/14, 1775	" Margaret	George Clark	221
Oct. 30, 1764	Sloan, Alexander	Elizabeth Sloan	214
June 5, 1780	" David	Jean Stewart	228
Oct. 30, 1764	" Elizabeth	Alexander Sloan	214
Mar. 16, 1752	" Mary	Isaac Dowglas	92
Mar. 19, 1754	" Mary	Hew Coulter	95
Aug. 17, 1756	" Mary	James Mitchel	141
Oct. 30, 1764	" Mary	John Thomson	214
Sept. 3, 1751	" Rachel	Robert Love	100
Jan. 2, 1777	Smith, Elizabeth	William Law	123
July 6, 1762	" Mary	David Mitchel	110
May 1, 1764	" Sam	Mary McCleary	121
Feb. 26, 1761	" Susan	John Morton	150
Oct. 17, 1780	Spencer, Elizabeth	Sam Little	178
Feb. 12, 1771	Spier, A.	Mt. Scott	113
Oct. 28, 1788	" James	Hanna(h) Lyttle	237
Nov. 8, 1757	Steven(son), Mary	John Thomson	143
Apr. 10, 1769	(Stew...?),	J. Dun(can)	217
Dec. 31, 1760	Stewart, Alexander	Jean Walker	149
Mar. 29, 1768	" Elijah	Ma. Paterson	161
Dec. 28, 1762	" Hew	Agnes Moor	69
Apr. 23, 1778	" James	Jean Reid	225
June 5, 1780	" Jean	David Sloan	228
Apr. 20, 1766	" John	Elizabeth Cooper	159
Mar. 17, 1767	" Margaret	Nath. Coulter	112
June 8, 1767	" Marjory	Robert Stewart	97
Apr. 10, 1764	" Mary	R. Paterson	110
Mar. 5, 1772	" Mary	James Walker	167
Oct. 22, 1767	" Reb.	James Muir	131
June 8, 1767	" Robert	Marjory Stewart	97
May 8, 1771	" Sam	Agnes Templeton	133
June 26, 1769	" Sarah	Sam Taylor	69
Feb. 15, 1757	" Susan	Thomas Finey	107
Feb. 26, 1777	Stuart, Margaret	Jas. Ramsay	92
Oct. 17, 1752	Strehon, Mary	Jo(hn) McCormick	92

14   REGISTER OF MARRIAGES AND BAPTISMS

Date	Name	Married to	Page
May 29, 1787	Sutherland, Hew	Sara Mehowl	183
Oct. 21, 1771	Swan, Jean	James Taylor	103
June 12, 1770	" Margaret	Thomas Finey	102
Feb. 5, 1770	(" ?) Sally	Robert Bell	102
May 18/19, 1767	Swansie, Martha	John Navin	94
Mar. 17, 1772	Tait, Joseph	Elizabeth Pattison	167
Oct. 21, 1771	Taylor, James	Jean Swan	103
Mar. 11, 1752	" Jo(hn)	Eliz. McClure	105
Dec. 25, 1759	" John	Mary Wilson	147
June 26, 1769	" Sam	Sarah Stewart	69
May 17, 1753	" Sarah	Jas. Calhoun	106
Feb. 21, 1788	Teenan, James	Jean Brown	183
May 8, 1771	Templeton, Agnes	Sam Stewart	133
Oct. 8, 1770	Thomson, Agnes	John Martin	165
Nov. 3, 1755	" Janet	Jo(hn) Mooney	72
Dec. 11, 1752	" Jean	George Williams	104
Nov. 8, 1757	" John	Mary Steven(son)	143
Oct. 30, 1764	" John	Mary Sloan	214
Jan. 12, 1773	" John	Mary Paterson	168
Jan. 31, 1764	" Mary	W. Greenlie	110
Oct. 13, 1775	" Mary	Robert McKee	258
Apr. 20, 1773	" Robert	Sally Mitchel	169
Apr. 25, 1765	" Sarah	William Loughhead	193
Apr. 17, 1769	" W.	Jean Duncan	94
May 19, 1772	" Wm. (Thom.)	Jean Johnston	188
June 4, 1761	Thompson, Ann	Thomas Morton	74
Dec. 11, 1752	Thorn, Ann	Alexander McNair	104
Dec. 31, 1755	" Esther	William Wilson	210
May 8, 1764	" Isobel	And. Walker	76
July 5, 1762	" James	Mary Wilson	110
June 7, 1760	" Math	Agnes McKnaught	109
May 14, 1771	Torbit, Elizabeth	Charles Boyle	80
Dec. 24, 1762	Toulan, Agnes	Wa(lter) Buchanan	110
Jan. 17, 1769	Vogan, Jean	Joseph Rob(ertson?)	163
Dec. 15, 1762	Walace, John	Margaret Shenan	153
May 8, 1764	Walker, And.	Isobel Thorn	76
Nov. 19, 1761	" Gab.	Margaret Bell	151
Mar. 5, 1772	" James	Mary Stewart	167
Dec. 31, 1760	" Jean	Alexander Stewart	149
Aug. 14, 1753	" John	Rebecca Ross	138
Feb. 28, 1754	" Mary	James Young	139
June 25, 1765	" Mary	John Branan	158
Oct. 17, 1780	" Newport	Jean Broadly (Negroes)	178
Jan. 20/21, 1773	" Sarah	Gilbert Buchanan	168
Feb. 15, 1773	" William	Margaret Reid	91
Nov. 3, 1789	Weaver, Agnes	Jas. Quin	237
Jan. 22, 1782	White, Alexander	Jean Fulerton	179

Date	Name	Married to	Page
June 22, 1752	White, And.	Martha Miens	105
Oct. 3, 1765	(") Jean	John Buch(anan)	215
Jan. 5, 1752	Whiteside, Phinehas	Ann Couper	189
Feb. 13, 1770	Widrow, Joseph	Rebecca Dunlap	132
Dec. 11, 1752	Williams, George	Jean Thomson	104
Oct. 29, 1764	Wilson, Abig. (Wil.)	Sam Biggar	214
Oct. 25, 1762	" Ann	And. McMiens	240
July 1/2, 1767	" Elizabeth	Philip Scott	160
Nov. 11, 1773	" John	Mary Dinwoody	81
Nov. 21, 1758	" Margaret	John Crawford	211
Dec. 25, 1759	" Mary	John Taylor	147
July 5, 1762	" Mary	James Thorn	110
Oct. 29, 1765	" Mary	William Mitchel	77
Feb. 3, 1774	" Mary	George Mit(chel)	123
Feb. 8, 1759	" Peter	Jean Calbreath	145–146
Oct. 22, 1788	" Robert	Jean Maughlin	236
Feb. 25/26/27, 1772	" Sarah	James McYlahlin	123
Dec. 31, 1755	" William	Esther Thorn	210
May 21, 1753	Woods, Janet	Adam Calhoun	103
Mar. 11/12, 1776	" John	Ann (Fulerton?)	195
Oct. 9, 1753	" Sarah	David Carson	106
Sept. 21, 1769	" Wm.	Susanna Andrews	164
Mar. 1, 1757	Young, Alexander	Elizabeth Cany	191
Feb. 28, 1754	" James	Mary Walker	139
Nov. 23/24, 1763	" Margaret	George Henry	213
June 18, 1771	" Margaret	James Robertson	98
Mar. 25, 1762	" Wm.	Margaret Sconler (?)	212
Aug. 29/30, 1786	(9)	(9)	82
June 10, 1779	(4)	(4)	176

BAPTISMS

BAPTISMS

(No separate index is made of the parents of the children baptized. Surnames which appear to be similar are grouped together.)

Date	Name	Parent	Page
June 5, 1783	Alexander, Eleanor	Ezekial Alexander	201
June 5, 1783	" Janet	" "	201
June 5, 1783	" Thomas	" "	201
Apr. 12, 1752	Anderson, A. (daughter)	Thomas Anderson	71
May 22, 1757	" Agnes	" "	73
Dec. 7, 1755	" Alexander	James "	140
July 29, 1788	" Andrew	Wm. "	236
June 2, 1771	" Ann	James "	122
Aug. 24, 1767	" Elizabeth	James "	121
May 27, 1764	" Esther	James "	156
July 29, 1788	" James	Wm. "	236
Dec. 21, 1758	" Jean	James "	145
Sept. 1, 1751	" Jean	Thomas "	70-71
Nov. 16/17, 1765	" John	John "	90
July 29, 1788	" John	Wm. "	236
June 1, 1777	" Katharin	Joseph "	173
Nov. 8, 1752	" Martha	Jas. "	208
Apr. 27, 1760	" Martha	William "	148
Aug. 31, 1761 (30)	" Mary	James "	151
Nov. 12, 1765	" Rebekah	James "	121
Sept. 9, 1754	" Sarah	Thomas "	72
Mar. 26, 1769	" Silas	James "	122
Aug. 15, 1773	" Wm.	John "	130
July 29, 1788	" Wm.	Wm. "	236
May 16, 1779	Andrew, Arthur	John Andrew	176
Mar. 8/9, 1775	" Isobel	John "	171
Nov. 19, 1772	" James	John "	168
Feb. 19/24, 1753	" Mary	Robert "	187-188
Aug. 7, 1757	" Moses	Robert "	142
July 13, 1777	" (?) Robert	(See James Ross)	173
June 1, 1777	Andrews, Agnes	John Andrews	173
Apr. 27, 1760	" Agnes	Robert "	148
Jan. 23, 1780	" Elizab(eth)	Francis "	228
May 28, 1755	" Humphrey	Robert "	140
Mar. 17, 1778	" James	Francis "	224
Aug. 12, 1764	Archibald, Abigail	John Archibald	250
May 4, 1766	" Jean	John "	250-251
Oct. 16, 1774	" Jesse	John "	252
Oct. 16, 1774	" John	John "	252

19

Date	Name	Parent	Page
Oct. 12, 1760	Archibald, Joseph	John Archibald	250
Oct. 8, 1769	" Margaret	John "	251
Apr. 29, 1772	Armstrong, Elizabeth	Thomas Armstrong	98
June 3, 1761	Ayers, Agnes	W. Ayers	74
Feb. 5, 1756	" James	Elizabeth "	185
Oct. 10, 1758	" Margaret	Eliza. "	145
Apr. 29, 1787	Ayres, Agnes	James Ayres	235
Sept. 24, 1769	" Alexander	Margaret "	164
Dec. 24/25, 1776	" Elizabeth	Eliz. Ayre(s)	172
Mar. 7, 1764	" William	Betty Ayres	155
Oct. 17, 1784	Ayrs, John	James Ayrs	233
Feb. 27, 1765	Baldridge, Mary	Alexander Baldridge	157
Mar. 24, 1762	" Wm.	A. "	212
Apr. 27, 1760	Barber, John	Agnes Barber	148
June 10, 1759	" Robert	Agnes "	147
Oct. 18, 1761	" Sam	Agnes "	151
June 10, 1759	" Sus.	Agnes "	147
Mar. 20, 1771	Barclay, James	Wm. Barclay	166
July 22, 1786	Barg. ..... , Elizabeth	John Barg.	182
Sept. 3, 1788	Beaty, Agnes	Alexander Beaty	200
Sept. 3, 1788	" Agnes	James "	200
Sept. 3, 1788	" Elizabeth	Hugh "	200
Apr. 19, 1772	Beggs, Agnes	Mat. Beggs	70
Aug. 22, 1773	" Mary	Matthew "	81
Nov. 19, 1786	Bel, Mo.	Han. Bel (Hen.?)	114
Sept. 20, 1772	Bell, James	Robert Bell	114
June 10, 1787	" James	Henry "	114
July 18, 1784	Berry, John	John Berry	181
July 1, 1760	Berryhill, Wm.	(Took engagements)	128
Aug. 29, 1757	Berrykil, Martha	Widow Berrykil	142
Nov. 13, 1757	" Sarah	Widow "	143
Sept. 19, 1762	Black, Eleanor	Hew Black	153
Nov. 7, 1786	" Hugh	James "	234
Feb. 12, 1760	" James	T. "	192
Sept. 7, 1788	" Jean	James "	236
Feb. 11/12, 1761	" Jerem(iah)	Hew "	149–150
Aug. 1, 1770	" John	Thomas "	113
Aug. 3, 1764	" Mary	Thomas "	111
June 16, 1761	" Margaret	T. "	150–151
May 3, 1767	" Richard	Thomas "	160
May 2, 1762	" Thomas	Thomas "	152
Nov. 16, 1758	Blakch, Jean	James Blakch	73
May 16, 1766	Blair, Robert	John Blair	260
May 16, 1766	" Wm.	John "	260
Sept. 28, 1766	Blakely, Agnes	James Blakely	77
June 14, 1767	" Benjamin	John "	121
Aug. 28, 1768	" Edward	James "	78

Date	Name	Parent	Page
Apr. 8, 1755	Blakely, James	Jo. Blakely	72
Aug. 3, 1762	" Katharine	James "	75
Apr. 8, 1755	" Kathrine	James "	72
Aug. 22, 1762	" John (Blakly)	John " (Blakly)	75
May 6, 1759	" Margaret	John "	74
Mar. 28/29, 1770	" Margaret	James "	79
Mar. 14, 1765	" Rachel	John "	157
July 26, 1752	" Thomas	James "	71
July 26, 1752	" William	James "	71
June 25, 1760	" William	John "	121
Sept. 23, 1779	Boal, Elizabeth	Charles Boal	84
Sept. 23, 1779	" Thomas	Charles "	84
Aug. 22, 1773	Bole, Martha	Charles Bole	81
Apr. 27, 1756	Bonar, John	Robert Bonar	95
Apr. 22, 1753	" Thos.	Robert "	99
Mar. 30, 1760	" William	Robert "	93
Aug. 29/30, 1786	Bourns, James	(See John Burns)	
Aug. 27, 1783	Boyd, Elias	R. Boyd	254
May 5, 1752	" George	John "	189
Dec. 28, 1763	Brady, Robert	William Brady	155
May 7, 1769	Braedy, Eliz.	James Braedy	78
Aug. 16, 1767	" James	James "	77
Mar. 4, 1761	Broedy, David	James Broedy	150
Feb. 15, 1765	" John	James "	157
Mar. 1, 1769	Braeden, Mary	W. Braeden	163
Aug. 28, 1768	" Joseph	James "	78
Aug. 6, 1771	" Walter	James "	94
Aug. 22, 1773	" Wm.	W. "	81
Dec. 7/8, 1762	Broeden, Jean	Wm. Broeden	153
Oct. 31, 1762	" Thomas	James "	153
Oct. 31, 1762	" Wm.	James "	153
May 12, 1771	Braester, Martha	Mary Braester	79
Sept. 24, 1769	Branon, Martha	Mary Branon	164
Sept. 9, 1770	Branwood, Elizabeth	And. Branwood	79
Mar. 27, 1768	" Isobel	And. "	77
Apr. 12, 1772	" James	And. "	80
Oct. 21, 1764	" Jean	And. "	76
Apr. 4, 1762	" Sarah	Andrew "	75
Apr. 18, 1756	Bratan, Sam	Hor(ace) Bratan	72
Apr. 13, 1760	Braton, Mary	Braton	74
Sept. 18, 1753	Bratton, Mary	Horace Bratton	89
Nov. 10, 1751	" Robert	Horace "	89
Feb. 20/21, 1782	Brigs, Mary	John Brigs	98
Feb. 5, 1764	Brison, Jean	Robert Brison	96
May 1, 1757	" James	Robert "	142
Aug. 18, 1766	" Sam	Robert "	97
May 18/19, 1761	" Wm.	Robert "	96

Date	Name	Parent	Page
May 9, 1754........	Broomfield, Charles.......John	Broomfield........	70
May 22, 1757........	" Daniel.......John	"	73
Sept. 1, 1751........	" James.......Jo(hn)	" 70–71
June 25, 1760........	" Robert.......John	" (Brom.)...121
May 16/17, 1770....	Brousler, Elizabeth......Mary Brousler...........		79
May 16/17, 1770.....	" Joseph.........Mary	"	79
May 16/17, 1770.....	" Mary..........Mary	"	79
Feb. 12, 1764.......	Brown, Alexander.......James	Brown........	90
Nov.(21), 1763......	" David...........Benjamin	" 110
Sept. 1, 1754........	" Elizabeth........Benjamin	" 106
Mar. 12, 1758 . . .	" Elizabeth........Alexander	" 108
May 24, 1761........	" Elizabeth........Ben	" 109
Apr. 25, 1762........	" Hanah...........Mat.	" 110
Sept. 22, 1751........	" Hannah..........Ja...	" 105
Oct. 15, 1768........	" Hannah.........Benjamin	" 112
Feb. 5, 1764........	" Henry...........A.	" 96
May 14, 1761........	" James...........James	" 90
June 1, 1770........	" Jean............Matthew	" 91
Oct. 12, 1752........	" John............James	" 105
Mar.(11), 1753......	" John............Alexander	" 105
Jan. 21, 1759........	" John............Ben(jamin)	" 108
Feb.(18), 1753......	" Margaret........Matthew	" 137
Nov. 6, 1751........	" Martha.........Alexander	" 105
July (20), 1755......	" Mary...........Alexander	" 107
Jan. 30, 1757........	" Mary...........Benjamin	" 95
Feb. 9, 1764........	" Mary...........Math.	" 90
Sept. 19, 1762........	" Matthew........Matthew	" 153
Apr. 13, 1768........	" Sara(h)..........Matthew	" 91
July 13, 1755........	" Thomas.......... (?)	" 190
May 10, 1772........	" Thomas.........Matthew	" 114
Aug. 14/15, 1771.....	" Thomas.........Ben	" 113
Jan. 17, 1758........	" William..........Matthew	" 143
Mar. 12, 1758........	" William.........James	" 108
Oct. 20, 1765........	" William.........Ben	" 111
Aug. 13, 1772........	Brownlie, Hew...........James Brownlie..........		129
Jan. 9, 1754........	" Isobel..........John	" 185
Sept. 19/20, 1770.....	" John...........James	" 194
Dec. 17, 1751........	Brownlies, Helen........Jo Brownlies.............		184
Dec. 17, 1751........	" John..........Jo	" 184
Dec. 17, 1751........	" Mary.........Jo	" 184
May 1, 1757........	Buchanan, Agnes.........Walter Buchanan........		142
June 14, 1772........	" Agnes.........John	" 219
Nov. 19, 1772........	" Agnes.........Walter	" 168
Aug. 31, 1766........	" Andrew.......John	" 216
July 27, 1757........	" Ebenezer......John	" 211
Nov. 14, 1762........	" Elizabeth......George	" 213
Aug. 19, 1753........	" Elizabeth......Wm.	" 209

Date	Name	Parent	Page
Apr. 16, 1752	Buchanan, George	Jo(hn) Buchanan	208
June 22, 1766	" George	George "	215
Apr. 6, 1783	" George	John "	232
Feb. 21, 1781	" Isaac	Gilbert "	98
Mar. 15, 1752	" Jas.	Walter "	91–92
July 27, 1757	" James	Wm. "	211
May 18/19, 1761	" James	Walter "	96
June 14, 1761	" James	Walter "	150
Aug. 31, 1768	" (an) James	J. "	217
May 3, 1752	" Janet	Walter "	136
Mar. 29, 1776	" Jean	John "	222
Dec. (5), 1778	" Jean	Wm. "	226
May 19, 1754	" John	George "	209
Feb. 17, 1757	" John	Walter "	95
Apr. 14, 1761	" John	John "	238
Sept. 4, 1763	" John	Walter "	154
Dec. 28, 1755	" Margaret	William "	210
May 20, 1759	" Margaret	Walter "	93
Oct. 23, 1768	" Margaret	Walter "	162
Apr. 9, 1770	" Martha	John "	218
Jan. 26, 1777	" Martha	Wm. "	223
June 2, 1757	" Mary	George "	211
Apr. 14, 1761	" Mary	George "	238
July 1, 1764	" Mary	(For John Marlin)	214
July 31, 1774	" Mary	John Buchanan	220
Mar. 26, 1783	" Mary	Gilbert "	92
Sept. 7, 1788	" Mary	James "	236
Oct. 4, 1778	" Thomas	John "	226
Oct. 30, 1774	" Walter	Gilbert "	170
May 1, 1759	Buc(hanan) William	Geo. Buc(hanan)	212
Aug. 29/30, 1786	Burns, James	John Burns (Bourns)	82
July 23, 1756	" James	Arch(ibald) Burns	72
Dec. 4, 1753	" Janet	Arch(ibald) "	138–139
Nov. 12, 1780	" Jean	Francis "	253
Nov. 12, 1780	" John	Francis "	253
Mar. 4, 1761	" Letitia	Richard "	150
Mar. 25, 1759	" Loetitia	Richard "	146
Nov. 7, 1773	" Margaret	John "	81
Mar. 24, 1763	" Mary	Rich. "	75
Mar. 10, 1765	" Thomas	Richard "	76
July 10, 1768	Cachy, Elizabeth	Sam Cachy	162
Nov. 3, 1771	" Esther	Sam "	167
June 8, 1766	" James	Sam "	159
Nov. 2, 1755	" Janet	Sam "	140
June 21, 1761	" John	Sam "	151
Nov. 26, 1758	" Nathaniel	Sam "	145
May 27, 1753	" Samuel	Sam "	138

Date	Name	Parent	Page
Mar. 27, 1764.......	Cachy, William.........	Sam Cachy..............	156
Aug. 20, 1769.......	Cairn, Jean..............	Mary Cairn..............	78
July 31, 1755.......	Cal. Samuel...........	Sam Cal................	95
Oct. 12, 1762.......	Calbreath, Agnes.........	Wm. Calbreath........	90
Nov. 13/14/15, 1765..	" (Daniel).......	(J. C.)......100
Mar. 27, 1761.......	" Francis.......	Henry " 150
Sept. 8, 1751........	" Hannah......	Robert " 134
May 30, 1754........	" James (ad.)....	Wm. " 190
Oct. 27, 1765........	" Margaret.....	Henry " 76
Sept. 18, 1763........	" Robert.......	Henry " 75
Apr. 22, 1759........	" Sam.........	Robert " 146
Dec. 21, 1758........	" Samuel.......	Henry " 145
May 28, 1782.......	Caldwell, Ann...........	John Caldwell...........179
Aug. 22, 1773........	" Matthew......	Matthew Caldwel(l)...... 81
Aug. 22, 1773........	" William.......	Matthew " 81
Sept. 1, 1754.......	Calghoun, Mathew......	James Calghoun..........106
May 29, 1768........	Calqhoun, Mary.... ...	Sam Calqhoun........... 97
Jan. 31, 1762........	Calhoun, Agnes..........	James Calhoun........109
Apr. 3, 1765........(	") Agnes..........	Sam (")........ 92
Dec. 3, 1786........	" Amelia........	Matthew " 182
May 10, 1772........	" Ann...........	Sam " 114
Feb. 4, 1762........	" David.........	Sam " 96
Mar. 5, 1770........	" Isobel.........	James " 217
May 10, 1772........	" Isobel.........	Sam " 114
Oct. 25, 1767........	" James.........	James " 112
Nov. 24, 1765........	" Mary..........	James " 111
Oct. 21, 1787........	" Matthew......	Matthew " 124
Apr. 26, 1763........	" Robert........	Sam " 96
June 12, 1763........	" Sarah.........	James " 110
Sept. 21, 1766........	" Sarah.........	Sam " 97
Jan. 15, 1772........	" William........	J(ames) C(alhoun) (?) 186–187
Sept. 23, 1753........	Colghoun, James........	Sam Colghoun........... 93
Feb. 17, 1760.......	Colhoun, Janet........	Sam Colhoun...........148
Mar. 16, 1760........	" Martha........	James " 108–109
Aug. 3, 1769.......	Colqhoun, Ann...........	S(am) Colqhoun.......... 97
Mar. 15, 1752........	" Jean..........	Adam " 91–92
Mar. 12, 1758.......	Colquhoun, David.......	James Colquhoun........108
Nov. 11, 1751........	" Jo(hn)......	Sam. " 99
June 2, 1782.......	Carson, Hew............	Wm. Carson............179
Aug. 4, 1754........	" Margaret.......	David " 120
May 16, 1756........	" Mary..........	David " 141
May 18, 1766.......	Carswel, David.........	Nathaniel Carswel....259–260
Nov. 28, 1764.... ...	Caruthers, Mary........	William Caruthers........ 87
Dec. 2, 1767........	" Sam..........	W. " 77
May 24, 1761.......	Cha. Isobel.........	John Cha. 109
Aug. 31, 1755.......	Chalmers, Elisha........	John Chalmers...........107
Oct. 2, 1774.......	Clark, John.............	Sam Clark.....257–258

Date	Name	Parent	Page
Oct. 2, 1774	Clark, Mary	Sam Clark	257–258
Dec. 29, 1782	(" ?) Mary Rowan	Margaret "	232
Oct. 21/22, 1769	" Wm.	Sam "	257
Oct. 27, 1751	Clyde, Jean	Mich. Clyde	199
Oct. 10, 1773	Coates, Sarah	John Coates	169–170
Apr. 30, 1761	Cochran, Eleanor	J. Cochran	117
Nov. 19, 1751	" George	Jo. "	125
Aug. 31, 1772	" Janet	T. "	80–81
Apr. 14, 1756	" Jean	John "	116
Apr. 20, 1755	" John	Jo. "	127
Mar. 25, 1753	" Mary	Joseph "	126
Aug. 31, 1772	" Robert	T. "	80–81
Aug. 24, 1766	Colins, Cornelius	Corn. Colins	159
June 13, 1756	" Eliza	Cornelius "	191
May 25, 1760	" James	Cornelius "	148
May 23, 1762	" Wm.	Cornelius "	152
Feb. 24, 1754	Collins, Agnes	Corn. Collins	189
Sept. 11, 1768	" David	Corn. "	162
June 18, 1758	" Esther	Cornelius "	144
May 3, 1759	Cooper, Hannah	William Cooper	74
Apr. 4, 1758	" William	William "	73
May 17, 1752	Couper, John	Wm. Couper	136
May 24, 1770	Cotter, Mary	(Adult)	194
Jan. 2, 1759	Coulter, Agnes	Hew Coulter	145
Aug. 16, 1774	(") Agnes	N. " (C.)	170
Aug. 16, 1774	(") Elijah	N. " (C.)	170
Oct. 31, 1779	" Esther	Nathaniel Coulter, Sr.	176
Apr. 18, 1765	" Grizzel	Nathaniel Coulter	157
Nov. 12, 1775	" Hugh	Nath. "	171
June 5, 1757	" Isobel	Hugh "	142
Mar. 16/17, 1763	" Janet	Nath. "	153
Dec. 21/22, 1767	" John	H(ugh) "	161
Jan. 22, 1771	" Josiah	Nath(aniel) "	166
Apr. 13, 1779	" Margaret	Nathaniel "	176
Apr. 18, 1765	" Mary	Hew "	157
Aug. 3, 1788	" Mary	Nathaniel "	200
Feb. 18, 1759	" Nathaniel	Natha, "	146
Apr. 30, 1769	" Samuel	Nath, "	163
Feb. 21, 1768	" Sarah	Nath. "	161
Apr. 8, 1777	" Sarah	Nathaniel "	173
Feb. 8, 1761	" William	N. " (Cou.)	149
May 11, 1766	C(owan), Sarah	J. or Eph. Cowan	257
June 2, 1782	Craig, Wm.	James Craig	179
Apr. 20, 1760	Crawford, Esther	John Crawford	212
Apr. 19, 1763	" William	John "	121
May 29, 1766	Crawfurd, Esther	Joseph Crawfurd	251
May 24, 1768	" James	John "	193

Date	Name	Parent	Page
June 9, 1765	Crawford, John	John Crawfurd	76
Mar. 11, 1770	" Margaret	John "	122
Apr. 13, 1760	Crook, James	John Crook	74
Aug. 13, 1772	Crooks, Alice	John Crooks	129
May 23, 1771	" Alice	James "	129
Nov. 15, 1773	" Jean	John " Jun	130
May 14, 1764	" Jean	J. "	76
Mar. 27, 1768	" John	John "	77
Mar. 30, 1766	" Margaret	John "	77
Oct. (5), 1756	" Mary	John "	141–142
Mar. 26, 1770	" Mary	John "	78
Apr. 4, 1762	" Rachel	John "	75
Aug. 18, 1772	" Rob	James "	129
Mar. 26, 1758	" William	John "	73
May 28, 1755	Crosan, Sam	T. Crosan	140
Apr. 29, 1759	Crossen, John	Jean Crossen	146
Mar. 14, 1765	Cross, Esther	Jean Cross	157
Sept. 14/15, 1763	" Esther	Thomas "	121
Aug. 10, 1760	" Sam	T. "	149
Mar. 31, 1768	" Thomas	Thomas "	122
Apr. 30, 1761	Crunckeltons, Elizabeth	Robert Crunckeltons	117
Apr. 30, 1761	" Sari	Robert "	117
Apr. 13, 1763	Crunckleton, Samuel	R. Crunckleton	128
Aug. 9, 1752	Cumins, Jean	Jonathan Cumins	136
May 27, 1764	Cuthbertson, John	Rev. John Cuthbertson	156
May 21, 1762	" Sarah	Rev. John "	152
July 9, 1769	" Walter	Rev. John "	164
Nov. 30, 1756	Davidson, James	James Davidson	142
May 29, 1771	" Joseph	James "	129
June 17, 1759	" Mary	James "	127–128
Nov. 29, 1761	" Rebecca	James "	87
Mar. 24, 1765	" Wm.	Jas. "	128
Nov. 6, 1777	Davison, Hew	Agnes Davison	224
Nov. 6, 1777	" Sam	Agnes "	224
Mar. 26, 1775	Davies, John	Hugh Davies	221
Jan. 20, 1789	Diliri (3 sons)	Malcom Diliri	183
Aug. 10, 1755	Dinwiddy, David	David Dinwiddy	72
Oct. 8, 1758	" James	David "	145
Apr. 19, 1761	" Sarah	David "	74
Mar. 18, 1753	(") Sarah	Jo. (") (?)	82
Mar. 18, 1753	(") Thomas	Jo. (") (?)	82
Sept. 1, 1751	Dinwoddy, Mary	David Dinwoddy	70–71
Feb. 19, 1764	Dinwoody, Hew	David Dinwoody	155
July 22, 1753	Dunwoody, John	David Dunwoody	82
Mar. 27, 1768	" Wm.	D. D.	77
Nov. 4, 1774	(Dixon), David	(S. Dixon)	220
Feb. 12, 1777	Do(bbin), James	Do(bbin)	81

Date	Name	Parent	Page
Mar. 17, 1776........Dougharty,	Agnes........	John Dougharty.....	221–222
Aug. 9, 1769........Dougherty,	Alexander....	Thomas Dougherty......	122
July 31, 1774....... "	Andrew......John	"	220
Aug. 9, 1769....... "	Eleanor......Thomas	"	122
Aug. 4, 1754....... "	Elizabeth....Thomas	"	120
Mar. 22, 1778....... "	Elizabeth.....John	"	...224–225
Aug. 9, 1769....... "	James.......Thomas	"	122
Aug. 4, 1754....... "	Jean........Thomas	"	120
Aug. 9, 1769....... "	John........Thomas	"	122
Aug. 4, 1754....... "	Margaret.....Thomas	"	120
July 31, 1774....... "	Margaret.....John	"	220
Aug. 9, 1769....... "	Martha......Thomas	"	122
May 3, 1772....... "	Robert......Thomas	"	123
Aug. 9, 1769....... "	Sarah......Thomas	"	122
Aug. 4, 1754....... "	Thomas.....Thomas	"	120
Jan. 20, 1789.......Downie,	David...........	Wm. Downie............	183
Mar. 30, 1752.......Dr.	Jean...........	——— Dr. (Lowry?)..	119
Oct. (23), 1763......Dranon,	Jean...........	Robert Dranon..........	155
Sept. 26, 1779.......Drenan,	David...........	John Drenan.............	84
Sept. 26, 1779....... "	Martha.........John	"	84
Sept. 13, 1770.......Dunbar,	Alexander......	James Dunbar..........	79
Dec. 20, 1772....... "	James..........John	"	204
Dec. 8, 1771....... "	John..........John	"	167
Sept. 13, 1770....... "	Margaret.......James	"	79
Nov. 16/17, 1765..... "	Mary..........James	"	90
Nov. 16/17, 1765..... "	Robert.........John	"	90
Aug. 28, 1768....... "	Robert.........Jas.	"	78
Dec. 24, 1769....... "	Thomas........John	"	204
June 12, 1757.......Duncan,	Ann............	Robert Duncan..........	191
Nov. 6, 1777....... "	Eleanor........John	"	224
July 13, 1755....... "	James..........James	"	190
Nov. 23, 1783....... "	James..........John	"	232
May 14, 1758....... "	Jean...........James	"	144
Jan. 23, 1780....... "	Jean...........John	"	228
May 18, 1755....... "	John..........James	"	139–140
Feb. 5, 1756....... "	John..........Robert	"	185
Apr. 9, 1786....... "	John..........John	"	234
June 6, 1762....... "	Mary..........Widow	"	152
Feb. 19/24, 1753..... "	Sarah.........James	"	187–188
Mar. 29, 1776....... "	Sarah.........John	"	222
Jan. 23/25, 1770......Dun.	Joseph (?)......John	Dun. (See Joseph Stewart).	186
Nov. 29, 1774....... "	Agnes..........J.	Dun.	204
Nov. 29, 1774.......(")	Mary..........	(?)	204
Jan. 4, 1759.......Dunlap,	Hanna.........J.	Dunlap..........	188
Sept. 22, 1778....... "	James..........Rebecca	" or Woodrow.	175
Sept. 22, 1778....... "	Lydia..........Rebecca	"	175

Date	Name	Parent	Page
Sept. 22, 1778	Dunlap, Margaret	Rebecca Dunlap	175
Dec. 8, 1763	" Martha	John "	155
Aug. 16, 1774	" Sarah	(Adult) "	170
May 15, 1763	" Sarah	John "	154
Apr. 4, 1756	Dunlop, Isobel	Jo. Dunlop	141
Mar. 26, 1781	" James	W. D(unlap)	178
Mar. 28, 1780	" John	Wm. "	177
Sept. 4, 1752	" Joseph	Jas. "	208
Mar. 31, 1771	" Thomas	John "	166
Apr. 26, 1752	" Wm.	John "	136
July 29, 1753	" Wm.	John "	138
Nov. 12, 1777	Edminston, David	Helen Edminston, Widow.	174
Nov. 12, 1777	" Henry	Helen " "	174
Nov. 12, 1777	" Mary	Helen " "	174
Nov. 12, 1777	" William	Helen " "	174
Mar. 5, 1754	Elliot(?), Margaret	John Elliot (?)	190
Apr. 27, 1755	E. Joseph	James E.	120
May 14, 1769	Ervin, James	John Ervin	163
Dec. 13, 1753	Erwin, Martha	James Erwin	126
July 2, 1758	Ewen, James	James Ewen	144
Oct. 13, 1751	Ewen, Wm.	James Ewen	135
Apr. 2, 1775	Ewin, James	Alexander Ewin	221
Dec. 5, 1776	" Jean	John "	223
Mar. 15, 1773	" Sam	John "	81
Oct. 11, 1784	Ewing, Alexander	Alexander Ewing	233
Mar. 27, 1777	" Eliz.	Wm. Ewi(ng)	173
Dec. 22, 1768	" Helen	Alexander Ewing	163
May 14, 1771	" Henry	John "	80
Apr. 22, 1779	" Henry	A. "	227
Sept. 5, 1779	" James	Wm. "	176
June 10, 1765	" Joshua	John "	157
Sept. 16, 1781	" Margaret	Wm. "	179
May 2, 1773	" Martha	Alexander "	220
Jan. 13, 1771	" Mary	Alexander "	218
May 4/5, 1778	" Mary	Wm. "	123
June 6, 1784	" Mary	Alexander "	233
Apr. 16, 1777	" Rebec(ca)	Alexander "	223
July 24, 1782	" Thomas	Alexander "	231
Feb. 27, 1781	" Wm.	John "	178
July 8, 1787	Farmer, Hanna	Gregory Farmer	235
Nov. 7, 1786	" Margaret	Gregory "	234
Nov. 12, 1775	Fegan, Janet	Agnes Fegan	171
Nov.(14), 1756	Fergus, Hew	Hew Fergus	142
Nov.(14), 1756	(" ?) John	Sam (" ?)	142
Oct. 8, 1758	" Mary	Hew "	145
June 3, 1764	" Robert	Hugh "	156
Oct. 13, 1754	" Thomas	Hew "	139

Date	Name	Parent	Page
Aug. 10, 1788	Ferguson, Mary	John Ferguson	195
Apr. 21, 1765	Ferrier, Agnes	And. Ferrier	214
Nov. 1/2, 1763	" Elizabeth	And. "	238–239
May 19, 1768	" James	And. "	128
Nov. 17, 1760	" John	And. "	212
May 19, 1768	" Sam	And. "	128
Mar. 28, 1762	" Thomas	And. "	212
June 10, 1759	" William	And. " (Ferier)	147
May 27, 1759	Finey, Agnes	Thomas Finey	108
July 29, 1764	" Agnes	Thomas "	110–111
Apr. 7, 1765	" And	James "	111
Oct. 20, 1765	" Elijah	Thomas "	111
Mar. 12, 1758	" James	Thomas "	108
Feb. 1, 1767	" James	Thomas "	186
June 16, 1771	" James	Thomas "	97
Feb. 4, 1770	" Janet	Thomas "	113
Mar. 16, 1760	" John	James "	108–109
Mar. 12, 1758	" Margaret	James "	108
Sept. 20, 1772	" Martha	Thomas "	114
Oct. 10, 1779	" Martha	James "	114
July 4, 1762	" Mary	James "	110
May 10, 1767	" Robert	James "	112
Jan. 22, 1761	" Sam	T. "	109
Oct. 9, 1768	" Sarah	Thomas "	112
Oct. 4, 1762	" Thomas	T. "	110
Jan. 31, 1764	" William	T. "	110
Oct. 28, 1753	Finlay, Abel	Abel Finlay	138
May 7, 1769	Finley, Abel	James Finley	78
Oct. 2, 1771	" Abel	John "	80
Feb. 21, 1773	" Elizabeth	John "	130
Oct. 2, 1771	" George	Wm. "	80
Oct. 2, 1768	" Hugh	John "	128
Mar. 21, 1769	" Margaret	John "	129
Oct. 21, 1764	" Sarah	John "	76
Dec. 21, 1755	Finton, Adam	William Finton	107
Aug. 18, 1754	" Samuel	William "	106
Nov. 21, 1784	Forsyth, Ann	Elijah Forsyth	182
Nov. 21, 1784	" Mary	Elijah "	182
Oct. 27, 1765	Frazer, Francis	David Frazer	76
Aug. 25, 1782	Fulerton, Adam	Wm. Fulerton	231
Mar. 25, 1763	" And	William "	213
May 5, 1752	" Ann	Humphrey "	189
Feb. 28, 1773	" David	Humphrey "	168
Nov. 6, 1757	" Elizabeth	Humphrey "	142–143
Sept. 19/20, 1770	" Humphrey	Humphrey "	194
June 2, 1754	" John	Margt. "	190
Feb. 11, 1787	" Margaret	W. " (Ful.)	235

Date	Name	Parent	Page
June 9, 1765........	Fulerton, Margaret.......	Robert	Fulerton...... 76
Apr. 21, 1765........	" Mary..........	William	" 214
Oct. 12, 1767........	" Mary..........	Humphrey	" 160
Nov. 1/2, 1763......	" R..............	William	" .238–239
June 9, 1765........	" Robert........	Robert	" 76
Apr. 30, 1780........	" Robert........	William	" 228
Oct. 13/14, 1784.....	" Samuel........	(Wm.)	" 233
May 29, 1757........	" Sarah..........	Robert	" 73
May 27, 1760........	" Thomas.......	Humphrey	" 148
Apr. 25, 1765........	" William........	H.	" (Fu.)....193
June 9, 1765........	" William.......	Robert	" 76
Oct. 4, 1778........	" William........	W.	" 226
Feb. 2/11, 1753	Fulson, Margaret..............	Fulson (?)........137	
Mar. 15, 1752........	Gardner, James (Jas.) ....Jo.	Gardner..........91–92	
Apr. 16, 1754........	" James..........	John " 103	
Aug. 26, 1762........	" Margaret.......	John " 100	
Aug. 3, 1758........	" Rachel..........	John " 144	
Aug. 8, 1756.......	Garner, Elizabeth........	Jo Garner............. 95	
Oct. 28, 1764........	" John.............	John " 93	
Apr. 7, 1754........	Gay, Ann.........	Sam Gay............. 95	
Jan. 10, 1760........	Gebby (Gabby), Janet ....John Gabby............186		
Sept. 27, 1761........	" John.............	John Gebby..........117	
Mar. 21, 1769........	" David............	J. " 129	
May 1, 1768........	" Janet............	Wm. " 216	
Mar. 24, 1765........	" James...........	John " 128	
Sept. 11, 1763........	" Jean............	William " (Geb.).......213	
Apr. 8, 1770........	" John............	William " 217	
Feb. 28, 1773........	" Marion..........	John " 168	
July 7, 1765........	" Mary............	William " 214	
June 2, 1771........	" Thomas..........	John " 122	
Mar. 24, 1765........	" Wm.............	John " 128	
Sept. 1, 1776........	" William McMn....Ann	" 222	
Nov. 1, 1789........	Gerry, Elizabeth........	Alexander Gerry........237	
Sept. 19, 1752.......	Gibb. Robert..........	Hew Gibb. 87	
Nov. 11, 1751.......	Gibson, Ann.............	Robert Gibson........... 99	
May 21, 1758........	" Ann.............	Hugh " (Gib.).......192	
June 29, 1755........	" David..........	H. " 87	
Aug. 10, 1754........	" Margaret........	Robert " 99	
Feb. 12, 1760........	" Rachel..........	H. " (Gib.).......192	
Nov. 11, 1751.......	Giffan, And.............	And. Giffan........... 99	
Mar. 1, 1757........	" Martha..........	Andrew " 191	
Apr. 2, 1769.......	Giffen, Agnes...........	John Giffen............. 91	
July 15, 1753........	" Wm............	And. " 93	
Sept. 23, 1759........	Gilchrist, Agnes..........	John Gilchrist.......249–250	
May 4, 1766........	" Archibald.......	John " 250	
Sept. 11, 1774........	" Charles........	John " 251	
Aug. 12, 1764........	" Eleanor.......	John " 250	

Date	Name	Parent	Page
Sept. 23, 1759	Gilchrist, Helen	John Gilchrist	249–250
Sept. 23, 1759	" John	John "	249–250
June 23, 1754	" Katharine	John "	250
Sept. 2/3, 1783	Gilespy, Nathaniel	Sam Gilespy	255
June 29, 1755	Gilmor, Benjamin	James Gilmor	87
Sept. 19, 1752	" Martha	Jas. "	87
Apr. 28/29, 1783 (27)	" Wm.	James "	181
May 8/9, 1752	Gilmore, Sarah (Twin)	John Gilmore (Jo.)	136
May 8/9, 1752	" Wm. (")	John " (")	136
Feb. 24, 1768	Girvan, David	John Girvan	161
Feb. 24, 1768	" Mary	John "	161
Nov. 13, 1760	" William	John "	212
July 18, 1779	Glen, Agnes	James Glen	176
Mar. 26, 1783	" Jean	James "	92
Mar. 26, 1781	" Joseph	James "	178
Dec. 20, 1775	" Rebecca	James "	92
Aug. 31, 1777	" Walter	James "	174
Dec. 20, 1775	" William	James "	92
Mar. 21, 1758	Glendining, Katharine	John Glendining	95
Aug. 21, 1751	" Jo.	Jo. "	91
Apr. 14, 1754	" Sam	John "	89–90
Aug. 8, 1784	Glover, Mary	Jas. Glover	182
Oct. 2, 1768	Gordon, James	Ar. Gordon	128
Oct. 21, 1787	" Wm.	John "	124
Dec. 20, 1772	Graham, Alexander	John Graham	204
Dec. 24, 1769	" David	Mr. "	204
Dec. 2, 1763	" Edward	George "	203
Feb. 4/5, 1767	" Eleanor	James "	102
Nov. 9, 1772	" Elijah	John "	98
Oct. 14, 1761	" George	G. "	203
Nov. 5, 1751	" Helen	Jo. "	101
Aug. 15, 1756	" Henry	John "	107
June 29, 1759	" Isobel	George "	203
Nov. 26, 1754	" Janet	George " (s)	203
June 7, 1768	" Jean	James " (Grah.)	102
Dec. 5/6, 1769	" Martha	James "	113
Feb. 14, 1773	" Ruth	James "	114
June 4, 1782	" (?) Mary Newberry	James "	179
May 9, 1753	Grahams, Esther	John Grahams	106
Oct. 27, 1751	Gray, George	James Gray	199
Feb. 4/5, 1767	Greenlie, David	James Greenlie	102
Apr. 30, 1765	" James	W. "	111
Feb. 4/5, 1767	" Sarah	Wm. "	102
Oct. 9, 1768	" Mary	W. "	112
Mar. 1, 1759	Greer, Elizabeth	Robert Gree(r)	211
Oct. 13, 1765	" Jean	Robert Greer	215
Aug. 27, 1757	" John	Wm. " (Gr.)	142

Date	Name	Parent	Page
Aug. 27, 1757	Greer, Margaret	Wm.	Greer (Gr.)	142
June 27, 1762	" Mary	Wm.	" 153
Mar. 1, 1759	" Moses	Robert	" (r)	211
Mar. 1, 1759	" Robert	Robert	" (r)	211
May 7, 1758	" Sarah	William	" 144
June 27, 1762	(" Sarah ?)	(William | " ?)	153
Nov. 1/2, 1763	" Thomas	Robert	" 238–239
July 30, 1760	Greers, Susan	W. Greers	149
Mar. 28, 1762	Grier, Mary	Robert Grier	212
Aug. 9, 1769	Guthrie, Mary	John Guthrie	122
May 18/19, 1761	Hail, Daniel	Hugh Hail	96
Nov. 20, 1758	" Katharine	Hew "	240
Apr. 15, 1764	Hains, David	Barth. Hains	96
Mar. 16, 1760	" Hannah	Bartho. " (Ha.)	108
Feb. 3, 1771	" Helen	Bartholomew "	186
Jan. 31, 1762	" James	Bartholomew "	109
Aug. 22, 1788	" John	Jonathan "	115
Aug. 10, 1766	" Jonathan	Bartholomew "	112
May 13, 1753	" Joseph	Bartholomew "	106
May 5, 1757	" Margaret	Bar. "	108
Mar. 10, 1752	" Mary	Bartho. "	105
June 30, 1752	Hall, John	Henry Hall (Hail?)	82
Sept. 7, 1760	Hamilton, Alexander	William Hamilton	149
Jan. 15/16, 1787	" Elizabeth	... " (?)	182
Sept. 7, 1760	" Jean	William "	149
June 14, 1761	" Mary	William "	150
May 8, 1763	" William	William "	154
Mar. 30, 1788	Hanna, Robert	Henry Hanna	235
Jan. 15/16, 1787	" Thomas	Henry "	182
June 5/6, 1790	" Wm.	Hen. " (Hana.)	238
Oct. 11, 1784	Harbison, Elizabeth	John Harbison	233
Oct. 11, 1784	" Margaret	John "	233
Mar. 31, 1776	Henry, George	Wm. Henry	222
Mar. 17/18, 1779	" George	Wm. "	227
Apr. 4, 1779	" John	(Wm.?) "	176
Dec. 14, 1777	" John	Wm. "	224
May 15, 1774	" Margaret	William "	220
Sept. 14, 1788	" Mary	(See McHenry)	
Dec. 18, 1777	Hill, Mary	Helen Hill	174
Oct. 24, 1784	Hilton, Elizabeth	Elizabeth Hilton	114
June 16, 1771	" Jean	John "	97
June 1, 1765	Hodge, Francis	John Hodge	76
May 17, 1764	" Margaret	Sam "	99
Oct. 27, 1765	" Sarah	John "	76–77
Aug. 29, 1784	Hood, John	James Hood	182
Aug. 29, 1784	" Rachel	James "	182
Oct. 29, 1767	Howston, Agnes	James Howston	97

Date	Name	Parent	Page
May 10, 1772	Howston, Christopher	James Howston	114
Aug. 7, 1766	" Rebecca	James "	96–97
Jan. 28, 1770	" Susanna	James "	113
Aug. 27, 1753	Hutchieson, Eliz.	John Hutchieson	71
June 9, 1765	" Jon. (Ad.)	John " Jun.	76
Sept. 1, 1751	" Rose-Anne	John "	70–71
Apr. 1, 1766	" Thomas	——	77
Apr. 3, 1768	Hutchinson, James	John Hutchinson	77
Mar. 26, 1770	" John	John "	78
Apr. 10, 1763	Innes, Elizabeth	Francis Innes	75
Apr. 10, 1763	" Francis	Francis "	75
May 11, 1759	" James	James "	74
Sept. 21, 1755	" Mary	James "	190
Sept. 19, 1783	Jackson, Benj.	Robert Jackson	255
Sept. 19, 1783	" Jacob	Robert "	255
Sept. 19, 1783	" Joseph	Robert "	255
Sept. 19, 1779	Jamieson, Mary	Robert Jamieson	83
Oct. 7, 1771	January, Deborah	Peter January	129
June 29, 1760	" Ephr.	Peter "	128
Aug. 17, 1762	" Hannah	Peter "	128
Aug. 1, 1756	" James	Peter "	116
Aug. 29, 1767	" John	Peter "	121
Mar. 26, 1765	" Samuel	Peter "	128
May 5, 1754	" Sarah	Peter "	126–127
June 10, 1765	Jones, Elizabeth	Eliz. Jones	157
June 10, 1765	" Helen	Eliz. "	157
June 10, 1765	" Katharine	Eliz. "	157
June 10, 1765	" Margaret	Eliz. "	157
June 10, 1765	" Thomas	Eliz. "	157
Aug. 13, 1783	Jordon, John	Jonathan Jordon	254
Aug. 13, 1783	" Robert	Jonathan "	254
Apr. 14, 1754	Junken, Agnes	Joseph Junken	89–90
May 17, 1761	" Benjamin	Joseph "	96
Apr. 26, 1763	" Eliz.	Joseph " (s)	96
Apr. 27, 1756	" John	Joseph "	95
Nov. 28, 1762	Kain, John	John Kain	203
Aug. 26, 1753	Kenedy, Thomas	John Kenedy	71
June 28, 1789	Kennedy, Agnes	Stewart Kennedy	237
Dec. 15, 1765	Kennety, Alexander	George Kennety	204
Dec. 16, 1770	" Elizabeth	Thomas "	87
May 6, 1772	" John	Thomas "	113–114
Mar. 14, 1764	" William	George "	203
Jan. 3, 1753	Ker, Jean	The. Ker	185
May 20, 1770	" Josiah	Alexander "	79
June 5, 1757	" Josiah	Jos. "	142
May 3, 1752	" Mary	Joseph "	136
Nov. 12, 1754	" Sarah	William "	185

Date	Name	Parent	Page
Aug. 2, 1772	Ker, Sarah	Alexander Ker	80
Oct. 16, 1759	" William	Jos. "	203
Aug. 31, 1760	Kilgore, Cha.	—— Kilgore	109
Mar. 8, 1770	" Elizabeth	Charles "	91
May 6, 1772	" Janet	Charles " (C.)	113–114
Oct. 12, 1762	" Jesse	Charles "	90
Mar. 23, 1758	Kilgour, Esther	Charles Kilgour	99
Aug. 30/31, 1780	Kilpatric, Jean	Robert Kilpatric	178
July 26, 1778	Kilpatrick, Nathaniel	Robert Kilpatrick	175
Mar. 10/11, 1783	" Peter	Robert "	180
Aug. 15/16, 1776	Kirkpatrick, Ann	Robert Kirkpatrick	222
Feb. 21, 1775	" Mary	Robert "	170–171
Sept. 8, 1751	Kincaid, Jo.	Jo. Kincaid	134
Aug. 12, 1753	Kinkead, Sam	John Kinkead	138
July 27, 1760	K. Hanna	James K.	148–149
June 13, 1756	Lackey, John	Alex. Lackey	191
Sept. 8, 1751	" Mary	Alexander "	134
Feb. 21, 1775	Laecky, Margaret	(Adult)	170
June 11, 1767	Lecky, Robert	Alexander Lecky	128
June 1, 1765	Lochy, Alexander	A. Lochy	76
June 1, 1765	" Ann	A. "	76
Aug. 5, 1753	Lockey, Wm.	Alex. Lockey	94–95
Mar. 1, 1759	Loekey (son)	Hanna Loekey	211
May 12, 1765	Laferty, John	(Adult)	94
Mar. 15, 1752	Laverty, Isaac	Alex. Laverty	91–92
Jan. 15/16, 1787	Lefarty, Elizabeth	(See Hamilton)	182
Feb. 6, 1777	Leffarty, Sarah	(Adult)	223
June (3), 1754	Laieder, Mary	Mary Laieder	190
Aug. 23, 1755	Laird, Esther	Lodowick Laird	107
Apr. 24, 1757	" James	Lodowick "	142
June 25, 1752	" John	Josovick "	118
Feb. 16, 1752	Lauchlin, John	Wm. Lauchlin	135
Aug. 17, 1788	Law, Agnes	Cornelius Law, Holander	115
Sept. 22, 1782	" Elizabeth	Wm. "	180
Aug. 17, 1788	" Hanna	Cornelius " "	115
May 13, 1756	" Janet	Robert "	141
Mar. 23, 1780	" John (La.)	W. " (La.)	177
Nov. 12, 1777	" Robert	Wm. "	174
Aug. 17, 1788	Lawson, Ann	John Lawson	115
Jan. 20, 1754	Leech, Elizabeth	(See Moore)	202
Mar. 27, 1763	Leiper, Archibald	Sam Leiper (Lieper)	213
July 28, 1754	" Elizabeth	John "	127
Mar. 22, 1761	" Elizabeth	Sam "	150
Nov. 11, 1770	" Elizabeth	James "	129
Aug. 15, 1769	" James	James "	78
Apr. 16, 1758	" Jean	Sam "	211
Aug. 30, 1752	" John	Sam. "	137

Date	Name	Parent	Page
Apr. 26, 1772	Leiper, John	James Leiper	98
Sept. 2, 1753	" Mary	Sam. "	126
Oct. 17, 1762	" Robert	John "	96
Apr. 21, 1755	" Sam	Sam "	127
Apr. 21, 1765	" Sara	Sam "	214
Feb. 12, 1766	Leipers, Sarah	Sam Leipers	92
Aug. 6, 1775	Lind, Matthew	"Brother" Lind	91
Aug. 16, 1772	Lynd, Adam	William Lynd	129
Sept. 8, 1751	Little, John	And. Little	134
July 23, 1756	" Sarah	Jo "	72
Dec. 4, 1753	" Susa(n)	And. "	138–139
May 10, 1759	" Susanna	John "	74
Apr. 9, 1752	" Wm.	Jo. "	71
Aug. 18, 1788	Lyttle, Andrew	John Lyttle	200
Aug. 10, 1788	Livingston, Adam	Rebekah Livingston	195
Apr. 4, 1756	Lochhead, David	James Lochhead	141
Feb. 13, 1758	" Janet	James "	143
Aug. 12, 1770	" Janet	Wm. "	165
Dec. 4, 1774	" Rebecah	Wm. "	170
Apr. 13, 1766	" Robert	Wm. " (Loch.)	158–159
Aug. 15, 1767	" Robert	James "	77
Feb. 10, 1760	" W. (son)	James "	148
Sept. 1, 1787	Loughhead, Agnes	(?)	235
June 19, 1768	" Eleanor	Wm. "	162
Dec.(15), 1754	" Elizabeth	James " (Lough.)	139
Sept. 26, 1779	" Hannah	Jos. "	84
Sept. 26, 1769	" John	James "	193
May 27/28, 1772	" Joseph	Eleanor "	194
Oct. 14, 1770	" Margaret	Joseph "	165
July 17, 1763	" Martha	Robert "	154
Oct. 30, 1768	" Mary	Joseph "	162
Jan. 11, 1773	" Rebecca	Joshua "	168
Nov. 11, 1753	" Robert	James "	138
Feb. 24, 1765	" Sarah	Joseph "	157
Oct. 26, 1766	" Susanna	Jos. "	159
Aug. 11, 1765	" Thomas	James "	158
Sept. 6, 1772	" William	William "	168
Sept. 8, 1751	Lockhart, Mary	Moses Lockhart	134
June 21, 1778	Long, James	Wm. Long	174
Nov. 23, 1783	Logue, James	James Logue	232
Feb. 7/9, 1757	Love, Alexander	Robert Love	107
Mar. 16, 1760	" Rachel	Robert "	108
Sept. 30, 1753	" Robert	Robert "	106
June 1, 1766	Lowdon, John	Robert Lowdon (London?)	251
June 1, 1766	" Lydia	Robert " "	251
Jan. 27, 1754	Lowrie, James	And. Lowrie	202
May 28, 1758	" Mary	And. "	202

Date	Name	Parent	Page
Jan. 27, 1754	Lowrie, Robert	And. Lowrie	202
Aug. 4, 1754	" Sarah	John "	120
Nov. 28, 1762	Lowry, Eleanor	Widow Lowry	203
June 22, 1755	" Elizabeth	Andrew "	202
Aug. 25, 1751	" Eliz.	Jo "	118
Aug. 25, 1751	" Ja	Jo "	118
Oct. 5, 1783	" Janet	Alexander "	255
Oct. 1, 1759	" Jean	Andrew "	203
Mar. 30, 1752	(" ?) Jean	(See Dr.)	119
Oct. 1, 1786	McBeth	(See Macbeth)	88
Sept. 23, 1759	McBride, Arch.	Arch. McBride	249
Oct. 31, 1780	" Archibald	James "	253
Oct. 16, 1774	" Bess (Negroe)...	——	252
Apr. 3, 1777	(" ?) Eliz.	Ar. " (McCurdy?)	173
July 1, 1753	" Jas.	Ach "	249
Oct. 29, 1775	" James	Fran. "	252
Sept. 11, 1774	" Janet	Francis "	251
Sept. 23, 1759	" Mary	Arch. "	249
July 1, 1753	" Patrick	Ach "	249
Apr. 17, 1766	McCalester, Robert	Alexander McCalester	159
May 14, 1775	McCalister, Alexander	Alexander McCalister	221
May 14, 1775	" Hannah	Alexander "	221
May 25, 1777	" James	Alexander "	224
Apr. 30, 1780	" Jean	Alexander "	228
June 22, 1766	" Wm.	Alexander "	215
Nov. 2, 1784	McCallen, Mary	John McCallen	98
Nov. 21, 1784	McCamon, John	John McCamon	182
Nov. 21, 1784	" Martha	John "	182
Sept. 20, 1772	McClaughlin, William	(See McGlaughlin)	
Oct. 1, 1752	McClean, Mary	David McClean	208
Nov. 20, 1769	McCleary, And.	And. McCleary	122
Apr. 20, 1777	" And.	John "	223
Dec. 12, 1780	" Andrews	Alexander "	229
Nov. 16, 1777	" Benjamin	Alexander "	174
May 1, 1768	" Eliz.	John "	216–217
May 1, 1768	" George	And. "	216–217
Nov. 11, 1771	" George	And. "	219
June 29, 1766	" Jean	And. " (Mc.)	159
Sept. 11, 1763	" John	And. "	213
July 8, 1770	" John	John "	218
Oct. 21, 1787	" John	Robert "	124
Feb. 14, 1766	" Martha	Andrew "	215
July 23, 1775	" Martha	John "	221
May 11, 1783	" Robert	Alexander "	232
Aug. 26, 1779	" Sarah	John "	228
June 5, 1776	" William	Alexander "	195
July 31, 1765	McClelan, Agnes	Catharine McClelan	158

Date		Name	Parent		Page
July 31, 1765	McClelan,	Joseph	Catharine McClelan		158
Sept. 26, 1771	McClellan,	Agnes	Thomas McClellan		80
July 15, 1753	"	Daniel	John	"	93
May 14, 1764	"	Daniel	T.	"	76
Oct. 22, 1758	"	James	John	"	145
Mar. 29, 1767	"	James	Katharine	"	97
Aug. 21, 1751	"	John	Jo.	"	91
June 3, 1765	"	John	Thomas	"	76
Sept. 26, 1771	"	John	Thomas	"	80
Aug. 3, 1755	"	Mary	John	"	93
Nov. 10, 1765	McClenachan,	James	James McClenachan, Jun.		82
May 29, 1774	"	James	John	"	130
Nov. 10, 1765	"	John	James	"	" 82
May 29, 1774	"	Margaret	John	"	130
May 26, 1771	" (McClen.)	Mary	James	" (McClen.)	129
Nov. 14, 1773	"	William	James	"	130
Aug. 25, 1751	McCl.	(daughter)	Jo.	McCl.	118
June 16, 1761	McClung,	Charles	Matthew McClung		150-151
Aug. 24, 1762	"	Charles	John	"	90
Apr. 12, 1782	"	Charles	Math.	"	195
Oct. 12, 1788	"	David	Matthew	"	196
Apr. 27, 1755	"	Elizabeth	John	"	120
Apr. 15, 1753	"	Esther	Jo.	"	89
Jan. 24, 1764	"	Hew	Math.	"	192
Oct. 21/22, 1769	"	James	John	"	257
Nov. 29, 1769	"	John	M.	" (Mc.)	193
Feb. 29, 1784	"	Martha	M.	"	195
Oct. 24, 1758	"	Mathew	Mathew	"	192
Nov. 5, 1758	"	Mathew	John	"	90
Aug. 10, 1788	"	Sarah	Charles	"	195
Aug. 10, 1788	"	Sarah	Matthew	"	195
May 5, 1752	"		(See McMeling)		189
May 19, 1765	McConel,	Agnes	Agnes	McConel	94
Aug. 23, 1767	"	Alexander	John	"	121
Aug. 29, 1767	"	Alexander	Alexander	"	121
Oct. 1, 1779	"	Francis	Matthew	"	206
Oct. 31, 1752	"	Janet	Robert	"	125-126
Feb. 18, 1773	"	Jean	John	"	123
May 3, 1761	"	John	Robert	"	74
Oct. 1, 1779	"	John	Matthew	"	206
July 28, 1754	"	Margaret	Robert	"	127
Aug. 23, 1767	"	Margaret	John	"	121
Sept. 23, 1770	"	Martha	Agnes	"	194
Sept. 26, 1756	"	Mary	Robert	"	141
Aug. 23, 1767	"	Prudence	John	"	121
May 22, 1768	"	Thomas	John	"	122
Aug. 27, 1751	"	Will	Robert	"	124

Date	Name	Parent	Page
May 28, 1770	McConel, William	John McConel	194
Nov.(21), 1763	McCord, (David?)	James McCord (?)	110
Sept. 20, 1772	" Elizabeth	James "	114
Aug. 21, 1783	" Hanna	James "	254
Oct. 7, 1770	" James	James "	165
Jan. 29, 1762	" John	Ja. "	109
Oct. 20, 1765	" John	James "	111
June 2, 1768	" Thomas	James "	112
July 30, 1769	McCormick, Agnes	Henry McCormick	112–113
May 15, 1770	" Benjamin	Ben "	79
Mar. 15, 1767	" David	Henry "	112
Sept. 25, 1763	" (k) Elizabeth	Benj. " (k)	75–76
Oct. 7, 1753	" Henry	John "	106
Aug. 28, 1765	" Henry	Hen. "	111
Mar. 27, 1768	" Hew	Ben "	77
Mar. 12, 1758	" Isobel	John "	108
Mar. 17, 1760	" Isobel	Henry "	109
Mar. 22, 1761	" James	Benj. "	150
Aug. 4, 1765	" James	John "	111
Sept. 20, 1772	" James	Henry "	114
Nov. 13, 1757	" John	Ben "	143
May 1, 1763	" John	Henry "	213
Apr. 16, 1769	" John	John "	112
Sept. 20, 1772	" John	John (")	114
Dec. 29, 1754	" Margaret	Ben "	139
Dec. 21, 1755	" Margaret	John " (k)	107
May 23, 1756	" Margaret	John "	107
Feb. 25, 1759	" Mary	Ben. "	146
July 26, 1761	" Sarah	John "	151
Jan. 31, 1762	" Wm.	Henry " (McCor.)	109
May 11, 1788	McCready, Hew	Dan McCready	183
May 21, 1782	" Margaret	Arch "	179
Mar. 3, 1789	McCuchon, Sarah	Hugh McCuchon	183
May 8, 1759	McCulloch, Agnes	R. McCulloch	116
May 12, 1754	" Andrew	Robert "	71
Feb. 9, 1777	" Jean	Alexander "	223
Sept. 10, 1786	" Jeany	Sam "	234
Sept. 1, 1751	" Isobel	Robert "	70–71
Feb. 14, 1773	" John	John "	114
June 27, 1779	" John	John "	227
June 25, 1786	" John	Alexander "	234
June 28, 1789	" Lititia	Sam. "	237
Apr. 21, 1765	" Margaret	John "	214
Aug. 15, 1779	" Margaret	Alexander "	227–228
Feb. 4, 1787	" Margaret	S. McCul. (")	234–235
Jan. 28, 1787	" Margaret to	Dr.? Sam "	234
June 7, 1789	" Sarah	Robert "	237

BAPTISMS 39

Date	Name	Parent	Page
Oct. 12, 1788........	McCullogh, Sarah........	Alexander McCullogh....	196
Sept. 1, 1787........	(See Loughhead)	Robert McCullough....	235
Sept. 2, 1759........	McCurdy, Agnes........	Robert McCurdy........	147
May 5, 1752........	" Jean.........	Robert "	189
Oct. 19, 1777........	" Martha.......	Arch "	174
Sept. 14, 1760........	" Robert.......	Robert "	149
Apr. 3, 1777 ......(	" ?) Eliz..........	Ar. (See McBride)	173
Oct. 6, 1782........	McDowel, Wm..........	Sam McDowel	180
Nov. 10, 1774........	(McFadden), Robert......	H. M. (McFacklen?)	220
May 24, 1752........	McFadgean, Eliz........	Dorby McFadgean	136
May 24, 1752........	" Mary.......	Dorby "	136
Nov. 20, 1769........	McFadzean, Agnes......	Hugh McFadze(a)n	122
Oct. 11, 1784........	" An.........	Hugh McFadzean	233
July 20, 1777........	" Hugh.......	Hew "	224
May 29, 1781........	" John.......	Hew "	229–230
Mar. 27, 1771........	" Margaret....Hew	"	219
June 22, 1779........	" Margaret....Hugh	"	227
Apr. 7, 1771........	" Mary.......Hew	"	166
June 28, 1789........	" Sarah.......Hugh	"	237
Jan. 31, 1771........	McGlauchlin, Agnes......	James McGlocghlin	186
Dec. 18, 1774........	Maglaughlin, James......	James Maglaughlin	220
Oct. 1, 1779........	McGlaughlin, James......	James McGlaughlin	206
Sept. 1, 1776........	" Janet......	James "	222
Mar. 21, 1779........	" John......	James "	227
Sept. 20, 1772........	McClaughlin, William.....	James McClaughlin	114
Aug. 13, 1752........	McGown, Agnes..........	George McGown	136–137
Feb. 22, 1756........	" Alexander......	George "	141
June 2, 1754........	" John..........	George "	190
Sept. 6, 1784........	" Margaret.......	John "	124
Dec. 17, 1752........	" Moses........	George "	137
Jan. 20, 1789........	" Moses........	—	183
Aug. 10, 1788........	" Rob..........	John "	195
Jan. 20, 1789........	" Wm..........	—	183
Sept. 14, 1788........	McHenry, Mary.........	John McHenry (Henry?)..	103
Aug. 18, 1788........	McKee, Elizabeth.......	By Mary McKee, Sister...	200
June 15, 1780........	McKitterick, Katharin....	Al. McKit..............	240
Sept. 17, 1787........	" Kathrine....	Alexander McKitterick....	235
June 24, 1770........	McKnaight, John......	John McKnaight	165
June 25, 1769........	McKnaught, Agnes.......	James McKt........	97
Nov. 9, 1772........	" David......James	"	98
Feb. 11/12, 1761.....	" David......John	"	149–150
Sept. 23, 1764........	" David......And.	McKnaught.	156
June 16, 1765........	" Hanna(h)...John	"	157
Mar. 16, 1760........	" Henry......James	"	108–109
Apr. 19, 1770........	" James......And.	McKt........	194
Apr. 29, 1759........	" James......Jos.	"	146
July 29, 1764........	" James......James	McKnaught	110–111

Date	Name	Parent	Page
Mar. 12, 1758........	McKnaught, John........	James McKnaught.	108
June 5, 1763........	" John........	And. "	154
Aug. 10, 1766........	" Mary......	James McKts.	112
Jan. 24, 1768........	" Mary......	John McKt.	161
Aug. 20, 1751........	" Mary Ann...Jo.	McKnaught.	105
Sept. 16/19, 1751.....	" Marjory....	Neal "	189
Jan. 3, 1768........	" Mary......	John "	161
Apr. 25, 1770........	" Sidney.....	Francis "	188
Apr. 14/15, 1772.....	McKnaughtan, John.....	Thomas McKnaughtan	194
June 11, 1753........	" Margaret..	Neal " (McK.).	.189
May 9, 1773........	McKnightan, Joseph.....	And. McKnightan	169
Apr. 25, 1762........	**McKown, Dan........	James McKown	110
May 5, 1752........	McMeling, Charles......	McMeling (McClung?)	...189
Nov. 19, 1751........	McMichan, Hanna(h)....	James McMichan	125
Dec. 2, 1751........	McMien, John...........	Jo. McMien	125
Dec. 2, 1751........	" Robert........	Jo. "	125
Aug. 29, 1767........	McMiens, James........	And. McMiens	121
Aug. 13, 1769........	" Jean...........	And. "	129
May 9, 1764........	McMeans, Mary........	And. McMeans	128
Oct. 11, 1758........	McMillan, Ebenezer.....	John McMillan	211
Oct. 2, 1751........	" Jo.............	Jo. "	184
Oct. 2, 1751........	" Margaret......	Jo. "	184
Aug. 16, 1752........	McMurray, Benjamin.....	Robert McMurray	137
Sept. 20, 1756........	McM. James........	J. McM.	210
Sept. 20, 1756........	" Samuel......	Joseph "	210
Nov. 17, 1773........	McNaghtan, Neal........	Thomas McNaghtan (*)	... 81
Nov. 14, 1762........	Mc. Sam........	Jo. Mc(Millan?)	213
Aug. 12, 1781........	McReady, Eliz...........	Dan McReady	179
May 2, 1787........	" Margaret......	Arch "	182–183
Feb. 16/17/18, 1780..	" Mary.........	Dan "	228
Apr. 7, 1763........	McWilliams, James......	Mary McWilliams	102
Apr. 26, 1778........	McWhorter, Jean........	Moses McWhorter	225
Aug. 16, 1774........	Maeben, John...........	John Maeben	170
Mar. 26, 1780........	" Mary..........	J. "	177
Apr. 12, 1767........	Maben, Jean.............	John Maben	160
Feb. 18, 1770........	" Margaret.......	John "	164
Oct. 1, 1786........	Macbeth, Wm...........	John Macbeth	 88
	Maglaughlin, James......	(See McGlaughlin)	
Dec. 28, 1755........	Mahafey, Mary..........	Mar. Mahafey	210
Dec. 28, 1755........	" Mar. (son)......	Mar. "	210
Mar. (4), 1753......	Mahaffy, Esther..........	Martin Mahaffy	209
Apr. 12, 1752........	Mair, Jean...............	Mary Mair	 71
Jan. 29, 1769........	Mair, Jean.............	(?)	112
Apr. 9, 1787........	Marky, Elizabeth.......	Martha Marky	124
Apr. 20, 1760........	Marlin, Eliz.............	George Marlin	212
Mar. 5, 1782........	" James..........	Jean " (Widow)	230

** (See also McGown.   * See also McKnaughtan.)

BAPTISMS

41

Date	Name		Parent	Page
June 9/10, 1788	Marlin, James	John	Marlin	236
May 1, 1768	" Jean	Wm.	" (Mar.)	216–217
Apr. 8, 1770	" John	John	"	217
Apr. 8, 1770	" John	William	"	217–218
Apr. 9, 1786	" John	John	"	234
Sept. 17, 1752	" John	Geo.	" (Mar.)	208
Aug. 31, 1768	" John (?)	(Possibly James to John)		217
Mar. 1, 1767	" Mary	Wm.	Marlin	216
Mar. 23, 1766	" Rachel	George	"	117
Nov. 11, 1771	" Rachel	W.	"	219
Aug. 9, 1767	" Rachel	John	"	216
June 1, 1755	" Samuel	George	"	140
June 25, 1786	" Sar(ah)	John	"	234
Sept. 17, 1752	" Susanna	Geo.	" (Mar.)	208
Apr. 5, 1772	" William	John	"	219
Dec. 11, 1752	Martin, Eleanor	Sam.	Martin	104
Nov. 19, 1751	" James	Jo.	"	125
Oct. 31, 1752	" Janet	Jo.	"	125–126
Aug. 26, 1771	" Jean	John	"	113
Nov. 19, 1751	" Martha	Jo.	"	125
Nov. 1, 1758	" Samuel	Sam.	"	145
Aug. 18, 1788	Mason, John	John	Mason	200
Oct. 5/6, 1784	Mauson, John	David	Mauson	233
Aug. 26, 1781	Maughlin, Agnes	Wm.	Maughlin	230
Mar. 1/2, 1790	" Ann	Jean	" (Wilson ?)	237
Jan. 3, 1769	" Jean	Wm.	"	217
July 20, 1777	" John	Wm.	"	224
Dec. 1, 1788	" John	W.	" (Maugh.)	237
Mar. 24, 1771	" Margaret	Wm.	"	218
Mar. 3/4, 1779	" Margaret	Wm.	"	226
June 11, 1775	" Thomas	Wm.	"	221
Nov. 23, 1783	" Wm.	W.	"	232
May 2, 1773	Muchlin, Martha	Wm.	Muchlin	220
Sept. 30, 1770	Meek, Robert	Katharine	Meek (Kath.)	113
May 10, 1772	" Samuel	Katharine	" (")	114
Aug. 6, 1769	" Wm.	Katharine	"	97
Aug. 1, 1762	Meredith, Thomas	Francis	Meredith	75
Mar. 27, 1754	Miens, Adam	John	Miens	106
Sept. 22, 1751	" Eleanor	John	"	105
Dec. 14, 1755	" Joseph	John	"	107
Feb. 25, 1771	Mil. Sarah	Y.	Mil.	97
Oct. 31, 1780	Millar ?, Hugh Melvin	Gavin	Millar ?	253
Sept. 26, 1771	Mitchel, Agnes	Matthew	Mitchel	80
Aug. 25, 1751	" And.	Jo.	"	118
Apr. 21, 1754	" Ann	Alexander	"	120
June 20, 1779	" Ann	John	"	227
Apr. 27, 1755	" Ann	Jo.	" (?)	120

Date	Name	Parent	Page
Jan. 1, 1777.......	Mitchel, Ben............George	Mitchel........123
July 4, 1762........	"　David...........Thomas	"　......110
Feb. 20, 1764........	"　Eliz............David	"　......155
Oct. 25, 1767........	"　Elizabeth........T.	"　......112
Feb. 18, 1773........	"　Elizabeth........Jesse	"　......123
Oct. 11, 1778........	"　Elizabeth........John	"　......226
Apr. 25, 1756........	"　Gavin...........Alexander	"　......120
Sept. 9, 1753........	"　George..........George	"　......120
Feb. 22, 1764........	"　George..........James	"　......213
Mar. 13, 1782........	"　George..........John	"　......231
Apr. 5, 1772........	"　Hannah.........James	"　......219
July 5, 1752........	"　Isobel...........Jo.	"　......119
Oct. 6, 1779........	"　Isobel...........John	"　...... 84
Apr. 3, 1766........	"　James..........David	"　...... 96
Feb. 18, 1773........	"　James..........Nathaniel	"　......123
May 1, 1775........	"　James..........G.	"　......171
Nov. 13, 1768........	"　Janet..........Matthew	"　...... 78
July 8, 1770........	"　Janet..........James	"　......218
Oct. 6, 1779........	"　Janet..........Ebenezer	"　...... 84
Jan. 9, 1754........	"　Jean...........William	"　......185
Aug. 29, 1757........	"　Jean...........Widow	"　......142
July 30, 1764........	"　Jean...........T.	"　......133
May 26, 1778........	"　Jean...........John	"　......225
Apr. 1, 1753........	"　John...........Jo.	" Sr........119
May 4, 1755........	"　John...........George	"　......120
Nov. 12, 1765........	"　John...........James	"　......121
Apr. 22, 1779........	"　John...........George	"　......227
Feb. 15, 1758........	"　Joseph.........George	"　......143
July 1, 1764........	"　Joseph.........James	"　......214
Nov. 17, 1751........	"　Katharine......George	"　......118
Apr. 27, 1755........	"　Margaret.......Gov.	" (Geo.?)....120
May 27, 1770........	"　Margaret.......David	"　......194
Apr. 23, 1752........	"　Mary..........Wm.	"　......185
Aug. 3, 1755........	"　Mary..........John	"　...... 93
Mar. 17, 1761........	"　Mary..........G.	"　......121
Mar. 30, 1758........	"　Mary..........James	"　...... 73
Aug. 25, 1751........	"　Moses..........Jo.	"　......118
May 1, 1768........	"　Rachel (Mi.).....James	" (Mi.) .216–217
Aug. 25, 1751........	"　Sarah..........Ja.	"　......118
Apr. 11, 1756........	"　Sarah..........R.	"　......127
Feb. 28, 1773........	"　Sarah..........David	"　......168
Feb. 18, 1773........	"　Sarah..........James	"　......123
Mar. 26, 1769........	"　Thomas.........Wm.	"　......122
Aug. 29, 1757........	"　Wm.............Widow	"　......142
Feb. 14, 1766........	"　Wm.............James	"　......215
Sept. 26, 1770........	"　William ....James	"　......122
May 3, 1772........	"　William ....Wm.	"　......123

Date	Name	Parent	Page
Oct. 6, 1779	Mitchel, Wm.	Matth. Mitchel	84
Dec. 21, 1758	Money, Margaret	John Money	145
Oct. (5), 1756	Mooney, Isaac	John Mooney	141
Oct. 2, 1774	Mony, Ann	John Mony	257-258
Feb. 26, 1764	" James	John "	213
Feb. 26, 1764	" Margaret	John "	213
May 6, 1753	Montgomery, Margaret	Thos. Montgomery	103
Jan. 16, 1752	" Samuel	Thomas "	189
Aug. 22, 1762	Moor, Amos	Wm. Moor	75
Oct. 21, 1764	" Ann	William "	76
Aug. 26, 1753	" Eleanor	" (M.)	71
Jan. 20, 1754	" Elizabeth (Leech)	Walter "	202
Apr. 18, 1756	" James	Sam "	72
June 5/6, 1787	" James	John "	103
Jan. 20, 1754	" Mary	Walter "	202
Jan. 20, 1754	" Sarah	Walter "	202
Nov. 1, 1770	" Temperance	Wm. "	122
Apr. 2, 1758	Moore, Martha	Mary Moore	73
Oct. 21, 1764	Morton, Ann	John Morton	76
May 27, 1753	" Mary	John "	138
Apr. 2, 1770	" Mary	John "	79
Mar. 15, 1773	" Thomas	John "	81
Jan. 7, 1762	" William	John "	152
July 29, 1788	Mulligan, Grizel	John Mulligan	236
July 29, 1788	" James	John "	236
July 29, 1788	" Janet	John "	236
July 29, 1788	" John	John "	236
July 29, 1788	" Samuel	John "	236
Aug. 8, 1783	Munell, John	John Munell (Nunnel ?)	254
Apr. 13, 1760	Murphey, Hew	John Murphey	74
Aug. 10, 1755	" James	John "	72
Mar. 26, 1758	Murphy, John	John Murphy	73
Nov. 21, 1773	Murray, (?)	John Murray	81
July 26, 1752	" Esther	Jeremiah "	71
July 14, 1754	" Elizabeth	Jer. "	71
Sept. 8, 1751	" Jean	Jeremiah "	134
Aug. 31, 1768	(") Jean	Janet (")	217
Apr. 19, 1772	" Jeremiah	John "	70
Aug. 31, 1768	(") John	Janet (")	217
Mar. 25, 1770	" Margaret	John "	78
May 22, 1757	" Mary	Jeremy "	73
Oct. 6, 1771	Neal, Esther	John Neal	129
Apr. 26, 1772	Neil, John	John Neil	98
July 22, 1753	Neelie, Sam	Thomas Neelie	82
Feb. 23, 1752	Neilil, Wm.	Chas. Neilil	115
June 4, 1782	Newberry, Mary	(See Graham)	179
Sept. 23, 1781	Newport, Thomas (Negro)	Newport	179

Date	Name	Parent	Page
June 8, 1788.......	Nicol, Elizabeth.........	Antony Nicol...........	236
Apr. 16, 1758.......	" Hugh............	William "	211
June 10, 1753.......	" James............	Wm. "	209
Apr. 20, 1760.......	" Sam.	William "	212
Sept. 19, 1756.......	" Sarah............	Wm. "	210
Sept. 19, 1756.......	" Wm.............	Wm. "	210
Aug. 20, 1786.......	Nicols, Mary...........	Antony Nicols...........	234
Apr. 4, 1756.......	Nugent, Arthur..........	Pat. Nugent..........	141
Feb. 24, 1760.......	" Margaret.......	Patrick "	148
Aug. 11, 1755.......	O'hail, Margaret........	Hew O'hail..............	82
Apr. 8, 1788.......	Oliva, John.............	James Oliva.............	236
Oct. 1, 1775.......	Oliver, James...........	Wm. Oliver.............	247
Aug. 4, 1788.......	Orr, George...........	Wm. Orr..............	200
Aug. 4, 1788.......	" John.............	Wm. "	200
Aug. 4, 1788.......	" Katharine..........	Wm. "	200
Aug. 4, 1788.......	" Margaret..........	Wm. "	200
Aug. 4, 1788.......	" Martha............	Wm. "	200
Aug. 4, 1788.......	" Wm.............	Wm. "	200
Aug. 5, 1765.......	Owens, Martha.........	Mary Owens (or Swan)...111
Aug. 5, 1765.......	" Rebecca.........	Mary " " " ...111
Feb. 20/21, 1782.....	Padon, Eliza............	John Padon..............	98
May 7, 1762.......	Park, Agnes............	John Park..............	188
June 5, 1764.......	" James............	John "	192
May 20, 1770.......	" Robert...........	John "	79
May 11, 1760.......	" Wm.............	John "	148
Aug. 31, 1772.......	Parks, Margaret.........	John Parks............80–81
Dec. 18, 1777.......	" Sam.............	Jas. "	174
Mar. 7, 1773.......	Parkhill, Jean...........	David Parkhill...........	81
Nov. 14, 1770.......	" John...........	David "	79
Aug. 20, 1769.......	" Sarah..........	David "	78
Aug. 10, 1754.......	Parkieson, Benjamin.....	William Parkieson........	99
Mar. 21, 1758.......	" David........	William "	95
Oct. 5, 1783.......	Parshal, David.........	David Parshal.........	255
Oct. 2, 1751.......	Paterson, Agnes.........	Peter Paterson........	184
Aug. 22, 1756.......	" Agnes.........	Wm. "	191
Sept. 5, 1762.......	" Agnes.........	Peter "	186
Oct. 31, 1762.......	" Alex..........	Thomas "	153
Feb. 1, 1770.......	" Eleanor.......	William "	113
Mar. 9, 1766.......	" Elizabeth......	W. "	112
Oct. 14, 1770.......	" Eliz...........	Thomas " ? (Pa.).....	165
Feb. 21, 1775.......	" Eliz...........	James " 170–171
Mar. 7, 1764.......	" Florence.......	James "	155
Dec. 17, 1751.......	" James.........	Jo " (John?).....	184
May 18, 1755.......	" James.........	Thomas " 139–140
Nov. 2, 1755.......	" James C.......	James "	140
Aug. 22, 1756.......	" James.........	Peter "	191
Mar. 1, 1758.......	" James.........	William "	143

Date		Name		Parent	Page
Oct. 26, 1766	Paterson,	James	Robert	Paterson	159
Sept. 13, 1767	"	James (?)	James	" (?)	160
Apr. 17, 1768	"	James	Wm.	"	91
July 2, 1777	"	James	Jas.	"	173
Dec. 17, 1751	"	Janet	Jo	" (John?)	184
Sept. 8, 1751	"	Jean	Wm.	"	134
Nov. 26, 1752	"	Jean	Wm.	"	137
Feb. (18), 1753	"	Jean	Thomas	"	137–138
Nov. 12, 1769	"	Jean	R.	"	164
Feb. 20, 1770	"	Jean	James	" Jr.	164
Apr. 22, 1753	"	John	Wm.	"	99
Dec. 17, 1751	"	John	Thomas	"	184
June 5, 1757	"	John	James	"	142
June 8, 1760	"	John	Peter	"	109
Mar. 20, 1763	"	John	James	"	153–154
Feb. 21, 1775	"	John	Robert	"	170
Feb. 20, 1764	"	Margaret	T.	"	155
June 28, 1761	"	Margaret	James	" (Paters.)	151
Feb. 18, 1766	"	Margaret	James	"	158
June 5, 1757	"	Mary	Thomas	"	142
Feb. 27, 1765	"	Mary	James	"	157
Apr. 7, 1765	"	Mary	Peter	"	111
Apr. 9, 1780	"	Mary	Robert	"	177
Oct. 12, 1767	"	Robert	James	"	160
May 21, 1769	"	Robert	James	"	163–164
Feb. 2, 1768	"	Samuel	Robert	"	161
Apr. 29, 1759	"	Sarah	James	"	146
Nov. 13, 1760	"	Sarah	James	"	212
Oct. 21, 1764	"	Sarah	T.	"	76
Apr. 23, 1765	"	Sarah	Robert	"	157
Oct. 26, 1760	"	Susanna	Thomas	"	149
Sept. 26, 1779	"	Susanna	James	"	84
Oct. 6, 1754	"	Thomas	Peter	"	139
Feb. 5, 1756	"	Thomas	Jo (John?)	" (Adopted)	185
June 11, 1758	"	Thomas	Peter	"	144
Oct. 8, 1758	"	Thomas	Thomas	"	145
Sept. 27, 1772	"	Thomas	William	"	98
Mar. 10/11, 1783	"	Thomas	R(obert)	" (Pat.)	180
Dec. 17, 1751	"	William	Thomas	"	184
Jan. 7, 1762	"	William	Wm.	"	152
Sept. 13, 1767	"	Wm.	James	"	160
Apr. 28, 1771	"	William	Robert	"	166
Apr. 4, 1773	Patterson,	Ann	Sam	Patterson	168
May 21, 1778	"	Elijah	Robert	"	225
Apr. 1, 1772	"	Hanna(h)	James	"	167
Mar. 2, 1773	"	Jean	T.	" (Patt.)	81
Mar. 28, 1773	"	Robert	Robert	"	168

Date	Name	Parent	Page
May 12, 1782	Patterson, Samuel	James Patterson	179
May 21, 1778	" Thomas	Robert "	225
May 23, 1773	Pattison, Agnes	Hew Pattison	169
Oct. 4, 1771	" Arthur	Thomas "	80
Mar. 23, 1758	" Rob.	William "	99
Dec. 31, 1771	" Samuel	Hew "	194
Mar. 20/21, 1775	" Sarah	Hugh "	195
Oct. 24, 1762	Paxton, Benjamin	Sam Paxton	75
Aug. 23, 1772	" David	Sam "	80
Jan. 8, 1756	" George	Sam "	141
July 3, 1760	" Grizzel	Esther "	74
Feb. 24, 1754	" Isobel	Esther "	189
Aug. 28, 1769	" John	T. "	193
Sept. 28, 1755	" Margaret	Th. "	140
Dec. 17, 1758	" Martha	T. "	192
Oct. 1, 1758	" Moses	Sam "	145
Sept. 20, 1761	" Thomas	T. "	75
Mar. 26, 1758	Poa, Ann	Alexander Poa	73
Aug. 28, 1768	" James	Alexander "	78
June 1, 1765	" John	Alexander "	76
May 11, 1755	" Margaret	Alexander "	72
Sept. 22, 1761	" Mary	Alexander "	75
Apr. 16, 1777	Polloch, Jean	Sam Pollock	223
Mar. 27, 1771	Pollogh, Grizzel	Sam Pollogh	219
June 21, 1772	Polly, John	T. Polly	167
Mar. 28, 1780	Port. ———	——— (Negro)	177
Sept. 3, 1780	Porter, John	John Porter	229
Nov. 30, 1777	" Mary	John "	174
Sept. 20, 1789	Purdie, Andrew	James Purdie	184
June 17, 1753	" Elizabeth	John "	202
June 17, 1753	" Martha	John "	202
Nov. (?), 1787	Purdy, James	....	183
June 29, 1753	Rainey, Christian	Jas. Rainey	249
Sept. 19/20, 1759	" David	James "	249
Oct. 31, 1780	" Elizabeth	Sam " (Raney)	253
June 29, 1753	" Esther	Jas. "	249
Sept. 11, 1774	" James	Sam "	251
Aug. 13, 1783	" Janet	Sam "	254
Aug. 13, 1783	" John	David "	254
June 29, 1753	" Ruth	Jas. "	249
June 29, 1753	" Sam	Jas. "	249
Aug. 13, 1783	" Sarah	Sam "	254
Sept. 19/20, 1759	" Susanna	James "	249
Oct. 31, 1780	" Wm.	Sam " (Raney)	253
Feb. 23, 1766	Ramsay, Agnes	T. (Ramsay?)	158
Apr. 6, 1788	" Agnes	James Ramsay	235
Feb. 2, 1752	" Ann	Robert " ...	135

Date	Name	Parent	Page
Sept. 28, 1755	Ramsay, Ann	Thomas Ramsay	140
June 14, 1778	" Ann	John "	174
Oct. 31, 1773	" Barbara	John "	170
May 21, 1782	" Elizabeth	John "	179
Dec. 3, 1770	" Elizabeth	Susana "	166
Nov. 3, 1754	" James	Joseph "	133
Apr. 21, 1771	" James	Robert "	166
Apr. 8, 1781	" James	James "	229
Sept. 5, 1779	" James	John "	176
Aug. 31, 1768	" Jean	T. "	217
Feb. 20, 1766	" Jean	James "	158
Nov. 3/4/5, 1779	" Jean	James "	177
July 29, 1753	" John	Thomas "	138
Jan. 7, 1759	" John	James "	145
Sept. 29, 1771	" John	James "	80
Sept. 9, 1764	" John	James "	156
Mar. 3, 1789	" John	John "	183
Jan. 5, 1769	" Joseph	James "	163
June 2, 1754	" Margaret (Mt.)	Robert "	190
Aug. 21, 1763	" Martha	James "	154
June 1, 1753	" Mary	Jas. "	189
Dec. 3, 1770	" Mary	Susana "	166
Jan. 10, 1771	" Mary	Thomas "	218
Mar. 5/6, 1776	" Mary	John "	172
Apr. 23, 1769	" Robert	Jean "	163
Dec. 3, 1770	" Robert	Susana "	166
Mar. 29, 1776	" Robert	T. "	222
Mar. 28, 1762	" Sam	Thomas "	212
June 22, 1766	" Sam	T. "	215
Dec. 24, 1766	" Sam	James "	160
May 26, 1776	" Samuel	James "	172
Mar. 30/31, 1774	" Sarah	James "	194
Mar. 8, 1772	" Susanna	John "	167
Sept. 29, 1751	" Susannah	Thomas "	133
Mar. 27, 1757	" Thomas	James "	191
Oct. 23, 1757	" Thomas	T. "	142
May 11, 1760	" Thomas	James "	148
July 1, 1764	" Thomas	Thomas "	214
Apr. 9, 1786	" Thomas	James "	234
Nov. 21, 1762	" Wm.	James "	153
Oct. 27, 1771	" William	James "	167
May 2, 1773	" Wm.	T. "	220
Sept. 5, 1773	" Wm.	Robert "	169
Nov. 8, 1778	Rankin, Hannah	Wm. Rankin	87
Oct. 13, 1774	Rea, Elizabeth	Jean Rea	252
Oct. 13, 1774	" James	Jean "	252
Apr. 1, 1784	" James	(Adult)	181

Date	Name	Parent	Page
Apr. 1, 1784	Rea, Wm.	James Rea	181
May 20, 1770	Reddick, James	John Reddick	79
June 3/4, 1767	" Rebecca	John "	77
Apr. 12, 1772	" Robert	John "	80
Mar. 31, 1768	" William	John "	122
Mar. 14, 1779	Reed, Jean	John Reed	226
Dec. 24, 1782	" Wm.	W. " (Red)	232
Oct. 2, 1751	Reid, Agnes	Jo. Reid	184
Aug. 20, 1786	" Agnes	John "	234
Apr. 5, 1787	" Agnes	Will "	182
Oct. 17, 1784	" Elizabeth	Wm. "	233
Nov. 14, 1751	" Henry	James "	118
Nov. 14, 1751	" Janet	James "	118
Aug. 15, 1759	" Jean	John "	186
May 23, 1754	" John	John "	209
Oct. 3, 1779	" John	John " (J.R.)	84
Mar. 1/2, 1790	" John	John "	237
Oct. 15, 1758	" Joseph	James "	145
Apr. 9, 1787	" Joseph (Adopted)	By John Branon	124
Nov. 28, 1784	" Thomas	John Reid	233
Dec. 4, 1751	Reynolds, Elizabeth	Geo. Reynolds	116
Dec. 4, 1751	" John	Geo. "	116
Apr. 27, 1760	" John	Margaret "	148
Aug. 15, 1759	" Joseph	Hew "	186
Apr. 7, 1763	" Joseph	Margaret "	102
Apr. 18, 1758	" William	Margaret "	101
May 24, 1767	Richie, Ann	Matthew Richie	77
May 29, 1754	" David	Mathew "	139
May 21, 1769	" David	John "	163–164
July 2, 1758	" Isobel	Mat. "	144
Mar. 12, 1765	" James	Mathew "	193
June 23, 1765	" Jean	Adam "	158
May 29, 1754	" John	Mathew "	139
Aug. 6, 1771	" Margaret	Matthew "	94
Aug. 10, 1760	" Mary	Ada. "	149
Oct. 24, 1762	" Matthew	Matthew "	75
Aug. 10, 1760	" Rachel	Math. "	149
June 6, 1773	" Rebecca	John " (*)	169
June(26), 1763	" Rebekah	John "	154
Dec. 7, 1755	" Robert	Mathew "	140
June 16, 1765	" Thomas	Ad. "	157–158
Mar. 16/17, 1763	" William	Adam "	153
May 12, 1769	" Wm.	Mat. "	193
Aug. 17, 1761	Richy, Jean (wife)	Adam Richy	151
Aug. 17, 1761	" Sarah	Adam "	151
June 16, 1765	Ritchie, Agnes	John Ritchie	157

* Possibly Richieson.

Date	Name	Parent	Page
Oct. 24, 1784	Ritchy, Ann	David Ritchy	114
Jan. 26/27/28, 1779	" David	James Ritchy	175
June 8, 1777	" Margaret	James "	173
Sept. 24, 1780	" Mary	James "	178
Sept. 27, 1768	Richieson, Margaret	Adam Richieson	78
Apr. 25, 1784	Ritchard, Alexander	John Ritchard	181
Apr. 25, 1784	" Martha	John "	181
Apr. 14, 1761	Roan, Margaret	John Roan (Rowan?)	238
Apr. 14, 1761	" Mary	John "	238
June 4, 1755	Rowan, Agnes	Andrew Ro(wan)	188
June 4, 1755	" James	Andrew "	188
Dec. 29, 1782	" Mary	(See Clark)	232
Apr. 15, 1759	Robb, John	John Robb	146
Feb. 18, 1761	Rob. John	—— Rob.	150
Oct. 10, 1758	Robeson, John	John Robeson	145
June 28, 1761	(")James	John Rob. (*)	151
Jan. 10, 1760	" Jospbel	John Robs. (*)	186
Feb. 8, 1766	(Robieson), Abigail	Wm. Rob., Jr. (*)	158
Sept. 13, 1767	(")Agnes	John Rob. (*)	160
Feb. 13/17, 1753	" Alexander	William Robieson	185
May 1, 1775	" Alexander	Al. "	171
Feb. 21/22, 1770	(")And	John Rob. (*)	193
June 16, 1765	(")Ben	Sam " (*)	157–158
Jan. 21, 1761	" David	W. Robieson	212
Feb. 21/22, 1770	(")Elijah	Sam Rob. (*)	193
Mar. 28, 1773	" Eliz(abeth)	Alexander Robieson	168
Jan. 18, 1780	(")Eliz(abeth)	J. Rob. (*)	228
Dec. 17, 1758	" Eliz.	Wm. Robieson	192
Oct. 16, 1763	" Elizabeth	David "	154
Aug. 26, 1781	" George	James Robison	230
Nov. 12, 1775	(")Hamilton Dicky	Sam Rob.	171
July 29, 1759	" Hannah	W. Robieson	147
June 21, 1774	(")Hannah	Joseph Rob. (*)	170
Oct. 10, 1779	" Hanna(h)	John Rob-son	114
Sept. 29, 1787	(")Helen	Sam Rob. (*)	124
Sept. 19, 1762	(")Isobel	John " (*)	153
Apr. 29, 1770	(")Isobel	Joseph " (*)	165
May 15, 1768	" Isobel	David Robieson	78
May 18, 1755	" James	Wm. "	139–140
Sept. 11, 1757	" James	Wm. "	133
Feb. 28, 1765	(")James	John Rob. (*)	193
May 3, 1778	(")James	Sam " (*)	174
June 25, 1780	(")James	Jos. " (*)	177
Feb. 6, 1757	" Jean	Wm. Robieson	107
Aug. 15, 1790	(")Jean	Jos. Rob. (*)	184
Dec. 17, 1751	" John	William Robieson	184–185
Feb. 14, 1766	" John	David "	215

* See footnote, page 50.

Date	Name	Parent	Page
June 21, 1767........ Robieson,	John............Wm.	Rob. (*).......160
May 31, 1778........ "	John............James	Robieson.......226
July 26, 1778........ "	John............Joseph	Rob. (*) 175
Feb. 6, 1757........ "	Joseph.........Joseph	(Robieson).....107
Sept. 13, 1767........ "	Joseph.........Sam	Rob. (*).......160
Apr. 8, 1777........ "	Joseph.........John	" (*).......173
Aug. 1, 1784........ "	Josiah.........Joseph	" (*)...181–182
May 23, 1773........ "	Margaret.......Joseph	" (*).......169
Dec. 17, 1751........ "	Mary..........William	Robieson...184–185
Mar. 3, 1752........ "	Mary..........Wm.	" 104
Apr. 14, 1765........ "	Mary..........Alexander	" 157
Jan. 30, 1776.......("	)Mary..........John	Robs.?(*).....171
Sept. 5, 1779........ "	Moses.........John	Rob. (*).......176
July 12, 1772........ "	Sam...........John	" (*)......168
Dec. 2, 1772........ "	Sam...........Sam	" (*)......194
Jan. 21, 1783........ "	Sam...........James	Robs. (*).......180
Mar. 5, 1769........ "	Sarah.........Alexander	Robieson.......163
May 3, 1772........ "	Sarah.........Hew	" 123
Oct. 10, 1779........ "	Sarah.........John	(Rob-son)(*)....114
Oct. 6, 1776........ "	Thomas........Jas.	Robieson...222–223
May 17, 1772........ "	Walter.........James	" 219
Oct. 10, 1779.......("	)Wm............John	(Rob-son)(*)....114
Nov. 13, 1757........ "	Wm............John	Rob. (*).......143
June 23, 1771........ "	Wm............Joseph	" (*).......166
Mar. 16/17, 1763..... "	William........Sam	" (*).......153
Dec. 12, 1784........ Robinson,	Alexander......James	Robinson......234
May 12, 1771........ "	Eleanor........B. (?)	" 79
Apr. 10, 1788........ "	James.........—	" 236
Aug. 24, 1777........ "	Thomas........Alexander	" 174
Aug. 8, 1756........ Rose,	Agnes............Wm.	Rose............ 95
June 23, 1752........ "	Rachel............Wm.	" 94
Aug. 29, 1767........ "	Rebecca...........Wm.	" 121
Apr. 7, 1754........ "	Ruth.............William	" 95
Sept. 19, 1776........ Ross,	Isobel.............James	Ross..............172
May 27, 1764........ "	James.............James	" 156
Feb. 21, 1759........ "	John.............James	" 211
June 21/22, 1768..... "	John.............James	" 217
Sept. 19, 1762........ "	Margaret.........James	" 153
Sept. 17, 1769........ "	Margaret.........Wm.	" 164
Apr. 20, 1766........ "	Mary.............James	" 159
Sept. 19, 1776........ "	Moses.............James	" 172
Aug. 27, 1770........ "	Phoebe............Js.	" 165
July 13, 1777........ "	Robert Andrew.....James	" 173
Jan. 27, 1754........ Scot,	And.............John	Scot............202
Oct. 7, 1779........ "	John.............Sa.	" 84

(*) Abbreviations. Surname may be any one of the several names used in Diary beginning with "Rob."

BAPTISMS

Date	Name	Parent	Page
Apr. 26, 1752	Scot, Joseph	Arthur Scot	136
Oct. 7, 1779	" Margaret	Sa. "	84
Sept. 17, 1769	Scott, Agnes	Thomas Scott	164
Mar. 2, 1768	" Alexander	Thomas "	161
Mar. 3, 1765	" Arthur	Thomas "	193
Mar. 3, 1765	" Elizabeth	Thomas "	193
Aug. 13, 1772	" James	Mary "	129
Oct. 24, 1752	Scroggs, James	Allan Scroggs	89
Nov. 8, 1758	Scrogs, Allan	Al. Scrogs	90
Aug. 6, 1754	" Eleanor	Alan "	90
Aug. 9, 1756	" Jean	Alan "	90
Nov. 8, 1758	" Margaret	Alex. "	90
Oct. 21/22, 1769	Selfridge, Agnes	Wm. S(elfridge)	257
Aug. 19, 1764	" Edward	William Selfri(d)ge	256
Aug. 19, 1764	" Martha	Oliver Self(ridge)	256
Oct. 2, 1774	" Martha	W. Selfridge	257–258
Oct. 2, 1774	" Neal	Oliver "	257–258
Oct. 8, 1775	" Robert	Oliver "	258
Oct. 2, 1774	" Wm.	W. "	257–258
June 24, 1784	Shuttles, Agnes	Widow Shuttles	233
Aug. 10, 1755	Silluck, Thomas	Mary Silluck	72
Aug. 24, 1766	Sinclair, Elijah	Da. Sinclair	159
Apr. 5, 1772	" Hannah	Dan " (Sinclar)	219
Apr. 8, 1770	" Mary	Dan "	217–218
Oct. 31, 1762	" Mathew	Dan "	153
Jan. 31, 1768	" Rachel	Dan "	216
Jan. 29, 1764	Sloan, Agnes	James Sloan	110
Apr. 16, 1758	" And.	Da. "	211
Feb. 14, 1762	" Andrew	Js. (")	109–110
Feb. 14, 1762	" David	James "	109–110
July 5, 1772	" Helen	Isobel "	219
Nov. 1/2, 1763	" Isobel	Isobel "	238–239
Nov. 5, 1751	" James	James "	101
Dec. 28, 1755	" Jean	David "	210
Nov. 17, 1760	" Martha	Isobel "	212
May 20, 1776	" Mary	Wm. "	114
Feb. 14, 1766	" Rose-Ann	D. "	215
May 27, 1759	" William	James "	108
May 20, 1759	Smielie, Arch.	John Smielie	93
May 20, 1759	" Mary	John "	93
May 20, 1759	" Thomas	John "	93
May 20, 1759	" William	John "	93
Dec. 3, 1786	Smilie, Ann	Thomas Smilie	182
Dec. 3, 1786	" David	Thomas "	182
Dec. 3, 1786	" John	Thomas "	182
Aug. 28, 1768	Smith, Alexander	Wm. Smith	78
Feb. 5, 1756	" Charles	(Adopted by Wm. Smith)	185

Date	Name	Parent	Page
June 28, 1789........Smith, Esther............George Smith...........237
Aug. 26, 1769........   "   James............W.   "   78
July 30/31, 1771 .....   "   Jean............Wm.   " 219
May 28, 1782.......   "   John Murray.....John   " Rev........179
May 30, 1765.......   "   Samuel...........William   "   76
Aug. 26, 1753.......Spadie, Eleanor..........M. Spadie (?).......... 71
Aug. 26, 1753.......   "   Jas.............Wm.   "   71
Feb. 19, 1764.......Speddy, Sarah..........William Speddy..........155
May 3, 1759.......Spoedie, Elizabeth.......William Spoedie.......... 74
Feb. 27, 1757........   "   James...........Wm.   " 72–73
Apr. 13, 1755........   "   Mary...........Wm.   "   72
Mar. 18/19, 1761.....Spoedy, Martha....... ...Wm. Spoedy............. 96
Apr. 1, 1770.......Speer, John.............Robert Speer............ 79
Oct. 14, 1764.......Speir (son)..............James Speir.............192
Apr. 3, 1768.......Spier, Agnes.............Robert Spier............ 77
Apr. 14, 1765........   "   Alexander.........Robert   " 157
Apr. 19, 1767........   "   Elizabeth..........James   " 193
June 6, 1762........   "   Robert............James   " 152
Apr. 17, 1772........   "   Robert...........Robert   "   80
Nov. 19, 1770.......Steel, Hew..............Joseph Steel............ 79
Mar. 8, 1773........   "   Jean.............Joseph   " 123
Mar. 8, 1773........   "   John.............William   " 123
Nov. 19, 1770........   "   Jos...............W.   "   79
Nov. 13, 1768........   "   Wm.............W.   "   78
Jan. 2, 1781........S. Letitia.............W.   S. 229
Oct. 21, 1764.......Stevenson, Alice.........Robert Stevenson........ 76
Apr. 15, 1755........   "   David.........Robert   "   70
May 6, 1759........   "   Isobel.........Robert   "   74
July 14, 1754........   "   Mary.........Robert   "   71
July 23, 1756........   "   Mary.........Robert   "   72
Apr. 5/6, 1763......   "   Robert.......Robert   " (R.)....... 70
Sept. 20, 1761........   "   Wm...........Robert   "   75
May 15, 1774.......Stewart, Agnes...........John   Stewart...........220
Dec. 3, 1786........   "   Agnes...........Sam   " 182
Dec. 3, 1786........ " (?) Alexander......Sam   " (?)..........182
May 18, 1766........   "   Ben.............Sam   " 259–260
June 7, 1756........   "   Charles.........Andrew   " 131
May 18, 1766........   "   Cynthia.........Sam   " 259–260
May 17, 1753........   "   Eleanor.........And.   " 106
Aug. 20, 1751........   "   Eliz..............S.   " 105
Sept. 2, 1752........   "   Elizabeth........Hugh   " 241
Mar. 16, 1760........   "   Hugh...........Hugh   " 108–109
Jan. 29, 1764........   "   James...........Hew   " 110
June 27, 1779........   "   James Henry....John   " 227
	(James & Henry?)
June 29, 1783........   "   James...........Elijah   " 187
Dec. 3, 1786........   "   James...........Sam   " 182

Date	Name		Parent	Page
May 27, 1759	Stewart, Janet	Robert Stewart		108
May 27, 1759	" John	Robert	"	108
Mar. 14, 1764	" John	R.	"	203–204
Sept. 9, 1770	" John	Robert	"	79
Jan. 31, 1771	" John	Elijah	"	186
Sept. 1, 1776	" John	John	"	222
May 18, 1766	" Jonathan	Joseph	"	259–260
May 18, 1766	" Jonathan	Wm.	"	259–260
Jan. 23/25, 1770	" Joseph	Hew	"	186
Apr. 9, 1770	" Margaret	John	"	218
May 18, 1766	" Martha	Sam	"	259–260
Aug. 11, 1763	" Mary	William	"	154
Sept. 2, 1752	" May	Hugh	"	241
Apr. 5, 1772	" Rebecca	John	"	219
Aug. 11, 1763	" Rebekah	William	"	154
Nov. 13, 1768	" Robert	Robert	"	78
Apr. 7, 1765	" Robert	Hew	"	111
Dec. 3, 1786	" (?) Robert	Sam	" (?)	182
Apr. 5, 1767	" Samuel	Hew	"	102
Nov. 9, 1772	" Samuel	Elijah	"	98
Mar. 7, 1773	" Samuel	Robert	"	81
May 18, 1766	" Sarah	Wm.	"	259–260
June 17, 1770	" Sarah	Elijah	"	113
May 18, 1766	" Solomon	Joseph	"	259–260
Jan. 26, 1772	" Sus.	H.	"	113
June 29, 1783	" Susanna	Elijah	"	187
May 27, 1759	" William	Robert	"	108
Jan. 1, 1777	Strain, Jas.	Andrew Strain		123
May 11, 1755	Strobridge, James	John Strobridge		72
Nov. 5, 1751	Swan, Agnes	Alex. Swan		101
July 4, 1762	" Alexander	Alexander	"	110
Apr. 29, 1753	" James	Alexander	"	105
Aug. 28, 1760	" James	Alexander	"	102
Apr. 18, 1758	" Sam	Alexander	"	101
Jan. 28, 1756	" Samuel	James	"	210
Dec. 22, 1755	" Sarah	A.	"	101
Aug. 21, 1751	Swansie, Jean	Henry Swansie		91
Apr. 7, 1763	Tagert, James	(See Mary McWilliams)		
Apr. 17, 1768	Taylor (Son)	John Taylor		91
May 31, 1778	" Agnes	John	"	226
Feb. 6, 1757	" Alexander	John	"	107
Aug. 1, 1770	" Barbara	Sam	"	113
Nov. 2, 1784	" Barbara	Sam	"	98
Sept. 7, 1788	" Barbara	George	"	236
Nov. 9, 1772	" George	John	"	98
Aug. 20, 1751	" Helen	Matthew	"	105
Jan. 27, 1766	" James	John	"	111

Date	Name	Parent	Page
Jan. 18, 1761	Taylor, Jean	John Taylor	109
Aug. 1, 1770	" John	John "	113
Oct. 21, 1787	" John	Sam "	124
Nov. 9, 1772	" Martha	James "	98
Mar. 14, 1754	" Mathew	Math. "	106
May 13, 1753	" Matthew	John "	106
Nov. 6/13, 1763	" Matthew	John "	110
Feb. 14, 1762	" Sam	John "	109
May 17, 1772	" Sar(ah)	Sam "	219
Oct. 5, 1783	Telfair, David	Wm. Telfair	255
Dec. 3, 1786	Templeton, Wm.	Robert Templeton	182
June 18, 1770	Thomson, David	Wm. Thomson	188
Sept. 5, 1762	" Elizabeth	John "	186
Oct. 15, 1752	" Isaac	Jo. "	105
Nov. 26, 1758	" Isaac	John "	145
Mar. 22, 1761	" Janet	John "	150
Jan. 21, 1759	" Jean	John "	108
Oct. 12, 1760	" Jean	James "	250
July 31, 1763	" Jean	Jo. "	154
May 8, 1757	" John	John "	108
Aug. 12, 1764	" John	James "	250
Aug. 12, 1764	" Rosanna	James "	250
Aug. 1, 1773	" Sarah	Wm. " (Thom.)	114
Sept. 5, 1762	" Susannah	John "	186
Aug. 10, 1788	" Wm.	Wm. "	195
Apr. 1, 1753	Thorn, Esther	Jo. Thorn	119
Feb. 12, 1764	" Esther	James "	90
June 22, 1783	" Francis	James " (Th.?)	181
Nov. 16/17, 1765	" James	James "	90
Nov. 5, 1751	" John	John "	101
May 29, 1768	" Margaret	James "	97
Aug. 25, 1751	" Martha	Jo. "	118
Mar. 15, 1758	" Matthew	John "	108
Sept. 30, 1770	" William	James "	113
Apr. 9, 1775	Todd, Jean	John Todd	87
May 20, 1781	" John	John " (Tod)	178
Aug. 4, 1776	" Margret	John " (")	172
Nov. 8, 1778	" Mary	John " (")	87
Oct. 24, 1784	Tom, John	W. Tom	114
Aug. 26, 1764	Trapp, Eliz.	Kaesy Trapp (Trap)	250
Oct. 12, 1760	" James	Kaesy " (")	250
Oct. 26/27, 1769	" Martha	Kaesy "	251
Oct. 9, 1774	" Ruth	Kaesy " (")	252
Aug. 26, 1764	" Sarah	Kaesy " (")	250
Oct. 26/27, 1769	" Susanna	Kaesy "	251
Oct. 31, 1780	" Wm.	W. " (")	253
Aug. 20, 1783	Turner, James	Thomas Turner	254

Date	Name	Parent	Page
Aug. 20, 1783.......	Turner, John............	Thomas Turner.........	254
Aug. 20, 1783.......	" Mary...........	Thomas "	254
Aug. 20, 1783.......	" Thomas.........	Thomas "	254
Aug. 20, 1783.......	" Win............	Thomas "	254
June 8, 1788.......	Valentine, George.......	Wm. Valentine..........	236
Oct. 10, 1784.......	" Mary.........	W. "	233
Mar. 7, 1782.......	" Sam..........	Wm. "	231
Mar. 29, 1764.......	Walker, Agnes..........	Isaac Walker.........	156
Sept. 8, 1751.......	" Andrew.........	Joseph "	134
Feb. 3, 1752.......	" Andrew.........	Jo. "	135
July 1/2, 1767.....	" Andrew.........	John "	160
Nov. 20/21, 1771.....	" Ann...........	John "	167
Apr. 27, 1756.......	" David..........	W. " (W.).......	95
Mar. 1, 1769.......	" Hannah........	John "	163
Feb. 20/21, 1782.....	" Hanna(h).......	John " Jun........	98
Sept. 7, 1760.......	" Isaac..........	Isaac "	149
Feb. 13/14, 1776.....	" Isaac..........	James "	172
May 3, 1752.......	" James..........	Isaac "	136
May 13, 1756.......	" James..........	John "	141
May 13, 1756.......	" Jean...........	Isaac "	141
May 12, 1774.......	" Jean...........	James "	220
Apr. 7, 1754.......	" John...........	William "	95
May 1, 1757.......	" John...........	Joseph "	142
Nov. 19, 1772.......	" John...........	John "	168
May 9, 1784.......	" John...........	Jas. " (Wal.)......	181
Feb. 5, 1764.......	" Jonathan.......	W. "	96
Feb. 20/21, 1782.....	" Joseph..........	James "	98
June 6/9, 1763.......	" Joseph..........	John "	154
July 13, 1766.......	" Margaret.......	Isaac "	159
May 6, 1778.......	" Margaret.......	Jas. "	174
June 2, 1754.......	" Martha.........	John "	190
July 18, 1779.......	" Martha.........	John "	176
Aug. 16, 1752.......	" Mary...........	Jas. "	137
June 5, 1753.......	" Mary...........	Isaac "	138
May 23, 1759.......	" Mary...........	W. " (Wal.)......	95
Dec. 3, 1761.......	" Mary...........	John "	151
Oct. 1, 1779.......	" Mary...........	Robert "	206
Jan. 4, 1759.......	" Moses..........	John "	188
June 3, 1759.......	" Nathaniel.......	Isaac "	146
May 7, 1762.......	" Rebecca........	Isaac "	188
Mar. 28, 1780.......	" Rebec(ca).......	Jas. "	177
Sept. 8, 1751.......	" Samuel.........	Joseph "	134
May 26, 1754.......	" Sarah..........	Isaac "	190
Feb. 28, 1765.......	" Sarah..........	John "	193
Oct. 1, 1779.......	" Sarah..........	Robert "	206
Dec. 4, 1783.......	" Sarah..........	James " (?)..........	98
Sept. 11, 1768.......	" Walter.........	Isaac "	162

Date	Name	Parent	Page
June 23, 1752.......	Walkter, Groyn.........	Wm. Walkter............	94
June 29, 1759.......	Wallace, Ann............	John Wallace............	203
Mar. 16, 1760........	" William.........	John " (Walace)......	108
July 26, 1752.......	Watt, Ezekial...........	John Watt..............	71
May 29, 1757........	" Hanah...........	John "	73
Sept. 15/16, 1788....	Whigham, Agnes........	Wm. Whigham...........	104
Sept. 15/16, 1788.....	" Ann...........	Wm. "	104
Nov. 2, 1784	" Robert.......	Wm. " 98–99
Sept. 15/16, 1788.....	" Sam...........	Wm. "	104
Nov. 2, 1784........	" Thomas.......	Wm. " 98–99
Oct. 28, 1761.......	Whiteside, Ann.........	Phinehas Whiteside......	192
Dec. 22, 1763........	" Edward.......	P. "	192
Dec. 21, 1752........	" John.........	Phinehas "	189
Oct. 28, 1761.......	" Mary........	Robert (")......	192
Mar. 30, 1756.......	" Peter........	Phinehas "	190
May 18, 1758........	" Thomas......	Phinehas " (P.W.)....192
June (3), 1754......	" Wm..........	Phinehas "	190
Oct. 12, 1760........	Wilkin, George...........	W. Wilkin...........	250
Aug. 12, 1764........	" James...........	William "	250
Oct. 8, 1769........	" Joseph...........	William "	251
May 4, 1766........	Wilkings, Robert........	William Wilkings.........	250
Sept. 23, 1759........	Wilkins, Daniel.........	William Wilkins.....249–250
Sept. 11, 1774........	" Elizabeth........	W. "	251
Sept. 23, 1759........	" Jean............	William " 249–250
Nov. 12, 1780........	" John...........	Wm. " Junior......253
July 1, 1753........	Wil. Wm...........	Wm. Wil.	249
May 9, 1753........	Williams, Jean..........	George Williams..........	106
June 5, 1764........	Wilson, Agnes.	Peter Wilson..........	192
Nov. 19, 1751........	" Eliz.............	Jo. "	125
Nov. 19, 1751........	" Elizabeth.......	James "	125
June 2, 1773........	" Elizabeth.......	Peter "	169
Oct. 7, 1779.......	" Elizabeth.......	S. "	84
May 25, 1757........	" Hugh...........	Thomas "	73
Nov. 20/21, 1771.....	" Isobel...........	Peter "	167
Jan. 14, 1754........	" James (Adopted)..Jo.	"	139
Mar. 17, 1761........	" James..........	James "	121
Apr. 18, 1770........	" James..........	Peter "	92
Sept. 26, 1779........	" James..........	Aaron "	84
Oct. 20, 1755........	" Jean.............	James "	140
Apr. 14, 1756........	" Jean.............	Jo "	116
Feb. 15, 1758........	" Jean.............	James "	143
May 7, 1762........	" Jean.............	Peter "	188
Jan. 7, 1768........	" John.............	Peter "	161
Sept. 23, 1770........	" Margaret........	Sam "	194
Jan. 10, 1753........	" Martha.........	Robert (")..........	137
Nov. 4, 1762........	" Martha........	James "	188
Feb. 25, 1766........	" Mary...........	Peter " (Wil.)......158

Apr. 11, 1756	Wilson, Rebecca	James	Wilson	127
Apr. 21, 1755	" Robert	James	"	127
July 26, 1752	" Sam	Thomas	"	71
Jan. 10, 1753	" Sarah	Ja.	"	137
Jan. 14, 1754	" Sarah	Sam (")		139
July 14, 1754	" Sarah	Thomas	"	71
Sept. 26, 1779	" Sus.	Isa.	"	84
Apr. 13, 1760	" Thomas	Thomas	"	74
Sept. 2, 1753	" Zacheus	James	"	126
Dec. 17, 1751	Wishart, Elizabeth	Joseph Wishart		184
Sept. 22, 1778	Woodrow	(See Rebecca Dunlap.)		175
July 28, 1784	Woods, John			181
July 29, 1787	Wylie, Janet	Robert Wylie		195
Mar. 29, 1752	" Margaret	Jo.	"	119
Mar. 29, 1752	" Mary	Jo.	"	119
Mar. 23, 1758	Young, Agnes	Alexander Young		99
July 8, 1770	" And	Wm.	"	218
Feb. 16, 1766	" Elizabeth	Wm.	"	215
May 1, 1768	" James	Wm.	"	216
Nov. 1/2, 1763	" John	William	"	238–239
Apr. 2, 1775	" Margaret	W.	"	221
Sept. 1, 1776	" Margaret	Wm.	"	222
Oct. 8, 1778	" Mary	William	"	226

Imperfect Baptismal Records:

Feb. (25), 1753	——— David	——— A———	138
Apr. 27, 1755	——— Ann	Jo—— (McClung?)	120
Oct. 20, 1754	——— John	Joseph ———	139
Apr. 1, 1753	——— James	——— (Mitchel?)	119
Feb. 23, 1766	——— Agnes	——— T———	158
Oct. 5, 1788	——— S	——— ———	187
Mar. 5/10, 1753	——(Born) Henry	Ja—— ———	115
Oct. 13, 1753	——— Matthew	Matthew ———	106
Feb. 14, 1762	——— Andrew	Js.—— ———	109–110
June 11, 1766	———	———	159
June 11, 1766	———	———	159
Aug. 30, 1761	———	———	151
Oct. 13, 1777	———	———	82
Oct. 13, 1777	———	———	82
Oct. 13, 1777	———	———	82
Oct. 13, 1777	———	(Adult)	82
Oct. 12, 1783	———	———	255
Oct. 12, 1783	———	———	255
Oct. 12, 1783	———	———	255
Nov. 26, 1786	———	(A number)	114
Mar. 18, 1753	——— Sarah	John ———	82
Mar. 18, 1753	——— Thomas	John ———	82

INDEX OF LOCATIONS

INDEX OF LOCATIONS

PENNSYLVANIA

Adams County:

Abbottstown, 69
Bear's Tavern, 69
Carroll's Tract, 70
Flowe's Furnace, 70
McGahy's Mill, 70
Marsh Creek, 70–82
Redland, 82
The Quarter, 82
Three Springs, 82
Toms Creek, 83
Track Irrasens, 83
Two Taverns, 83

Allegheny County:

Allegheny Creek, 83
Forks of Yough, 83–84

Bedford County:

Bedford, 84
Juniata River, 84

Berks County:

Chapel Potts, 85
Pine Forge, 85
Maiden Creek, 85
Reading, 85
Reading Furnace, 85
Reeits Mills, 85
Weidenhammer's Tavern, 85
Weiser's Tavern, Conrad, 85

Bucks County:

Deep Run Meeting, 85
Durham Furnace, 86
Neshaminy, 86
Quakertown, 86
Shamony Old Meeting-house, 86
Tohicken, 86
Wards Bridge, 86

Chester County:

Brandywine, 86–88
Compass, 88
Dean's Meeting-house, 88
East Fallowfield, 88
Elk, 88
Forks of Brandywine, 88
French Creek, 88
New Londonderry, 88
Oxford, 88
Pickering, 89
Wantsmill, 89
Warwick's Furnace, 89
White Horse, 89

Cumberland County:

Big Spring, 89–91
Blane's Tavern, 91
Canandugwinet Creek, 91–92
Carlisle, 92–94
Hogestown, 94
Hopewell, 94
Junken Tent, 94–99
Leteart Spring, 99
Middle Spring, 99
Pennsborough Meeting-house, 99
Pine Ford, 100
Salem, 100
Sawglass, 100
Sherman Valley, 100
Shippensburg, 100
Stiglestown, 100
Susquehanna River, 100
Taeff's Ferry, 101

Dauphin County:

Beaver Creek, 101
Blue Mountain, 101–103
Derry Meeting, 103
Hummelstown, 103–104
Lisburn, 104
Little Swatara, 104

Dauphin County—(Continued)
Manadie Township, 104
Martin's Mill, Sam, 104
Murray's Gap, 104
Ormostogg, 104
Overtakes, 104
Paxton, 105–115
Susquehanna, 115
Swatara, 115
Tait's Meeting-house, 115

Delaware County:
Chester, 115
Darby, 115

Fayette County:
Juniata River, 115
Laurel Hill, 115
Redstone, 116

Franklin County:
Antietam (Little), 116
Conococheague, 116–117
Greencastle, 117–118
Guilford, 118
"Kittachtinnan," 118
Rocky Spring, 118–124

Fulton County:
Licking Creek and The Cove Society,
124–130
Scrub, 130
Sharp's Fort, 130
Sideling Hill, 130
Upper Settlement, 130

Lancaster County:
Anderson's Ferry, 130
Blue Ball, 130
Brown's Mill, 130
Colerain Township, 131
Conestoga, 131
Conewago, 131
Donegal, 131
Dorbus, 131
Downie's Mill, 131
Dutch Tavern, 131
Gates Hill Ford, 132

Graham Bridge Meeting-house, 132
Greer's Mill, W., 132
Half-Way-House, The, 132
Ker's Mill, Joseph, 132
Lancaster, 132–133
Level, 133–134
McDowell's Mill, 134
Middle Octoraro, 134–184
Muddy Run, 184–187
New Holland, 187
Octoraro Creek, 187–188
Peach Bottom, 188
Pequea, 189–196
Poedleh, 196
Robert's Mills, 178
Rocky Valley, 196
Seceder Meeting-house, 196
Sign of The Plow, 196
Silver Mine, 196
Sneider's Tavern, 196
Stoner's Dam, 196
Susquehanna River, 196
Tavern Third, 196
The Gap, 131

Lehigh County:
Allentown, 197

Montgomery County:
Abington, 197
Blue Ball, 197
Goldsmith's T., 197
Hickorytown, 197
Merion, 198
Plymouth, 197
Potts Grove, 198
Pottstown, 198
Seven Stars, 198
Swamp, 198
Swedesford, 198
Upper Merion, 198
Welsh Tract, 198
White Marsh Church, 198

Northampton County:
Bethlehem, 199
Easton, 199
Twimmins Mills, 199

Northumberland County:
   Chillisquaque, 199
   Indian Wigwam, 199
   Northumberland, 200
   Rutherford, 200
   Sunbury, 200
   Warrior Run, 200
   White Deer Hole, 200

Philadelphia County:
   Cather's School, 201
   Delaware River, 201
   Frankford, 201
   Germantown, 201
   Holton's Tavern, 201
   Moreland, 202
   Pennypack Creek, 202
   Philadelphia, 202–205
   Sorrel Horse Tavern, 205
   Spread Eagle, 205

Schuylkill County:
   Schuylkill, 205

Snyder County:
   McClure's Gap, 206
   Mt. Pleasant, 206

Somerset County:
   Fort Mills (Hills?), 206
   Laurel Hill, 206

Washington County:
   Chartiers, 206
   Miller's Run, 206

York County:
   Burkholder, 207
   Chamber's Tavern, 207
   Chanceford, 207
   Cold Spring, 207
   Deadman's Road, 207
   Dutch Shoe, 207
   Dutch Tavern, 207
   Latta's School, Mr., 207
   Lower Chanceford Society, 208–238
   Mount Difficult, 238

   Muddy Creek, 238–239
   Muddy Run Meeting-house, 239
   Neilson's Ferry, 239
   Price's Ferry, 239
   Ramsay's Tent, Thomas, 239
   Ross's Tent, Col., 239
   Somerville, 239
   Susquehanna River, 239
   The Island, 239
   The White Horse, 240
   Twelve Tavern, 239
   York, 240

DELAWARE

Kent County:
   Dover,* 240–241
   New Castle, 241
   Newport, 241
   Pencader, 241
   Red Lion, 241
   St. Georges, 241
   Whiteclay Creek, 241
   Wilmington, 241

MARYLAND

Allegheny County:
   Cumberland, 242

Baltimore City:
   Baltimore, 242
   Old Town, 242

Frederick County:
   Cedar Creek Meeting-house, 242
   Frederick, 242
   Opicken, 242
   Opicken Meeting-house, 242

Harford County:
   Crossroads, Bush, Joppa, Trap, 243

Montgomery County:
   Morgan's Mill, 243

   * Possibly in York County, Pa.

NEW JERSEY

Bergen County:
Dekaes Mills, 243
Hackensack, 243

Essex County:
Newark, 243

Gloucester County:
Rambo's Ferry, 244

Hunterdon County:
Amwell, 244

Morris County:
Dutch Tavern, 244
Morristown, 244

Passaic County:
Ringwood's Furnace, 244

Somerset County:
Basking Ridge, 244
Lakes Miln, 244–245
Raritan, 245
Wells Ferry, 245

Sussex County:
Andover, 245

Warren County:
Hackettstown, 245
Lewistown, 245
Moravian Mills, 245
Muskingoe, 245
Sewitz' Tavern, 245
Quaker Tavern, 245

NEW YORK

Albany County:
Albany, 246
Ferry (Dumback's?), 246

Greene County:
Coxsackie, 246
Esopus ("Sopoze"), 246–247
Kaaterskill, 247
New Paltz, 247

Orange County:
Florida, 247
Goshen, 247–248
Gracehill's Tavern, 248
Hudson River, 248
Little Britain, 248
Sterling, 248
Valley of The Walkill, 248–255

Renssalaer County:
Hoosick, 255
Sanhoit, 256

Saratoga County:
Halfmoon, 256

Ulster County:
Rosendale, 256
Shawangunk ("Shamgam"), 256

Washington County:
Buskirks Bridge, 256
Cambridge, 256–258
Melopard, 258
The Settlement, 258

Weschester County:
Dobbs Ferry, 258
Bedford, 258
Plains (White?), 258

MASSACHUSETTS

Berkshire County:
Coliver's Bridge, 259
Sheffield, 259
Williamstown, 259
Windsor, 259

Franklin County:
Colerain, 259–260

Hampton County:
Blandford, 260
Westfield, 260

Hampshire County:
Hadley, 260
Northampton, 260
Pelham, 260

CONNECTICUT

Fairfield County:
Botsford, 261
Danbury, 261

Newtown, 261
Ridgefield, 261

Hartford County:
Farmington, 261
Painthorn, 261
Simsbury, 261

Litchfield County:
Canaan, 261
Woodbury, 261

New Haven County:
Waterbury, 261

QUOTATIONS FROM DIARY OF REV. JOHN
CUTHBERTSON

QUOTATIONS FROM DIARY OF REV. JOHN CUTHBERTSON

For nearly forty years Mr. Cuthbertson ministered to the Covenanter Societies in Lancaster, Dauphin, Cumberland, Franklin, Fulton, Adams and York Counties, Pennsylvania. His trips took him into other Pennsylvania Counties as far west as the Ohio River, and as far as the Delware River on the East. He journeyed into Maryland, Delaware, Virginia, New Jersey, New York, Connecticut and Massachusetts. Everywhere he went, whether into homes or to regular meeting places, we find him preaching, lecturing, baptizing, marrying, rebuking, examining, etc., often all in one day.

(a) The marriage and baptism entries are placed under the locations where solemnized. Children were sometimes carried long distances to be baptized.

(b) Spaces and short lines under quotations are intended to bring out more clearly consecutive trips.

PENNSYLVANIA

ADAMS COUNTY

Abbotstown

1769 Mar. 9   "rode 38 miles to Abbot's T.   S. Duncan's; bad road." (From Hugh Ross's.)

Bear's Tavern

1762 Dec. 28   "rode 18 miles to Bear—married Hew Stewart and Agnes Moor.—" (From Stewart's.)

1766 Apr. 7   "rode 33 miles with Lr. to Bear's Tav.—wet day." (From Marsh Creek.)

1767 Feb. 9   "rode 20 miles in snow ice etc. to the Bear—G. Kerson." (From W. Brown's.)

1769 June 26   "rode 18 miles; bear; married Sam Taylor and Sarah Stewart." (Then 35 miles home on 27th.)

Carroll's Tract

1754 May 7   "Rode 28 to Carrols Tract, Br. Burns exhausted exceedingly." (From Sus.)

"   9   "Preached psalm 147:1 lectured 1 Thessalonians 4:15–L and examined 30 persons and baptized Charles, son to John Broomfield—John W."

1755 Apr. 14   "Rode 8 miles to the Tract. conversed with Jo. Wat. denies sin R.—." (From Marsh Creek.)

"   15   "Preached psalm 133 lectured John 3:14–18 and examined 20 persons, baptized David, son to Robert Stevenson, give praise to God." (At Carroll's Tract.)

1757 May 27   "Rode 9 miles to and from John Withrows and to David Dinwiddys sold tract." (From Carroll's Tract.)

1758 Mar. 24   "Rode 28 miles to sister's—Burns died the 11 at 1 o'clock." (From Carlisle.)

1760 Jan. 15   "Married Francis Meredith and Sister Burns." (In Carroll's Tract.)

1763 Apr. 5, 6   "rode 20 miles to R. Stevenson's—preached psalm 30:4–8 and Corinthians 1:30, 31. Baptized Robert son to him—went W. and Di—." (At Carroll's Tract.)

1772 Apr. 19   "Sabbath; preached 40:1—lectured Isaiah 8:11—and preached Luke 24. rode 9 miles to Tract. Baptized Jeremiah son to John Murray and Agnes to Mat. Beggs." (From David Dunwoody's.)

"   20   "Married Nathaniel Mitchel and Jat. Burns." (At Carroll's Tract.)

Flowe's Furnace

1760 Oct. 17   "rode 40 miles home to Flowe's Furnace, Dinwiddy's, K's, etc. good health." (From White Horse.)

McGahy's Mill

1763 Apr. 4   "rode 8 miles to Da. McGahy's Miln and sisters." (From David Dinwoody's.)

Marsh Creek Society (Rock Creek)

1751 Aug. 30   "Rode 8 miles over Mash Creek to David Dinwithiers, tired but safe." (From Robert Ready's.)

Sept. 1   "Sabbath.—Rode 2 miles to and from the Tent. Preached psalm 9:15–1. Lectured Luke 12:41–49 and

Marsh Creek Society (Rock Creek)— *Continued*

preached Galatians 5:1 and baptized Jean, daughter to Thomas Anderson and Isobel, daughter to Robert McCulloch and Rose-Anne, daughter to Jo. Hutchieson, and James, son to Jo. Broomfield and Mary, daughter to David Dinwoddy. Made a large offer of Christ. Had a session . . . praise to my God."

1752 Apr. 9   "Preach. Ps. 78:7–12 lectured Jer. 3:12–16 bap. Wm. son to Jo. Little." (At Robert Reddick's—then rode 10 miles to David Dunwoody's.)

" 12   "Sab. Rode 2 miles to 3.—preach. Ps. 22:1–6. lect. So. 1–4 preach Titus 1–2 and bap. A—daughter to Thomas Anderson and Jean daughter to Mary Mair rode 2 miles—." (From David Dunwoody's.)

July 26   "Sab. Rode 2 to and from the tent, preach. Psa. 27: 1–5 lectured So. 9:9–L and preach. Hos. 2:14 baptized Sam son to Thomas Wilson and Esther daughter to Jeremiah Murray. Thomas and William sons to James Blakely and Ezekial son to John Watt give all praise to God." (From David Dunwoody's.)

1753 Apr. 8   (See Rocky Spring, Franklin Co. for ordination of David Dunwoody, Jeremiah Murray and Thomas Wilson as elders.)

Aug. 26   "Sab. rode—mi. preached Ps. 42:5–9 lectured 1 Peter 5:8 Hebrews 3:12 and baptized Thomas son to John Kenedy, Jas. son to Wm. Spadie and Eleanor daughter to M. (From David Dunwoody's.)

" 27   "Rode 14 mi. John Hutchieson's preach Ps. 23, lectured Mat. 28:16–76 baptized Elizabeth daugh. to him and came to John Kenedy's 6 Jo. McC-" (Then rode 10 miles to Robert Redick's Joh Wats.—x x."

1754 May 12   "Sabbath. preached psalm 55:20–L lectured Amos. 1: 6–13 preached Hebrews 10:23 g.a. and baptized Andrew, son to Robert McCulloch, praise to my God." (David Dunwoody's.)

July 12   "Rode 5 miles to Crooks, after wandering to Da. Dinwoody's, where I set out."

" 14   "Sabbath—preached psalm 63:1–6—Lectured Amos 3: 8–L and preached Malachi 4:2 g.a. Baptized Sarah daughter to Thomas Wilson; Mary, daughter to Robert Stevenson and Elizabeth, daughter to Jer. Murray— rode 7 miles to Brothers."

Marsh Creek Society (Rock Creek)— *Continued*

1754 Sept. 9 "Rode 18 miles to John Broomfield's—preached psalm 121: 1-5 and preached Romans 4: 11 and baptized Sarah, daughter to Thomas Anderson—give all praise to God." (From James McKts—then rode 10 miles to Archibald Burns' on 10th.)

" 12 "Rode 7 miles to Da. Porter's old meeting-house, Da. Dinwiddy's, etc." (From Archibald Burns', Carroll's Tract.)

" 13 "Held session 10 hours, rectifying disorders, removing differences."

1755 Apr. 8 "Rode 12 miles to Br. Arch. Tract. (from John Bromfield's) after preaching psalm 78: 19-24 and examined 22 persons and baptized James son to Jo. Blakely and Kathrine daughter to James Blakely give all praise to my gracious God." (Then rode 8 miles to David Dunwoody's.)

" 13 "Sabbath—preached psalm 71: 20-L, Lectured Matthew 3: 1—preached Jeremiah 4: 14 and baptized Mary, daughter to Wm. Spoedie explained psalm 68: 1-10. give all praise to God." (At David Dunwoody's.)

May 11 "Sabbath, preached psalm 72: 15-L., lectured Matthew 4: 12-L. Preached Jeremiah 4: 14 and baptized James son to John Strobridge and Margaret daughter to Alexander Poa give all praise to my gracious God (Paid W. W. 1-7-0)." (At David Dunwoody's.)

Aug. 10 "Sabbath preached psalm 76: 7-L, lectured Matthew 5: 17-21, baptized David son to David Dinwiddy, Thomas son to Mary Silluck and James son to John Murphey: preached Micah 5: 5 and rode 6 miles to N." (At David Dunwoody's.)

Nov. 3 "Rode 13 miles to Humphrey Fulerton's after marrying Jo Crooks and Margaret McClure and Jo. Mooney and Janet Thomson—etc."

1756 Apr. 18 "Sabbath preached psalm 86: 6-12; lectured Matthew 9: 8-14 and preached Mark 9: 23 and baptized Sam son to Hor. Bratan and James son to Sam Moor; good health; give all praise to my gracious God." (At David Dunwoody's.)

July 23 "Rode 7 miles to David Dinwiddys after preaching (at Jer. Murrays) psalm 145: 17-L; catechized 40 persons and baptized Mary daughter to Robert Stevenson, James son to Arch Burns and Sarah daughter to Jo Little o.a."

1757 Feb. 27 "Sabbath. Rode 7 miles to J. B. am safe; preached psalm 102: 1—lectured Matthew 16: 6-13 and preached

Marsh Creek Society (Rock Creek)— *Continued*

2 Chronicles 20: 12 and baptized James son to Wm. Spoedie." (At David Dunwoody's.)

1757 May 22 "Sabbath. Preached psalm 104: 1–6: lectured Matthew 18: 19–23; preached Zephaniah 2: 1 g.a. and baptized Daniel son to John Bromfield, Mary daughter to Jeremy Murray and Agnes daughter to Thomas Anderson; exhausted." (At David Dunwoody's.)

" 25 "Rode 7 miles to brothers; preached psalm 60: 1—catechized 42 persons and baptized Hugh son to Thomas Wilson; rs 9–6 to little John Carr." (From Gibson's.—)

" 27 "Rode 9 miles to and from John Withrows and to David Dinwiddys sold tract." (From Archibald Burns, Carroll's Tract.)

" 29 "Sabbath. Rode 6 miles to John Crooks; preached psalm 104: 7–14; lectured Matthew 18: 23–L; preached Zephaniah 2: 1 and baptized Sarah daughter to Robert Fulerton and Hanah daughter to John Watt. give all praise to my gracious God." (From David Dunwoody's.)

1758 Mar. 26 "Sabbath—preached psalm 113: 1–7, Lectured Matthew 26: 47–57 preached psalm 94: 12 and baptized John son to John Murphy; William, son to John Crooks; and Ann, daughter to Alexander Poa." (At David Dunwoody's.)

" 30 "Fast Day—rode 7 miles to D.D. Preached psalm 80: 1—preached Isaiah 33: 2 and baptized Mary, daughter to James Mitchel—give all praise to God." (From W. or J. Withrow's.)

" 31 "rode 14 miles to and from—Married And. Branwood and Sarah Gibson—conversed—A. Cook drunk." (From David Dunwoody's.)

Apr. 2 "Sabbath—preached psalm 113: 7–L. Lectured Matthew 26: 57—preached psalm 94: 12 x x and baptized Martha, daughter to Mary Moore—g.a. etc." (At David Dunwoody's.)

" 4 "Preached psalm 97: 8–L. Preached Isaiah 28: 16 and baptized William son to William Cooper; praise to my gracious God." (At William Cooper's.)

Nov. 16 "rode 7 miles to D. D. after preaching psalm 89: 15; preaching John 2: 4 and baptizing Jean, daughter to James Blakch." (From Neal McKnaughtan's.)

Marsh Creek Society (Rock Creek)—*Continued*

1759 May 3 "rode—preached psalm 11:3 and exer. Matthew 11: 28–L and baptized Hannah, daughter to William Cooper; and Elizabeth daughter to William Spoedie." (At William Cooper's.)

"   6 "Sabbath—preached psalm 135:1–6. Lectured Philippians 1:5–11 and preached Malachi 3:16 and baptized Isobel, daughter to Robert Stevenson; and Margaret to John Blakely o.a. praise to my gracious God." (At David Dunwoody's.)

"   10 "rode 8 miles T. Wils.—preached psalm 30:4–9. Examined 40—baptized Susanna, daughter to John Little at Widow Murray's." (From J. Watts'—Carroll's Tract.)

"   11 "rode 8 miles to and from Na. Paxton's—preached psalm 27:11—preached Jeremiah 31:33 and baptized James son to James Innes—tired." (Then rode 6 miles from Thomas Wilson's to David Dunwoody's on 12th.)

1758 "   22 "rode 20 miles to T. Kennedy's, N. Duff's, and John Neily's." (From Robert Gilmore's.)

1760 Apr. 9 "rode 7 miles to D. D.—conversed 2 hours with Hans Hamilton."

"   13 "Sabbath—preached psalm 147:16. Lectured Habakkuk 1:5–12. Preached Romans 8:30 and baptized James, son to John Crook; Thomas, son to Thomas Wilson; Mary, daughter to —— Braton; and Hew, son to John Murphey—give all praise to God." (At David Dunwoody's.)

July 3 "Rode 16 miles to Widow Gibsons; preached psalm 80:1—catechized 40; baptized Grizzel daughter to Esther Paxton; went to Bays, D. McClellans." (Then tramped 2 miles to David Dunwoody's on 5th.)

1761 Apr. 19 "Sabbath preached psalm 18:30–36; lectured E. 2:15–16; preached psalm 39:4 and baptized Sarah daughter to David Dinwiddy, give all praise to God." (At David Dunwoody's.)

May 3 "Sabbath—preached psalm 18:41; lectured Ephesians 2:19–20 preached psalm 39:4 and baptized John son to Robert McConel presented by the mother." (At Widow Wilson's.)

June 3 "Rode 24 miles; Sis; removed; preached psalm 37:19–L, preached Revelation 1:18; baptized Agnes daughter to W. Ayers; presented by father." (At Carroll's Tract?)

"   4 "Married Thomas Morton and Ann Thompson; sick."

PENNSYLVANIA 75

Marsh Creek Society (Rock Creek)— *Continued*

1761 Sept. 20 "Sabbath, preached psalm 25: 11–16; lectured 1 Corinthians 11: 21 preached Matthew 16: 24 and baptized Wm. son to Robert Stevenson; Thomas son to T. Paxton." (At David Dunwoody's.)

" 22 "rode 8 miles widow M's etc. preached psalm 102: 17; examined 35; baptized Mary daughter to Alexander Poa; wandered to R. Reddicks." (At Alexander Poa's —from David Dunwoody's.)

1762 Apr. 4 "Sabbath preached psalm 33: 15–L; lectured Ephesians 6: 15–16 preached Isaiah 30;—baptized Sarah to Andrew Branwood and Rachel to John Crooks." (At David Dunwoody's.)

Aug. 1 "Preached psalm 37: 26–33; lectured Zachariah 2: 10–L, preached psalm 19: 13 and baptized Thomas son to Francis Meredith." (At David Dunwoody's.)

" 2 & 3 "Rode 17 miles to Jos. Kers and T. Wilson's; preached psalm 81: 8–12 and lectured Hebrews 3: 7–12 and baptized Katharine daughter to James Blakely." (From David Dunwoody's.)

" 22 "Sabbath. Rode 2 miles; preached psalm 38: 1 lectured Philippians 3: 13–16 preached John 6: 29 and baptized John son to John Blakly and Amos son to Wm. Moor." (From Thomas Anderson's.)

Oct. 24 "Sabbath preached psalm 40: 6–9; lectured Philippians 2: 12–17 and preached James 2: 12, baptized Benjamin son to Sam Paxton, explained psalm 69: 11–19, and baptized Matthew son to Matthew Richie." (At David Dunwoody's.)

1763 Mar. 24 "rode 7 miles James Paterson's—preached psalm 63: 1–5. Lectured Isaiah 55: 1–4 and baptized Mary, daughter to Rich. Burns." (From Humphrey Fulerton's—then rode 6 miles to John McMillan's.)

Apr. 10 "Sabbath—preached psalm 46: 9–L. Lectured Zechariah 8: 1–7—preached Hebrews 10: 23 g.a. and baptized Francis and Elizabeth, to Francis Innes." (At R. Stevenson's.)

" 18 "rode 14 miles to T. A's—married John Brakenridge and Mary Boyd." (Then rode 15 miles to James Reid's on 19th.)

Sept. 18 "Sabbath—preached psalm 55: 20. Lectured Zechariah 14: 20–L and preached Isaiah 27: 9 and baptized Robert son to Henry Calbreath—give all praise to God." (At David Dunwoody's.)

" 25 "Sabbath—preached psalm 55: 20–L—lectured Matthew 26: 26–33 preached Isaiah 27: 9 and baptized Elizabeth,

Marsh Creek Society (Rock Creek)— *Continued*

daughter to Benjamin McCormic—edict." (At David Dunwoody's.)

1763 Sept. 26   "rode 16 miles S. Hodges—married John Hutchinson and Eliz. Craw——." (From David Dunwoody's.)

1764 May 8   "rode 16 miles—preached psalm 137:1 and lectured Zechariah 14: 4–10 and married And. Walker and Isobel Thorn—rode to T. Wilson's." (From David Dunwoody's.)

"   14   "rode 3 miles—exc. Hebrews 7: 25—baptized Jean to J. Crooks; and Daniel to T. McClellan—tired." (3 miles from David Dunwoody's.)

Oct. 21   "Sabbath—preached psalm 73: 25–L—preached Colossians 2: 12–16—preached Hebrews 12: 29 (at David Dunwoody's) and baptized Sarah, daughter to John Finley; Jean, daughter to And. Branwood; and Alice to Robert Stevenson—rode 8 miles to Thomas Paterson's—preached psalm 80: 1 Exc. John 3: 16, 17 and baptized Ann, daughter to John Morton; Sarah to T. Paterson; and Ann to William Moor."

1765 Mar. 10   "Sabbath—preached psalm 78: 14–20. Lectured Colossians 3: 18–L and baptized Thomas, son to Richard Burns—headache." (At David Dunwoody's.)

May 30   "Fast—prayed—preached psalm 74: 18–L. Preached Isaiah 59: 34 x x—baptized Samuel son to (William Smith) x x." (At David Dunwoody's.)

June 1   "preached psalm 69: 11–19—preached Isaiah 38: 14—baptized Francis son to John Hodge; Alexander and Ann, son and daughter to A. Lochy—pr—and John to Alexander Poa. Cons. distributed the tokens good health, praise God."

"   3   "preached psalm 15—preached Philip 4: 6, 7, 8 and baptized John son to Thomas McClellan, a most sweet time, etc.—very tired." (At David Dunwoody's.)

"   9   "Sabbath—preached psalm 79: 1–6. Lectured Luke 24: 13–28—preached Matthew 6: 20, 21 and baptized John son to John Crawfurd and Robert, Margaret and William, sons and daughter to Robert Fulerton; and Jon. adopted son to John Hutchieson, Jun.—give all praise to my gracious God—weary." (At David Dunwoody's.)

Oct. 27   "Sabbath preached psalm 86: 11–15; lectured John 14: 1–2, preached Hebrews 9–L, and baptized Francis, son to David Frazer; Margaret to Henry Calbreath and

Marsh Creek Society (Rock Creek)— *Continued*

Sarah, daughter to John Hodge, g.a.—cold day." (At David Dunwoody's.)

1765 Oct. 29 "rode 10 miles—married William Mitchel and Mary Wilson; and Matthew Mitchel and Mary Richie—received nothing." (From David Dunwoody's.)

1766 Mar. 30 "Sabbath—preached psalm 91: 9–14. Lectured Hebrews 10: 30–34. Preached Jude—baptized Margaret to John Crooks." (At David Dunwoody's.)

Apr. 1 "Fast-day preached psalm 19: preached Jeremiah 31: 19 baptized Thomas Hutchieson—rode 8 miles to Jos. Ker's." (At David Dunwoody's.)

Sept. 28 "Sabbath preached psalm 103: 12–26; lectured Romans 3: 26—preached last verse baptized Agnes daughter to James Blakely." (At David Dunwoody's.)

1767 May 24 "Sabbath—preached psalm 107: 31–39; lectured John 6: 41–52, preached Jude and baptized Ann daughter to Matthew Richie; praise to my good God." (At David Dunwoody's.)

June 3, 4 "rode 9 miles to J. Kers; preached psalm 94: 14–18 and explained Mark L: 14–17 and baptized Rebecca daughter to John Reddick.o.a." (From David Dunwoody's.)

Aug. 15 "walked 2 miles to and from John Reed's visited sick and baptized Robert son to James Lochhead." (From David Dunwoody's.)

" 16 "Sabbath—preached psalm 111: 1–5; lectured Proverbs 1: 24–L; preached Habakkuk 3: 2 and baptized James son to James Braedy o.a. praise to my gracious God." (At David Dunwoody's.)

Dec. 2 "rode 2 miles Dan. Mc.—preached psalm 27 lectured Romans 8: 1–4 and baptized Sam son to W. Caruthers." (Then rode 8 miles on 3rd Jat. Gilm. to David Dunwoody's.)

1768 Mar. 27 "Sabbath—preached psalm 119: 33–37. Lectured 1 John 5: 13–16 and preached verse 14 o.a. Baptized Isobel, daughter to And. Branwood; and Hew, son to Ben McCormick. Exercised 1 Thess. 4: 13—and baptized Wm. son to D. D., and John son to John Crooks." (At David Dunwoody's.)

Apr. 3 "Sabbath from 37–4; Lectured 5: 16–L and preached verse 18 and baptized James son to John Hutchinson; and Agnes, daughter to Robert Spier." (At David Dunwoody's.)

Marsh Creek Society (Rock Creek)—*Continued*

1768 May 15   "Sabbath—preached 60: 65. Lectured 1 Peter 4: 12–17—preached 17 and baptized Isobel to David Robieson." (At David Dunwoody's.)

Aug. 28   "Sabbath—preached psalm 121–24. Lectured Jeremiah 3: 12–16—preached Revelations 3: 11 and baptized Alexander, son to Wm. Smith; Joseph, son to James Braeden; Edward to James Blakely; James to Alexander Poa; and Robert, son to Jas. Dunbar." (At David Dunwoody's.)

"   29   "rode 30 miles to Smeizar's—married David Parkhill and Martha Murray—received dol.—"

Sept. 27   "Fast-day—prayed, rs causes, preached psalm 51: 11–L and preached Isaiah 55: 7 and baptized Margaret, daughter to Adam Richieson—rode 9 miles to sister's." (At David Dunwoody's.)

Nov. 13   "Sabbath—rode 12 miles—preached 161–7—preached Proverbs 15: 9 and baptized Robert, son to Robert Stewart: Janet, daughter to Matthew Mitchel at night. Exercised 2 hours Isaiah 63: 1–4 and baptized Wm. to W. Steel." (At David Dunwoody's.)

1769 May 7   "Sabbath preached psalm 137: 1—lectured Matthew 5: 33–38; preached Isaiah 26: 9 and baptized Abel son to James Finley and Eliz. daughter to James Braedy." (At David Dunwoody's.)

"   11   "rode 20 miles; married Alexander Ker and Sarah Murray." (At Neil McKnight's.)

Aug. 15   "rode 12 miles R. McCull. preached psalm 91: 14 and lectured 1 Corinthians 6: 1–8: x x and baptized James son to James Leiper and married John Robertson and Mary Lowry." (At Robert Crunkleton's.)

"   20   "Sabbath preached 7–L; lectured Luke 22: 19–24; preached Matthew 22: 11, etc. and baptized Sarah daughter to David Parkhill and Jean daughter to Mary Cairn." (At David Dunwoody's.)

"   26   "Preached psalm 84: 4–10; preached Mark 6: 50 and baptized James to W. Smith." (At David Dunwoody's.)

1770 Mar. 25   "Sabbath—2 miles—preached psalm 5: 1 lectured Isaiah 26: 5–10 and preached Jeremiah 12: 13 and baptized Margaret, daughter to John Murray—give all praise to God." (From David Dunwoody's.)

"   26   "rode 20 miles, visited McKt. preached and exercised psalm 138: 5 and baptized John, to John Hutchinson and Mary, to John Crooks." (At Neil McKnight's.)

Marsh Creek Society (Rock Creek)— *Continued*

1770 Mar. 28, 29   "rode 8 miles J. Mur.—preached psalm 40: 1 lectured Colossians 2: 5, 6 & 7 and baptized Margaret, daughter to James Blakely o.a." (From John Murray's.)

Apr.   1   "Sabbath preached 5: 7 lectured Isaiah 26: 10 & 15— preached Jeremiah 17: 14 and baptized John, son to Robert Speer, give all praise to my gracious God." (At John Murray's.)

"   2   "rode 8 miles Jos. Ker's. Married Matthew Begs and Martha McKinley—exercised psalm 30: 1–5—and baptized Mary daughter to John Morton."

May 15   "rode 8 miles back; preached psalm 34: 11; catechized 50 persons, and baptized Benjamin son to Ben McCormick o.a. s. night." (From T. Wilson's to D. D's.)

"   16, 17   "rode 17 miles—married George Duffield and Eliz. McNaughtan—held session—exercised psalm 34: 17– L and baptized Elizabeth, Mary and Joseph to Mary Brousler, McNight."

"   20   "Sabbath—preached 5: 1–4; lectured Isaiah 65: 1–9; preached 41: 10 and baptized Josiah to Alexander Ker, Robert to John Park and James to John Reddick; give all praise to God. Rode 8 miles to sisters."

Sept.   9   "Sabbath preached psalm 16: 7–L; lectured John 8: 1– 12; preached Isaiah 63: 7 and baptized John son to Robert Stewart and Elizabeth to And. Branwood." (At David Dunwoody's.)

"   13   "rode 7 miles D. D's after preaching (at Neal Mc-Knaughtan's) 51: 7—and lectured Matthew 13: 18–24 and baptized Alexander and Margaret son and daughter to James Dunbar."

Oct.   8   (See Middle Octoraro.)

Nov. 14   "Preached psalm 51: 1—exercised Acts 10 afterwards baptized John son to David Parkhill o.a. praise God." (Then rode 8 miles to David Dunwoody's.)

"   19   "rode 11 miles Wm. Steel's: preached psalm 19: 7 exercised Acts 2: 37—baptized Hew son to Joseph Steel and Jos. to W." (From David Dunwoody's.)

1771 May 12   "Sabbath preached 5: 9; lectured Romans 4: 1–9; preached Isaiah 26: 12 and baptized Eleanor to B. Robinson and Martha to Mary Braester, o.a. praise God etc., foot getting better." (From D. B., Leonard Mc'shel P. Burg.)

Marsh Creek Society (Rock Creek)— *Continued*

1771 May 14   "rode 6 miles after preaching 19: 7—lectured Numbers 23: 19–22 and baptized Henry son to John Ewing; married Charles Boyle and Elizabeth Torbit, went to John Murp." (At David Dunwoody's.)

Sept. 26   "rode 8 miles to D. D's; preached 119: 9—catechized 53 persons, and baptized Agnes daughter to Matthew Mitchel and Agnes and John to Thomas McClellan." (From T. Wilson's.)

"   29   "Sabbath rode 9 miles (from David Dunwoody's) to James Spiers; after preaching 33: 6–10; lectured Luke 13: 10–18; preached Jude and baptized John to James Ramsay." (Then rode 5 miles to Francis Meredith's, Carroll's Tract.)

Oct. 2   "rode 8 miles after preaching 103: 6–13; catechized 34 persons baptized George son to Wm. Finley and Abel son to John Finley went to widow S." (From John Cochran's.)

"   4   "preached 103: 13—catechized 28 and baptized Arthur son to Thomas Pattison." (8 miles from John Cochran's.)

1772 Apr. 12   "Sabbath; preached 39: 7-L; lectured Isaiah 8: 1–11; preached Luke—L. 29 and baptized James son to And. Branwood, and Robert son to John Reddick; give all praise to my gracious God." (At David Dunwoody's.)

"   17   "preached psalm 76: 1–7; lectured 7–L and baptized Robert son to Robert Spier." (At David Dunwoody's.)

Aug. 2   "Sabbath; preached 14–18; lectured Jude 7–L and preached psalm 119: 132 and baptized Sarah daughter to Alexander Ker, g.a. intimate sacrament." (At David Dunwoody's.)

"   19   "rode 26 miles to D. D's., married John Burns and Esther Murray." *

"   20   "rode 19 miles to McCork. married Matth. Caldwel and Margaret Reid; went to Jos. Walkers and Neal McKnaughtan's." (Then rode 8 miles to David Dunwoody's.)

"   23   "Sabbath, preached 45: 4–7; lectured 1 Corinthians 10: 12–22 preached 1 Corinthians 5: 8, of Christ, baptized David son to Sam Paxton; give all praise to my gracious God." (At David Dunwoody's.)

"   31   "Preached 85: 6—discoursed Acts 9: 6; x x—baptized Janet and Robert (to T. Cochran and and his wife Mar-

* Same as Murphy, Morrow.

Marsh Creek Society (Rock Creek)— *Continued*

garet) and Margaret daughter to John Parks, g.a. rode 12 miles to T. Cross'; very tired." (At David Dunwoody's.)

1773 Mar. 2 "rode 3 miles—preached 61: 1—lectured 2 Corinthians 5: 1–11. Baptized Jean to T. Patt." (From D. McCur.—Crook's.)

" 7 "Sabbath: rode 2 miles—preached 16–L. Lectured 27 and baptized Samuel son to Robert Stewart; and Jean daughter to David Parkhill." (From David Dunwoody's.)

" 15 "rode 11 miles to John Parks; preached 119: 1—lectured Hosea 61–4 and baptized Thomas to John Morton; and Sam son to John Ewin T.P. 1." (From David Dunwoody's.)

Aug. 21 "rode 3 miles from John Murphy's to W. B's and D. Dunw."

" 22 "Sabbath preached 14–L. Isaiah 39—preached same and baptized Wm. son to W. Braeden; William, son to Matthew Caldwel; and Matthew, son to Matthew; and Mary daughter to Matthew Beggs; and Martha, daughter to Charles Bole—give all praise to my benignant God & Mitchel."

" 24 "rode 34 miles—married Wm. Paterson and Jean Murray. And Sam Marshal and Mary Murphy—came to Smeizar's." (From David Dunwoody's.)

Nov. 7 "Sabbath—preached 6–L and lectured Isaiah 43: 1–14 and baptized Margaret daughter to John Burns, o.a. praise my gracious God." (At David Dunwoody's.)

" 11 "rode 15 miles to D. D's John Mur.—married John Wilson and Mary Dinwoody—give all praise to God." (David Dunwoody's or John Murphy's.)

" 17 "rode 3 miles to sis.—preached 27: 1—preached 4th verse—baptized Neal son to Thomas McNaghten g.a." (From Hugh Dunwoody's.)

" 21 "rode 8 miles—preached 64: 5–L. Preached Philip 3: 3 and baptized to John Murray—rode to Jos. Ker's." (From David Dunwoody's.)

1777 Feb. 11 "rode 22 miles to S. D., John Park's, Mr. Dobin's, Lind came."

" 12 "rode 6 miles—Mr. Lynd preached Revelations 12: 1, 2 —baptized James Do(bin?)." (Then rode 10 miles to J. Park's on 13th.)

M: rsh Creek Society (Rock Creek)— *Continued*

1777 Oct. 13   "Mr. Dobin preached psalm 89: 31–38 and preached Hebrews 11: 9. Baptized 3 children, adult."

1786 Aug. 29, 30   "rode 17 miles to Coch., Gebby's, and James Crooks preached 86: 11–15 Exer. 2 Kings 7: 3, 4 and baptized James to John Bourn's, C. Married 9." (From John Bourn's.)

Redland

1752 June 30   "Rode 15 miles to James Dills redland preached Psa. 129; lectured Ps.. 26: 20–21, preached Amos 5, 6 and baptized John to Henry Hall." (From Carlisle.)

1753 Mar. 13   "Rode 20 miles over Susquehanna to James Dill's, having insomnia."

"   14   "Rode 4 miles to Robert Bonar's in Balmondyean." (Ballymoney.)

1755 Aug. 11   "Rode 15 miles to John Dill's, preached psalm 23, lectured Zephaniah 2: 1–4 and baptized Margaret to Hew O'hail, give all praise to God. Conversed." (From David Dunwoody's.)

The Quarter

1765 Nov. 7   "rode 5 miles to and from the Quarter—visited Leiper, Rankin, Gebby." (From John Cochran's, J. McClenachan's.)

"   10   "Sabbath—preached psalm 87—preached Hebrews 4: 16. Baptized James and John, sons to James McClenachan, Jur.—exc. Mark 10: 10–46–L."

1769 Mar. 22   "rode 10 miles Quarter; preached psalm 23: 1–3; lectured John 1: 36–40 and married James Brownlie and Eliz. Rankin, James Leiper and Margaret Brownlie went to R. Crunk's. rs 2–2–6." (Robert Crunckleton's about 3 miles from James McClenachan's.)

Three Springs

1752 Nov. 5   "Sab. Rode 8 miles 3 spr. preach. Ps. 31: 11–15 lect. So. 5: 13–L. preach. 2 Cor.—" (From B. W's.)

1753 Mar. 18   "Sab. rode 2 mi. 3 springs, preach Ps. 36: 1–7 lectured 1 Peter 1: 17—preached Lev. 20: 7 and baptized Thomas and Sarah son and daugh. to Jo.—" (From David Dunwoody's.)

July 22   "Sab. rode 3 mi. to and from 3 Springs preached Ps. 40: 9–12 lectured 1 Peter 4: 10–12 preached Jer. 3: 4 g.a.—baptized Jo... son to David Dunwoody and Sam son to Thomas Neelie." (From David Dunwoody's.)

Toms Creek

1770 Mar. 27 "rode 18 miles to Tams Creek—married Thomas Armstrong and Jean McCrea; James Scott and Mary Rankin—went to John Murray's—roads bad, bad—rec'd 17 s." (From McKt's.)

" Tract Irrasens "

1767 May 25 "rode 15 miles to and from Tract Irrasens F. Meredith." (From David Dunwoody's.)

Two Taverns

1762 Apr. 12 "Rode 28 miles to the 2 Tavern; rs 1-0-0 from W. Cooper." (Then 32 miles home on 13th.)

ALLEGHENY COUNTY

Monongahela Society

Rev. John Cuthbertson made his only recorded trip into Allegheny County and into Washington County in the fall of 1779, visiting the Society known as the Monongahela, distributed over a large area of country along the Monongahela and Youghiogheny Rivers, some twenty miles southeast of Pittsburgh, the central point of which was the Forks of the Yough. Perhaps the earliest settlement was in 1769, when James Wilson and his son Zaccheus left the Cove Mountain, east of the Alleghenies, and settled in this vicinity, moving to the Forks of the Yough the following year, accompanied by Robert McConnell. They were soon joined by the families of Robert and Matthew Jamison; Andrew McMeans; Matthew Mitchell.

Allegheny " Creek "

1779 Sept. 15 "Rode 30 miles Cumberl. Fort Mills (or Hills), Creek Alegheny, Tomlinson." (From Old Town.)

Forks of Yough

1779 Sept. 17 "Rode 37 miles Laurelhill, Mr. Greer's, Forks of Yough, Mr. Simson's."
" 18 "Rode 12 miles to Col. Cook's by Aaron to Zaccheus Wilson's. Good health."
" 19 "Sabbath—rode 3 miles preached 37: 7–12; lectured Hebrews 6: 13–L and baptized Mary daughter to Robert Jamieson, o.a. praise my gracious God."
" 20 "rode 5 miles down Yough to James Finey's, agreed not."

Forks of Yough— *Continued*

1779 Sept. 21 "rode 10 miles from Ben Brown's to Joseph Caldwel's, T. Morton."

" 23 "rode 3 miles to James Finey's, after preaching, 91: 1-7 and lecturing 7-L and baptized Thomas and Elizabeth to Charles Boal; o.a. praise God, etc."

" 24 "rode 3 miles to David Robinson's; received $39 from James Finey."

" 26 "Sabbath—preached 12: 19; lectured Hebrews 12: 1-4 g.a. and baptized Sus. to Isa. Wilson, James to Aaron, Hannah to Jos. Loughhead, David and Martha to John Drenan and Susanna to James Paterson; rode 3 miles to and from J. Drenan."

Sept. 28
to   } (See Washington County.)
Oct. 1

Oct. 3 "Sabbath—rode 3 miles from —— to John Reid's; preached 37: 19-24; lectured Hebrews 11: 1-7 and baptized John son to J. R. give all praise to my gracious God."

" 4 "rode 10 miles with John Reid to and from plantation, good." (At West Middletown, Washington Co.)

" 5 "rode 12 miles to Widow Reed's, over Monongahela; Hen. Nisby's etc."

" 6 "preached 22: 28—catechized 50 and baptized Wm. to Matth; Janet to Ebenezer and Isobel to John Mitchel; o.a. praise God."

" 7 "rode 14 miles, 6 to Sam Wilson's; preached 51: 1— preached Hebrews 13: 14 and baptized Elizabeth to S. Wilson John and Margaret to Sa. Scot, then rode 8 miles to Peter Paterson's, Red Sto."

" 8 "rode 10 miles to and from Wm. Patter., John Robies., James Pa., John Stewa."

BEDFORD COUNTY

Bedford

1779 Oct. 14 "rode 38 miles Glades Mountains, etc., to Bedford—a fall, etc." (From Glades.)

Juniata River

1779 Oct. 15 "rode 35 miles over Juniata, Sideling Hill, Scrub, rs. D. McC." (From Bedford.)

BERKS COUNTY

Chapel (or Chapel Potts)

1764 Aug. 29 "rode 42 miles to Chapel Potts, Furnace, 6 to Grove, and T. Kenety's." (From Jacob Glein's.)

Pine Forge

1760 Sept. 29 "rode 44 miles to Schulkil, Pine-forge. priests, Jacob Glein's etc." (From Thomas Kennedy's.)

Maiden Creek

1752 Oct. 4 "Rode 34 miles over maiden C. by Stairs, Con. Wisers, Reeits Mills, etc."

Reading

1754 July 2 "Rode 40 miles—25 Reading Town, 15 Con. Wiser, with Rynford ——." (From Jost Henricks.)

1780 Oct. 24 "rode 33 miles through Reading to Mr. Widenhammers Tavern." (On way to Allentown.)

Reading Furnace

1764 Aug. 7 "rode 36 miles to Reding Fur. French Creek, White Horse to Stoffields." (On way to Allentown from Robert Gilmore's.)

" Reeits Mills "

1752 Oct. 4 (See Maiden Creek.)

Weidenhammer's Tavern

1780 Oct. 24 (See Reading.)

Weiser's Tavern, Conrad

1752 Oct. 4 (See Maiden Creek.)

1753 July 6 "Rode 50 miles to Tavern at Conrad Woesers no good rest cards played."

1754 July 2 (See Reading.)

BUCKS COUNTY

Deep Run Meeting (Dyerstown)

1766 June 4 "rode 20 mils to Alexander Mickleroy's; preached psalm 4, preached 1 Timothy 1: 15, then came by Deep Run meeting-house to R. Robieson's Tavern." (From Old Forge and Ferry.)

1779 Nov. 23, 24 "rode 13 miles to Deep Run M. Mr. McHenry's. John Bates." (From Bartholomew Weaver's.)

Durham Furnace

1769 Nov. 1   "rode and walked 36 miles Dur. Furn. and Jacob Couker's." (From Hacket's T. and T. Lecken's.)

1775 Sept. 26   "rode 40 miles to Thievley's. (9) Trumbour's (10 miles)
Dur. F. (18), Jones 2." (From Pine Forge and Mr.
Richard's.)

Neshaminy and " Shamony old meeting-house "

1753 June 18   " Received 30 letters from S.— rode 28 miles to Shamony,
Toehicken Wm. Morris (Moore's?) " (From Walter
Moore's.)

"   19   "Preached there Ps. 132: 12–L and preached John 3:
14, 15 conversed Patterson, Boles."

1754 June 10   " Rode 16 miles to Robert Henderson's after preaching
psalm 78: 5–12 and preaching Amos 5: 6 at Shamony
o. meeting-house give all praise to God ——." (From
Walter Moore's.)

1757 June 23   "Rode 16 miles to Shamony; preached Psalm 2: 1–9
and preached Isaiah 26: 20." (From Walter Moore's.)

1758 Sept. 16   "rode 7 miles to Wm. Smith's, Shamony dead in spirit,
etc."

Dec. 8   "rode 17 miles to father's and to James Edem's at
Shamony." (From Frankfort.)

Quakertown

1783 Aug. 2   "rode 28 miles to Quaker Town, Pitts. T, 2 Buski.
Ben M." (From Pickering's.)

Tohicken

1753 June 18   (See Neshaminy.)

" Ward's Bridge "

1783 Sept. 22   "rode 8 miles Wards Bridge, John Coulter's and Wm.
Dalgliesh.—3." (Returning from New York.)

CHESTER COUNTY

Brandywine

1751 Sept. 9   (See East Fallowfield.)

1752 Jan. 27   (See Forks of Brandywine.)

1752 May 12   " Rode 11 miles to Thomas Kennedy's. Preached psalm
129 and preached 2 Cor. 8: 21 . . . to Ro. Gilmore 5 s.
and to S. K. 4—etc. continued 4 hours concerning
agreements, etc." (From Humphrey Fullerton's.)

Sept. 18   "Rode 28 miles to Poequay then to Robert Gilmor's
and 'Thos. Kennedy's—."

Brandywine— *Continued*

1752 Sept. 19 "Gave a history preach. Ps. Rom. 3:27 spoke of the covenant and baptized Robert son to Hew Gibb. and Martha daugh. to Jas. Gilmor."

1754 Jan. 29 "Rode 22 miies—6 to Jo. McGee's—5 Jacob's Shop— 11 Thomas T., Thomas K." (From Seven Stars.)
" 30 "Rode 3 miles Robert Gilmor's after preaching psalm 23 and preaching E. 5:15. Received from T. K. and R. G. 15 and from Ja. Garner 5—from adw. 5—from W. 3."

1755 June 29 "Sabbath. Preached psalm 74:12–15 lectured Amos 8:8–L preached John 8:36 and baptized Benjamin son to James Gilmor and David son to H. Gibson." (At Thomas Kennedy's—then rode 3 miles to R. G. x x am to see James Ga ——.)
1759 June 16 "rode 11 miles to Robert Gilmor's, Brandawine—to Leech." (From Pequea.)

1761 Nov. 28 "Rode 30 miles with John Ker to Thomas Kennetys; good health." (From Holton's Tavern.)
" 29 "Sabbath preached psalm 48:1—lectured Song of Solomon 5:4–9 and Baptized Rebecca daughter to James Davidson; slept none."

1764 Nov. 27 "rode 26 miles (from home) to William Caruther's John Lindsay's Kennet—."
" 28 "rode 3 miles after preaching psalm 102:13—lectured Titus 2:11–15 and baptized Mary daughter to Wm. Caruthers—give all praise to God."

1770 Dec. 15 "rode 22 miles to R. Lyon, T. Kennety's."
" 16 "Sabbath preached 19:7–11; lectured Isaiah 63:10–17 and baptized Elizabeth daughter to Thomas Kennety o.a. praise my gracious God."

1775 Apr. 9 "Sabbath—preached 5–9, Lectured 17–L. Baptized jean, daughter to John Todd." (At Thomas Kennedy's, Brandywine.)

1778 Nov. 4, 5 "rode 24 miles to H. F's, Compass, and Tho. Ken."
" 8 "Sabbath—preached 42–45. Lectured Heb. 6:15–L and baptized Hannah to Wm. Rankin and Mary to John Tod o.a."

Brandywine—*Continued*

1784 Aug. 30   "rode 3 miles to Mordecai Persals T. Ken. John Tod's from Jas. Nis."

Compass

1777 June 23   "rode 10 miles to the Compass—visited Sam McClellan and wife (2½ Joes from An Ken)." (Then 12 miles home on 24th.)

1783 Nov. 3   "rode 18 miles from John Tod's, compass Js. Loughhead's, home, all well."

Dean's Meeting-house

1751 Sept. bet.
16 & 19   "Rode 7 miles to the Forks of Brandawine at Deans Meeting-house. . . ."
"Preached psalm 4: 1–6 and preached Daniel 7: 13 . . . then rode 16 miles to Hum. Ful."

East Fallowfield

1751 Sept. bet.
9 & 14   "Rode 36 miles: very tired, to Jo. Fleming's East Fallowfield Brandawine." (From Philadelphia.)

Elk

1752 Sept. 1   (See Bencadar, Del.)

Forks of Brandywine

1752 Jan. 27   "Rode 15 miles to Thomas Kennedy's, forks Brandawine."

"   28   "Rode 5 miles to meeting-house. Preached psalm 4: 6–L and preached Heb. 2: 3.—9: 3 and a Do.—rd. Nickleduff and to Jo. Culberts."

French Creek

1764 Aug. 7   (See Reading Furnace, Berks Co.)

New Londonderry Manor

1751 Aug. 7   "Rode 15 miles to Jo. Rosses, Mannor of New London Derry, weary, etc. . . ." (Then 8 miles to Joseph Walker's, Middle Octoraro on 9th.)

Oxford

1786 Sept. 30
& Oct. 1   "Sabbath—20 miles Oxford, preached 73: 25, lectured 19–L, preached Titus 2: 14 and baptized Wm. son to John Macbeth C." (From Carroll's Tract.)

Pickering

1783 Aug. 1   "rode 31 miles to Pickering's, Quakers." (On way to Quakertown.)

" Wantsmill "

1751 Oct. 16   " Rode 16 miles to Wantsmill—Thomas Tsennedys where preached psa. 76 . . . and lectured Mark 19–25. . . ." (Then 7 miles to James Gilmore's on 17th.)

Warwick's Furnace

1754 Jan. bet.
16 & 18   (See Swedesford, Mont. Co.)

White Horse

1754 June 5   "Rode 50 miles—15 Red—Ly; 5, White Horse; 15 Swede's Ford; 15 Sa White Horse." (On way to Walter Moore's from Thomas Kennedy's.)

1756 Jan. 20   "Rode 28 miles to John Neallie's; White Horse—tired but well." (On way to Pequea from Walter Moore's.)

1758 Aug. 12   "rode 55 miles to White-horse—my wife rode 35 and John Kain—etc. dying." (From York Co.)

CUMBERLAND COUNTY

Big Spring (Near Newville)

1751 Nov. 8   "Rode 12 miles to And. Ralstons Big spring Pennsbo. T." (From Carlisle.)

" 10   "Sabbath. Preached psalm 16: 1–6. Lectured Gal. 3: 1–5. Preached Jer. 3: 19 and baptized Robert son to Horace Bratton presented by the Mother.—Give all praise to God."

1752 Mar. 21   "Rode 22 miles to Big Spring. c. ov. Carried in canow. Carl. Ch. Shel ——." (From Walter Buchanan's.)

Oct. 24   "Rode 5 miles A. Rals. preached Ps. 103: 17–22 and preach. Rev. 3: 2 praise to God and bap. James son to Allan Scroggs wrote letters to . . . ." (From Charles Kilgour's—then rode 22 miles to Dunlop's Ship.)

1753 Apr. 15   "Sab. preach. Ps. 37: 12–19 lectured 1 Peter 2: 6–9 and preached Lev. 7–L. bap. Esther daugh. to Jo. McClung weary." (At Andrew Ralston's, Big Spring.)

Sept. 18   "Rode 14 mi. Hopewel preach. Ps. 125 lectured Hos. 2: 10–L and baptized Mary daughter to Horace Bratton 3 hours give praise to God—old wife." (Then rode 5 miles to Charles Kilgore's on 19th.)

1754 Apr. 14   "Sabbath. Rode 7 miles to C. Kilg., after preaching psalm 54. Lectured Joel 3: 9–15 (at Fran. McNicol's) and preached Amos 5: 6 and baptized Agnes, daughter

Big Spring (Near Newville)— *Continued*

to Joseph Junken, and Sam, son to John Glendining."
Give all praise to my God."

1754 Aug. 6 "Rode 16 miles to Alan Scrogs—exer. 2½ hours psalm 23 and baptized Eleanor daughter to him—then came to Charles Kilgours." (From Wm. Dunlop's—then rode and walked 9 miles to Fran. McNichol's.)

1756 Aug. 9 "Rode 20 miles to Ch. Kilgores; received 15 sh. preached psalm 125, examined 20; baptized Jean daughter to Alan Scrogs; came to Joseph Junkens give all praise to God."

1758 Nov. 5 "Sabbath—preached psalm 119—16th part. Lectured Micah 2: 10–L—preached Nahum 1: 7 o.a. and baptized Mathew, son to John McClung wet day, etc." (From Francis McNicol's—then 8 miles to Carlisle on 6th.)

"   8 "rode 10 miles to C. Kilg. after preaching psalm 78: 5–12. Lectured Acts 5: 29–33 and baptized Allan, son to Al. Scrogs; and Margaret daughter to Alex." (At Big Spring.)

17 61 May 14 "Preached psalm 80: 5–9 and lectured Matthew 28: 16–L and baptized James son to James Brown; give all praise to God, sick; old Roan sick." (At Charles Kilgore's.)

1762 Aug. 24 "Rode 8 miles to John Agnews; preached psalm 24: 11–17; lectured Acts 2: 37–41 baptized Charles to John McClung married John Giffan and Eleanor Heron." (From John McClung's.)

Oct. 12 "Preached psalm 69: 13–16; lectured Mark 10: 47–L and baptized Jesse son to Charles Kilgore and Agnes daughter to Wm. Calbreath." (At Charles Kilgore's.)

1764 Feb. 9 "rode 6 miles to Math. Brown's—preached psalm 62 Preached Hebrews 7: 25 and baptized Mary, daughter to him—had a great cold." (From W. Parkieson's.)

"   12 "Sabbath—preached psalm 64: 1–5 and preached 1 Corinthians 16: 13 and baptized Alexander, son to James Brown and Esther daughter to James Thorn." (Then rode 6 miles to Carlisle from Charles Kilgore's on 13th.)

1765 Nov. 16 & 17 "—Sabbath—rode 6 miles—preached psalm 88: 1–8. Lectured John 14: 15–22—preached Hebrews 4: 16 and baptized James son to James Thorn; Robert, to John Dunbar; and Mary daughter to James Dunbar—exc. psalm 37: 3 and baptized John, son to John Anderson." (From Ch. Kilgore's—then rode 6 miles to William Parkieson's to General Meeting on 18th.)

Big Spring (Near Newville)— *Continued*

1768 Apr. 12 "rode 30 miles—married Robert Hamilton and Eleanor Giffe(n)." (From John Mitchel's.)

"   13 "rode 10 miles—preached psalm 34: 3–8. Lectured 1 John 5: 10–14. Baptized Sara. daughter to Matthew Brown (received 10 from And. St.) "

"   17 "Sabbath—preached 44–49. Lectured Isaiah 56: 6–9. Preached 26: 3 and baptized —— son to John Taylor; and James, son to Wm. Paterson."

1769 Apr. 2 "Sabbath preached psalm 135: 6–12; lectured Romans 3: 19–L; preached 5: 1 and baptized Agnes daughter to John Giffen; very sick; give all praise to God." (At Charles Kilgore's.)

1770 Mar. 8 "rode 30 miles (from Chas. Kilgore's)—preached psalm 51: 1—lectured 6, 7 and 8 verses—baptized Elizabeth to him."

June 1 "rode 10 miles and preached psalm 42: 1—preached Zech. 13: 1 and baptized Jean daughter to Matthew Brown g.a." (From Charles Kilgore's; then rode 5 miles to Wm. Parkieson's.)

1773 Feb. 15 "rode 14 miles to Ch. Kilg.—married William Walker and Margaret Reid." (At Big Spring.)

1775 Aug. 6 "Sabbath—Mr. L. prayed and preached. I preached Romans 6: 4—baptized Matthew son to Brother Lind. g.a. praise God—a great rain, etc." (At Mr. Lind's o. h.)

Blane's Tavern

1782 May 15 "rode and walked 14 miles to Martin's, Latta's, Mr. Smith's Blanes Tavern." (From old John Reagh's on way to Pequea.)

Canandugwinet Creek (See also Junkin Tent)

1751 Aug. 20 "x x Then rode 18 miles to Walter Buchanan's upon side of Cannodugwin Creek; tired but safe." (From Wm. Brown's, Paxton.)

"   21 "Preached psalm 76: 10–1. Preached psalm 8: 4 and baptized Jo., son to Jo. Glendining; John, son to Jo. McClellan and Jean, daughter to Henry Swansie. Give all praise to God. Then rode 20 miles to . . . near the great Spring, weary, molested. . . ."

1752 Mar. 12 "Rode 12 miles over Susquehanna (Dr. Plum) to Walter Buchanan, Cannondug."

"   15 "Sabbath. Preached psa. 20: 6–L. Lectured Gal. 6: 6–10 and preached 1 Cor. 15: 22. x x x and then bap-

Canandugwinet Creek (See also Junkin Tent)— *Continued*

tized Jas. son to Walter Buchanan, Jas. son to Jo. Gardner, Isaac son to Alex Laverty and Jean daughter to Adam Colqhoun."

1752 Mar. 16   "Married Isaac Dowglas and Mary Sloan. Then preached psa. 34: 1–6 and exam. 20 persons—exhausted —Wm. Gardner tho is married to his wife's sister, etc. and desires w. write the president."

"   25   "Rode 18 miles to Jo. Wylies at Cannondug. Cr. x x." (From Carlisle.)

1765 Apr.   3   "rode 8 miles to Walter Buchanan's—preached psalm 66: 13–L and lectured Hebrews 12: 1, 2; at Sam Calhoun's preached psalm 94. Lectured Hebrews, etc. Baptized Agnes."

1766 Feb. 12   "rode 3 miles W. Buchanan's—preached psalm 119: 105—catechized 28—baptized Sarah to Sam Leipers." (From James McKnaught's.)

1770 Apr. 17   "rode 21 miles to Wal. B.   Married Alexander McCulloch and Hannah Dixon—went by R. Fulton's—very tired."   (From home.)

"   18   "rode 4 miles preached psalm 34: 1–5 catechized 25, etc. Baptized James, son to Peter Wilson, conversed, etc."

1775 Dec. 20   "rode 4 miles to W. Buch—preached 66: 7, Lectured Haggai 2: 1–7.   Baptized William son to James Glen and Baptized Rebecca (his daughter)."   (From W. Richy's.)

"   21   "rode 4 miles to John Walker's—preached 11–14 and catechized 22 persons."

1777 Feb. 26   "rode 8 miles—married Jas. Ramsay and Margaret Stuart at Wal. Buch. preached 32: 5—preached Micah 6–9—went to John Alison's."   (From Sam Poak's.)

1783 Mar. 25   "rode 11 miles to Mar. Collins and Walter Buchanan's." (From home.)

"   26   "rode 4 miles—preached 19.   Catechized 20 and baptized Jean to James Glen and Mary to Gilbert Buchanan o.a.   Went to J. Bigham's."

Carlisle

1752 Oct. 17   "Rode 17 miles married Jo. McCormick and Mary Strehon to . . ."   (Then rode 9 miles to Carlisle.)

Carlisle— *Continued*

1753 July 12 "Rode 9 miles to Carlisle John Paterson's tired 1 mi. to Fr. McNic." (From Walter Buchanan's.)

"   15 "Sab. Preach. Ps. 40: 5–9 lectured 1 Peter 4: 6–10 and preached Jer. 3: 4 and baptized Daniel son to John McClellan and Wm. son to And. Giffen g.a."

Sept. 23 "Sab. Preached Ps. 44: 1–9 lectured 2nd Peter 1: 4–8 and preached Luke 12: 32 and baptized James son to Sam Colghoun ——." (At Francis McNicol's.)

1754 Apr. 11 "Rode 7 miles to Carlisle and Francis McNicols. Am to preach Js. Dil."

Sept. 4 "Rode 4 miles to Carlisle—talked with Gus Smith— got thread, stockings." (From Wm. Parkieson's.)

"   5 "Tramped 1 mile to Francis McNichols—good health, praise to God, but tired, etc."

1755 Aug. 3 "Sabbath preached psalm 76: 1–7, lectured Matthew 5: 13–17, preached Micah 5: 5 g.a. and baptized Mary and Mary daughters to John McClellan and John Mitchel." (At Francis McNichol's.)

Sept. 22 "Rode 26 miles to Carlisle, married Reid and Margaret Hamilton." (From Neal McKnaught's.)

1756 Aug. 5 "Rode 7 miles to F. McKni. and tramped to and from Carlisle; G. Henry, etc." (From Jas. McKnaught's.)

1759 May 20 "Sabbath—preached psalm 135: 12–16. Lectured Phillipians 1: 15–19—preached Malachi 3: 6–9 (at Frances McNickle's) and baptized Arch, Thomas, William, and Mary, to John Smielie and Margaret daughter to Walter Buchanan, o.a.—praise God." (Then rode and walked 9 miles to William Parkieson's on 21st.)

1760 Mar. 30 "Sabbath—preached psalm 147: 12–18. Lectured Nahum 3: 14–L. Preached Ephesians 1: 4 and baptized William, son to Robert Bonar—give all praise to God." (At Francis McNickle's.)

1763 Apr. 25 "rode 11 miles to Carlisle, Gembels and W. Parkieson's." (From Chas. Kilgore's.)

1764 Oct. 25 "tramped 2 miles to Carlisle—saw Lr. (Fr.?) Fulton Tib sold."

"   28 "Sabbath—preached psalm 74: 1–5. Lectured Colossians 2: 16–20—preached Hebrews 7: 25 and baptized John son to John Garner—give all praise to God."

Carlisle— *Continued*

1765 Apr.   1   "rode 10 miles to Carlisle, McNickle's, Hew McCormic's." (From Chas. Kilgore's.)

"   2   "rode 5 miles to William Parkieson's x x."

May 12   "Sabbath—preached psalm 78: 56–62. Lectured Matthew 26: 26–30—preached Isaiah 44: 5 and baptized John Laferty, adult at Wm. Parkieson's." (Then rode 5 miles to Francis McNickol's, Leteort Spring, on 13th.)

"   19   "Sabbath—preached psalm 78: 62–68—lectured Mark 9: 20–25—preached Isaiah 44: 5 and baptized Agnes, daughter to Agnes McConel." (At And. Giffen's.)

1767 May 18, 19   "rode 17 miles; married John Navin and Martha Swansie; preached psalm 116: 1–8, examined 32 persons; went to widow McNickles." (From Joseph Junkin's.)

1769 Apr. 17   "rode 12 miles to W. Cairn's; married W. Thomson, Jean Duncan." (From David Mitchel's—then 28 miles home on 18th.)

1771 Aug.   6   "rode 19 miles widow McNicols after preaching and lectured psalm 43 and baptized Walter son to James Braeden and Margaret to Matthew Richie." (From Neal McKnaughtan's.)

1781 Oct. 16   "rode 22 miles to Mr. Poak's, Carlisle, Ralph Marlins, Josh." (From Hugh Hail's.)

Hogestown

1762 Feb. 1, 2   "Rode 18 miles to Hogs-town and W. Buchanan." (Then 3 miles to Joseph Junken's on 3rd.)

Hopewell

1753 Sept. 18   (See Big Spring.)

Junken Tent

Near Kingston and about ten miles from Harrisburg, on the farm of Joseph Junken. Later on the farm of James Bell, a Ruling Elder, one mile west. Mr. Cuthbertson's first Communion in America was held at this tent on Aug. 23, 1752. About 200 communed.

1752 June 23   "Rode 7 miles to W. By. (from David Plum's). Preached psa. 89: 49–L. Lectured Heb. 10: 19–25. Baptized Rachel daughter to Wm. Rose and Groyn, daughter to Wm. Walkter, then rode 3 miles to Jo. Glendinings."

Dec. 12   "Rode 10 mi. to Da. M. Married Jas. Loughhead and Eleanor M." (From Sam. Martin's.)

1753 Aug.   5   "Sab. Rode 8 mi. to D. M. preach Ps. 41: 1–7 lectured 1 Peter 4: 14–18 preach John 5: 40 and baptized Wm.

Junken Tent— *Continued*

son to Alex. Lockey went to Dan McClellans." (At
David Mitchell's.)

1753 Oct. 22 "Rode 16 mi. to Da. Mit. Married Ben. Brown and
Mary Mitch." (From Wm. Brown's?)

1754 Mar. 19 "After riding 5 miles to Jo. Sloans, marrying Hew Coulter and Mary Sloan; disturbed etc. back." (From
David Mitchel's.)

Apr. 4 "rode 3 miles to Joseph Junkens, after preaching psalm
119: 123. Lectured Jeremiah 45, examined 34 persons
and married Walter Buchanan and Mary Coulter."

" 7 "Sabbath. Preached psalm 53: 3–L. Lectured Joel 3:
4–9, preached Amos 5: 6; very pub. g.a. baptized Ann,
daughter to Sam Gay; John, son to William Walker
and Ruth, daughter to William Rose, presented by the
mother, father gone to ——."

1755 July 31 "Rode 2 miles to Joseph Junken's, after preaching psalm
111: 6–L, lectured John 6: 15–22 examined 32 persons
and baptized Samuel to Sam Cal." (Then 8 miles to
Carlisle on August 1.)

1756 Apr. 27 "Rode 8 miles to W. Walkers after preaching psalm 33:
11–19, and preaching Jeremiah 59: 12 and baptizing
John son to Joseph Junken and John son to Robert
Bonar." (From Carlisle.)
Rode 7 miles to W. Walkers explained psalm 46 and
baptized David son to W. W."

Aug. 8 "Sabbath, preached psalm 89: 47–50; lectured Matthew
11: 25–L and preached Hebrews 10–L and baptized
Agnes daughter to Wm. Rose—and Elizabeth daughter
to Jo Garner (Gardner)."

1757 Jan. 30 "Sabbath. Preached psalm 99: 6–L; lectured Matthew
15: 10–21 and baptized Mary daughter to Benjamin
Brown, g.a. great—" (At David Mitchel's, whose wife
died the 19th.)

Feb. 17 "Rode 1 mile to Joseph Junkens; preached psalm 37:
1–6; preached Titus 2: 11, 12 and baptized John son
to Walter Buchanan; give all praise to God—strong."
(From Wm. Walker's.)

1758 Mar. 21 "preached psalm 119: 1–8 and baptized Katharine
daughter to John Glendining—Rode 4 miles to William
Parkieson's and explained Hosea 3: 3. Baptized David, his son o.a." (At Joseph Junken's.)

1759 May 23 "rode 1 mile William Walker's—preached psalm 78: 5—
sick—Lectured 1 Peter 3: 1–5 and baptized Mary,
daughter to W. Wal. catechized 2—." (At Jos. Gardner's.)

1760 Mar. 27 "rode 3 miles to and from W. Walker's—saw John
Drumond." (From Joseph Junken's.)

Junken Tent—*Continued*

1761 May 17 "Sabbath—preached psalm 19: 1–7; lectured Ephesians 3: 1–2; preached Romans 2: 12 and baptized Benjamin son to Joseph Junken; sick." (At T. McNickle's.)

" 18, 19 "rode 9 miles W. Walkers; preached psalm 102: 13; preached Hosea 4: 6—and baptized James to Walter Buchanan; Wm. son to Robert Brison; Daniel son to Hugh Hail and Martha daughter Wm. Spoedy o.a. praise my gracious God."

1762 Feb. 4 "Rode 4 miles to W. Parkiesons after preaching psalm 95; lectured Hebrews 3: 12 and baptized David son to Sam Calhoun; W. Hog ——." (From Joseph Junken's.)

Sept. 1 "Rode 7 miles to Jos. Junkens new key, Lv. Gemie." (From Carlisle.)

Oct. 17 "Sabbath preached psalm 40: 5–7 and lectured Colossians 3: 3 and preached Ephesians 6: 13—o.a. and baptized Robert son to John Leiper——." (At John Wade's —then rode 8 miles to Sharp's, John Mitchel's on 18th.)

1763 Apr. 26 "rode 3 miles to Jo. Junken's—preached psalm 44: 17—lectured John 15: 1–6 and baptized Robert son to Sam Calhoun and Eliz. to Joseph Junkens."

1764 Feb. 3 "rode 2 miles to Jos. Junkens—held session all day, etc." (From W. Walker's.)

" 5 "Sabbath—preached psalm 63. Lectured Philip 4: 4–9. Baptized Henry son A. Brown; Jonathan, son W. Walker; Jean, daughter to Robert Brison—sick."

Apr. 15 "Sabbath—rode 15 miles to D. M's (from Paxton)—preached psalm 68: 5—lectured Philip 4: 15–L.—Preached Revelations 3: 3 and baptized David, son to Barth. Hains." (Then rode 40 miles home on 16th.)

May 22 "rode 15 miles to D. Mitchel's—preached psalm 103: 13 and lectured. Married Alexander Robieson and Martha McCormick." (From Wm. Brown's, Paxton.)

1765 Nov. 25, 26 "rode 35 miles to D. M's. etc. Married James Grahams and Ruth Little." (Then rode 20 miles home on 27th.)

1766 Apr. 3 "rode 2 miles T. Paterson's—preached psalm 89: 15. Lectured Isaiah 63: 1–7 and baptized James, son to David Mitchel—rs Belamy Dial." (From David Mitchel's.)

Aug. 7 "rode 6 miles W. W. preached psalm 65: 1–5; lectured Romans 6: 12–18 and baptized Rebecca daughter to

Junken Tent— *Continued*

James Howston. Reb. Joseph Junken o.a. praise God." (From Wm. Parkieson's.)

1766 Aug. 18 "Rode 15 miles D. M.—prayed and preached; I concluded the service with John 7: 31; and baptized Sam son to Robert Brison—give all praise to our God." (At David Mitchel's?)

Sept. 21 "Sabbath preached psalm 108: 8–12; lectured Romans 3: 23–27—preached; lectured and baptized Sarah, daughter to Sam Calhoun o.a. praise God." (At Wm. Parkieson's.)

1767 Mar. 29 "Sabbath preached psalm 106: 28–34; lectured Hebrews 13: 15–20; preached Micah and baptized James son to Katharine McClellan." (Probably at Joseph Junken's.)

June 8 "rode 10 miles; fasted after marrying Robert and Marjory Stewart at Sam Bell's." (From David Dunwoody's.)

Oct. 29 "rode 8 miles James etc. preached psalm 78: 5–ᶜ, lectured Romans 8: 24–28—at night exercised 2 hours psalm 23., baptized Agnes daughter to James Howston." (From Jos. Junken's and Wm. Parkieson's.)

1768 May 29 "Sabbath—preached psalm 119: 70–73 Lectured 9: 18–23—preached Revelations 11: 15 and baptized Mary, daughter to Sam Calqhoun and Margaret to James Thorn." (W. Parkieson's.)

1769 Mar. 24 "rode and walked 4 mile from D. M's married And Reid and Esther McBryar; received 15 shillings John Wat. and David Mitchel quarreling." (Then rode 15 miles to James Mitchel's on 25th.)

June 25 "Sabbath preached psalm 139: 17–21; lectured Isaiah 52: 1–7 and preached 2 Kings 5: 13 and baptized Agnes daughter to James McKt. give all praise to my gracious God." (David Mitchel's and B's.)

Aug. 3 "preached psalm 37: 1–5; catechized 57 and baptized Ann to S. Colqhoun." (At W. Parkieson's.)

" 6 "Sabbath preached (at W. Parkieson's) 141: 1–5: lectured Haggai 1: 7 and preached Matthew 23: 11; x x baptized Wm. (son to Katharine Meek or Parkieson)."

1771 Feb. 25 "rode 27 miles to David Mitchel's: preached 27–3—lectured Acts 20: 37–41 and baptized Sarah to Y. Mil. and married Thomas Kennedy and Mary McCallin; went to W. Cairns." (From Ben Brown's.)

June 16 "Sabbath preached 29: 1 lectured Romans 5: 14–L; preached Galatians 2–16 and baptized James son to Thomas Finey and Jean daughter to John Hilton." (Probably at Joseph Junken's.)

Junken Tent— *Continued*

1771 June 18   "rode 19 miles; 6 places; married John Brown and Mary Guililand, James Robertson and Margaret Young; went to D. Mitchel's after preaching 116: 1—lectured Isaiah 38: 9–18; bought Roan Filly at 14 pounds, paid." (From John Duncan's.)

1772 Apr. 26   "Sabbath; preached 5–9; lectured Isaiah 9: 1–8; preached Luke L 29 and baptized Johns sons to James Leiper and John Neil, g.a." (Then rode 13 miles to Joan Morison's on 27th.)

"   29   "rode 8 miles to David Mitchel's then preached 4: 1–6: lectured Isaiah 1: 15–19; baptized Elizabeth daughter to Thomas Armstrong, g.a."

Sept. 27   "Sabbath—preached 5–8: lectured Mark 15: 1–15; preached psalm 50: 15 and baptized Thomas son to William Paterson, went to D. Mitchels."

Nov. 9   "rode 15 miles (from Wm. Brown's); preached 30; re-capitulated, etc., baptized Samuel son to Elijah Stewart; Elijah to John Graham; George to John Taylor; David to James McKt., and Martha daughter to James Taylor; give all praise to God."

1773 Aug. 11   "rode 18 miles to D. Mit. and to Widow Morison's— Janet married—received 10-10—." (From T. Anderson's.)

1775 Dec. 19   "rode 16 miles J. Mns., W. Richy's.   Married Wm. Clark and Margaret Rowan." (Rode 4 miles to Walter Buchanan's on 20th.)

1781 Feb. 21   "rode 5 miles to Gilb. preached 71: 1—preached Revelations 3: 20; baptized Isaac son to Gilbert Buchanan great rain." (From Walter Buchanan's.)

1782 Feb. 20, 21   "rode 8 miles Gilb. Buch. preached 40: 1 and catechized 35 concerning ex. and baptized Joseph to James Walker, Mary to John Brigs; Hanna to John Walker Jun. and Eliza to John Padon; came to Walker's." (From W. Buchanan's.)

1783 Dec. 3   "rode 5 miles to Gilbert Buchanan's and James Walkers."

"   4   "rode 2 miles preached 42, preached 42: 5–9, preached Zechariah 13: 1—and baptized Sarah." (Then rode 9 miles home on 5th.)

1784 Nov. 2   "Two miles, preached psalm 19: 7 preached Philippians 3: 10 and baptized Barbara to Sam Taylor born Nov. 23, 1783 and Mary to John McCallen born Sept. 1st, '82 and Thomas and Robert sons to Wm. Whigham

Junken Tent—*Continued*

born March 24th 1779, and March 4th, 1783, rode 3 miles to and from James Calhoun's."

1787 Oct. 3 "rode 13 miles to Carlisle, Stony Ridge, widow J.
" 4 "rode 6 miles to Parkeson's, Jean Brown's 2d."
" 6 "Sabbath—preached 14–L; lectured 11: 1–7 and preached Isaiah 36: 10."
" 8 "rode 4 miles to W. Walker's, John Pringlered."
" 9 "rode 10 miles to Loneb, Mr. Boyd's."

" Leteart Spring "

bet.
1753 Apr. 19 & 21 "Rode 15 miles to Isaac D. preach. Ps. 119: 129–34 lectured Eph. 6: 11–18 and preached Rev. 3: ᵔ v. pub. went to Francis McNichols Loetert Spring."
" 22 "Sab. preach. Ps. 37: 20–25 lectured 1 Peter 2: 9–13 and preached Lev. 20–7 g.a. and baptized John son to Wm. Paterson and Thos. son to Robert Bonar."
1754 Aug. 10 "Sabbath—psalm 62: 1 Lectured Isaiah 8: 9–15. Preached Malachi 4: 2 and baptized Benjamin, son to William Parkieson and Margaret, daughter to Robert Gibson— give all praise to God—very hot—great rain." (At Francis McNickol's.)
1758 Mar. 23 "preached psalm 96: 1–6. Preached John 3: 14, 15 and baptized Rob. son to William Pattison; Esther, daughter to Charles Kilgour; and Agnes, daughter to Alexander Young. Then rode 5 miles to James Mc-Knaughts—very tired." (At Francis McNickle's.)
1764 May 17 "rode 16 miles F. McN.—preached psalm 103: 1–5. Lectured Ephesians 2: 19–L and baptized Margaret, daughter to Sam Hodge o.a. praise God." (At Francis McNickle's.)

Middle Spring

1760 June 21 "Rode 16 miles to G. Cunninghams—mid. Spring." (From Chas. Kilgore's.)
" 22 "Sabbath preached psalm 8; lectured Habakkuk 3: 16–L and preached Isaiah 7: 9 give all praise to my God."

Pennsborough Meeting-house (See also Big Spring)

1751 Nov. 11 "Rode 3 miles to Pensbourough Meeting-house, Preached psalm 72: 13–1 . . . preached psalm 95: 7 and baptized Jo. son to Sam. Colquhoun, And. son to And. Giffan and Ann daughter to Robert Gibson, g.a. Then rode 4 miles to Charles Gilgours—good health, praise to God."

Pine Ford

1753 May 3   "Rode 15 miles to Pine-Ford Jas. Ireland and David Mitchel catechiz." (From James McKnaught's.)

1754 Mar. 26   "Rode 9 miles to Pine f. etc. with Mar. Blaflum, James Riters." (Then 9 miles to Wm. Brown's, Paxton.)

Salem (Church)

1781 Mar. 16, 17   "James Talbot, Salem, Baptist, etc., Mr. Marsh."
"   18   "Sabbath—preached 16: 1–7 and lectured Galatians 3: 19–23 o.a. praise my gracious God."

1788 Oct. 23   "rode 3 miles Squire Reid's and went to John Reid's salem." (From Fulerton's and Stewart's.)

"Sawglass"

17,'1 Feb. 27   "rode 8 miles to and from Stiglestown; Sawglass." (From W. Cairn's.)

Sherman Valley

1754 Apr. 15   "Rode 20 miles over Mountain up Sheermans Valey to John Gardners." (From C. Kilgore's.)

1762 Aug. 25   "Rode 12 miles to Sheerman's Valey—James Thorn's praise God." (From John Agnew's.)
"   26   "Preached psalm 119: 132–137—preached Matthew 4: 20 and baptized Margaret daughter to John Gardner o.a. praise God."

Shippensburg

1765 Nov. 13, 14, 15   "rode 30 miles—Shipp. W. Calb., J. Brown's and Ch. Kilgore's—preached Psalm 19: 12–L and lectured Mark 10: 46–L and baptized Daniel son to J. C."

1769 Mar. 28   "rode 28 miles to Shipp. and Alexander McConel's; Agnew." (Then 10 miles to Charles Kilgore's on 29th.)

"Stiglestown"

1771 Feb. 27   (See Sawglass.)

Susquehanna River

Crossed many times between Lancaster and York Counties, Cumberland and Dauphin Counties.

1751 Sept. 3   "Rode 18 miles the River Sus. Married Robert Love and and Rachel Sloan at the River, then came 10 miles to Lancaster."

" Taeff's Ferry "

1777 Oct. 14   "rode 25 miles to Walkers, Taeff's Ferry, etc., W. Brown's."

DAUPHIN COUNTY

Beaver Creek

1752 June 1   "Rode 12 miles over Beaver and Manadie Creeks to Alex. Swan. Preached psa. 48: 11–L and preached Gen. 17: 1—lost point. . . . Rode 3 miles over S. ara in canoe, etc. Came to David Mitchels where I preached psa. 93: 3–L and examined 24 persons. Give all praise to my God." (From Wm. Brown's.)

Blue Mountain

1751 Oct. 29   "Rode 40 miles. Went to And. Super's on the side of the Blew Mountain—very tired. My horse . . . once fed and I not. Lay in my scab at stove, etc. Heard nothing that was said, etc."

"   30   "Rode 36 miles to Calfmans Mills on the Blew Mountain and wandered along until 8 at night, the L(ord) brought me to Isa. Gushwa's."

Nov. 4   "rode 13 miles to Alex. Swans at the Blew Mountain in Manadie Township."

"   5   "Preached psalm 142. Lectured Hag. 1: 1–6 and baptized James, son to James Sloan, Helen, daughter to Jo. Graham, John son to Jo. Thorn, and Agnes, daughter to Alex. Swan, g.a.   Then rode 12 miles to Wm. Browns in Paxton, Ex. Alex. Brown."

1753 May   8   "Rode 6 miles to Jo. Sloan etc. Ad. Reid's and then to A. Swan's." (From Sam Sloan's.)

1754 July   3   "30 miles from 11 o'clock to Jo. Sloan's, Alex. Swans, to —serv. to Burd." (From Con. Wiser's.)

1755 Dec. 22   "Rode 21 miles to A. Swans, expounded, psalm 9: 1–7 and baptized Sarah daughter to him—praise God." (From Wm. Brown's.)

1758 Apr. 18   "Rode 9 miles over Susquehanna—held session— preached psalm 74: 20–L explained Acts 2: 39–40 and baptized Sam, son to Alexander Swan; and William son to Margaret Reynolds, Brownlie in." (Then rode 11 miles home on 19th.)

Blue Mountain—*Continued*

1760 Aug. 27 "rode 12 miles to Alex. Swan's—could sleep non, etc." (From home.)

"   28 "rode 12 miles back, after preaching psalm 73: 24— preached 1 Corinthians 15: 29 and baptized James son to Alexander Swan and visited William Robiesen."

1762 Aug. 18 "rode 12 miles over Blew Mountain—John Wilson's— tired." (From J. Davidson's.)

1763 Apr. 7 "Fast-day—prayed, etc.—preached psalm 69: 5–10— preached Zechariah 12: 10 and baptized Joseph, son to Margaret Reynolds and James to Mary McWilliams x x explained causes, etc."

June 14 "rode 14 miles to William Strehorn's, sick and Alexander Swan's." (From Wm. Brown's, Paxton.)

"   15 "rode 8 miles to R. Robeson's, after preaching psalm 124 and lecturing 9: 9–L."

1767 Feb. 3 "rode 12 miles by D. Strehor's to Alexander Swan's." (From J. Duncan's.)

"   4, 5 "Tramped 3 miles; preached psalm 6: 6—lectured Hebrews 12: 9–18 etc. baptized David son to James Greenlie, Eleanor to James Graham and Sarah to Wm. Greenlie."

Apr. 1, 2, 3 "rode 26 miles, Thomson's, A. Swan's, etc. catechized 25."

"   5 "Sabbath—preached psalm 106: 34–40; lectured Hebrews 13: 20–L; preached Micah L. L. and baptized Samuel son to Hew Stewart, o.a. praise God."

1768 June 6 "rode 12 miles to and from A. S.—preached psalm 39: 7–L and lectured 2 Thess. 4: 13–L."

"   7 "preached psalm 2: 4–8 and catechized 70 concerning the offices of Christ. Catechized 52 and baptized Jean, daughter to James Grah——."

1770 Feb. 5 "rode 12 miles to A. Swan's; married Robert Bell and Sally." (From W. Brown's.)

June 12 "rode 14 miles to F's, A. Swan's—married Thomas Finey and Margaret Swan."

Blue Mountain—*Continued*

1771 Oct. 21 "rode 12 miles to A. Swan's; married James Taylor and Jean Swan."

1787 Jun. 4, 5, 6 "rode 17 miles, visited, 9 families, 7 A. S. preached 42: 6–9, lectured Luke 19: 1–9 and baptized James son to John Moor born March 22d, 1786, o.a." (From W. B.)

Derry

1751 bet. Sept. 15 and 20 "2 miles to Derry,* David McNair. Preached psalm 110: 1. Lectured Hebrews . . . 1: 3. Three hours." (From Donegal.)

" 23 "Rode 15 miles to Connowagon, Da. Mcanairs where married Richard Crain and Jean Espie. Then rode 25 miles to Lancaster. Exhausted." (From Wm. Brown's.)

Nov. 3 "Sabbath. Rode 10 miles to and from Derry Meeting-house, where preached psalm 15, Lectured Gal. 2: 17–1, and preached Jer. 3: 19—o. ass. God directing." (From David Mitchel's.)

1753 May 6 "Sab.—rode 12 mi. to and from Derry meeting preach. Ps. 37: 33–37 lectured 1 Peter 2: 18–21 and preach. Luke 12: 1 and bap. Margaret daugh. to Thos. Montgomery." (From Pine Ford. Then rode 6 miles to Sam Sloan's on 7th.)

" 21 "Rode 18 miles after marrying Adam Calhoun and Janet Woods, to Derry Meeting, reasoned and caviled 5 hours before the meeting Roan quite wrong after yielding called the one—par. and 14 ant. stuff." (From Andrew Stewart's.)

" 22 "Preach. Ps. 61: 1–6 and preach Mark 11: 24 after marrying Wm. Finton and Helen Brattan very weary give praise to God." (At Derry Meeting.)

1754 Apr. 16 "Rode 6 miles to and from David McNairs after preaching psalm 110. Preached Hosea 2: 19 and baptized James, son to John Gardner. Give all praise to God." (From John Gardner's.)

Hummelstown

1788 Sept. 14 "Sabbath—rode 7 miles, preached 19–L; lectured Jeremiah 30: 18–L, preached verse 17 and baptized Mary to John McHenry, born Mar. 8, 1788, went to Hugh Esteman's." (Then rode 3 miles to David Hummel's, Hummelstown on 15th and 16th.)

* About 9 miles from Paxton.

Hummelstown— *Continued*

1788 Sept. 15, 16   "Rode 3 miles to David Humel's, Hum. Town, preached psalm 4: 1–6 and lectured Matthew 11: 12— and baptized Sam, born Aug. 8, 1788 and Agnes born April 1784 and Ann, born April 10, 1787, o.a. to Wm. Whigham." (From Hugh Easteman's—then rode 3 miles to Hugh Stewart's on 17th.)

Lisburn

1780 Aug. 16   "rode 10 miles to Lisbon Robert McCall's, by widow Brison's." (From Alexander Brown's.)

Little Swatara

1751 Oct. 31   "Rode 20 miles to Paden T. over Little Sw. ara and cold peheela, and so merciiully arrived at Da. Mitchel's." (From Isa. Gushwa's.)

Manadie Township

1752 Mar. 2   "rode 12 miles to Alex. Swans.   Manadie Hans Township."

"   3   "Preached psa. 32: 5–6. Lectured Zecn. 1: 1–8 and baptized Mary daughter to Wm. Robieson."

Martin's Miln, Sam

1752 Dec. 11   "Rode 5 miles to Sam Martin's preach. Ps. 105: 16–23 lectured 3: 27–L. and bap. Eleanor daugh. to him, after marrying George Williams and Jean Thomson and Alexander McNair and Ann Thorn." (From Paxton.)

1758 Oct. 29   "Sabbath—rode 9 miles to and from Sa. Martin's Miln— preached psalm 119: 15th part. Lectured Micha 2: 9–10 and preached Luke 24: 17—o.a. praise God." (From Ben Brown's.)

Murray's Gap

1754 Apr. 17   "Rode and traveled 12 miles over Murrays Gap to John Agnews." (From John Gardner's.)

" Ormostogg "

1778 June 2   (See Overtakes.)

" Overtakes "

1778 June 2   "rode from Jos. Reid's to Ormostogg, overtakes, Lane, over Cannowago to Michael—Shanks—tired etc. 40 miles." (Then 14 mi. through Hummelstown etc. on 3rd.)

Paxton (and Paxtang) Society

1751 Aug. 20 "Preached psalm 102: 13–16. Lectured Hebrews 4: 14
. . . and baptized Eliz. daughter to S . . . Stewart;
Helen, daughter to Matthew Taylor; and Mary Ann,
daughter to Jo. McKnaught. Then rode 18 miles to
Walter Buchanan's upon the side of Cannondugwin
Creek; tired but safe."

Sept. 22 "Sabbath. Preached psalm 10: 11–15. L: Galatians 1:
1–5 and preached Galatians 5: 1—and baptized Eleanor, daughter to Jo. Miens and Hannah, daughter to
Ja. Brown. Praise to my God." (At Wm. Brown's.)

Nov. 6 "Rode 6 miles to Andrew Stewarts, where I preached
psalm 61: 1–6 and lectured Mal. 3: 16–1 and baptized
Martha daughter to Alexander Brown. g.a." (From
Wm. Brown's, Paxton.)

1752 Mar. 4 "Examined, conversed, etc. Rode 12 miles to Wm.
Brown's Paxton." (From Alex. Swan's.)

"   8 "Sabbath. Preached psa. 20: 1–6 L. Gal. 6: 1–6 and
preached Isa. 45: 23 give all praise to God."

"   9 "General meeting—held session—causes examined Geo.
Williams etc."

"   10 "Preached psa. 31: 1–5. Preached Rom. 3 last Rev. G.
Wil. and baptized Mary daughter to Bartho. Hains.
Married Jas. Ferguson and Mary McCormick. Then
examined 42 persons. Great snow, etc."

"   11 "Married Jo. Taylor and Eliz. McClure. Then rode 6
miles to S. Mar." (At Wm. Brown's, Paxton.)

June 22 "Rode 17 miles to A. Stews. Married And. White and
Martha Miens. Then rode 7 miles to David Plu——
x x." (From Wm. Brown's.)

Oct. 12 "Preach. Ps. 34: 17–L. and preach. Zeph. 3: 12 and baptized John son to James Brown." (At Widow Brown's.)

"   15 "Sab. Wm. B. preach. Ps. 30: 4—etc. lectured So. 5:
3–6 and preach. 2 Pet. 1: 4 g.a. and baptized Isaac son
to Jo. Thomson rs. K letters from Scott praise to
God."

1753 Mar. (11) "Sabbath—preached Psa. 35: 33–L. lectured 1 Peter 1:
13–18 and preached Leviticus 20–7 and baptized John
son to Alexander Brown—very cold day, exhausted,
etc." (At William Brown's.)

Apr. 29 "Sab. Preach. Ps. 37: 25–33 lectured 1 Peter 2: 13–18
preach. Lev. 20: 7–3, sign and bap. James son to Alexander Swan give all praise to my gracious God." (At
Wm. Brown's.)

Paxton (and Paxtang) Society— *Continued*

1753 May 9 "Rode 12 miles to Wm. Brown's after preaching Ps. 80: 14–L. preach. Luke 12: 1 bap. Esther daugh. to John Grahams and Jean daugh. to George Williams and examined 40 persons give praise to God." (From A. Swan's.)

"   13 "Sab. preach. Ps. 37: 37–L., lectured 1 Peter 2: 21–L and preach. Romans 9: 32 and bap. Joseph son to Bartholomew Hains and Matthew son to John Taylor." (At Wm. Brown's.)

"   17 "Rode 10 miles to and from And. Stewarts explained Ps. 23 bap. Eleanor daugh. to him after marrying Jas. Calhoun and Sarah Taylor." (From Wm. Brown's.)

Sept. 30 "Sab. rode 14 mi. to Wm. B. after preach. Ps. 44: 9–17 lectured 2 Peter 1: 8–12 preach. Luke 12: 32 and baptized Robert son to Robert Love praise to my gracious God." (From David Mitchel's.)

Oct. 7 "Sab.   preached Ps. 44: 17–L. lectured 2 Peter 1: 12–16 preached Luke 12: 32 g.a. and baptized Henry son to John McCormick ——." (At Wm. Brown's.)

"   9 "Married David Carson and Sarah Woods conversed with the people etc." (At Wm. Brown's.)

"   13 "on 13 bap. Matthew son to —do—." (Matthew?) (At Wm. Brown's?.)

1754 Mar. 14 "Fast day, prayed, prefaced and preached psalm 89: 38–46 and Hosea 14: 1 and baptized Mathew, son to Math. Taylor g.d." (At Wm. Brown's.)

"   27 "Rode 9 miles to William Brown's, after preaching psalm 105: 1—lectured Hebrews 10: 35–L. baptized Adam, son to John Miens and catechizing 25 persons. o. ass. by the kindness of God." (From Pineford.)

Aug. 18 "Sabbath—preached psalm 62: 5–9. Lectured Ephesians 2: 1–11 and preached Malachi 4: 2 and baptized Samuel son to William Finton—F. D. prayed, preached at 2 o'clock Jeremiah 14: 20—give all praise." (At Wm. Brown's.)

Sept. 1 "Sabbath—preached psalm 62: 5–9. Lectured Isaiah 12 and preached Malachi 4: 2—give all praise to God. Baptized Mathew, son to James Calghoun and Elizabeth, daughter to Benjamin Brown; had some unusual appr. of death. Col. 3 ——." (At Wm. Brown's.)

1755 Apr. 1 "Rode 16 miles Ch. Kilgores (Big Spring) after marrying Peter Peters and Agnes McCormick rs. for S—sent letter to Bro. o.a."

Paxton (and Paxtang) Society—*Continued*

1755 July (20) (Sabbath)—"Psalm 75: 1–5, lectured Malachi 5: 1–7, preached Micha 5: 5 g.a. and baptized Mary daughter to Alexander Brown—very pub. all day." (At W. Brown's.)

" 28 "Rode 16 miles to T. McCormic's, married Wm. Paterson and Mary McCormic—to James Brown, preached psalm 27: 1 examined 24." (From Wm. Brown's.)

Aug. 23 "Preached psalm 119: 57–61, preached 1 Kings 3: 5, baptized Esther daughter to Lodowick Laird, held session, distributed tokens 50 subscribing." (At Wm. Brown's.)

" 31 "Sabbath. Preached psalm 77: 12–16, lectured Matthew 5: 27–33, preached 1 Peter 9—and baptized Elisha son to John Chalmers give praise to God. rode." (At W. Brown's.)

Dec. 14 "Sabbath. Preached psalm 79: 5–9, lectured Isaiah 30: 15–18, preached Isaiah 26: 30 and baptized Joseph son to John Miens, g.a. received the causes." (At Wm. Brown's.)

" 21 "Sabbath. Preached psalm 79: 9–L. Preached Isaiah 26: 20 and baptized Adam son to William Finton and Margaret daughter to John McCormic g.a. etc." (At Wm. Brown's.)

1756 May 21 "Rode 2 miles to Wm. Browns in good health praise to my gracious God." (From Sam Stewart's in Paxton.)

" 23 "Sabbath, preached psalm 88: 8–13; Lectured Isaiah 59: 1–5; preached Isaiah 26: 16 and baptized Margaret daughter to John McCormick g.a."

Aug. 15 "Sabbath, preached psalm 89: 49–L; lectured Micah 7: 1–8; preached Hebrews 10–L and baptized Henry son to John Graham give all praise to my gracious God." (At Wm. Brown's.)

1757 Feb. 6 "Sabbath preached psalm 100; lectured Matthew 15: 21–29; and baptized Alexander son to John Taylor; Jean daughter to Wm. Robieson; and Joseph son to Joseph ———." (At Wm. Brown's.)

" 7/9 "—16–L and examined 30 persons concerning God e—a—and baptized Alexander son to Robert Love, thoughtful concerning—." (At Wm. Brown's.)

" 15 "Rode 14 miles after marrying James McK. and Martha Milroy and Thomas Finey and Susan Stewart, to and from Rj." (At Wm. Brown's.)

Paxton (and Paxtang) Society— *Continued*

1757 May 5 "Rode 13 miles; explained psalm 28: 1–6; preached He-
brews 7: 25 and baptized Margaret daughter to Bar.
Hains o.a.—a little tender went to Wm. Browns Pax."
(From George Espies.)

"   8 "Sabbath. Preached psalm 103: 17–20; lectured Matthew 18: 7–15; preached Zephaniah 2: 1 and baptized
John son to John Thomson o.a. was sick all day, the
cold, etc."

"   16 "Rode 18 miles over R.   W. W. after marrying Joseph
Espie and Elizabeth McCormick."   (At Wm. Brown's,
Paxton.)

1758 Mar. 12 "Sabbath—preached psalm 112: 1–6—lectured Matthew
26: 39 and preached psalm 94: 12 and baptized David
son to James Colquhoun; James, son to Thomas Finey;
John son to James McKnaught; William son to James
Brown; Isobel daughter to John McCormick; Margaret,
daughter to James Finey; Elizabeth, daughter to Alexander Brown."   (At William Brown's.)

"   13 "tramped 4 miles—visited—still uneasy—pp secure."

"   14 "rode 10 miles to James and Ben. Browns—family all
well."

"   15 "Rode 9 miles back. Preached psalm 54; Lectured
Zephaniah 3: 14–L and baptized Matthew son to John
Thorn—in good health, praise to my God."

1759 Jan. 18 "tramped 2 miles—Married Henry McCormick and
Eliz. Còlhoun."   (At Wm. Brown's.)

"   21 "Sabbath—preached psalm 123: preached psalm 57: 1
and baptized John son to Ben. Brown and Jean daughter
to John Thomson o.a."   (At Wm. Brown's.)

"   29 "rode 16 miles to Bar. Hews, after marrying James Miens
and Ha. B——."   (From J. Brown's, Paxton.)

May 27 "Sabbath—preached psalm 135: 16–L. Lectured Phil. 1:
19–22. Preached Malachi 3: 10–17 and baptized William, son to James Sloan; Janet, John and William to
Robert Stewart; and Agnes, daughter to Thomas
Finey."   (At Wm. Brown's.)

1760 Mar. 16 "Sabbath—preached psalm 147: 1–6. Lectured Nahum
3: 1–8. Preached Ephesians 1: 7 and baptized Rachel,
daughter to Robert Love; Hannah, daughter to Bartho.
Ha - - - - .   William, son to John Walace; Hugh, son to

Paxton (and Paxtang) Society—*Continued*

Hugh Stewart; John, son to James Finey; Martha, daughter to James Colhoun; and Henry, son to James McKnaught." (At Wm. Brown's.)

1760 Mar. 17 "Rode 10 miles—preached psalm 68: 18—preached Galatians 3: 27 and baptized Isobel daughter to Henry McCormick—o.a.—praise God." (At Wm. Brown's—then rode 9 miles to James and A. and B. Brown's."

June 7 "Rode 15 miles to W. Brown's, married Math. Thorn to Agnes McKnaught—bad with cold." (From David Mitchel's.)

" 8 "Sabbath. Preached Psalm 2: 1–7, lectured Habakkuk 3: 5–10, preached 1 John 3: 23 and baptized John son to Peter Paterson, very sick, cold, etc." (At W. Brown's—then rode 13 miles to W. Strehorn's.)

Aug. 31 "Sabbath—rode 8 miles—preached psalm 7: 6. Lectured Zephaniah 2: 12–L and preached So. 8: 5. Baptized Cha. Kilgore—very sick—went to A. Brown's.

1761 Jan. 18 "Sabbath—preached psalm 15—lectured Hosea 4: 1–6 and baptized Jean, daughter to John Taylor." (At Wm. Brown's.)

" 22 "rode 4 miles T. Finey's—explained psalm 84: 6–I. and baptized Sam. son to him." (From Wm. Brown's.)

" 27 "rode 14 miles to James Brown's—married Math. Brown and Eleanor McCormick rs. from 76 and ge."

May 24 "Sabbath preached psalm 19: 7—lectured Ephesians 3: 2 and preached Romans 2: 12 and baptized Elizabeth daughter to Ben Brown and Isobel to John Cha——. (At W. Brown's.)

" 25 "rode 15 miles to James Campbel's; widow Halls; married Thomas Girvan and Mary McNiely ——." (From Wm. Brown's.)

1762 Jan. 29 "Rode 9 miles; preached psalm 86: 1–4; lectured 5–L; baptized John son to Ja. McCord." (At Paxton.)

" 31 "Sabbath preached psalm 31: 15–19; preached Isaiah 30: 18 and baptized Wm. son to Henry McCor; Agnes daughter to James Calhoun, and James son to Bartholomew Hains; g.a." (At Ben Brown's.)

Feb. 14 "Sabbath preached psalm 31: 22–L; preached Isaiah 30: 18 and baptized Sam son to John Taylor, David son to

Paxton (and Paxtang) Society—*Continued*

James Sloan and Andrew Js.—." (At Wm. Brown's— then rode 14 miles to David Mitchel's.)

1762 Apr. 25 "Sabbath preached psalm 34: 12–18; lectured Ephesians 6: 21–L; preached Isaiah 30: 18 and baptized Dan son to James McKown and Hanah daughter to Mat. Brown." (At Wm. Brown's.)

July 4 "Sabbath preached psalm 37: 7–10; lectured Zechariah 1: 12–16, preached John 3: 5 and baptized David son to Thomas Mitchel, Mary daughter to James Finey and Alexander son to Alexander Swan, give all praise to my gracious God." (At Wm. Brown's.)

" 5 "Rode 10 miles Harris's; married James Thorn and Mary Wilson."

" 6 "Rode 12 miles; married David Mitchel and Mary Smith."

Oct. 4 "Preached psalm 132: 12—preached Hosea 3: 3 and baptized Thomas to T. Finey." (At Wm. or Matthew Brown's.)

Dec. 24 "rode 10 miles and 25(th)—married Wal. Buchanan and Agnes Toulan." (From W. Brown's.)

1763 June 12 "Sabbath—preached psalm 50: 1–6. Lectured Zechariah 10: 9–L. Preached 1 Samuel 30: 6 and baptized Sarah, daughter to James Calhoun—give all praise to God." (At William Brown's.)

Nov.
(bet. 6 & 13) "preached psalm 59: 1–5. Lectured Phil. 1: 22–27 and preached Hebrews 10: 21, 22 and baptized Matthew son to John Taylor o.a. sick." (At Wm. Brown's.)

" (21) "rode 9 miles. Explained psalm 84: 4–L and baptized David son to Benjamin Brown and James McCord o.a. praise God—snow 18 inches."

1764 Jan. 29 "Sabbath—preached psalm 63: 1–6. Lectured Philip 3: 1–7 o.a. cold. Baptized James son to Hew Stewart and Agnes daughter to James Sloan." (At Wm. Brown's.)

" 31 "rode 6 miles A. S.—preached psalm 106: 1—preached Acts 2: 21 and baptized William son to T. Finey— married W. Greenlie and Mary Thomson g.a. (W. Brown off.) "

Apr. 10 "rode 11 miles back by J. T. (From W. Thomson's)— married R. Paterson and Mary Stewart."

July 29 "Sabbath—preached psalm 71: 1–7, Lectured Colossians 1: 6–10 and preached Hebrews 13: 14 and baptized

Paxton (and Paxtang) Society— *Continued*

James son to James McKnaught's and Agnes, daughter to Thomas Finey." (At Wm. Brown's.)

1764 Aug.   3   "rode 12 miles to R. Gilmor's after preaching psalm 27: 1–6.   Lectured Titus 2: 11 and baptized Mary, daughter to Thomas Black—43 miles T. K." (From Humphrey Fulerton's.)

1765 Apr.   7   "Sabbath—preached psalm 78: 35–40. Lectured Colossians 4: 10–L after preaching Hebrews 6: 12 and baptizing Robert to Hew Stewart; And. to James Finey; and Mary, daughter to Peter Paterson—give all praise to God." (At Wm. Brown's.)

"   8   "rode 35 miles Lan. after marrying James Howston and Isobel Neilson." (At Wm. Brown's.)

"   28   "Sabbath—preached psalm 78: 46–52. Lectured Acts 13: 30–38—preached Hebrews 3: 6 and baptized Henry, son to Hen. McCormick." (At Wm. Brown's, Paxton.)

"   30   "rode 8 miles—preached psalm 45: 5–10; catechized 52–3rd Co.—baptized James son to W. Greenlie." (At W. Greenlie's, 20 miles from Paxton.)

Aug.   4   "Sabbath—preached psalm 81: 1–8. Lectured Hebrews 7: 26–L. Preached psalm 17–L and baptized James son to John McCormick—o.a. praise my gracious God." (At Paxton.)

"   5   "rode 22 miles to A. S.—preached—lectured Isaiah 38: 9–17 and baptized Rebecca and Martha, daughters to Mary Owens x x—went to David Mitchel's."

Oct.   20   "Sabbath—preached psalm 86: 6–11, lectured Hebrews 9: 13–16; preached Hebrews 4: 6 and baptized John, son to James McCord; William, son to Ben Brown; and Elijah, son to Thomas Finey, o.a. praise to my kind God." (At Wm. Brown's.)

"   22   "rode 22 miles to Alexander Brown's after marrying James Greenlie and Agnes Guililand." (Then rode 6 miles to Francis McNickle's on 23rd.)

Nov.   24   "Sabbath—preached psalm 88: 8–13. Lectured John 14: 22–27 preached Hebrews 4–L and baptized Mary, daughter to James Calhoun—o.a. praise my gracious God." (At W. Brown's.)

1766 Jan.   27   "rode 20 miles D. Mitchel's, Mat. Taylor's—preached psalm 51: 9–15—lectured Acts 8: 10–15 and baptized James, son to John Taylor—o.a." (From home.)

Paxton (and Paxtang) Society—*Continued*

1766 Mar. 9   "Sabbath—preached psalm 90: 13–L—preached J. 17: 24 and baptized Elizabeth to W. Paterson." (At W. Brown's—then rode 3 miles to J. D's.)

Aug. 10   "Sabbath—preached psalm 102: 17–21; lectured 1 Corinthians 5: 6–9 preached John 6: 37 and baptized Jonathan son to Bartholomew Hains and Mary to James McKts." (At W. Brown's.)

1767 Mar. 15   "Sabbath preached psalm 106: 14–21; lectured 13 Hebrews 7–10 baptized David son to Henry McCormick, o.a. praise to my gracious God, got cold." (At W. Brown's.)

"   17   "rode 4 miles; married Nath. Coulter and Margaret Stewart."

May 10   "Sabbath—preached psalm 107: 15–22; lectured John 6: 26–35 and preached verse 35; baptized Robert son to James Finey, give all praise." (Then rode 7 miles to Sam Martin's.)

Oct. 25   "Sabbath preached 115: 10–L; lectured Jude 7–10; preached Titus last chapter verse 14 and baptized James son to James Calhoun, Elizabeth to T. Mitchel." (At W. Brown's.)

1768 June 2   "rode 9 miles—preached psalm 22: 27—catechized 22 and baptized Thomas son to James McCord—went to G. and J. Dun." (Then rode 3 miles to Wm. Brown's on 3rd.)

Oct. 9   "Sabbath—preached 145–49. Lectured Corinthians 11: 23—preached 139: 23, 24 and baptized Mary daughter to W. Greenlie; and Sarah, daughter to Thomas Finey." (At W. Brown's.)

"   13   "Fasted—prayed—preached psalm 79: 8–L and preached Zech. 13: 1 o.a. praise my God."

"   15   "preached psalm 42: –3–preached John 1: 46 and baptized Hannah, daughter to Benjamin Brown—give all praise to my gracious God." (At W. Brown's.)

1769 Jan. 29   "Sabbath—preached psalm 128; preached Hebrews 4: 1, 2 and baptized Jean Mair." (At W. Brown's.)

Apr. 16   "Sabbath—preached 135: 15–L; lectured Colossians 3: 1–5 and preached John 1: 12; g.a. and baptized John son to John McCormick; rode 15 miles David Mitchel's." (At W. Brown's.)

July 30   "Sabbath preached psalm 140: 9–L; lectured Isaiah 4;

Paxton (and Paxtang) Society— *Continued*

preached Matthew 22: 11 and baptized Agnes daughter to Henry McCormick." (At W. Brown's.)

1769 July   31   "rode 3 miles to John Duncan's, x x."

Dec. 5, 6   "rode 14 miles Widow Swan's—preached 71: 7–13 exercised Isaiah 26: 20 and baptized Martha daughter to James Graham—give all praise to God." (From Wm. Brown's.)

1770 Jan.   28   "Sabbath—preached 149: 5–L and lectured Isaiah 35 and baptized Susanna to James Howston. Give all praise to God." (6 miles from Alexander Brown's.)

Feb.   1   "rode 10 miles to and from William Paterson's; preached psalm 94: 11 preached Jeremiah 17: 13 and 14 and baptized Eleanor, daughter to him." (At Wm. Brown's.)

"   4   "Sabbath preached psalm 150, lectured Ephesians 6: 1–10 and baptized Janet daughter to Thomas Finey; give all praise to my gracious God." (At Wm. Brown's.)

June 17   "Sabbath psalm 9: 12–16; lectured Isaiah 66: 1–5; preached 41: 11 and baptized Sarah daughter to Elijah Stewart; give all praise to my gracious God." (Hum. Spr.—went to W. B's.)

Aug.   1   "rode 18 miles after preaching psalm 79: 5–9; preached Isaiah 58: 13, 14 and baptized John and John to Thomas Black and John Taylor; and Barbara daughter to Sam Taylor—was the first preaching there." (Then on 2nd and 3rd rode 8 miles to Wiggin's, Sts; Ben. Walaces, W. Brown's.)

Sept. 25   "rode 4 miles J. S.—married Thomas McKt. and E. B.

"   30   "Sabbath—preached 13–L. Lectured John 8: 26–33. Preached Isaiah 63: 8 and baptized William son to James Thorn and Robert to Kath. Meek." (At Alexander Brown's.)

1771 Feb. 12   "rode 9 miles Gilchrist's; married A. Spier and Mt. Scott." (From W. Brown's.)

Aug. 14, 15   "rode 17 miles to and from James McCords; preached 19: 7–1 preached Galatians 2: 16 and baptized Thomas son to Ben Brown; went to J. D." (From Wm. Brown's.)

"   26   "preached psalm 42: 8—preached Job 17: 9 and baptized Jean daughter to John Martin g.a." (At Wm. Brown's.)

1772 Jan. 26   "Sabbath; preached 19–24; lectured Jude 10–L and baptized Sus. to H. Stewart." (At W. B's.)

May   6   "rode 13 miles A. Brown's; preached 76: 10–L; lectured

Paxton (and Paxtang) Society—*Continued*

Romans 5: 12—and baptized John to Thomas Kennety and Janet to C. Kilgore." (From Charles Kilgore's.)

1772 May 10   "Sabbath; preached 13: L; lectured Isaiah 10: 1–13; preached Jude, g.a.   baptized Isobel and Ann daughters to Sam Calhoun, Thomas son to Matthew Brown; Samuel son to Kath. Meek, and Cristopher son to James Howston. g.a. sick once and again." (At Alexander Brown's—then rode 3 miles to Joseph Junkens.)

Sept. 20   "Sabbath; preached 46: 1–5; lectured Isaiah 20 and 21: 1–6; preached Genesis 46: 4 and baptized James son to Henry McCormick; John son to John; James to Robert Bell; Elizabeth daughter to James McCord; William son to James McClaughlin and Martha to Thomas Finey." (At W. Brown's—then rode 5 miles to John Hilton's, Jean Sloan's; dying; and J. Duncans on 21st.)

1773 Feb. 14   "Sabbath—preached 51: 5–8. Lectured 26: 1–12 and baptized John son to John McCulloch; and Ruth, daughter to James Graham." (Then rode 14 miles to Charles Kilgore's.)

Aug. 1   "Sabbath—preached   59: 1–6.   Lectured   37: 21–L. Preached Isaiah 2: 3 and baptized Sarah, daughter to Wm. Thom.—give all praise to God."

1776 May 20   "I preached 89—preached Job 17: 8, 9 o.a. and baptized Mary, daughter to Wm. Sloan—held Presb., etc.—appointed 13th June for a fast. Mr. Dob. sacrament on the 25th of August. I on F. beg." (At Wm. Brown's —then rode 20 miles to D. Mitchel's.)

1779 Oct. 10   "Sabbath—rode 8 miles; preached 24–29; 1 Samuel 7: 12—and baptized Martha and (to?) James Finey; Hanna, Sarah and Wm. to John Rob-son; went to S. Wilson, very weary; mare strayed."

1784 Oct. 24   "Sabbath—preached 64: 6–L; lectured Colossians 1: 12– 19, and baptized John son to W. Tom, born April 7th, 1782, Ann to David Ritchy born Jan. 1777 and Elizabeth to Elizabeth Hilton born Sep. 27, 1776, o.a. praise God." (At Wm. Brown's—Paxton.)

1786 Nov. 19   "Sabbath—preached 6–L and lectured 6–L and baptized Mo son to Han (or Hen) Bel. born Jan. 10." (W. B's.)

Nov. 26   "Sabbath—preached 76: 6–L and preached Jude v 21 and baptized." (On 28th rode 9 miles to Hugh Stewart's and to Mr. James Cluney's.)

1787 June 8   "rode 9 miles to W. B., Paxton."

" 10   "Sabbath—preached 80: 7–12, lectured Jeremiah 5: 19– L., preached same and baptized James to Henry Bell, born May 26th, 1787."

Paxton (and Paxtang) Society—*Continued*

1788 Aug. 17 "Sabbath—preached 91: 25, lectured 29: 15–24, preached same and baptized Ann daughter to John Lawson, born April 12, '87, and Hanna and Agnes, born April 1786 and 1788, to Cornelius Law, Holander, give all praise to God." (At Eleanor Brown's or S. S.)

"   22 "rode 11 miles, preached 51: 1–5 lectured 5: 6 and baptized John S. born Aug. 17, Inst. to Jonathan Hains. etc." (At Bartholomew Hains'.)

Susquehanna

(Crossed many times.)

Swatara

1752 Feb. 22 or 23 "Rode 8 miles to Sweetara great differences— passed Cannowagon, etc., etc. Sabbath. Preached Psa. 19: 1–9 lectured Gal. 5: 17–22 and baptized Wm. son to Chas. Neilil then rode 7 miles over Sweetara to James M. (Mitchel's?).

June 1 "x x Rode 3 miles over S(wata)ra in a canoe, etc. came to David Mitchel's where I preached psa. 93: 3–L and examined 24 persons give all praise to my God." (From Alex. Swan's.)

Tait's Meeting-house

1753 bet. Mar. 5 & 10 "Rode 34 miles to Calb. Miln, Tait's Meeting-house, born Henry, Ja. —." (Then rode 10 miles to Wm. Brown's, Paxton.)

Delaware County

Chester

1759 June 28 "Rode 31 miles to Chester, Darby, Philadelphia—left B. Leech." (From Wilmington—Marshal's.)

Darby

1759 June 28 (See Chester.)

Fayette County

Juniata River

1779 Oct. 15 "rode 35 miles over Juniata, Sideling Hill, Scrub, M. D. McC." (On way from Allegheny County, Pa.)

Laurel Hill

1779 Sept. 17 "rode 37 miles Laurel-hill Mr. Greer's Forks of Yough Mr. Simson's."

Oct. 13 "rode 30 over Laurel-hill, Glades, lay on straw at Mr. Spiegers." (On way to Bedford.)

Redstone

1779 Oct. 7 (See Forks of Yough, Allegheny County, Pa.)

FRANKLIN COUNTY*

(See also Cumberland County.)

Antietam (Little)

1752 Nov. 3 "Rode 22 miles to Antiturn (?) to Robert Redicks— bought 100 acres." (From Jas. McCorahan's.)

Conococheague Society

1751 Dec. 4 "Travelled 2 miles. Preached psalm 34:17–1 and preached 2 Kings 7:3–4. Give all praise to God and baptized John and Elizabeth son and daughter to Geo. Reynolds. . . ." (At George Reynolds, Antrim T.)

1755 Apr. 16 "Rode 24 miles to James McClenachans, deep snow eight inches—." (From Carroll's Tract.)

"   17 "Preached psalm 32:1–5 and preached Zechariah 13: 1 etc.

"   18 "Rode 9 miles to Da. Logan's and David McBryar's good health—."

1756 Apr. 12 "Rode 27 miles to James McClenachan's Connecho-jieg.—"

"   14 "Rode 20 miles to Sharp's Fort etc. after preaching psalm 79:1–6 lectured Joel 2:12–15 and baptized Jean and Jean daughters to Jo Wilson and John Cochran; all fly from the Indians, etc."

Aug. 1 "Sabbath. Preached psalm 89:40–47; lectured Matthew 11:16–25; preached Hebrews and baptized James son to Peter January; examined 14 persons." (At James McClenachan's.)

1759 May 7 "Rode 25 miles to A. Poa's and to James McClenachan's." (From David Dunwoody's.)

"   8 "preached psalm 147. Lectured Matthew 1:15–L— baptized Agnes, daughter to R. McCulloch."

* Regular preaching places in Franklin County where most of the Conococheague Society resided, were Lurgen, Roxbury, Strasburgh, Southampton, Green, Scotland, Fayetteville, Greenwood, Shady Grove, Waynesboro, Mercersburg, and Hamilton.

Conococheague Society— *Continued*

1761 Apr. 28   "rode 22 miles to A. Finley and James McClenachans; great rain." (From John Watt's.)

"   30   "rode 3 miles Robert Crunckeltons after preaching psalm 42: 1; preached Jeremiah 32: 40 and baptized Elizabeth and Sari to Robert Crunckeltons and Eleanor (to) J. Cochran."

May 1   "rode 10 miles to Robert Crunkeltons to Widow Wilsons."

Sept. 23   "Rode 27 miles to J. Cochran's and James McClenachans." (From R. Reddick's.)

"   27   "Sabbath preached psalm 25: 16—lectured 1 Corinthians 11: 28—preached Matthew 16: 24 and baptized John son to John Gebby give all praise to God; offer of Christ."

1766 Mar. 23   "Sabbath—preached psalm 91: 5–9. Lectured Hebrews 10: 25–30 and preached John 17: 24 and baptized Rachel, daughter to George Marlin, Ex. psalm 46– –." (At James McClenachan's, then rode 8 miles to J. Cochran's on Mar. 24.)

1768 Sept. 29   "rode 7 miles to James & Widow McClenachans—dull." (From J. Crook's.)

"   30   "preached psalm 80: 17–L and catechized 40 persons— o.a. praise God."

1770 Mar. 14   "rode and walked 18 miles to R. C. etc. Married James Crook and Mary Crunk(leton)."

"   16   "rode 2 miles, visited Letitia Niel and James McClenachan."

"   18   "Sabbath—preached 4: 6–L; lectured Isaiah 45: 20–L and preached Jeremiah 17, 13 and 14. o.a."

"   19   "rode 7 miles to James McClenachan's, D. McCurdy, John Crooks." (Then 9 miles to John Cochran's on 20th.)

Greencastle

1786 Aug. 31   "rode 8 miles or 9 miles to G. Clark's, Green Castle good health, praise God, rain."

Greencastle— *Continued*

1786 Sept. 3 "Sabbath—preached 73: 1–10; lectured 1 Peter 1: 22–L and preached John 3: 16, rode 4 miles R. C."

1787 Sept. 26 "rode 16 miles Greencastle, Fulert. Mr. Lind's." (From John Burns'.)

Guilford

1771 Feb. 4, 5, 6 "rode and walked 25 miles to Guil., Slo., widow and W. Robieson's."

1787 Sept. 27 "rode 14 miles Gulford, Chamber's, guage, R. S. J. Woods," (From Greencastle.)

" Kittachtinnan "

1752 June 24 "Rode 26 miles to John Glend. Kittachtinnan, Sheerman's—."

" 25 "Rode 2 miles to Jo. Kilogh. Preached psa. 23. Lectured Mark 10: 46–L and preached Luke 13: 3 and baptized John son to Josovick Laird—talked Crawfurd etc."

Rocky Spring Society

The " Tent " was near George Mitchel's house.

1751 Aug. 22 "Preached psalm 121 and lectured Matthew 17: 4. . . . Then rode 22 miles to Ja. Mitchel's near Rocky Spring." (From Walter Buchanan's.)

" 25 "Sabbath. Preached psalm 9: 10–15. Lectured Luke 12: 35–41 and preached at 2 o'clock Amos 4 . . . and baptized And. and Moses, sons to Jo. Mitchel; and Ja. and Eliz. son and daughter to Jo Lowry; and Martha, daughter to Jo. Thorn, and Sarah, daughter to Ja. Mitchel and - - - daughter to Jo. McCl(ung.) v. pub. Praise to God."

Nov. 14 "Preached psalm 20: 1. Preached Tit. 3: 8 and baptized Janet and Henry, daughter and son to James Reid. Then rode 12 miles to Ja. Mitchel's." (At James Reid's.)

" 17 "Sabbath. Preached psalm 16: 6–1. Lectured Gal. 3: 5–10 and preached Jer. 3: 19 and baptized Katharine to Geo. Mitchel Ex. psalm 54: 1–1."

1752 Mar. 26 "Rode 9 miles to George Mitchel's after preach. Ps. 122: 1–7 and preached Jonah 2: 8." (At Jo. Wylie's.)

" 27 "Preached Ps. 19: 7–12 and exam. 28 persons conversed R. McCon(el)."

Rocky Spring Society— *Continued*

1752 Mar. 29   "Sabbath. Rode 4 miles to and from Ja. Mitchels preached Ps. 21: 5–9 lectured Gal. 6: 14 and preach. 1 Cor. 15: 22 and bap. Mary and Margaret to Jo. Wylie."

"   30   "Rode 20 miles to Jo. Lowries preach. Ps. 57: 1—lect. Phillipians 2 and bap. Jean daughter to Dr.—then came to Ja. McMichans."

July   5   "Sabbath. Rode 4 miles to and from J. M. preached Psa. 25: 16–L lectured So. 3: 1–4 preached Jos. 2: 14 and baptized Isobel, daughter to Jo. Mitchel, Janet. . . ." (From Geo. Mitchel's.)

"   10   "Rode 2 miles to James Mitchel's—Jo. Leiper. . . ."

"   12   "Sab. preached Psa. 26: 1–9, lectured So. 3: 3–6 and preached Hos. 55: 16–L. praise to God."

"   13   "Married Thomas Jones and Elizabeth Blakely x x."

Oct.   25   "Rode 22 miles to Dunlop's Ship: owing lodging and to G. Mitch."

1753 Mar. 30   "Rode 3 miles to George Mitchel's great rain. Give all praise to my God." (From Jo. Thorn's.)

Apr.   1   "Sab.—Rode 2 mi. to Joseph Mitchel preached Ps. 37: 4–7 lectured 1 Peter 2: 1–4 and preach. Lev. 20, 7 and baptized John son to Jo. Mitchel senior James son to - - - and Esther daugh. to Jo. Thorn, d. Day excited at honor."

"   2   "Married Peter January to Debora McMichan preach. Ps. 91: 1—lectured John 6: 15–22 and exam. 30 persons, rode 2 miles."

"   3   "Birthday—entering me into the 35th year of life from 1718. March 24, O.S. cried to the Lord with Sev.- - -"

"   6   "Rode 2 miles to Jas. Mitchels, examined 7 persons, 2 ruling elders."

"   8   "Sab. preach. Ps. 37: 7–12 lectured 1 Peter 2: 4, 5 and preach. Lev. 20: 7 praise to God. preach. Eph. 4: 8 and ordained 6 elders Jos. Wilson and Jas. Wilson George Mitchel, Jer. Murray, David Dinwoody and Thomas Wilson, then explained Ps. 58; 7 hours and a half employed today, give praise to God."

Sept.   6   "Traveled 6 mi.—Dan Havisha's place 280 acres—went to Jas. Mitchel's." (From Lowry's.)

"   7   "Conversed with 4 persons concerning Testimonies, Government Alex. Mitchel—"

Rocky Spring Society— *Continued*

1753 Sept. 9   "Sab. Preach. Ps. 43: 1–4 lectured 1 Peter 5: 10–L. and preached Hos. 3: 3 concerning So. League and baptized George son to George Mitchel pro. vow, oath and covenant."

"   10   "Rode 2 miles to Geo. Mitchel's feeble but God preserved."

"   14   "Rode 2 mi. to James Mitchel's—weak—."

―――――

"   17   "Rode 14 miles to Jo. Wy. and Jo. Reid after marrying John Morton and Elizabeth Mtear's.—" (From James Mitchel's—then 14 miles to Hopewell on 18th.)

―――――

1754 Apr. 19   "Rode 11 miles to John Wylies and George Mitchels—exhausted, etc." (From James Reid's.)

"   21   "Sabbath. Rode 4 miles tent, preached psalm 55: 1 lectured John 3: 15–18. preached Hebrews 10: 23 and baptized Ann, daughter to Alexander Mitchel. Give all praise to my God."

―――――

―――――

Aug. 1   "Rode 2 miles to John and James Mitchel's 2 Day, sweet - -, water cold. Offered old M. 14, 26 lib."

"   4   "Sabbath—preached psalm 61: 5–L. Lectured Isaiah 26: 3–L. Visited and preached Malachi 4: 2 and baptized Elizabeth, Margaret, Jean and Thomas to Thomas Dougherty; and Sarah, daughter to John Lowrie; and Margaret, daughter to David Carson; and exer. 2 hours psalm 66: 1–10—give all praise to God."

―――――

―――――

1755 Apr. 24   "Rode 2 miles to George Mitchel's in good health, praise to my gracious God."

"   27   "Sabbath. Rode 4 miles preached psalm 72: 7–11, lectured Matthew 3: 13–L. Preached baptized Elizabeth, daughter to John McClung, Ann daughter to Jo——. Margaret daughter to Gov. (or Geo.) Mit. and Joseph son to James E——."

―――――

May 4   "Sabbath, preached psalm 72: 11–15. lectured Matthew 4: 1–12, preached Jeremiah 4: 14 and baptized John son to George Mitchel. g.a. unhamp. offer of Christ."

1756 Apr. 25   "Sabbath. Rode 7 miles to N. M. preached Ps. 86: 12–15, lectured Matthew 9: 14–20; preached Mark 9: 23 and baptized Gavin to Alexander Mitchel." (From Arch. Burns.)

Rocky Spring Society— *Continued*

1760 June 25 "Rode 3 miles to James Mitchels, preached psalm 66: 8—lectured Zephaniah 3: 8—and baptized William son to John Blakely and Robert son to John Bromfield." (From John Wade's.)

1761 Mar. 17 "rode 7 miles to John McCleary's; preached psalm 111: examined persons and baptized James son to James Wilson and Mary, daughter to G. Mitchel." (From James Wilson's.)

1763 Apr. 19 "rode 15 miles James Reid's—preached psalm 56: 8— and lectured Isaiah 4: 1—and baptized William son to John Crawford." (From T. A's.)

Sept. 14, 15 "rode 11 miles after preaching psalm 94: 10–16 preached Mark 8: 34 and baptized Esther, daughter to Thomas Cross—came to John Ker's." (From David Mitchel's.)

1764 May 1 "rode 14 miles to Hammond's—married Samuel Leiper and Sarah McCleary; Sam Smith and Mary McCleary all—." (From Wm. Gemmil's.)

1765 Nov. 11 "rode 20 miles to James Mitchel's, R. Spring—good health."

"   12 "rode 3 miles to T. And. preached psalm 17: 13–L. Lectured Hebrews 7: 23–L. Baptized John son to James Mitchel and Rebekah to James Anderson."

1767 June 12 "Rode 18 miles with James Mitchel to his house." (From Robert Crunckleton's.)

"   14 "Sabbath preached psalm 108: 1–7; lectured John 6: 61–66; preached Titus 2: 14 and baptized Benjamin son to John Blakely; give all praise to my gracious God."

Aug. 21 "rode 20 miles to James Mitchel's with him hot."

"   23 "Sabbath preached psalm 111: 5–L; lectured Isaiah 64: 7–L; preached Habakkuk 3: 2 and baptized Margaret, Alexander and Prudence to John McConel."

"   24 "rode 3 miles to and from W. Cal. 25th.—preached psalm 119: 113; baptized Elizabeth daughter to James Anderson; catechized about 40 persons." (From James Mitchel's.)

"   29 "preached psalm 51: 1—preached Romans 7: 6 I baptized Alexander son to Alexander McConel, John son to Peter January, James son to And. McMiens, and Rebecca daughter to Wm. Rose; constituted session; distributed the tokens ——." (At James Mitchel's.)

Rocky Spring Society— *Continued*

1768 Mar. 31   "rode 8 miles T. Wilson's—preached psalm 89:1—preached 2 Thess. 2:11, 12. Baptized Thomas, son to Thomas Cross, and William son to John Reddick—Jean Cross presented." (Then rode 7 miles to David Dunwoody's April 1st.)

May 22   "Sabbath—preached 65–70 lectured 1 Thess. 4:13—preached 1 Peter 4:17 and baptized Thomas, son to John McConel—give all praise to God, etc." (At James Mitchel's.)

Oct. 3   "rode 20 miles to James Mitchel's—held session—agreed Fin. and Spier." (From Widow McClenachan's.)

———

1769 Mar. 25   "rode 15 miles to James Mitchel's; very tired." (From David Mitchel's.)

" 26   "Sabbath preached 134:1—preached Genesis 22:3–8; preached Galatians 2:16 and baptized Silas to James Anderson and Thomas to Wm. Mitchel; give all praise to my gracious God."

" 27   "rode 5 miles—Paterson, Calb. Anderson and Wade."

———

Aug. 7   "rode 40 miles to R. Spring, McClung's etc. with James Mitchel." (From W. Parkieson's.)

" 9   "rode 8 miles James Anderson's; preached psalm 46:8 preached Titus 3:5 and baptized John, Sarah, James, Eleanor, Alexander and Martha to Thomas Dougherty and Mary to John Guthrie."

———

Nov. 20   "etc. 21st—rode 7 miles—preached psalm 91:14—lectured 1 Corinthians 6:12–L—x x baptized Agnes to (Hugh McFadzean) and And. to And. McCleary—give all praise to God—conv.—strain."

1770 Mar. 11   "Sabbath—preached psalm 4:1–6; lectured Ephesians 6:1–10 baptized Margaret daughter to John Crawfurd o.a. praise God." (At T. Dough.)

Sept. 26   "rode 24 miles J. Mitchel's—preached 47:1. Lectured Jeremiah 31:1–7 and baptized William, son to James Mitchel."

Nov. 1   "rode 7 miles preached 110:1–5; preached Acts 2:38–39 and baptized Temperance to Wm. Moor." (At W. Moore's.)

———

1771 May 31   "rode 13 miles to James Mitchel's, very tired but well." (From David Mitchel's.)

June 2   "Sabbath preached 28–1; lectured Romans 5:1–10; preached Jude and baptized Thomas son to John Gebby; Ann to James Anderson."

———

Rocky Spring Society— *Continued*

1772 Feb. 25, 26, 27 "rode 20 miles; preached; catechized; married James McYlahlin and Sarah Wilson, went to George Mitchels." (From John Walker's.)

May 3 "Sabbath; preached 40: 9–13; lectured 9: 8–L; preached Luke 1–32 and baptized Robert son to Thomas Dougherty; Wm. to Wm. Mitchel and Sarah daughter to Hew Robieson; visited B. M's." (At James Mitchel's.)

1773 Feb. 17 "rode 22 miles with Mr. Roger to Ship—to James Mitchel's R."

" 18 "rode 5 miles—preached 84: 8—preached Deuteronomy 7: 22—baptized James, son to Nathaniel Mitchel; Jean to John McConel; Sarah to James Mitchel; and Elizabeth to Jesse Mitchel."

Mar. 8 "rode 10 miles T. Cross—preached 51: 7—exercised Isaiah 27: 5 and baptized John, son to William Steel; and Jean, daughter to Joseph Steel." (From David Dunwoody's.)

" 9 "rode 7 miles to Matt. R's after marrying Joseph McMurray and Martha Cross (at Thomas Cross's)—married Benjamin Brown and Agnes Ritchie—sick, wet, etc."

Aug. 9 "rode 40 miles—married Thomas Kennedy and Eliz. Lowry, etc." (From Alex. Brown's, at James Mitchel's.)

1774 Feb. 3 "rode 6 miles—married Geo. Mit. and Mary Wilson— 10 shillings." (From Widow and H. Ewin's.)

" 4, 5 "rode 7 miles to and from G. Mitchel's."

1777 Jan. 1 "rode 3 miles—preached 51: 5—lectured 1 Peter 5: 6, 7 and baptized Ben, son to Geo. Mitchel; and Jas. to Andrew Strain." (From G. M.)

" 2 "rode 7 miles R. Laws—married William Law and Eliz. Smith."

1778 May 4, 5 "rode 35 miles to G. Mitchel's, Jas. Wilson's, preached 41: 1–5. Lectured 1 Thessalonians 4: 14–L and baptized Mary, daughter to Wm. Ewing." (Then rode 11 miles home on 6th.)

Rocky Spring Society—*Continued*

1784 Sept. 6 "rode 14 miles, preached 51: 1–6, lectured Acts 8: 35—baptized Margaret daughter to John McGown C. Sept. 3, 1784, rs. 1–18–4, from all went James Lo—." (From James Nisbet's.—then 5 miles to widow McClures, Paton, D. McCready's, home, etc. D-s on 7th.)

1787 Apr. 9 "rode 5 miles, preached 7: 11, lectured Acts 2: 37–L and baptized Elizabeth to Martha Marky, the husband absent born Feb. 19th, ult. and Joseph Reid, adopted by John Branon born Dec. 3rd, 1778." (From Alexander McCullough's.)

Sept. 29 "N. M. 30th.—Sabbath—preached 86: 8–14; lectured 17–L, preached John 4: 29 and baptized Helen daughter to Sam Rob. C. April 24." (From Gulford, etc. J. Woods'.)

Oct. 21 "Sabbath—preached 88: 1–8, lectured 12 and preached Matthew 11: 28 and baptized John son to Robert McCleary born Sept. 26 ult. Matthew son to Math. Calhoun born Aug. 21st and Wm. son to John Gordon born Dec. 3, 1786, Exc. Zechariah 12: 9, 10 and baptized John son to Sam Taylor, born Aug. 21 ult. give all praise to God; rs 10 or 12 dollars. (At A. Alie.—then rode 9 miles to Ben Sayres and Thomas Mitchel's on 23rd.)

FULTON COUNTY

Licking Creek and The Cove Society

Licking Creek and The Cove Society was located near the Franklin County line about 10 miles west of Mercersburg. Covenanters were here as early as 1748. This Society is sometimes called "Timber Ridge." The Wilsons were the principal members, moving to Western Pennsylvania later. Other members moved elsewhere, those remaining worshiping with other Societies in Franklin County.

1751 Aug. 26 "Rode — miles to Jo. Cochran's, Upper Settlement, exhausted." (From James Mitchel's.)

"   27 "Rode 4 miles to Ja. Wilson's; preached psalm 125 and lectured Mark 10: 46—and baptized Will son to Robert McConel in the big Cave; blew ——. Then rode 8 miles to Jus. Smith's; tired but yet safe; praise to God."

"   28 "Preached psalm 23 and preached Hebrews 3, last g.a.; then rode 4 miles; Ja. McEld. . . ."

Nov. 18 "Rode 16 miles to James Wilsons Lickencreek. In good health, praise to God." (From James Mitchel's.)

Licking Creek and The Cove Society— *Continued*

1751 Nov. 19   "Preached psalm 46: 1–6. Preached Jer. 3: 7 and baptized Hanna daughter to James McMichan Martha and James daughter and son to Jo. Martin; George son to Jo. Cochran; Eliz. daughter to Jo. Wilson and Elizabeth daughter to James Wilson. Then rode 2 miles to . . . Camp. Conversed concerning Christ's univ. Do. Fa. etc. agreeing."

"   29   "Rode 13 miles to Mr. Camp and 12 miles back 8 watch dropped . . . and 2 miles to James W. Lickencreek; my W. where 3 lifted a whi. . . ." (From Morgan's Mill.)

"   30   "Rode 8 miles to James McMichans—praise to my God, etc."

Dec. 1   "Sabbath,—preached psalm 17: 6–13. Lectured Gal. 3: 15–20 and preached Heb. 4: 12."

"   2   "Rode 11 miles to Jo. Wilson's in the big cave. preached psalm 74: 1–6 and lectured Luke 24: 28–38 and baptized John and Robert sons of Jo. McMien. Then rode 2 miles to Adam McConnels. Conversed concerning various things."

1752 Apr. 6   "Rode 8 miles to Jas. (or Jus) Smith's, Ind. of Cum. studies etc." (From Ja. McMichan's.)

"   7   "Rode 7 miles to and from Ja. McClellan's preach Ps. 76: 10 lectured Ezek. 17: 12–19 - -."

July 13   "x x x rode 20 miles to Adam McConnell's in the big cave—exhausted fleas."

"   14   "Rode 4 miles to and from Jo. Wilson's preach. Psa. 74: 6–12, lectured Heb. 10: 23 and preach. Luke 24: 32, 5 hours, g.a. praise to God, talked concern various things, etc."

"   16   "Rode 12 miles to James McMichan's, exhausted, conversed about various things."

"   17   "Rode 3 miles to James Wilson's Licken Creek, tired of the ungodly."

"   19   "Sab. preach. x x."

Oct. 31   "Rode 12 miles to the Cam. conversed—says of Christ's purchase not a drop of water—to the elect of the Rep. in an offer of Christ, owns it the duty of w. to - -. Wilson's pref. Ps. 78: 5–9, preached Luke 12: 1 and

Licking Creek and The Cove Society— *Continued*

baptized Janet daugh. to Robert McConel and Janet daugh. to Jo. Martin. Church holds form to the rule of diety with the precept. wrote a letter to Roan, false representation told." (From Jus. Smith's—then rode 12 miles to George Reynolds, etc.)

1753 Mar. 25   "Sab. preach. Ps. 36: 7–L lectured 1 Peter 1: 22–L and preach. Lev. 20–7 and bapt. Mary daugh. to Joseph Cochran exhausted." (At Jos. McClenachan's.)

"   26   "Rode 6 miles to Jo. Cochran lectured Ps. 132: 10–L examined persons to Wm. Mores." (From Jos. Mc-Clenachan's.)

"   27   "Rode 12 mi. to Jo. Wils. Big Cave tired distressed."

"   28   "Rode 12 miles to Jas. McMich. to John Thorn's tired." (Three miles from George Mitchel's.)

Apr. 8   (James Wilson and Jos. Wilson ordained elders at James Mitchel's, Rocky Spring, Franklin County.)

Aug. 30   "Rode 13 miles to Jus. Smith's Maxwell's and Jas. Wilson's." (From Jas. McClenachan's.)

Sept. 2   "Sab. preached Ps. 42: 8–L. lectured 1 Peter 5: 7–10 and preached Hos. 3: 3 g.a. and baptized Zacheus son to Jas. Wilson—and Mary daugh. to Sam. Leiper."

"   3   "Rode 12 mi.—to Big Cove in good health praise my gracious God—." (From James Wilson's.)

"   4   "Preach. x x."

Dec. 11   "Rode 9 miles to James Wilson's—reason etc." (From Robert Loughhead's.)

"   12   "Rode 4 miles to Widow Calbreath's—conversed with Seceder, etc."

"   13   "Rode 6 miles, after preaching psalm 121 and lecturing Zephaniah 3: 8–14 and baptizing Martha, daughter to James Erwin, to John Rosses—good health, praise to God."

1754 Apr. 29   "Rode 20 miles to McDowels, then to the Big Cave James Wilson's." (From John Lowry's.)

"   30   "At Jo. W. preached x x."

May 5   "Sabbath. Preached psalm 55: 15–20 lectured Amos 1: 1–6, 'preached Hebrews 10: 23 and baptized Sarah,

Licking Creek and The Cove Society— *Continued*

daughter to Peter January explained psalm 65: 6–L."
(At Sam Leiper's.)

1754 July 21 "Sabbath preached psalm 60: 6–L.. Lectured Amos 4:
1–8 and preached Malachi 4: 2., g.a."
"   22 "Rode 3 miles to McMichan's: talked with Mary, James,
children, etc.—good health."
"   23 "Rode 15 miles to Sm. Alexander's, Jo. Cochran's,
Camp, Thomas Dougherty's."

"   28 "Sabbath—Rode 12 miles G. M. after preaching psalm
61: 1–5. Lectured Amos 4: 8–L.; preached Malachi 4: 2
and baptized Margaret, daughter to Robert McConel,
and Elizabeth, daughter to John Leiper." (From John
Cochran's.)

1755 Apr. 19 "Rode 5 miles to Jo. Cochran's x x." (From Da. Logan's and David McBryar's.)
"   20 "Sabbath—Preached psalm 72: 1–7 lectured Matthew
3: 7–13 preached Jeremiah 4: 14 and baptized John
son to Jo. Cochran give all praise to my God."
"   21 "Rode 5 miles to James Wilson's; preached psalm 74:
20–L. Lectured Zephaniah 3: 1–4 and baptized Robert
son to him and Sam son to Sam Leiper and examined."
"   22 "Rode 13 miles to James McMich. Coch. and Jo.
Leiper's in good health."

Sept. 8, 9 "Rode 2 miles and 12 miles to Jo. Lowrie's and to John
Cochran's—good health, praise God."
"   10 "Preached psalm 61: 1–5, preached Isaiah 32: 2 g.a.
hours and ½ conversed, etc."
"   11 "Rode 5 miles to James McMichan's and to James Wilsons, good health."
"   14 "Sabbath preached psalm 78: 1–6, lectured Matthew 5:
43–L, preached 1 Peter 5: 8 and explained psalm 69:
1–5."
"   15 "Rode 13 miles to Da. Logan's, McClenachan's exer. 2
hour psalm 22."

1756 Apr. 11 "Sabbath. Rode 16 miles, preached psalm 86: 1–6,
lectured Matthew 9: 1–8, preached Mark 9: 2 and baptized Rebecca daughter to James Wilson, and Sarah
daughter to R. Mitchel." (From Arch. Burns'.)
1759 June 17 "Sabbath. Preached psalm 136: 21–L. Lectured Philip-
pines 2: 1–5 and preached Hebrews 3: 18—give all

Licking Creek and The Cove Society— *Continued*

praise to God (g.a.l.D.) and baptized Mary, daughter to James Davidson—." (At Robert Gilmore's.)

1760 June 29 "Sabbath. Rode 16 miles to J. McClenachan; at widow Wilsons, preached psalm 4: 1–5; lectured Zephaniah 1: 1–4 and preached Isaiah 7, 9 and baptized Ephr. son to Peter January give all praise to my gracious God." (At Wm. Morison's.)

July 1 " Preached psalm 37: 3—preached Jeremiah 32: 40; catechized 26 persons and baptized Wm. Berryhill; took on the engagements himself, etc." (At Widow Wilson's—then rode 24 miles to John Watts and Withrows in Carroll's Tract.)

1762 Aug. 17 "rode 1 mile J. Davidson's—preached psalm 119: 37–61—preached Isaiah 30: 18 and baptized Hannah daughter to Peter January." (From Widow Wilson's —then 12 miles over Blew Mountain to John Wilson's.)

1763 Apr. 13 "rode 3 miles R. Crun.—preached psalm 85: 6–L. Lectured Luke 18: 15 and baptized Samuel, son to R. Crunkleton." (From James McClenachan's.)

1764 May 9 "rode 8 miles—preached psalm 116: 1—catechized 42— baptized Mary, (to) A. McMeans, And.—then came to Tract sisters." (Then rode 10 miles to David Dunwoody's on 11th.)

1765 Mar. 24 "Sabbath—preached psalm 78: 28–32 and lectured Colossians 4: 1–6 and baptized Wm. and James to John Gebby; and Wm. son to Jas. Davidson." (6 miles from John Cochran's—then rode 12 miles to Robert Crunkleton's.)

" 26 "rode 5 miles Sam Kyle's—preached psalm 57: 1–4. Lectured Colossians 3: 1–4 and baptized Samuel, son to Peter January, o.a." (At James Davidson's—then rode 18 miles to Thomas Anderson's.)

1767 June 11 "Preached psalm 119: 1–7; lectured Luke 18: 1–9; preached Titus 2: 11, 12 and baptized Robert son to Alexander Lecky, presented by the mother." (At James McClenachan's.)

1768 May 19 "rode 12 miles to James Davidson's—preached psalm 68: 11—preached verse 3 and 23 and baptized James and Sam. sons to And. Ferrier." (From Robert Crunkleton's.)

Oct. 2 "Sabbath—preached 142–45. Lectured Matthew 26: 32–47—preached Hebrews 2: 1 and baptized Hugh to John Finley; and James to Ar. Gordon." (At James and Widow McClenachan's.)

Licking Creek and The Cove Society— *Continued*

1769 Mar. 21   "rode 12 miles; preached psalm 31: 14—preached Romans 5: 1 and baptized Margaret daughter to John Finley and David to J. Gebby and married W. Finley and Mary Cochran, John Neil and Letitia McClenachan received 17." (From John Cochran's.)

Aug. 13   "Sabbath preached psalm 5: 7; lectured Habakkuk 1: 12–L; preached Matthew 22: 11 and baptized Jean daughter to And. McMien's; give all praise to my gracious God." (At Robert Crunkleton's.)

1770 Nov. 11   "Sabbath preached 28: 33; lectured Ephesians 4: 7–13; ordained John Cochran and Wm. Finley ruling elders; baptized Elizabeth to James Leiper." (At John McClenachan's.)

1771 May 23   "rode 7 miles (from John Crook's) to J. McClen. after preaching 110: 1—lectured Acts 2: 32–L and baptized Alice daughter to James Crooks; give all praise to God."

"   26   "Sabbath preached 11–L; lectured Jude 16–L; preached Jude baptized Mary, James McClen. give all praise to God." (Then rode 4 miles to Robert Crunkleton's.)

"   29   "rode 12 miles to James Davidson's; preached psalm 65: 1; lectured Isaiah 48: 16–L, and baptized Joseph son to him went W. Morison's." (From Robert Crunkleton's o.h.)

Oct. 6   "Sabbath preached 33: 10–15; lectured Isaiah 56: 1—preached John 17: 3 and baptized Esther to John Neal." (At Robert Crunkleton's.)

"   7   "rode 13 miles Jean Morison; preached 9: 9; lectured John 15: 1–7 and baptized Deborah daughter to Peter January." (From John Cochran's.)

1772 Aug. 13   "rode 5 miles to W. McClenachans; preached psalm 48: 10–L: lectured Mark 8: 34–L and baptized Hew son James Brownlie, James son to Mary Scott and Alice to John Crooks." (From D. McCurdy's.)

"   16   "Sabbath; preached 45: 1—lectured Isaiah 18; preached 1 Corinthians 5: 7, 8 and baptized Adam son to William Lynd, a gust, give all praise to God." (Then rode 12 miles to James W. Downy's Rankin's and John Crooks on 17th.)

"   18   "rode 3 miles to J. Cochran's after preaching psalm 51: and lecturing Acts 2: 37–41 and baptized Rob son to James Crooks, give all praise to God."

Licking Creek and The Cove Society— *Continued*

1773 Feb. 21   "Sabbath; preached 51: 8–13; lectured Isaiah 26: 12–L and baptized Elizabeth daughter to John Finley, o.a. praise my gracious God." (At John McClen.)

Aug. 15   "Sabbath—preached 11–14. Lectured Isaiah 38: 9–L and preached 2: 3 and baptized Wm. son to John Anderson—give all praise to my gracious God 5½." (At John McClenachan's.)

———

Nov. 14   "Sabbath—preached 64: 1—lectured 14–L and baptized William son to James McClenachan g.a." (At John McClenachan's.)

"   15   "rode 7 miles to John Crooks—preached psalm 27: 1— and lectured 1 Thess. 4: 13—and baptized Jean to John Crooks, Junior—give all praise to my gracious God."

———

1774 May 29   "Sabbath preached 33–L; lectured Isaiah 51: 7–9; preached 1 John 4: 9 and baptized Margaret and James, daughter and son to John McClenachan." (At Ker's —then rode 24 miles to sister's on 30th.)

Scrub (Ridge) and Sideling Hill

1779 Oct. 15   (See Fayette Co.)

Sharp's Fort

1756 Apr. 14   (See Conococheague, Franklin County.)

Upper Settlement

1751 Aug. 26   (See Licking Creek and The Cove.)

LANCASTER COUNTY
Anderson's Ferry

1758 Apr. 5   "Rode 27 miles over Susquehanna to Anderson's Ferry with C. Betty." (From John Crook's and Wm. Cooper's.)

1768 May 11 or
12   "—37 miles And's Ferry—Baird's." (On way to David Dunwoody's.)

Blue Ball (Tavern)

1769 Nov. 30   "Rode 14 miles to Lan. and Blew Ball with A. Swan." (From Mat. McClung's—8 mi. from home.)

Brown's Mill

1758 July 10   "rode 14 miles to and from Jas. McKts., Brown Mill x x.", (From home.)

Colerain Township

1751 Sept. 5 "Rode 20 miles to Colerain Township. Daniel McClellans. Exhausted." (From Lancaster.)

Conestoga

1756 June 1 "Rode 16 miles to Humphrey Fulerton's after preaching psalm 140: 4–10 and preaching Hebrews 7: 25 at John Boyds Conestogoe." (From Lancaster.)

Conewago

1761 Sept. 16 "rode 10 miles to Wm. Coopers Connewago; weary." (From Hugh Ross's.)

Donegal

1781 Nov. 14 "rode 23 miles to Poedleh to James Paterson's, Donegl." (From home.)

" 29, 30 "—closed with Union, rode 54 miles Doneg. (From Wm. Brown's, Paxton.)

Dec. 2 "Sabbath—preached 25: 1–8 and lectured 1 John 3: 11—g.a."

" 3 "rode 8 miles to and from Edw. Wahub's paid his wife 2 dollars."

"Dorbus"

1756 bet. Nov. 9 and 24 "Rode 4 miles to Dorbus widow Littles; visit and to Robert Lochheads—." (From home.)

Downie's Mill

1758 July 14 "rode 7 miles to Dan McClellan's and Downie's Mill with—." (From home.)

1776 Mar. 7 "rode 7 miles to J. Paxton's, Downie's x x." (From home.)

Dutch Tavern

1767 Oct. 22 "rode 22 miles Dutch—married James Muir and Reb. Stewart." (From Matthew McClung's.)

1773 Nov. 23 "rode 45 miles to Dutch Tav.—3 miles from Lancaster." (From John Park's.)

Gap, The

1756 June 7 "x x Gap. exer. psalm 23 and baptized Charles son to Andrew Stewart; give all praise to my gracious God." (9 miles from Robert Lochhead's.)

1759 " 5 "rode 22 miles—visit to Pequea, the Gape and home— tired." (From home.)

1764 Mar. 8 "rode 13 miles to and from the Gap; R. Thomson's, preached 1 Corinthians 16: 13." (From home.)

Gates Hill Ford

1752 Feb. 11   "Rode 14 miles to James Wilson's at Gateshills Ford, Octorara." (From John Duncan's.)

Graham Bridge Meeting-house

1757 Apr. 25   "Tramped 2 miles to and from meeting house; —at Graham bridge." (From Robert Lochhead's.)

Greer's Mill, W.

1758 July 28   "rode 15 miles to and from W. Greer's Mill, visited old W. Andrews." (From home.)

1761 Nov. 3   "Rode 14 miles to and from Greers Miln; rs. Baxter's life." (From home.)

Half-Way-House, The

1770 Feb. 12   "rode 22 miles to Widow Laughlin's to the half way house—John Dun." (From home.)

"   13   "Married Joseph Widrow and Rebecca Dunlap—received 17–6."

Ker's Mill, Joseph

1761 Feb. 27   "Rode 9 miles home after visiting Jos. Ker's Mill."

Lancaster

Rev. John Cuthbertson rode many times to and from Lancaster from his home in Middle Octoraro, there being 72 trips recorded in his Diary between the years 1751 and 1784. These were mostly for the purpose of making purchases of "various things." Only such as refer to people in connection therewith are quoted here."

1751 Aug. 15   "Rode 40 miles to Lancaster, Sweetara-Creek and Ja. McKnaught's." (From Humphrey Fullerton's.)

1752 Feb. 18   "Rode 12 miles to Lancaster—talked with Miller and Holl(and) about printing S(ermon.)" (From Humphrey Fullerton's.)

"   19   "Preached psa. 62: 7–11 and preached Acts 2: 39 in the Town-house etc. Then supped etc. with —— Polson Scot, who goes to Charlestown."

May 26   "Rode 12 miles Lancaster. Spoke with Holland about sermon—printing." (From Humphrey Fullerton's.)

July 28   "Rode 26 miles over Susquehanna to Lancaster, preach. Ps. 63: 1–5 preach. 2: 29 then rode to Wm. Allans, tired but safe." (From Dutch Tavern in York, then rode 8 miles to Humphrey Fullerton's in Pequea.)

Lancaster—*Continued*

1761 Apr. 1   "rode 16 miles Lanc.; married Gab. Holms (or Helms) and Mary Moore." (From home.)

Oct. 7   "Rode 34 miles to Baileys Lanc. and home—sick, weary." (From home.)

1762 Feb. 17   "Rode 25 miles to Lancaster Mr. Helms, bought 1-10-0." (From Da. Mitchel's, then rode 15 miles home on 18th.)

1763 May 3   "rode 25 miles to Lancaster—married D. Mitchel—." (From David Mitchel's, then 15 miles home on 4th.)

1764 Jan. 25   "rode 10 miles to Lancaster—Mr. Bigham's—sick—sturgeon." (From Matthew McClung's.)

July 30   "rode 40 miles to Lancaster—preached psalm 72: 15–L and lectured Titus 2: 11–L and baptized Jean, daughter to T. Mitchel—give all praise to God." (From Wm. Brown's, then 15 miles home on 31st.)

Nov. 13   "rode 24 miles to Lan.—married H. Duncan and Jean Mitchel." (From David Mitchel's.)

1765 June 11   "rode 34 miles to York, And. Ferry and Lancaster, Wat. Sug." (From Lynch's—then 15 miles home with Sally on 12th.)

1767 Apr. 6   "rode 37 miles to Shearer's, Stigles, Lancaster, tired." (From Alex. Swan's, then 15 miles home on 7th.)

1769 Jan. 25   "Rode 15 miles to Lancaster; left 4 doll. with Mr. Bickam." (From home.)

1770 Feb. 7   "rode 27 miles to Lancaster—Padlehouser; home, well."

1771 May 8   "rode 15 miles Lancaster; married Sam Stewart and Agnes Templeton (10) parted with Y. next day." (From home.)

1772 Sept. 1   "rode 48 miles (from T. Cross's) to Lancaster with Mrs. Inglis, fv." (Then 15 miles home on 2nd.)

1783 July 14   "rode 20 miles to Lancaster to from Millars, T. Keneats, Jos. Ash." (On 15th rode 17 miles home by McIrvine.")

Level

1751 Sept. 29   "Sabbath. Preached psalm 10: 15–1: Galatians 1: 5–12 and preached Galatians 5: 1 praise to my God then baptized Susannah, daughter to Thomas Ramsay." (At James Robieson's, Level, then rode 1 mile to John Duncan's.)

1754 Nov. 2   "Rode 10 miles to Joseph Kers. Killed a viper snake. Good health, praise to God." (From Humphrey Fullerton's.)

" 3   "Sabbath—Preached psalm 65: 5–9. Lectured Luke 24: 13–25 preached verse 17—o.a. - - -. Baptized James, son to Jos. Ramsay in the Level."

1757 Sept. 11   "Sabbath. at home; preached psalm 106: 12–18 and preached Ephesians 2: 8 and baptized James son to Wm. Robieson; level. Ague ¼ hr."

Level—*Continued*

1757 Sept. 27   "Married John Robieson—lev. and Jean Boyd."

1759 Aug. 28   "rode 15 miles, conveying—and Mr. Smith in the Level."

McDowall's Mill

1752 Feb. 12   "Rode 6 miles to McDowals Miln and Jo. Calbreaths—good health." (From Gateshills Ford, Octoraro.)

Middle Octoraro Society

The principal Society of Mr. Cuthbertson was at Middle Octoraro from August, 1751 to March, 1783, when he was released by the Presbytery. There seems to have been little secession in his work in this locality, however. The church in which he preached was built in 1754, and was rebuilt by the Associate Congregation in 1849. This church went into the Union in 1858, becoming a United Presbyterian Church. The building is now abandoned, but there is hope that it may be restored. As early as 1740 a Covenanter Society formed in the vicinity of Octoraro. Mr. Cuthbertson's first sermon in America was preached here in a tent three miles from the house of Joseph Walker. After his marriage in 1756, Mr. Cuthbertson made his home on a farm about two miles from the stone church. (See pages xvii and xviii for pictures of home and church.)

1751 Aug. 9   "x x rode 8 miles to Joseph Walker's in Mid. Octorara, weary." (From Jo. Ross's, Manor of Newlonderry.)

"   11   "Sabbath. Rode 3 miles to the Tent. Preached psalm 8. Lectured Luke 12: 22–31 and preached Song of Solomon 3."

"   12   "Rode 9 miles to Janet and Robert Loch-head. At Craighead's. . . ."

Sept. 5   (See Colerain Tp.—Daniel McClellan's.)

"   8   "Sabbath—Rode 7 miles to and from the Tent (From Dan McClellan's). Preached psalm 10: 1–6. Lectured Luke 12: 49–54 and preached Galatians 5: 1. Baptized Jo., son to Jo. Kincaid; Mary, daughter to Alexander Lackey; Jean, daughter to William Paterson; Hannah, daughter to Robert Calbreath; John, son to And. Little; Jean, daughter to Jeremiah Murray; Samuel, and Andrew, sons to Joseph Walker; and Mary, daughter to Moses Lockhart, wt. give all praise to my God."

Middle Octoraro Society— *Continued*

1751 Oct. 6 "Sabbath. Rode 6 miles to and from Octorara preached Psa. 11 and Galatians 1: 12–1 preached Acts 10." (From Robert Lochhead's.)

" 9 "Rode 7 miles to Jo. Calbreath's."

" 13 "Sabbath. Preached Psa. 12 and Galatians 2: 1–5, preached Acts 10: 42 and baptized William, s. to James Ewen. Praise to my gracious God."

" 14 "Rode 11 miles to Octorara, married George McKown and Janet Kilpatrick. Held session 3 hours and . . . then rode 3 quarters of a mile to Josias . . . (Ker's)."

1752 Jan. 1 "Concerned with the sins and deliverances of the past year. Rode 6 miles Joseph Walkers—conversed, tired but in good health." (From Poequey.)

" (5) "Sabbath. Rode 6 miles to the meeting, preached psalm 18: 17–23, lectured Galatians 4: 12–19 and preached Hebrews 4: 12. o.a. at William Lauglans, explained psalm 90, give all praise to God. Rode 6 miles to Matthew Ritchies, conversed, prayed, Jo. Walker's, Geo. Dinins and Thomas Givans, tired, sick, miserable. Rode 6 miles to William Kers etc., then to Hunphrey Fulertons. x x."

Feb. 1 "Rode 3 miles to Robert Loughhead's etc." (From Jos. Walker's.)

" 2 "Sabbath. Rode 4 miles. Preached psa. 18: 40–46. Lectured Gal. 5: 7 and preached Heb. 4: 12 and baptized Ann daughter to Robert Ramsay, give all, etc."

" 3 "Travelled 3 miles Wm. Lauchlins. Lectured Psa. 26: 1–6. Baptized Andrew son to Jo. Walker. Examined 26 persons etc."

" 14 "Rode 8 miles to Sam Jacksons and Robert Loughheads—held session." (From Jo Calbreath's.)

" 16 "Sabbath. Rode 10 miles to meeting-house. Preached psa. 18: 46–L. Lectured Gal. 5: 13–17. Preached Isa. 45: 23 and baptized John son to Wm. Lauchlin, pr by the wife. Then went to Wm. Kers, where exer. psalm 30 (gave 23 shillings and 6 pence for 2 shirts etc.)."

Middle Octoraro Society—*Continued*

1752 Feb. 17 "Rode 4 miles to Humphrey Fulerton's. Dejected, etc."

Apr. 26 "Sab. Rode 7 miles to and from meeting preach. Ps. 22: 11–17 lectured So. 1: 7–8 Titus 1.2. bap. Wm. son to John Dunlop and Joseph to Arthur Scot."

"   27 "Rode 1 mile to And. Works x x."

May 3 "Sab. rode 12 miles preached Ps. 22: 17–23 lect. So. 1: 9–12 preach. Titus 1.2 and bap. James S. Isaac Walker Mary daugh. to Joseph Ker and Janet daughter to Walter Buchanan." (From Robert Laughlin's.)

" (8 or 9) "—miles to Nathaniel Coulters married Sam Cachy and Esther Coulter preach. Ps. 77: 1–5 lect. Ephes. 2: 19–L and baptized Wm. and Sarah son and daugh. to Jo. Gilmore, twins, dined, then conversed Wm. Noble. . . ."

"   17 "Sabbath. Rode 13 miles to O. . . . Preached psalm 22: 27–L. Lectured So. 1: 15–L and preached Philip 2: 9 and baptized John son to Wm. Couper. Visited Ar. Scot. Rode to Dan McClellan's."

"   18 "Rode 4 miles to Robert Lochhead's—wrote . . Hall a long letter—good health praise to God."

"   23 "Travelled 2 miles to and from Mat. Richie and James Robieson's—conversed, etc., etc."

"   24 "Sabbath. Rode 4 miles to O.—preached psalm 23. Lectured So. 2: 1–4. x x Preached Philip 2: 9 and baptized Eliz. and Mary, daughters to Dorby McFadgean— came to Josias Kers—good health . . . 19. Preached S. 93: 3–L. Lectured Heb. 10: 19–25. Rebuked Jona. Cumin for Dr. in Exs."

Aug. 9 "Sab. Rode 4 miles (from John Walker's) preach. Ps. 27–7–11, lectured So. 4–4–7. preached 2d Peter 1.4, baptized Jean daughter to Jonathan Cumins good health and give all praise to God."

"   10 "Rode 5 miles, held session till night then went to Robert Lochhead's."

"   13 "Rode 5 miles to R. loch. preach Ps. 146: 1–6, lectured Matt. 17: 24–L. Exc: 30 and baptized Agnes daugh-

Middle Octoraro Society— *Continued*

ter to George McGown 12 years old 5 hours." (From David McClellan's.)

1752 Aug. 16 "Sab. Rode 6 miles, preach. Ps. 27: 11–L, lectured Hos. 14: 1–5, preach 2 Cor. 13: 5 and baptized Benjamin son to Robert McMurray and Mary daughter to Jas. Walker."

" 30 "Sab. Rode 6 miles to and from meeting preach Ps. 28: 1–6, lectured So. 4: 8–10 and preach. 2 Pet. 1–4 then baptized John son to Sam. Leiper give all praise to God." (From Robert Loughhead's.)

Nov. 24 "Rode 12 miles to Joseph Kers and Robert Andrews, went to Jo. K."

" 25 "Rode 3 mi. preach. Ps. 32: 1–5 lect. So. 6: 7–10 preach. Heb. 4: 1 and "

" 26 "Sab. bap. Jean daugh. to Wm. Paterson, then went to Humphrey Fulerton's."

Dec. 12 (See Rocky Spring, Franklin County.)

" 17 "Sab. Rode 4 mi. to preach. Ps. 33: 1–6 lectured So. 7: 1, 2 and preach. Heb. 4: 1 and bap. Moses son to George McGown and then uneasy—to Joseph K."

" 18 "Rode 9 mi. to Humphrey Fulerton's received 3 letters and a box full of B."

1753 Jan. 10 "Rode 4 miles to T. W. after preaching Psalm 84: 8–L. preached Matthew 11: 28–29 and baptized Sarah daughter to Ja. Wilson and Martha daughter to Robert." (At . . . Calbreath's.)

" 12 "Rode 8 miles to Matthew Brown's, Robert Loughhead's ——."

" 14 "Sabbath—Rode 4 miles to meeting, preached Psalm 34: 1–8. Lectured Song of Solomon 7: 10–L and preached Prov. 4: — and at night Wm. McClure's preached Ps. 91: 1—and preached Hebrews 7: —."

Feb. bet. 2 & 11 ". . . miles to . . Fulson's, Margaret to . . . ."

" (18) "Sabbath—Rode 5 miles to meeting house, preached Psalm 35: 8–13, lectured 1 Peter 1: 3–6, preached 1 Samuel 2–30, and baptized Margaret, daughter to Matthew Brown and Jean, daughter to Thomas Pater-

Middle Octoraro Society— *Continued*

son, at Wm. McClure's preached Psalm 71: 3–10 and lectured 1 Thessalonians 3: 13–L. g.a."

1753 Feb. (25) "Sabbath. Rode 6 miles, preached Psalm 35: 13–17, lectured 1 Peter 1: 6–10, preached . . . Mary Stev. (or Stew.) and Ex. Psalm 56, baptized David son to A. . . ." (At G. Brit.—then rode 6 miles to Dan McClellan's.)

Apr. 8 (For ordination of James Wilson as Elder see Rocky Spring, Franklin County.)

May 27 "Sab. Rode 12 mi. on Saturday and Sab. to and from meeting and John Walker's preach Ps. 38: 8–12, lectured 1 Peter 3: 5–8 and preached Romans 9: 32 and bap. Samuel son to Sam Cachy and Mary daugh. to John Morton."

June 5 "Lectured Ps. 25: 1–12 examined 40 persons and baptized Mary daugh. to Isaac Walker and rode 4 miles to Sam Jackson's." (At Jas. Wilson's—then rode 6 miles to Jeremiah McFadian's on 6th.)

July 29 "Sab. Rode 12 mi. (from Dan McClellan's). Preached Ps. 40: 12–L. lectured 1 Peter 4: 12–14 and preached Jer. 3, 4 and baptized Wm. son to John Dunlop and John son to Thomas Ramsay." (Then rode 9 miles to Joseph Ker's on Aug. 1.)

Aug. 12 "Sab. rode 7 mi. preach. Ps. 41: 7–L. lectured 1 Peter 4: 18–L and preached John 5: 40 g.a. and baptized Sam son to John Kinkead—offer of Christ." (From Robert Loughhead's.)

" 14 "Rode 5 mi. after marrying John Walker and Rebecca Ross (At Robert Loughhead's.)

Oct. 24 "Rode 7 miles to Robert Lochhead's—disorderly sale there." (From Robert Andrews.)

" 25 "Travelled 2 miles to And. Little—conversed, etc. with Martha etc."

" 28 "Sabbath. Rode 6 miles to and from M. preached Psalm 45: 6–10. Lectured 2 Peter 1: 19–L and preached Galatians 5: 17. Baptized Abel son to Abel Finlay. g.a. praise."

Nov. 11 "Sabbath. Rode 7 miles. Preached psalm 45: 14–L. Lectured 2 Peter 2: 4–7. Preached Galatians 5: 17 and baptized Robert son to James Loughhead—conversed etc. at night." (From Dan McClellan's.)

" 19 "Travelled 2 miles to and from W. McClure's. Married William Reid and Jean Muir." (From Joseph Ker's.)

Dec. 4 "Rode 7 miles to John Duncan's—good health, praise to my gracious God. (2 meetings Sabbath night,

Middle Octoraro Society— *Continued*

December 2nd.) Exercises at Ro(bert) L(ochheads) psalm 61—2 hours, and baptized Susa, daughter to And. Little and Janet, daughter to Arch. Burns, g.a."

1754 Jan. 14   "Rode 6 miles to Joseph Walker's after marrying (at John Walker's) James Brown and Mary McClellan. Then explained psalm 137 and baptized James, ad. son to Jo. Wilson and Sarah, daughter to Sam."

Feb. 28   "Rode 7 miles to etc. Married James Young and Mary Walker. Stayed late, cavilled with Math. R. and visited David Ryburn, by the favor of God." (From Dan McClellan's.)

May 29   "Held session 3 hours. Preached psalm 125: 1–L. Examined 40 persons and baptized David and John sons to Mathew Richie—Christ's 3 offices."

Oct. 6   "Sabbath—Rode 12 miles—preached psalm 64: 1–5. Lectured Amos 5: 6–11 and preached 2 Corinthians 5: 10—sick. Baptized Thomas, son to Peter Paterson. Went to Dan McClellan's."

" 10   "Rode 4 miles—still sick. Married Matthew Ritchie and Mary Ca.

" 13   "Sabbath—Rode 4 miles. Preached psalm 64: 5–L. Lectured Romans 13: 5 - - - preached Hebrews 4: 13. Baptized Thomas son to Hew Fergus. Give all praise to my God - - to Joseph - - -."

" 14   "Rode 3 miles to Jo. Walker's, after holding session 6 hours, etc."

" 20   "Sabbath. Rode 6 miles. (From Robert Loughhead's.) Preached psalm 65: 1–5. Preached 2 o'clock Hebrews 4: 13. Admitted to the office of Ruling Elders: Phin. Whiteside, Robert Calbreath, William Calbreath, Walter Buchanan, Jo. McMillan, Jo. Duncan, and Thomas Ramsay. Baptized John son to Joseph - - -."

" 22   "Rode 12 miles. Visited two sick people. Thomas and Jo. Dowglas, James, Walter, Charles - - -."

Dec. (15)   "Sabbath—Rode 4 miles. Preached psalm 65: 1–7. Lectured Luke 24: 41–49. Preached Romans 4: 23: g.a. etc. Baptized Elizabeth, daughter to James Lough(head)." (From Robert Loughhead's.)

" 29   "Sabbath. Rode 6 miles. Preached psalm 68: 11–18 and preached Romans 7: 23 and baptized Margaret, daughter to Ben McCormick. g.a." (From Robert Loughhead's.)

1755 May 18   "Sabbath. Rode 6 miles to meeting-house preached psalm 73: 1–11 lectured Amos 6: 7–L and preached

Middle Octoraro Society— *Continued*

Micah 5: 5—baptized James son to Thomas Paterson, James son to Wm. Robieson and John son to James Duncan give all praise to God." (From Robert Lochhead's.)

1755 May 27 "Rode 5 miles to Robert Andrews, the Creek Octorara." (From Robert Lochhead's.)

"   28 "Rode 5 miles to Matthew Brown's after preaching Psalm 146: 1–7. Examined 60 persons and baptized Humphrey son to Robert Andrews and Sam son to T. Crosan."

"   29 "Rode 6 miles to Jo Robieson's good health but Matthew Brown's in vain."

"   30 "Rode 4 miles to Da. McClellan,—after preaching psalm 83 and examining 70 persons."

June 1 "Sabbath. Rode 6 miles preached psalm 73: 16–23 lectured Amos 7: 10–L and preached Micah 5: 5 and baptized Samuel son to George Marlin—give all praise to God."

Sept. 28 "Sabbath. Preached psalm 78: 12–20, lectured Matthew 6: 9–14, preached 1 Peter 5: 8 and baptized Ann daughter to Thomas Ramsay, Margaret daughter to Th. Paxton." (At Joseph Ker's.)

"   29 "Rode 4 miles to Ro. Loughheads after catechizing 20 persons and preaching psalm 43."

Oct. 20 "Preached psalm 101, preached Revelations 3: 11 g.a. on night 18th and baptized Jean daughter to James Wilson Notingham." (At Joseph Ker's.)

Nov. 2 "Sabbath. Rode 6 miles preached psalm 78: 46–53, lectured Matthew 8: 31–L. preached Hosea 3: 3 baptized James C. son to James Paterson explained psalm 140: 1–9 and baptized Janet to Sam Cachy." (From Dan McClellan's.)

Dec. 3 "Tramped 2 miles to and from Math Richies. . . ." (From Robert Loughhead's.)

"   7 "Sabbath. Rode 6 miles, preached psalm 79: 1–5, lectured Matthew 7: 6–13, preached Hosea 3: 3 g.a. baptized Alexander S. to James Anderson explained psalm 68: 28–L and baptized Robert S. to Mathew Richie." (From Robert Loughhead's.)

1756 Jan. 7 "Rode 6 miles to Joseph Walker's, John Welsh—Removed hind shoes." (From Humphrey Fullerton's.)

Middle Octoraro Society— *Continued*

1756 Jan.   8   "Fast day—Rode 6 miles to Robert Loughheads—
Preached psalm 78: 5–12.   Preached Revelations 14:
7 and baptized George, son to Sam Paxton, presented
by the mother."

Feb. 22   "Tramped 1¼ miles, preached psalm 83: 1–9, lectured
Matthew 7: 13–21 and baptized Alexander, son to
George McGown, give all praise to God." (From
Joseph Ker's.)

Apr.   4   "Sabbath.   Rode 5 miles, preached psalm 85: 6–L, lec-
tured Matthew 8: 20–L, preached Mark 9: 22, baptized
Arthur son to Pat. Nugent and Isabel daughter to Jo.
Dunlop explained psalm 69: 1–9 and baptized David
son to James Lochhead g.a. very pub. against the sec."
(From Robert Lochhead's.)

"   5   "Rode 11 miles to J. Duncan's after marrying Robert
Calbreath and Elizabeth Camin." (Cumings?)

May 12   "Rode 4 miles to widow Calbreath's in a heavy thunder
gust etc." (From James Wilson's.)

"   13   "Preached psalm 146: 7–L and examined 40 persons and
baptized Jean daughter to Isaac Walker; James son
to John Walker and Janet daughter to Robert Law; a
great gust etc."

"   15   "Rode 10 miles to Robert Andrews; stayed 3 hours,
then to Dan McClellans."

"   16   "Sabbath.   Rode 6 miles; preached psalm 88: 1–8; lectured Hosea 13: 1–5 and preached 2d Chronicles 20:
20 g.a. and baptized Mary daughter to David Carson."

June 7   "Married James Paterson and Florence Dale; then
preached psalm 110 and examined 50 persons x x."
(At Robert Lochhead's.)

Aug. 17   "Five years this day since landing in America.(?)   Rode
21 miles to Jo Sloans; married James Mitchel and Mary
Sloan. psalm 76 and lectured 1 Samuel 12: 20–L g.a.
went to Dan McClellans." (From Wm. Brown's.)

Sept. 26   "Sabbath.   Rode 6 miles; preached psalm 91: 5–10;
lectured Matthew 12: 38–48 and preached psalm 119:
37 and baptized Mary daughter to Robert McConel;
good health." (From Robert Lochhead's.)

Oct. (5)   "Preached psalm 54: 8–L and preached psalm 20: 5 g.a.
(at home) baptized Isaac son to John Mooney and

Middle Octoraro Society— *Continued*

Mary to John Crooks, rode 9 ——." (Then 5 miles to Joseph Walker's.)

1756 Nov. (14) "Sabbath. Rode 6 miles, preached psalm 47: 7–14, lectured Matthew 13: 33–34 and preached —— and baptized Hew, son to Hew Fergus and John son to Sam ——." (From Middle Octorara or Robert Lochhead's.)

" 30 "Rode 18 miles to J. Neilies, after preaching psalm 1–6 and preaching 2d Corinthians —— (at Robert Gilmore's) and baptizing James son to James Davidson ——."

1757 Jan. 24 "x x bought Josias Kers plantation at 350 lib. paid 93 lib. lodged there." (At Middle Octoraro.)

Apr. 24 "Sabbath; tramped; preached psalm 103: 8–13; lectured Matthew 17: 28–L; and preached Matthew 21: 42 g.a. Baptized James son to Lodowick Laird." (At Robert Lochhead's.)

May 1 "Sabbath. Rode 8 miles; preached psalm 103: 12–17; lectured Matthew 18: 1–7 preached Matthew 21: 42 and baptized Agnes to Walter Buchanan and James son to Robert Brison. x x Baptized John son to Joseph Walker; dead. God's wrath." (From home.)

June 5 "Sabbath. Rode 4 miles to Joseph Kers; preached psalm 104: 13–19; lectured Matthew 19: 1–19; preached Zephaniah 2: 1 and baptized Josiah to Jos. Ker, Isobel daughter to Hugh Coulter, Mary daughter to Thomas Paterson and John son to James Paterson give all praise—in the night." (From Daniel McClellan's.)

Aug. 7 "Sabbath. Preached psalm 105: 32–40; lectured Matthew 21: 17–28 and preached Genesis 18: 27 and baptized Moses son to Robert Andrew o.a. etc." (At home.)

" 27 "Preached psalm 15: preached Solomon 2: 10 and baptized John and Margaret son and daughter to Wm. Gr(ier?)." (At Robert Lochhead's.)

" 28 "Sabbath preached x x 240 communing."

" 29 "Preached psalm 23; preached John 1: 29 and baptized Wm. and Jean son and daughter widow Mitchel and Martha to widow Berrykil."

Sept. 20 "Married Thomas Niely and Margaret Paterson; shaked 2." (At home.)

Oct. 23 "Sabbath sick; preached psalm 106: 29–36; lectured Matthew 22: 23–34 and baptized Thomas son to T. Ramsay—x x." (At home.)

Nov. 6 "Sabbath. Preached psalm 106: 43–L; lectured Mat-

Middle Octoraro Society— *Continued*

thew 23: 1–12 and baptized Elizabeth daughter to Humphrey Fulerton; sick." (At home.)

1757 Nov. 8   "Married John Thomson and Mary Steven.—." (At home.)

" 13   "Sabbath. Preached psalm 107: 1–9 and lectured Matthew 23: 13–23 and baptized John son to Ben McCormick, Wm. son to John Rob. and Sarah daughter to widow Berrykil." (At home.)

" 14   "Rode 9 miles to W. Greer's; married Nath. Coulter and Gr. Lough."

1758 Jan. 16   "Rode 8 miles to S. Cachys—R. Cou. and to Robert Lochheads." (From home.)

" 17   "Rode 3 miles to Mat. Browns—married John McKnaught and Mary Paterson—then preached psalm 126 and lectured Matthew 28 and baptized William son to Matthew Brown."

" 18   "Rode 3 miles back to Robert Lochheads—tired but well."

Feb. 1   "rode 4 miles to and from T. Ramsays etc.—visited." (From home.)

" 7   "Rode 5 miles to and from W. McClure's, D. Hannaes—cold." (From home.)

" 13   "Rode 4 miles to R. L's held session—preached psalm 139: 1–5. Lectured Acts 8: 35–38 g.a. Baptized Janet, daughter to James Lochhead—praise to my God." (From home.)

" 14   "Rode 8 miles to G. McGown, R. A's and W. Calbreath's."

" 15   "Rode 10 miles to and from Martha Laws and R. Andrews—preached psalm 138: 4–L preached Revelations 3: 1 and baptized Joseph, son to George Mitchel, Jean, daughter to James Wilson."

" 16   "Rode and walked 6 miles to and from H. Coulter's and R. Lochheads."

" 17   "Rode 4 miles home."

Mar. 1   "Rode 6 miles after preaching psalm 69: 1–5, lecturing Philippians 3: 13–L and baptizing James son to Wm. Paterson—give all praise to God—went to Dan McClellan's." (From John Duncan's.)

Middle Octoraro Society— *Continued*

1758 Mar. 2   "Rode 6 miles to A. Works etc. and home."

Apr. 24   "Married Andrew Ferrier and Jean Marlin." (At home.)

May 7   "Sabbath preached psalm 7–13; Lectured Matthew 27: 39–50. Preached Jeremiah 17: 9 and baptized Sarah, daughter to William Greer—give all praise to God." (At home.)

"   14   "Sabbath—preached psalm 116: 13–L. Lectured Matthew 27: 50–L. Preached Jeremiah 17: 9 and baptized Jean daughter to James Duncan—give all praise to God." (At home.)

June 11   "Sabbath—preached psalm 118: 12–17. Lectured Obadiah 1: 10. Preached Jeremiah 17: 9 and baptized Thomas, son to Peter Paterson o.a., praise to my gracious God." (At home.)

"   15   "rode 10 miles to and from R. L's—at McCarter's, child's burying."

"   16   "tramped 5 miles to and from T. Ramsays etc."

"   18   "Sabbath preached psalm 118: 17–22. Lectured Obadiah 10–17. Preached Jeremiah 17: 9 and baptized Esther, daughter to Cornelius Collins g.a. etc."

July 2   "Sabbath—preached psalm 119: 1–9. Lectured Jonah 1: 1–8. Preached Philippians 4: 5 and baptized James, son to James Ewen and Isobel, daughter to Mat. Richie."

"   4   "rode 10 miles to Widow Vernon's, married Thomas Black and Margaret McCubray. Then rode 5 miles— saw 300 sold—went to Humphrey Fulertons."

"   5   "Rode 10 miles to J. Elliot's, John Welsh's, Jos. Walker's —home off at ——."

"   7   "rode 11 miles F. Walker's—R. Loughhead's with —— then home."

"   8   "rode 8 miles to Dutch Dr. for Frank's throat—reaped rye."

Aug. 3   "Rode 8 miles to Matthew Brown's—preached psalm 60: 1–5 explained Ephesians 2: 19–L and baptized Rachel daughter to John Gardner—very hot." (From home.)

Middle Octoraro Society— *Continued*

1758 Oct.   1   "Sabbath—preached psalm 119—11th part. Lectured Micah 1: 1–6 and preached Genesis 42: 21, 22 and baptized Moses, son to Sam Paxton—presented by mother." (At home.)

"   8   "Sabbath—preached 119: 12th part. Lectured Micah 1: 6–10 and preached Genesis 42: 21, 22 and baptized Thomas son to Thomas Paterson; James, son to David Dinwiddy; and Mary, daughter to Hew Fergus." (At home.)

"   10   "rode 7 miles to John Robeson—Lectured John 15: 1–6 and baptized John son to John Robeson; and Margaret, daughter to Eliz. Ayers." (From home—then 8 miles to John McMillan's on 11th.)

"   15   "Sabbath—tramped 2 miles to and from meeting-house —preached psalm 119—13th part. Lectured Micah 1: 10 preached Ephesians 1: 7 and baptized Joseph, son to James Reid x x." (At home.)

"   22   "Sabbath—preached psalm 119—14th part. Lectured Micah 2: 1–6—preached Ephesians 1: 7 and baptized James, son to John McClellan—o.a. praise my gracious God." (At home.)

"   31   "Married James Paterson and Mary McCord 3.9." (At home.)

Nov.   1   "rode 6 miles to A. Stewart's after preaching psalm 68: 15–21 and lecturing Mark 4: 35–L and baptizing Samuel son to Sam. Martin, presented by the mother."

"   26   "Sabbath—preached psalm 119—19th part. Lectured Micah 3: 9–L. Preached Nahum 1: 7 and baptized Nathaniel, son to Sam Cachy; and Isaac, son to John Thomson." (At home.)

Dec.   20   "rode 8 miles to Dan McClellan's Mathew Brown's and James McKts." (From home.)

"   21   "rode 8 miles home after marrying Hew and Mary Black —preached psalm 98: 1—Explained Romans 13: 11–L. Baptized Samuel son to Henry Calbreath; Margaret daughter to John Money; and Jean daughter to James Anderson."

1759 Jan.   2   "rode 4 miles to R. Lochhead's—preached psalm 66: 8–15 and explained John 8: 28–33 and baptized Agnes daughter to Hew Coulter." (From home.)

"   7   "Sabbath—preached psalm 122: 1–6. Lectured Micah 4: 3–6 and baptized John, son to James Ramsay."

Feb.   8   "rode 7 miles—visited—married John Park and Isobel

Middle Octoraro Society— *Continued*

Calbreath; Peter Wilson and Jean Calbreath—went to J. D's." (Then rode 9 miles home on 9th.)

1759 Feb. 18 "Sabbath—preached psalm 127. Lectured Micah 5: 10–L and baptized Nathaniel son to Natha. Coulter had a sweet night." (At home.)

" 22 "rode 10 miles home—married Sam. Rob. and Eleanor Dicks(on?)." (From James Ross's.)

" 25 "Sabbath—preached psalm 128. Lectured Micah 6: 1–6. Preached Revelations 3: 11 and baptized Mary, daughter to Ben. McCormick." (At home.)

Mar. 9 "rode 6 miles to widow McCormick's, R. Ramsay's, etc. —visited."

" 23 "Margaret Bell was bound with me 2 years and 5 ——."

" 25 "Sabbath—preached psalm 132: 1–7. Lectured Micah 7: 5–9—preached John 12–28 and baptized Loetitia. daughter to Richard Burns—give all praise to my gracious God." (At home.)

Apr. 11 "rode 10 miles home—wife abroad—all well—praise to my gracious God." (From John Dunlap's.)

" 15 "Sabbath—preached psalm 132: 13–L. Lectured Micah 7: 14–18—preached James 4: 10 and baptized John, son to John Robb—give all praise to my gracious God favoring me, etc."

" 17 "br. and sis. off—married John Paterson and Sarah McCord 5 s."

" 22 "Sabbath—preached psalm 133. Lectured Micah 7: 3–1—visited and preached James 4: 10 g.a. and baptized Sam, son to Robert Calbreath praise to my gracious God."

" 29 "Sabbath—preached psalm 134. Lectured Phil. 1: 1–5 preached Malachi 3: 16, 17 and baptized John son to Jean Crossen; James son to Jos. McKt. and Sarah, daughter to James Paterson g.a. etc." (At home.)

" 30 "rode 10 miles with — — to Da. Marsh and John Duncan's g.a." (From home.)

June 3 "Sabbath—preached psalm 136: 1–9. Lectured Phil. 1: 22–27—preached Malachi 3: 17 and baptized Nathaniel son to Isaac Walker." (At home.)

Middle Octoraro Society— *Continued*

1759 June 6 "rode and walked 8 miles to Hanna Walker's, T. and home." (From home.)

"   10 "Sabbath—preached psalm 136: 9–21. Lectured Phil. 1: 27–L—preached Malachi 3: 17 and baptized William son to And. Ferier and Sus. and Robert, daughter and son to Agnes Barber—give all praise to God—sent J.- -"

"   12 "rode 19 miles to and from Betty Duncan's burial— out Lib. B. coure." (From home.)

"   19 "rode 10 miles home by John Eliot's—conversed." (From Humphrey Fulerton's.)

July 11 "rode 8 miles to and from R. Lochhead's—wife dyed asleep that night." (From home.)

" 12, 13 "rode 8 miles to and from Lochhead's—wife's burial, etc." (From home.)

"   19 "rode 16 miles to and from James McKnaught's visiting his wife." (From home.)

"   29 "Sabbath—preached psalm 139: 7–19. Lectured Philippians 2: 25–L and preached Galatians 3: 27—give all praise to God—and baptized Hannah, daughter to W. Robieson—great rain." (At home.)

"   30 "rode 9 miles to and from J. Kyle's, A. W's., etc., visiting sick, etc."

Aug. 1 "rode 9 miles home—wrote out J. Lowry's Journal." (From Humphrey Fullerton's.)

"   9 "rode 12 miles Kyle's—Married James Henry and Sus. McKnaught, etc."

Sept. 2 "Sabbath—preached psalm 140: 1–6. Lectured Philippians 3: 10–12—preached Galatians 3: 27 and baptized Agnes, daughter to Robert McCurdy o.a. praise God." (At home or Level.)

Dec. 17 "Tramped 6 miles to and from S. Paxton's: visited Nath. dying." (From home.)

"   24 "Rode 9 miles to Paxton's, W. Thomson's, paid 2-18-0." (From home.)

"   25 "Married John Taylor and Mary Wilson—snowed."

1760 Jan. 3 "Tramped and rode 8 miles; married Daniel Sinclar and Isobel Gray etc. received dol. from him." (From home.)

Middle Octoraro Society— *Continued*

1760 Jan. 31 "Married James Scot and Janet Alexander—x x." (At home.)

Feb. 3 "Sabbath—preached psalm 145: 1–8 and lectured Nahum 1: 10–L o.a. etc." (At home.)

" 7 "Rode 8 miles to T. G's, married James Broedy and Elizabeth Girvan."

" 10 "Sabbath—preached psalm 145–8–13 and preached 1 Peter 2: 3 and baptized W. son to James Lochhead. give all praise to my gracious God."

" 17 "Sabbath—preached psalm 145: 13–17; preached 1 Peter 2: 3 and baptized Janet daughter to Sam Colhoun, give all praise to God; x x." (At home.)

" 24 "Sabbath—Preached psalm 145: 17–L; preached 1 Peter 2: 3 and baptized Margaret, daughter to Patrick Nugent, give all praise to my gracious God." (At home.)

Mar. 4 "Tramped 3 miles; married Sam Leiper and Mary McDr. (Br.?) . . ." (From home.)

Apr. 27 "Sabbath—preached psalm 149: 1–5. Lectured Habakkuk 1: 14–L—preached Romans 8: 30. o.a. and baptized Agnes, daughter to Robert Andrews, Martha, daughter to William Anderson; and Johns, sons to Margaret Reynolds and Agnes Barber—hot, hot." (At home.)

May 7 "rode with Lr. (or Fr.) 8 miles to and from Noll's, Walker's, etc., etc. (From home.)

" 11 "Sabbath—preached 149: 7–L, lectured Habakkuk 2: 5–9 preached Romans 8: 30 g.a. Baptized Wm. son to John Park and Thomas son to James Ramsay." (At home.)

" 25 "Sabbath—preached psalm 1: 1–4, lectured Habakkuk 2: 15–L preached psalm 119: 37 and baptized James son to Cornelius Collins g.a., plain, etc." (At home.)

" 26 "rode 8 miles to Humphrey Fulertons."

" 27 "rode 8 miles home; preached psalm 119: 57–61, baptized B. Thomas son to Humphrey Fulerton."

June (2 or 3) "Rode 7 miles to and from James Wilson's to lease and release."

July 17 "rode 9 miles to H. Coulters R. L's. Joseph Millers and home." (From home.)

" 27 "Sabbath—preached psalm 5: 10—lectured Zephaniah

Middle Octoraro Society— *Continued*

1: 15 preached the same and baptized Hanna daughter to James K——." (At home.)

1760 July 30   "Rode 14 miles to and from W. Greers; preached psalm 93 examined 18; baptized Susan daughter to him."

Aug. 4   "Rode 8 miles to Thomsons, Joseph Walkers, etc. held session 3 hours." (From home.)

"   10   "Sabbath—preached psalm 6: 6–L; lectured Zephaniah 12: 4–8 preached Zechariah 1: 4 baptized Sam son to T. Cross, Mary daughter to Ad. Richie and Rachel daughter to Math. Richie. x x."

Sept. 7   "Sabbath—preached psalm 7: 9–14. Lectured Zephaniah 3: 1–5; preached Songs 8: 5 and baptized Isaac son to Isaac Walker; Jean and Alexander, daughter and son to William Hamilton." (At home.)

"   12   "rode 6 miles to and from John Wilson's, etc. bought y. cow 3-0-0 retu."

"   14   "Sabbath—preached psalm 7: 14–L. Lectured Zephaniah 3: 5–8—preached Songs 8: 5 and baptized Robert son to Robert McCurdy—give all praise to my gracious God."

Oct. 26   "Sabbath—preached psalm 2: 16–L. Lectured Zephaniah 3: 18–L. x x and baptized Susanna, daughter to Thomas Paterson." (At home.)

Nov. 7   "rode and walked 8 miles—married Thomas Montgomery and Sus. McG." (From home.)

Dec. 22   "rode 10 miles to and from T. Girvan's. Dr. sick dangerously." (From home.)

"   24   "rode 10 miles to and from R. L's, and Dun. Evans. etc."

"   31   "tramped 6 miles to and from W. T. and J. Walker's— married Alexander Stewart and Jean Walker—sick at night with cold." (From home.)

1761 Feb. 8   "Sabbath—preached psalm 17: 1–5. Lectured Ephesians 1: 18–21 and baptized William son to N. Cou." (At home.)

"   11, 12   "rode 15 miles to R. L's. and James McKt's. preached psalm 68: 18–21. Catechized 2—and baptized David

Middle Octoraro Society— *Continued*

son to John McKt. and Jerem. son to Hew Black."
(From home.)

1761 Feb. 17   "Rode 12 miles to Alex. Camp's—37 s for 10 books to
S. Rols."   (From home.)

"   18   "Rode 12 miles home; preached psalm 63: 1–6; preached
1 Corinthians 15: 29 and baptized John son (to) Rob."

"   24   "Rode 10 miles to John Duncan's.   Paid W. Gebby
8-19-9."   (From home.)

"   26   "Rode 18 miles, married John Morton and Susan Smith."
(From John Duncan's.)

"   27   "Rode 9 miles home after visiting Jos. Ker's mill."

Mar.   4   "Rode 4 miles to Jos. Walker's; preached psalm 103:
1–5; exam. 40 persons and baptized David son to James
Broedy and Letitia to Richard Burns."   (From home.)

"   19   "rode 9 miles home; married T. Ramsay and Betty
McDowel."   (From R. Andrew's.)

"   22   "Sabbath preached psalm 18: 14–18; lectured Ephesians
2: 6–9 and baptized James son Benj. McCormick, Janet
to John Thomson and Elizabeth daughter to Sam
Leiper; give all praise to my gracious God."   (At
home.)

"   26   "Rode 4 miles by J. Brigham's to Robert Loughhead's—
x x."

"   27   "Rode 4 miles home after session; preached psalm 49:
15–L; catechized 40 and baptized Francis son to Henry
Calbreath; good health praise God."

Apr.   6   "Married James Ramsay and Jean Birney; also T. Scott
and Janet Brown G. meeting etc. next June."   (At
home.)

June   8   "rode 36 miles to and from John Scotts; married Thomas
Mitchel and Sarah Scott; also Wm. Calbreath and Jean
Lowry."   (From home.)

"   14   "Sabbath preached psalm 21: 1–5; lectured Ephesians
3: 1–13 and preached 1 Corinthians 15: 28 and baptized James son to Walter Buchanan and Mary daughter to Wm. Hamilton; give all praise to my gracious
God."   (At home.)

"   15   "rode 8 miles to Humphrey Fulerton's after marrying
Wm. Cuthry and Esther Mc(Millan?)."

"   16   "rode 10 miles home; preached psalm 85; lectured Acts

Middle Octoraro Society— *Continued*

2: 27 and baptized Charles son to Matthew McClung, and Margaret to T. Black."

1761 June 21 "Sabbath—preached psalm 21: 5–9; lectured Ephesians 3: 13–16 preached John 3: 36 g.a. and baptized John to Sam Cachy—."

" 28 "Sabbath—preached psalm 21: 9 lectured Ephesians 3: 16–19. preached John 3: 36 and baptized James son to John Rob and Margaret daughter to James Paters."

" 30 "rode 10 miles etc. bought 3-6-0 books—Poak's."

July 26 "Sabbath—preached psalm 22: 15–21. Lectured Ephesians 4: 6–9—preached 2 Corinthians 15: 17 and baptized Sarah, daughter to John McCormick—great rain —o.a." (At home.)

Aug. 17 "Preached psalm 23; preached Titus 2: 11, 12; dismissed singing psalm 101 and baptized Jean and Sarah, wife and daughter to Adam Richy." (At home.)

" 30 "Sabbath—preached psalm 24: 6—lectured Ephesians 4: 17–20, preached Matthew 16: 24 and baptized." (At home.)

" 31 "Rode 6 miles; bought cow, Henry Rocky, 3-5-0; mowed, and baptized Mary daughter to James Anderson on the 30th g.a." (From home.)

Oct. 18 "Sabbath preached psalm 27: 1—lectured Ephesians 5: 1–5; preached same baptized Sam son to Agnes Barber. o.a. praise God. Very weary."

Nov. 6 "Rode 5 miles to and from McCarters—." (From home.)

" 19 "rode 6 miles to and from; married Gab. Walker and Margaret Bell." (From home.)

Dec. 2 "Rode 11 miles R. L's. and widow Galbreaths—Thos." (From home.)

" 3 "Rode 6 miles to Jo. Walkers after preaching psalm 98: 1–5 and lectured John 3: 1 and baptized Mary daughter to John Walker, o.a. praise God, etc."

" 4 "Rode 10 miles home; paid Joseph Miller 2-14-3 for the gall."

" 21, 22 "Rode 8 miles to Walkers and to see Ryburn at widow Smith's."

Dec. 30 &
1762 Jan. 1 "Rode 5 miles to D. Ryburns burial and to Edwards." (From home.)

Middle Octoraro Society—*Continued*

1762 Jan. 5 "Rode 7 miles; visited; to James Ramsays and James
Patersons."

"   6 "Rode 2 miles to W. P's, A. Thomsons and widow
Smiths."

"   7 "Rode 5 miles to John Marshals; preached psalm 42:
1–5; lectured Philippians 2: 1–6 and baptized Williams
sons to Wm. Paterson and John Morton."

"   8 "Rode 7 miles Mr. Works etc. W. Dennys and home;
sick."

Feb. 18 "Rode 15 miles home (from Lancaster), all well, etc.
bought Ax from Brewer—."

"   24 "Rode 9 miles with brother Fullton to Loch., Miller,
home." (From home.)

Mar. 18 "Rode 10 miles home (from Robert Andrew's); married
Andrew McKt. and Ann Blackburn."

May 2 "Sabbath preached psalm 34: 18–L; lectured Haggai 1:
1–7 and preached 2 Peter L and last v and baptized
Thomas to Thomas Black, o.a."

"   3 "6 miles to and from Hew Coulters; borrowed 10 pounds
till July."

"   4 "Tramped 3 miles; married John Patterson and Agnes
Scott."

"   6 "Married Joseph Brostrer and Mary McKnight." (At
home.)

" bet.
17 & 20 "35 miles with R. Loch. and wife by R. Thomson."
(From home.)

"   21 "10 miles before 8 morning; wife delivered of daughter
(Sarah), praise God."

"   23 "Sabbath preached psalm 35: 11–17; lectured Haggai 2:
6–10 and preached John 3: 5 o.a. baptized Wm. son to
Cornelius Colins; g.a." (At home.)

June 1 "Married Robert Lochhead and Martha McKnaught."

"   2 "Rode 10 miles to Robert Lochheads, Thomson's, Nolls
and home." (From Thomas Ramsay's.)

"   6 "Sabbath preached psalm 35: 21–L; lectured Haggai 2:
10–17 preached John 3: 5, and baptized Robert son to
James Spier and Mary, daughter to Widow Duncan."
(At home.)

Middle Octoraro Society— *Continued*

1762 June 27   "Sabbath preached psalm 37: 1–7; lectured Zechariah 1: 7–12 and preached John 3: 5 and baptized Mary daughter to Wm. Greer and Sarah ———." (At home.)

"   28   "Rode 18 miles to my friend R. Andrews burial."

"   29   "Rode 18 miles to Robert Lochheads; married John Ritchie and Margaret Lochhead."

Sept. 9   "Rode 8 miles Colin Brown's, J. Walker's, etc." (From home.)

"   19   "Sabbath preached psalm 39: 1–5; lectured Zechariah 3: 1–4; preached John 6: 29 and baptized Matthew son to Matthew Brown, Isobel daughter to John Rob, Margaret to James Ross, Eleanor to Hew Black." (At home.)

Oct. 31   "Sabbath preached psalm 40: 10–12; lectured Zechariah 3: 5–8 preached Matthew 16: 26 and baptized Mathew son to Dan Sinclair; Alex. son to Thomas Paterson. Thomas and Wm. sons to James Broeden o.a. praise to my gracious God."

Nov. 21   "Sabbath preached psalm 41: 1–5 and preached Matthew 16: 26 and baptized Wm. son James Ramsay." (At home.)

Dec. 7, 8   "Rode 16 miles to and from James McKt.; preached psalm 56, lectured Matthew 6: 31–L and baptized Jean daughter to Wm. Broeden." (From home.)

"   15   "Rode 16 miles—married John Walace, Margaret Shenan; and Th. McClellan and Mary Guthry—received 10 from W.—cold day." (From home.)

1763 Jan. 25   "rode 9 miles to . . . Works, and W. Stewarts conversed, etc." (From home.)

"   31   "rode 8 miles to Jos. Walker's, Eliot's, McCain's and H. Fulerton's." (From home.)

Feb. 15   "rode 5 miles to W. Downey's and R. Lochhead's, very cold, etc." (From home.)

"   16   "rode 4 miles home—catechized 40 persons—preached psalm 85: 6–L."

"   24   "in Gavin Kirkpatrick's married George Cumings and Margaret Kirkpatrick—agreeable company."

Mar. 16, 17   "rode 8 miles to and from W. Greer's. Preached psalm 39: 1–5 catechized 30 persons. Baptized Williams, sons to Sam Rob and Adam Richie; and Janet, daughter to Nath. Coulter." (From home.)

"   18   "rode 6 miles to and from Hugh Coulter's."

"   20   "Sabbath—preached psalm 45: 13–L and preached He-

Middle Octoraro Society— *Continued*

brews 4: 14. Baptized John, son to James Paterson. Lectured Zechariah 7: 1–4." (At home.)

1763 May 8 "Sabbath—preached psalm 48–6–11. Lectured Zechariah 9: 1–9. Preached Hebrews 10: 23 and baptized William son to William Hamilton." (At home.)

"   15 "Sabbath—preached psalm 48: 11–L. Preached Zechariah 9: 9–13. Preached Hebrews 10: 23 and baptized Sarah, daughter to John Dunlap—give all praise to God." (At home.)

June 5 "Sabbath—preached psalm 49: 14–L. Lectured Zechariah 10: 5–9. Preached Hebrews 10: 23 and baptized John son to And. McKnaught—give all praise to God." (At home.)

" bet.
6 & 9 "rode 16 miles to Widow Galbreath's and home. Preached psalm 119: 97—catechized 60 persons and baptized Joseph, son to John Walker."

"   (26) "Sabbath—preached psalm 50: 2–18. Lectured Zechariah 11: 7–12—preached 1 Samuel 30: 6 and baptized Rebekah, daughter to John Richie, o.a. praise to my gracious God." (At home.)

July 17 "Sabbath—preached psalm 51: 7–14. Lectured Zechariah 12: 6–10 preached Luke 1: 27 o.a. and baptized Martha, daughter to Robert Loughhead." (At home.)

"   31 "Sabbath—preached psalm 52: 1–6. Lectured Zechariah 13: 1–6 and preached Luke etc. Baptized Jean daughter to Jo. Thomson." (At home.)

Aug. 10 "rode 9 miles (from home) to and from Sam Hawthorn's —got 20 bus(hels)."

"   11 "Fast-day—prayed about the Causes—preached psalm 74: 18–L—preached Zechariah 12: 10 and baptized Rebekah and Mary to William Stewart."

"   21 "Sabbath—preached psalm 53: 4–L. Lectured Zechariah 14: 5–8—preached Luke 14: 27 and baptized Martha daughter to James Ramsay, g.a.—3 paid." (At home.)

Sept. 4 "Sabbath—preached psalm 55: 1–9. Lectured Zechariah 14: 12–16—preached Isaiah 27: 9 and baptized John son to Walter Buchanan g.a." (At home.)

Oct. 16 "Sabbath—preached psalm 57: 1–5. Lectured Philippians 1: 8–12—preached Hebrews 10: 12 and baptized Elizabeth daughter to David Robieson o.a." (At home.)

155

Middle Octoraro Society— *Continued*

1763 Oct. bet.
(17 & 21) "Rode 6 miles to and from Benjamin Side's." (From home.)

" (23) "Sabbath—preached psalm 57: 5–L. Preached Hebrews 10: 20—prayed, discoursed, debarred, invited, preached psalm 101: 1 and preached Hebrews 10: 12 and baptized Jean daughter to Robert Dranon o.a. etc. 180 communed." (At home.)

Dec. 8 "rode 22 miles Dow. (from Thomas Wilson's)—at John Dunlap's preached psalm 62; preached Hebrews 7: 25 and baptized Martha daughter to him o.a." (At home.)

" 25 "Sabbath—rode 8 miles to J. McKnaught's."

" 28 "Preached psalm 11. Lectured Romans 18: 11–L and baptized Robert, son to William Brady."

" 29 "rode 7 miles home."

1764 Jan. 10 "rode 8 miles to Widow Lough. Dorby's and Widow Andrews." (From home.)

" 11 "rode 9 miles home—preached psalm 85: 1–8 and lectured Songs 3: 1, 2 o.a."

" 19 "rode 8 miles home—married Joseph Loughhead and Jean Robieson." (From Sam Dixon's.)

Feb. 19 "Sabbath—preached psalm 64: 5. Lectured Phil. 3: 7–10. Preached 1 Corinthians 15, 13 and baptized Hew, son to David Dinwoody; and Sarah, daughter to William Speddy o.a." (At Dan McClellan's or Math. Richie's.)

" 20 "rode 14 miles W. Cooper's—preached psalm 62: 1— preached Hebrews 7: 25 and baptized Eliz. to David Mitchel and Margaret to T. Paterson." (At Daniel McClellan's?)

Mar. 7 "rode 14 miles to and from James Paterson's—preached psalm 19—catechized and baptized William son to Betty Ayres, and Florence to James Paterson." (From home.)

" 20 "rode 7 miles to D. Sinclair's wife's burial—an invalid up to this time." (From home.)

" 22 "rode 7 miles to and from J. Wilson's, Doc. J. Walker."

Middle Octoraro Society— *Continued*

1764 Mar. 27   "rode 8 miles—preached psalm 19—catechized 30 persons and baptized William son to Sam Cachy, at Hew Coulter's—visited Widow—." (From home.)

" 29   "rode 16 miles to and from James McKts. preached psalm 78—catechized and baptized Agnes, daughter to Isaac Walker—o.a. praise God."

May 24   "rode 6 miles to and from Gab. Walker's—payed off till that day." (From home.)

" 27   "Sabbath—preached psalm 68: 28–32. Lectured Malachi 2: 11–L—preached Ephesians 5–7 and baptized James, son to James Ross; Esther, daughter James Anderson, and John, my own son (born March 21st half past 8 in the morning." (At home.)

" 29   "rode 6 miles Felix's, John Walker's." (From home.)

" 31   "rode 10 miles to and from Works, Ramsay's, Hickman's." (From home.)

June 3   "Sabbath—preached psalm 68: 32–L. Lectured Malachi 3: 1–6. Preached Ephesians 5: 7 and baptized Robert, son to Hugh Fergus."

July 20   "rode 6 miles to and from Ch. McElheron's—wife dying." (From home.)

" 24   "rode 7 miles to John Walker's—visited Da. Anderson, etc." (From home.)

Sept. 3   "rode 6 miles to and from John Walker's—visited D. Anderson dying." (From home.)

" 9   "Sabbath—preached psalm 72: 12–16. Lectured Colossians 1: 19–21—preached Hebrews 12: 28, 29 and baptized John son to James Ramsay rs of — — McCl. differing, etc." (At home.)

" 10   "rode 6 miles to and from John Walker's; David Anderson's burial."

" 23   "Sabbath—preached psalm 73: 1–9. Lectured Colossians 1: 24–L preached Hebrews 12: 29 and baptized David, son to And. McKnaught." (At home.)

Oct. 1, 2   "rode 10 miles to Stiller's, Doc. Noll's, etc." (From home.)

Middle Octoraro Society— *Continued*

1765 Jan. 1 "rode 9 miles (from Humphrey Fullerton's)—married
              Da. McQuig and Margaret Aitken—came home—snow
              great."

      "   6 "Sabbath—read Owen on the 6th to the Hebrews." (At
              home.)

Feb. 15 "rode 6 miles to and from Gab. Walker's baptized John
          son to James Broedy." (From home.)

  "   24 "Sabbath—preached psalm 78: 1–5—preached Hebrews
          6: 12—baptized Sarah, daughter to Joseph Loughhead
          —give all praise to my God." (At home.)

  "   26 "rode 8 miles to Alexander Robieson's, etc."

  "   27 "preached psalm 37: 1—Lectured John 15: 1–9 and bap-
          tized Mary and Mary daughters to Alexander Baldridge
          and James Paterson."

— Mar. 14 "rode 7 miles—preached psalm 109: 21–27. Lectured
           Hebrews 10: 25–L and baptized Rachel to John Blakely;
           and Esther to Jean Cross." (From Thomas Pater-
           son's—then 3 miles to and from Daniel McClellan's on
           15th.)

Apr. 14 "Sabbath—preached psalm 78: 37–43. Lectured Gala-
          tians 5: 1–6. Preached Hebrews 8: 6 and baptized
          Alexander, son to Robert Speir; and Mary, daughter
          to Alexander Robieson." (At home.)

  "   18 "rode 10 miles to James McKnaught's; at H. Coulter's
          preached psalm 105: 1. Lectured Isaiah 57: 15–L.
          Baptized Grizzel and Mary to Nathaniel and Hew
          Coulter—a pistole to S. Coul." (From home.)

  "   23 "rode 10 miles—preached psalm 106: 43—Lectured He-
          brews 9: 11–14, and baptized Sarah, daughter to Rob-
          ert Paterson; and married William Barclay and Mar-
          garet Ramsay Sq. W's—home." (From Alexander
          Robieson's.)

June 10 "rode 24 (from David Dunwoody's)—married James
         Finley and Margaret Finley at T. Patterson's preached
         psalm 63: 1–5. Lectured Luke 24: 28–33 and baptized
         Joshua, son to John Ewing and Margaret, Katharine,
         Thomas, Helen, and Elizabeth, daughters and son to
         Eliz. Jones—give all praise to God—went to W.
         Cooper's and to Lynch's."

  "   16 "Sabbath—preached psalm 79: 6–10; lectured Jeremiah
          17: 5–11—preached Ecclesiastes 1: 2 and baptized Ag-
          nes to John Ritchie, Hanna to John McKnaught, Ben

Middle Octoraro Society— *Continued*

son to Sam Rob and Thomas son to Ada(m) Richie."
(At home.)

1765 June 23 "Sabbath—preached psalm 79: 10–L. Lectured Hebrews 7: 1–6—preached Ecclesiastes 1: 2 and baptized
Jean, to Adam Richie." (At home.)

"   25 "rode 6 miles to and from J. Walker's, W. T's—married
John Branan and Mary Walker." (From home.)

July 31 "rode 17 miles after preaching psalm 84: 7–L. Lectured Jeremiah 3: 12–16 and baptized Agnes and Joseph, daughter and son to Catharine McClelan, g.a."
(From W. Walker's.)

Aug. 11 "Sabbath—preached psalm 81: 8–12. Lectured He-
brews 8: 1–4 and preached psalm 17–L and baptized
Thomas son to James Loughhead—o.a. praise God."
(At home.)

Sept. 5 "rode 16 miles to and from Ag. Swan's and And. Ker's
burial." (From home.)

"   11 "rode 12 miles to and from Sam Paterson owing 1-0-0
of ——." (From home.)

1766 Jan. 7 "rode 10 miles to and from John Shirt's with Joan Porter." (From home.)

Feb. 8 "rode 14 miles Greer's—preached psalm 32: 1 catechized
32—baptized Abigail, daughter to Wm. Rob. Jr. Wm.
Greer, refuse ——." (From home.)

"   18 "rode 5 miles home (from McMurdy's Robert)—preached
psalm 62: 1–6—catechized 50—baptized Margaret
daughter to James Paterson (Jame's son)—about sacraments."

"   20 "rode 5 miles H. Coulter's—preached psalm 78: 1—
catechized 36 and baptized Jean, daughter to James
Ramsay—about sacraments."

"   23 "Sabbath—preached psalm 90: 5–10. Lectured Hebrews 10: 9–15, baptized Agnes to T ——."

"   24 "rode 6 miles to and from W. McClure's—preached
psalm 90: 8–11. Ex - -. 4: 13–L o.a."

"   25 "rode 10 miles Ex. at J. Wilson's John 15: 7–13 and
baptized Mary daughter to Peter Wil."

Mar. 4 "married John Maeben and Ag. Coulter." (At home.)

Apr. 13 "Sabbath—preached psalm 92: 1—Lectured Hebrews 10

Middle Octoraro Society— *Continued*

—preached John 17—baptized Robert to William Loch." (At home.)

1766 Apr. 14 "rode 5 miles to McDowels, Thomsons, meeting-house; held session."

" 17 "Fasted, prayed, preached psalm 60: 1-6; preached Galatians 3: 10 and baptized Robert son to Alexander McCalester, 18th at 1 o'clock Mr. McClellan's."

" 20 "Sabbath preached psalm 95: 6—preached Revelations 3: 20; preached, discoursed, debarred, invited; sung psalm 24 rs 1 Corinthians 11: 23 blessed brake, etc. McCl. 2 tables—200 meeting, preached Romans 5: 19–21 m. preached psalm 106–1—preached Matthew 5: 8. I concluded with an exhortation, preached and lectured psalm 148: 5; then baptized Mary to James Ross; married John Stewart and Elizabeth Cooper; held session; all well; praise to my gracious God (the 16th Sacrament in America)."

June 8 "Sabbath—preached psalm 98: 4–L; lectured Hebrews 11: 1-4 and baptized James to Sam Cachy in McClellans; preached Genesis 3: 9 o.a. praise God."

" 11 "rode 7 miles H. Coulters—McClellan's; preached and baptized 2 children." (Then rode 4 miles home on 12th.)

" 29 "Sabbath—preached psalm 100—lectured Hebrews 11: 8–11—preached — — 9, baptized Jean daughter to And. Mc. . . ."

July 11 "rode 5 miles to and from Wm. Downeys and R. F. etc." (From home.)

" 13 "Sabbath—preached psalm 101: 5–L; lectured Hebrews 11: 16–20 preached 2 Corinthians 5: 1 and baptized Margaret daughter to Isaac Walker o.a."

Aug. 24 "Sabbath. Preached Psalm 102: 21–25; lectured Hebrews 11: 28–32—preached Revelations 3: 20 and baptized Cornelius son to Corn. Colins; and Elijah to Da. Sinclair."

Sept. 1 "rode 20 miles home; ordered J. White sell p at 130 or 140."

Oct. 26 "Sabbath—rode 2 miles; preached 104: 5–10; lectured Hebrews 11: 2–5 and baptized James son to Robert Paterson and Susanna to Jos. Loughhead; o.a. all praise to my gracious God.- - -" (At home.)

Dec. 5 "rode 4 miles to and from Robert Thomson's with my wife." (From home.)

Middle Octoraro Society— *Continued*

1766 Dec. 8 "rode 3 miles to and from John Cunningham's, bought 2 hogs 35." (From home.)

"   10 "rode 4 miles to and from R. T's., burying his son."

"   12 "rode 4 miles to and from Joseph Walkers, bought 2 sides; L."

"   24 "rode 14 miles, A. Robieson's; preached psalm 97: 8— baptized Sam son to James Ramsay; catechized 40; rode W. B."

"   25 "rode 4 miles Jos. Walker's; preached psalm 86: 11–15, catechized 25."

"   26 "rode 9 miles home; very aguish; x x."

1767 Apr. 12 "Sabbath—preached psalm 106: 40–44, lectured Hebrews 13: 10—baptized Jean daughter to John Maben, o.a.—preached Colossians 2: 9 concerning Christ." (At home.)

May 3 "Sabbath preached psalm 107: 8—lectured Isaiah 25: 6—preached Acts 26: 9 and baptized Richard son to Thomas Black o.a. praise God." (At home.)

June 21 "Sabbath preached psalm 108: 7–11; lectured John 6: 66–L; preached Hebrews 3: 13 and baptized John son to Wm. Rob. o.a. praise to my gracious God." (At home.)

July 1, 2 "rode 24 miles to and from Widow And. and Calbreath's; preached psalm 3; lectured Romans 8: 1–5; baptized Andrew son to John Walker and married Philip Scott and Elizabeth Wilson, o.a." (From home.)

"   6 "rode 4 miles to and from Montgomery's; hurried and wearied." (From home.)

Sept. 13 "Sabbath—preached psalm 112: 3–1; lectured 1 John 2: 18–24; preached Habakkuk 3: 2 g.a. and baptized Agnes to John Rob. Joseph son to Sam Rob. and Wm. son to James Paterson, James his son." (At home.)

Oct. 4 "Sabbath preached psalm 114: 1–6; discoursed 1 Timothy 5: 17; ordained Humphrey Fulerton, T. Girvan, James Ramsay, Corn. Collins, and John Rob." (At home.)

"   12 "baptized Robert son to James Paterson and Mary daughter to Humphrey Fulerton." (At home.)

Nov. 6 "rode 14 miles to and from R. Tweed's burying etc." (From home.)

"   21 "rode 3 miles to R. R. Bur." (Robert Ramsay's burial —from home.)

Middle Octoraro Society— *Continued*

1767 Dec. 21, 22   "rode 9 miles—preached psalm 46: 1–6. Lectured Philip. 3: 15, 16, and baptized John son to H. Coulter (Presented by mother.) " (From home.)

1768 Jan. 3   "Sabbath—preached psalm 110: 24–L. Lectured 1 John 4: 11–16 and baptized Mary, daughter to John Mc-Knaught." (At home.)

" 7   "rode 3 miles to J. Wilson's—married Alexander and Frances Ewins—preached psalm 1: 1–5. Lectured Matthew 19: 16–23 and baptized John to Pet. Wilson." (From Hen. Ewin's—then rode 10 miles home on 8th.)

" 12   "rode 5 miles to and from W. McClure's burial." (From home.)

" 24   "Sabbath—preached 119: 5–9. Lectured 1 John 4: 16— and baptized Mary, daughter to John McKt.—g.a. praise to my gracious God."

Feb. 2   "eight miles home after preaching and catechizing 50 persons and baptizing Samuel, son to Robert Paterson." (At Alexander Robieson's.)

" 21   "Sab.—preached psalm 119: 22–26—baptized Sarah. daughter to Nath. Coulter give all praise to God." (At home.)

" 22   "rode 5 miles by Montgomery's."

" 24   "rode 8 miles T. G's.—preached psalm 51: 15—catechized 26 and baptized David and Mary, son and daughter to John Girvan." (At T. G's.—from Humphrey Fullerton's.)

Mar. 2   "rode 7 miles—preached psalm 91: 1—catechized 25 persons and baptized Alexander son to Thomas Scott o.a." (From Thomas Girvan's.)

" 12   "rode 6 miles with N. Coulter's child's burial." (From H. Coulter's.)

" 28   "rode 8 miles Josias Kers, in ordinary health." (From David Dunwoody's.)

" 29   "tramped 1 mile—married Elijah Stewart and Ma. Paterson—rs. 10 conversed, etc."

Apr. 20   "rode 6 miles to and from T. Girvan—John's wife dying." (From home.)

" 21   "rode 10 miles to and from James Loughhead's—saw Y. etc."

Middle Octoraro Society— *Continued*

1768 May 6   "rode 8 miles to and from H. and N. Coulter's, etc." (From home.)

June 14   "rode 9 miles with Mr. Clayton Wid." (From home.)

" 19   "Sabbath—preached psalm 119: 81–5. Lectured Isaiah 63: 1–7 and preached Revelations 11: 15 and baptized Eleanor, daughter to Wm. Loughhead."

July 10   "Sabbath—preached 93: 97. Lectured Jude 15 and 16 preached Revelations 3: 10 and baptized Elizabeth, daughter to Sam Cachy—give all praise to my gracious God, etc., etc." (At home.)

Aug. 8   "rode 3 miles to and from And. Frunks, etc." (From home.)

" 10   "rode 4 miles to and from Montgomery's, etc."

Sept. 11   "Sabbath—preached 129: 133. Lectured Jeremiah 3: 1–6. Preached Hebrews 2: 1 and baptized David, son to Corn. Collins; and Walter to Isaac Walker." (At home.)

" 12   "began 2 mowing—carr. 2 loads apples Peter Schever— rode 9 miles to and from Loughheads with a letter to P. Whiteside."

" 16   "rode 10 miles to and from H. C., J. Paisleys, J. Millers— brought Sally."

" 21   "rode 10 miles—received 3-0-0 from W. Denny." (From home.)

Oct. 23   "Sabbath—preached 149–53. Lectured Isaiah 30: 8–10 —preached Matthew 7: 21 and baptized Margaret daughter to Walter Buchanan." (At home.)

" 24   "rode 12 miles to Sides, Wid. Mill. Coul. Paisleys, Mon."

" 26   "rode 4 miles to and from Nolls, R. Ramsays, etc." (From home.)

" 30   "Sabbath—preached 153–57. Lectured Isaiah 30: 18– 27 and baptized Mary, daughter to Joseph Lough- head." (At home.)

" 31   "rode 14 miles to and from Cal.—married T. Kennety and Ann Calbreath—conversed Mr. Henderson."

Nov. 9   "rode and wandered 12 miles to Jos. Ker's—married

Middle Octoraro Society— *Continued*

John Murray and Mary Lochhart—received 3 dollars— good health." (From Abbotstown.)

1768 Dec. 15 "rode 4 miles to and from R. Thomson's, very cold, wrote." (From home.)

" 22 "rode 3 miles after preaching psalm 4:6-L; lectured Genesis 18:16–19 and baptized Helen daughter to Alexander Ewing, o.a. praise God." (From Widow Calbreath's—then 10 miles home on 23rd.)

1769 Jan. 5 "rode 7 miles home; preached psalm 97:10-L; lectured 2 Timothy 2:10–15 and baptized Joseph son to James Ramsay."

" 17 "rode 10 miles to W. Vogan's; married Joseph Rob. and Jean Vogan." (From home.)

Feb. 9 "rode 8 miles home with Y. family all well; Colin Brown sick."

" 20 "rode 8 miles to and from Colin Brown's a dying etc." (From home.)

" 27 "rode 6 miles to James Spier's, G. D. and J. K.'s R. and A. Work." (From home.)

" 28 "rode 8 miles J. Murghat's and Wal. Buchanan's."

Mar. 1 "rode 12 miles to Jo. Walker's; preached psalm 33:10; preached Romans 3:19–20 and baptized Mary to W. Braeden and Hannah to John Walker; went to J. Paxton's."

" 2 "rode 2 miles home; family all well; praise my gracious God."

" 5 "Sabbath preached psalm 132:7–12; lectured Isaiah 55: 3–6 and baptized Sarah daughter to Alexander Robieson g.a. etc."

Apr. 23 "Sabbath preached psalm 136:1—lectured Isaiah 63: 15, 16; preached John 1:12 and baptized Robert son to Jean Ramsay give all praise to God." (At home.)

" 30 "Sabbath preached psalm 136:17—lectured psalm 19: 7—preached John 1:12 and baptized Samuel son to Nath. Coulter, x x." (At home.)

May 14 "Sabbath preached 187:7-L; lectured Isaiah 26:1–5 and preached Isaiah 26:9 give all praise to my gracious God. Rode 8 miles S. psalm 51: exercised Romans 5: 12. Rode 8 miles x x and baptized James son to John Ervin." (8 miles from Neal McKnaughtan's.)

" 21 "Sabbath preached psalm 138:1—lectured Matthew 5:

Middle Octoraro Society— *Continued*

33—preached Isaiah 26: 9 and baptized David son to John Richie and Robert to James Paterson."

1769 June 12   "After sore labor wife was delivered of a son, about half an hour after 12."

July   6   "married Walter Moore and Martha Loughhead." (At home.)

"   9   "Sab. preached psalm 139: 21–L; preached 1 Corinthians 10: 1, 2 and baptized Walter (Cuthbertson) born June 12th at 1 o'clock, praise my gracious God." (In summary, July 9 baptized Walter.)

Sept. 17   "Sab. preached psalm 143: 5–10; lectured 15–18 and preached Jude and baptized Agnes daughter to Thomas Scott and Margaret daughter to Wm. Ross." (At home.)

"   21   "rode 9 miles to and from T. Girvan's; married Wm. Woods and Susanna Andrews; paid W. Prey 10 shillings." (From home.)

"   24   "Sabbath preached psalm 143: 10–L; lectured Romans 5: 18–L; preached Jude and baptized Alexander son to Margaret Ayres, rode 6 miles exercized Isaiah 1: 16; baptized Martha daughter to Mary Branon, at John Walker's."

Nov.   9   "rode 8 miles to Mos. Baird's, Humphrey Fullerton's— good health." (From home.)

"   10   "rode 9 miles by Widow Cooper's, Matt. McClung's, home."

"   12   "Sabbath—preached 145: 10—lectured Isaiah 5: 1–8 and baptized Jean to R. Paterson."

"   14   "rode 14 miles to and from Widow Lachlin's etc.— Marlin's, etc."

"   15   "rode 6 miles to McGuffey's—rs Gib's. "Refuge of Lies." "

"   23   "rode 18 miles home—married James Robieson and Sarah Dixon." (From John McMillan's with James McKnaught.)

Dec. 14   "rode 16 miles—married James Mitchel and Han. Peterson." (From home.)

1770 Feb. 18   "Sabbath—preached psalm 2: 1–7. Lectured Ephesians 6: 1–10 and baptized Margaret daughter to John Maben o.a. praise God." (At home.)

"   20   "rode 7 miles to James Paterson's preached psalm 61: 1–L and catechized 50 and baptized Jean, daughter to James Paterson, Jr."

Middle Octoraro Society— *Continued*

1770 Feb. 27   "rode 15 miles to and from James Paterson's. Married Sam Paterson and Margaret —— James McGlaughlin and Margaret Mitchel." (From home.)

Apr. 24   "rode 10 miles. Married Robert Ramsay and Mary Mitchel." (Then rode 8 miles to Widow Andrew's on 25th.)

"   29   "Sabbath—preached psalm 7: 1–6. Lectured Isaiah 64: 1–6 preached Matthew 24: 13 and baptized Isobel daughter to Joseph Rob. g.a. etc." (At home.)

May 1   "rode 17 miles—married John Andrews and Jean Cooper —went to Robert Laws—paid 11-4-0 to J. . . ." (From home.)

"   2   "rode 13 miles home."

"   8   "rode 7 miles to Widow Irvine's and Matthew Mc-Clung's." (From home.)

June 21   "rode 4 miles to and from R. Thomson's, John Ramsay's." (From home.)

"   24   "Sabbath—preached 16–L; lectured Isaiah 66: 9; preached 41: 11 and baptized John son to John Mc-Knaight o.a.—great heat and rain."

"   26   "rode 5 miles to and from R. Thomson's, R. Ramsay's, etc."

July 11   "from Henry Small received 4-7-6 hot harvest." (At home.)

Aug. 12   "Sabbath preached psalm 13: 4; lectured Acts 8: 12— Joshua 1: 10 and baptized Janet daughter to Wm. Lochhead o.a. praise God."

"   27   "Preached 101; preached 2 Thessalonians 1: 11, 12 and baptized Phoebe (to) Js. Ross." (At home.)

Oct. 7   "Sabbath—preached 18: 1—Lectured Luke 17: 1— preached Deuteronomy 33: L, and baptized James son to James McCord—give all praise to my gracious God."

"   8   "rode 28 miles Cairn's—married John Martin and Agnes Thomson."

"   9   "rode 28 miles home by G. Dinings—bought 10 yds. lin.—2-2."

"   14   "Sabbath—preached 18: 8–14. Lectured John 8: 33– 45—preached Deuteronomy 33–L and baptized Margaret to Joseph Loughhead, and Eliz. to Thomas Pa . . ."

Middle Octoraro Society— *Continued*

1770 Oct. 23   "rode 16 miles to and from R. C's. married John Shenan and Han. Calbre."

"   24   "hauled 720 rails."

Dec.   3   "rode 5 miles; preached psalm 137: 1—catechized 34 persons and baptized Elizabeth, Robert and Mary to Susana Ramsay." (From home.)

1771 Jan. 22   "rode 9 miles W. Down; received 9-10-0; paid J. Millar, preached psalm 77: 1—lectured Malachi 4: 7, 8; baptized Josiah son to Nath. Coulter; Samy dying." (From home.)

Mar.   6   "rode 4 miles to and from R. T. bought guth. T. and 12, 13 g.a. went to widow Owen." (From home.)

"   13   "rode 12 miles home; married John Ramsay and Phoebe."

"   20   "rode 8 miles to A. Robieson; preached 116: 1–7; preached Isaiah 51: 7, 8 and baptized James son to Wm. Barclay." (From home.)

"   31   "Sabbath 2 miles; preached 25: 1–8; lectured Isaiah 51: 9–17 and baptized Thomas son to John Dunlop Brandawine give all praise to God." (At home.)

Apr.   7   "Sabbath preached 8: 14; lectured Isaiah 51: 17–L and baptized Mary daughter to Hew McFadzean o.a. foot mending." (At home.)

"   11   "Married Archibald Shield and Jat. Buchanan."

"   21   "Sab. preached 26: 1–7 lectured Isaiah 52: 7–L and baptized James son to Robert Ramsay; give all praise to my gracious God." (At home.)

"   23   "rode 7 miles with Y. to Matthew McClungs in health." (From home.)

"   24, 25   "rode 12 miles to Howstons, Fulertons, and home, sore."

"   28   "Sabbath preached 7–L; lectured Isaiah 6 and baptized William son to Robert Paterson o.a. praise my gracious God."

June 23   "Sabbath preached 29: 5–L; lectured Romans 6: 1–6 preached Jude and baptized Wm. son to Joseph Rob. give all praise to God; exposed new light, Papist, etc." (At home.)

July 19   "rode 18 miles with Y. to and from James McKts., A. Russel's, etc." (From home.)

Sept. 6   "rode 12 miles to Gem. Thom., Hannas, Hains, home." (From home.)

"   10   "rode 18 miles to and from widow Lauch's, W. and Sam. Rob's." (From home.)

Middle Octoraro Society—*Continued*

1771 Oct. 27 "Sabbath preached 34: 8–14; lectured 1 Corinthians 1: 17–23 then preached Proverbs 27: 1 and baptized William son to James Ramsay, give all praise to God, etc." (At home.)

" 31 "rode 9 miles to and from John Wilson's, vendue, etc." (From home.)

Nov. 3 "Sabbath preached 14: 2; lectured Romans 10: 1–11 and baptized Esther daughter to Sam Cachy; give all praise to my gracious God." (At home.)

" 12 "rode 24 miles to Ag. Black home etc. all well, praise God." (From J. Marlin's.)

" 20, 21 "rode 20 miles to and from John Walkers; preached 18: 1—lectured Acts 2: 37–41; baptized Ann to him and Isobel daughter to Peter Wilson; bought 6 quarts timothy."

Dec. 8 "Sabbath preached 19: 24; lectured John 15: 1–9; preached James 4: 13 and baptized John son to John Dunbar; give all praise to gracious God."

1772 Feb. 24 "rode 5 miles to D. Hanna, John Walkers, wrote Widow." (From home.)

Mar. 2 "rode 10 miles to H. Ervins and John Andrews." (From Geo. Mitchel's.)

" 3 "rode 6 miles to John Rob's, after preaching 89: 19–24 and catechizing 30."

" 4 "rode 6 miles to A. McK. Corn; and James Ramsay's."

" 5 "rode 10 miles to S. Ram. married James Walker and Mary Stewart, got cold, etc."

" 8 "Sabbath; preached 38: 5–11; lectured Isaiah 5: 11–20; preached Luke L29 and baptized Susanna daughter to John Ramsay, g.a."

" 17 "rode 10 miles to R. C. and Hu. Coulter's; married Joseph Tait and Elizabeth Pattison; great snow; 10 s." (From home.)

" 24 "rode 4 miles to and from burial Charles Collins." (From home.)

" 26 "rode 3 miles to and from burial R. Ramsay's W."

Apr. 1 "rode 8 miles to Al. Robieson's; preached 119: 49; catechized 40 persons and baptized Hanna to James Patterson." (From home.)

June 21 "Sabbath; preached 9–L; lectured 13: 1–12; preached Jude and baptized John to T. Polly." (At home.)

Middle Octoraro Society— *Continued*

1772 June 23   "rode 8 miles; burial of Ralston; R. Thomson's." (From home.)

July 12   "Sabbath; preached 44: 1–4; lectured Jude 16–L; preached Jude and baptized Sam son to John Rob; give all praise to my gracious God." (At home.)

Sept. 6   "Sabbath; preached 45: 1–14; lectured Isaiah 19: 1–18; preached Genesis 46: 4; baptized William son to William Loughhead; held session." (At home.)

"   11   "rode 3 miles home; sick spleen; the day before Mr. McGill." (From H. Coulter's.)

Nov. 19   "rode 8 miles to N. Coulter's after preaching 44: 17: lectured Galatians 3: 26, 27 and baptized James son to John Andrew, John to John Walker, and Agnes to Walter Buchanan." (From Robert Lowry's.)

"   20   "rode 4 miles home."

"   24   "married Enos. McDonald and Rebecca Duncan." (At Mid. Oct.)

Dec. 29   "rode 9 miles—married George Mitchel and Martha Houston." (From home.)

1773 Jan. 7   "at home—married John Girvan and Mary Laughlin."

"   11   "rode 8 miles to James Paterson's—preached 63: 1— lectured 1 Corinthians 15: 51 and baptized Rebecca to Joshua Loughhead—g.a." (From home.)

"   12   "rode 7 miles visiting—married John Thomson and Mary Paterson."

"   20, 21   "rode 15 miles to P. Wilson, Wid. Buch.—married Gilbert Buchanan and Sarah Walker (daughter) to John Walker." (Then rode 9 miles home on 22nd.)

Feb. 28   "Sabbath: preached 51: 13–16—preached 2 Peter 1: 10 and baptized David son to Humphrey Fulerton; Marion to John Gebby; and Sarah to David Mitchel, presented by the mother." (At home.)

Mar. 28   "Sabbath—tramped 2 miles—preached 53: 1–4. Lectured 16–L and preached Luke 17: 10 and baptized Robert son to Robert Patterson; and Eliz. to Alexander Robieson."

Apr. 4   "Sabbath—preached 5–L. Lectured 29: 1–13 and baptized Ann, daughter to Sam Patterson, presented by the mother."

"   5   "rode 8 miles—received Mr. Moore's watch for John and 4 s. spoons for Sally. Paid bond with R. Ramsay

Middle Octoraro Society— *Continued*

for 12-0-8 to John Crawfurd, Warrington, Exr. etc.
etc." (Probably on death of Father-in-law, Walter
Moore.)

1773 Apr. 10   "was with J. Noble, etc.—died at 8—sowed oats."

"   19   "rode 6 miles to James Paterson with wife and Dr."

"   20   "rode 8 miles by Work's, Ram.—married Robert Thomson and Sally Mitchel."

"   22   "tramped and rode 3 miles—vendue 2-1-2 Mr. Smith's—6 vols. R." (From home.)

May   4   "rode 7 miles home family all well—praise my gracious God." (From Alexander Robinson's.)

"   9   "Sabbath—tramped 2 miles—preached 12:18. Lectured 31 and preached Isaiah 30:15 and baptized Joseph son to And. McKnightan o.a. praise God."

"   11   "rode 9 miles by Mr. Sharp's home." (From H. Fulerton's.)

"   23   "Sabbath—preached 22-L. Lectured 32:9-L. Preached verse 17 g.a. and baptized Margaret to Joseph Rob. and Agnes to Hew Pattison." (At home.)

"   31   "rode 12 miles with Y. to J. M., J. And., and Robert Law's." (From home.)

June 1   "rode 2 miles—married Robert Martin and Janet La(w)."

"   2   "rode 10 miles home—preached. Exercised Ezra 36–25 and baptized Elizabeth, daughter to Peter Wilson, g.a. etc."

"   6   "Sabbath—preached 7–L. Lectured 13–L and preached Isaiah 33:16 and baptized Rebecca, daughter to John Richie—give all praise to God."

"   23   "rode 25 miles to and from Hew Russel's with Y., etc., etc." (From home.)

Aug. 26   "rode 10 miles to McCumpry's, Thomson's, etc." (From home.)

Sept. 5   "Sabbath—preached 60:5–9. Lectured 12:22; preached Ephesians 1:5 etc. x x and baptized Wm." (son to Robert Ramsay).

Oct. 10   "Sabbath—preached 62:1–5. Lectured 20–L and

Middle Octoraro Society— *Continued*

preached from same o.a. and baptized Sarah, daughter to John Coates from Scotland." (At home.)

1773 Oct. 14 "rode 12 miles to and from John Marshal's W. Steel's." (From home.)

" 31 "Sab.—preached 63: 1–6 and preached from same— baptized Barbara, daughter to John Ramsay o.a. praise God, etc." (At home.)

Nov. 1 "rode 4 miles to John Ramsay's, White." (From home.)

Dec. 9 "rode 13 miles home—married Alexander Kilpatrick and Mary Andrew—nothing." (From John Walker's.)

1774 Jan. 11 "rode 3 miles to and from Mr. Smith's—sick at night with cold." (From home.)

May 11 "rode 13 miles to Mr. S. Marsh, Colier's, Poaks, Wal. Buch." (From home.)

June 21 "married Sam Fegan and Agnes Coulter." (At home.)

"   " "baptized Hannah daughter to Joseph Rob. g.a."

Aug. 16 "rode 8 miles to and from N. Coulter's; preached 18: 46—and lectured 1 Peter 3: 18—and baptized Sarah Dunlap, adult, Agnes and Elijah to N. C. and John to John Maeben, sweet time, praise God." (From home.)

Oct. 25 "rode 8 miles to and from Sam Cachy's; Nath. very sick." (From home.)

" 30 "Sabbath; preached 8–12 and lectured Isaiah 59: 16–L and baptized Walter son to Gilbert Buchanan; give all praise to my gracious God."

Nov. 14 "rode 22 miles to Molly Collins, saw dying girl; home." (From J. Reid's.)

Dec. 4 "Sabbath;—preached 75: 5–L and lectured Isaiah 62: 1–6 and baptized Rebecah daughter to Wm. Lochhead; give all praise to my gracious God."

1775 Jan. 10 "rode 9 miles to John Walkers with Christie, etc." (From home.)

" 12 "rode 3 miles to S. P's., married James Glen and Janet Buchanan." (On 13th rode 10 miles home.)

Feb. 21 "preached, catechized 32 and baptized Margaret Laecky, adult; John, son to Robert Paterson; Mary, to Robert

Middle Octoraro Society— *Continued*

Kirkpatrick Eliz. to James Paterson, o.a. praise God."
(At Robert Paterson's.)

1775 Feb. 22 "rode 9 miles home; James Millar's s(on's) burial."

" 28 "rode 8 miles to John Ritchies." (From home.)

Mar. 8, 9 "preached 41: 1–5—catechized 25 and baptized Isobel to John Andrew." (At home.)

Apr. 20 "rode 4 miles to R. R.—preached 22: 1–4; catechized 20 persons and visited E. Kinkend." (From home.)

May 1 "Mr. Dob. preached 89: 7–11 and preached Hebrews 11: 16., g.a. and baptized Alexander to Al. Robieson; and James to G. Mitchel—then held Presb. were harmon— dull mi ——." (At home.)

Aug. 24 "rode 8 miles to and from Widow Coul., Sam Fregan's burial." (From home.)

Nov. 5 "Sabbath—preached 8–13 and lectured Isaiah 6: 1–5 o.a. —N. Spier moved." (At home.)

" 8 "rode 9 miles to N. Coulter's John Brown's, Junr.— well."

" 12 "Sabbath—preached 13–L. Lectured Isaiah 6: 5–L and baptized Hugh, son to Nath. Coulter; Janet, daughter to Agnes Fegan; and Hamilton Dicky son to Sam Rob. o.a. praise God."

Dec. 11 "rode 6 miles to and from Mustering, etc." (From home.)

" 18 "rode 9 miles to H. Coulter's, J. R., Sam Poak's wife." (From home.)

" 22 "rode 10 miles to Jas Glen's and home—sal.—cold." (From John Walker's.)

1776 Jan. 9 "rode 7 miles to S. McDow., And. Works, and James Patterson's." (From home.)

" 10 "rode 1 mile—preached and catechized 30 persons— visited John and James Patt."

" 28 "Sabbath—walked 2 miles—preached 49–L and lectured Genesis 28: 16–L o.a. praise." (At S. Robs.)

" 30 "rode 3 miles—preached 50: 7—lectured from same— baptized Mary to John ——. (Then rode 3 miles home by Millar's on 31st.)

Middle Octoraro Society—*Continued*

1776 Feb. 13, 14 "rode 14 miles—preached, lectured Isaiah 57: 13–L and baptized Isaac, son to James Walker." (From home.)

"   15 "Married John Mitchel and Mary Buchanan."

Mar. 5, 6 "rode 5 miles R. R.—preached 37: 7 catechized 24— baptized Mary to John Ramsay—conv. Noll, etc.— went home."

"   7 "rode 7 miles to J. Paxton's, Downie's—settled s. and home."

"   13 "rode 6 miles home—left Y. Mr. Woodhul—tired." (From H. Fullerton's.)

May 26 "Sabbath—preached 11–16. Lectured Philip. 1: 25–L and preached 4: 13, etc. Baptized Samuel, son to James Ramsay." (At home.)

June 20 "rode 5 miles to Mr. Thom., Hanna's and Mr. Smith's." (From home.)

Aug. 1 "rode 8 miles John McGra.—exch. cap Ross's Comp., etc." (From home.)

"   4 "Sabbath—preached 98: 1–5. Lectured 15–L. Preached same and baptized Margret to John Tod." (At home.)

"   6 "rode 7 miles to and from John Ritchy's with Grif. Tod and Chi———."

Sept. 10 "rode thru rain 3 miles Comin, Jas. Miller's concerning Grif., and home." (From home.)

"   11 "rode 5 miles to Kron Kickman's (Hickman?), A. W., con. concerning Griff. rain."

"   12 "rode 5 miles home—met Ful. and Talbot—conversed etc."

"   19 "rode 15 miles to Cap. Ross's, Thom., home preached psalm 57: 5–8. Lectured Titus 2: 11–14 and baptized Moses and Isobel to Jas. Ross." (From home.)

Nov. 22, 23 "rode 8 miles to and from Jas. Loughhead's, John Ritchey's." (From home.)

"   25, 26 "rode 11 miles to Wid. Collin's, W. Steel's, Widow Ramsay's, home." (From home.)

Dec. 24, 25 "rode 12 miles to John Robs., Robert Paterson's— great frost—preached 144: 1—lectured Matt. 4: 1–12 and baptized Elizabeth to Eliz. Ayre." (From home.)

Middle Octoraro Society— *Continued*

1776 Dec. 26   "rode 5 miles home by John Maeben's—great snow— G. L. take—."

1777 Mar. 10   "rode 8 miles to and from Jos. Millar's—he and Paxton John voted." (From home.)

"   27   "rode 1 mile to John Wa. held session x x preached 18th psalm, 4–L verses—catechized 32 persons—baptized Eliz. to Wm. Ewi(ng)." (From James Walker's—then 12 miles home on 28th.)

Apr. 2   "rode 10 miles home—visited W. L. and Mrs. Graham bought 3 pounds cott." (From home.)

"   3   "Birthday—rode 4 miles—preached 144: 1–6—catechized 30—baptized Eliz. to Ar. M. (McBride or McCurdy.) Now entered in my 60th year. Death draws near." (From home.)

"   8   "rode 6 miles H. C's—preached 54: 1—catechized 35 persons baptized Joseph to John Rob; and Sarah to Nathaniel Coulter." (From home.)

May 26   "rode 16 miles home—found all well—received from John Stoner 20-2-6." (From J. Mc.)

June 1   "Sabbath—preached 107: 9-16. Lectured Jeremiah 2: 31–L and preached Joel 3: 16 and baptized Katharin to Joseph Anderson and Agnes to John Andrews." (At home.)

"   4   "rode 7 miles—visited Adam Barclay—paid Mrs. Graham 6 dol. for him."

"   8   "Sabbath—preached 16–23. Lectured Micah 7: 16–L. preached from same—baptized Margaret to Jas. Ritchy g.a. praise God." (At Capton Paxton's.)

July 2   "9 miles to Cap. Pax.—swore all. to John Pat.—preached psalm 15 exc. Jeremiah 4: 1, 2 and baptized James, son to Jas. Paterson." (From home.)

"   13   "Sabbath—preached 109: 1-8. Lectured John 15: 6–11—preached psalm 102: 16 and baptized Robert Andrew, son to James Ross—conversed Eld. concerning Lough. and Ritch."

"   14   "Reaped wheat, etc."

"   21   "rode 17 miles by S. Simpson's, home—all well." (From Wm. Maughlin's.)

Middle Octoraro Society— *Continued*

1777 Aug. 24   "Sabbath—preached 110: 1—lectured Ezekial 37: 1–11
—preached psalm 22: 30 and baptized Thomas, son to
Alexander Robinson o.a. praise God, etc." (At home.)

"   25   "rode 6 miles to Robert Gays, Jas. Lough., Jack went."

"   31   "Sabbath—preached 5–L. Lectured 11–15—preached
from same x x—baptized Walter, son to James Glen
o.a." (At home.)

Oct. 19   "Sabbath—preached 114: 1–L and lectured Isaiah 10: 1
and baptized Martha to Arch. McCurdy." (At home.)

"   22, 23   "rode 10 miles seeking hay—bought bushels beans
from Kisack."

Nov. 12   "rode 4 miles—preached psalm 66: 8–15—preached Titus
2: 11–L and baptized David, Mary, Henry and William
to Helen Edminston, widow; and Robert, son to Wm.
Law—went to John Andrews." (Then 11 miles home
on 13th.)

"   16   "Sabbath—preached 116: 1–7. Lectured Isaiah 34: 1–9
and baptized Benjamin son to Alexander McCleary."
(At home.)

"   30   "Sabbath—preached 13–L. Lectured Zechariah 8: 16–
20 and baptized Mary to John Porter."

Dec. 18   "Thank day—pr. rs. pro—preached 121—preached 1
Samuel 7: 12 and baptized Sam to Jas. Parks; and Mary
to Helen Hill, g. day."

1778 Jan. 1   "sold stallion to Jas. Porter—42 pounds spec. 10." (At
home.)

May 3   "Sabbath—preached 44: 49—preached 2 o'clock Corinthians 3: 10, 11 and baptized James son to Sam. Rob.
g.a. praise my gracious God." (At home.)

"   6   "rode 11 miles home—preached 94: 14–18. Exc. Acts 2:
37–L and baptized Margaret to Jas. Walker—was with
Mr. McCorkle." (From Jas. Wilson's.)

"   12   "rode 5 miles to Gr. Widow Moore's, with my ——."
(From home.)

June 14   "Sabbath—preached 65–70 and discoursed 2 o'clock 1
Corinthians 3: 15, 16 and baptized Ann to John Ram-
say—a mixed Assembly, Seceders and O. and N. Sides."
(At home.)

"   21   "Sabbath—preached 70–73. Discoursed 2 o'clock 1
Corinthians 3: 16, 17 and baptized James to Wm.
Long." (At home.)

Middle Octoraro Society—*Continued*

1778 June 25   "rode 9 miles to Mr. Corkles, Millar's, H. C.—Wars, Wars!" (From home.)

"   30   "rode 10 miles to J. Robs.,—married Nat. Coulter and Isobel Dunlap."

July 12   "Sabbath—preached 81–5 and lectured 1 Corinthians 3: 10–21 and preached last verse—Jas. Rea." (At home.)

"   14   "rode 9 miles to Mr. S., N. Coulter's, H., John Dunlap and home."

"   26   "Sabbath—preached 89–93 and lectured Micah 7: 1–7. Preached verse 7 and baptized Nathaniel son to Robert Kilpatrick; and John to Jos. Rob. o.a. praise God." (At home.)

"   29   "rode 9 miles to Calebs x x." (From home.)

Sept. 1   "tramped 2 miles to Calebs, Peters—paid 12 dollars—hard ——." (From home.)

"   22   "rode 6 miles to and from Nathan. Coulter's—preached 69: 1–4. Lectured Matt. 10: 13–28 and baptized Margaret, James and Lydia, to Rebecca Dunlap, alias Woodrow, o.a. praise my gracious God—received 34 dollars." (From home.)

Nov. 2   "rode 6 miles to Mr. S., John Maeben's, Will. McCorkles."

"   3   "rode 3 miles home—John half-soled my shoes."

Dec. 13   "Sabbath, Nil sick ague, spleen, left arm straitened, etc." (Home.)

"   15   "rode 6 miles R. Thomson's burial."

"   23   "Rode 9 miles to S. Cachy's at H. Cou., married Daniel Mcready and Agnes Coulter, cold, very sick." (From home.)

1779 Jan. 14   "rode 2 miles home; preached 19: 11 and catechized 18 at Sus. Ram."

"   18   "rode 10 miles to James Glen's, John Walkers, cold." (From home.)

"   26, 27, 28   "20 miles; preached 23; catechized 11 and preached 84; catechized 40 persons, and baptized David son to James Ritchy, James McCorkle." (From home.)

Middle Octoraro Society— *Continued*

1779 Feb. 2 "Rode 10 miles to John Andrews 3 pr. and catechized etc. rs. 340." (From home.)

"   4 "rode 8 miles to John Brown's, Robert Calb. Married Wm. Dunlap and Margaret Brown—breast, rib, etc. broke on —— sore distress." (From home.)

"   15 "rode 6 miles; sold my whiskey to H. Rocky 3 gallons." (From home.)

Apr.   1 "rode 6 miles to Nolls, Widow Ram., John—Jos. Walkers." (From home.)

"   3 "U. S. Birthday 61; preached, confers. rep. covenant, etc.—dead."

"   4 "Sabbath—preached 129; lectured 6–11 and baptized Henry's John." (At home.)

"   13 "rode 3 miles; preached 23: 1—exercised Revelations 12: 11; held session; baptized Margaret daughter to Nathaniel Coulter, son to Hugh o.a." (At home.)

May 16 "Sabbath: preached 133; lectured Hebrews 10: 1-5; preached verse 4 and baptized Arthur son to John Andrew, give all praise to my gracious God." (At home.)

"   19 "Tramped 4 miles Mr. S., Widow Thomson's, Mr. Marshal, etc." (From home.)

"   28 "held session, conversed Sally Patt. x x." (At home.)

June 10 "x x came home to meet J. 4 Wed. nil great rain."

July 12 "rode 14 miles to John Walkers, daughters burial, Mr. Smith's, etc." (From home.)

"   18 "Sabbath preached 21–L; lectured Hebrews 11: 1–4 and preached verse 4 and baptized Martha to John Walker and Agnes to James Glen." (At home.)

" 28, 29 "rode 18 miles to and from Sa. Cachy's, etc. Widow Bur. Young's." (From home.)

Aug.   3 "rode 6 miles to Mr. Sm. and to and from Janet Coulter's burial." (From home.)

Sept. 5 "Sab.—preached 138: 1–5; lectured 8–13 and preached verse 10 (at home); baptized Moses to John Rob. and James to Wm. Ewing, give all praise to God.   Rode 4 miles to and from John Ramsay's, preached 30: 5–L; exercised Matthew the last chapter 20, 21 and baptized James his son, rs. on 6–10 D."

Oct. 29, 30 "Raising roof Barn, etc., etc."

"   31 "Sabbath—preached 139: L–7 and lectured Hebrews 11: 13–17 and baptized Esther daughter to Nathaniel Coulter sen. give all praise to my gracious God." (At home.)

Middle Octoraro Society— *Continued*

1779 Nov. 1 "rode 16 miles to S. Hathorn's McLung's, widow Fuler-
              ton." (From home.)

      "   2 "rode 9 miles by John Ram., widow Moore, Robert
              Ramsay's, home."

  " 3, 4, 5 "rode 18 miles widow Collins, John Paterson's;
              preached 102:16–19 and baptized Jean daughter to
              James Ramsay; lectured 1 Corinthians 15:55–L; went
              to W. Works."

      Dec. 24 "rode 11 miles home by James Glens." (From John
               Dolaps or Dunlap's.)

1780 Mar. 23 "rode 10 miles to J. A. (John Andrew's) preached 37:
              1–7, catechized and baptized John, son to W. La(w)."
              (Then 10 miles home from James McKts. on 23rd.)

      "   26 "Sabbath—preached 145:1–8. Lectured 7–11 and bap-
              tized Mary to J. Maeben." (At home.)

      "   27 "rode 11 miles to John and Jas. Walkers." (From
              home.)

      "   28 "rode 12 miles—preached psalm 26 catechized persons
              and baptized Rebec., daughter to Jas. Walker; John to
              Wm. Dunlop; and Port. neg." (From home.)

      Apr. 5 "rode 4 miles to and from Widow McCoubray's R. R's.,
               Infair, sick, night." (From home.)

      "   9 "Sabbath—preached 15–19. Lectured 16–L and bap-
              tized Mary to Robert Paterson." (At home.)

      "   10 "rode 6 miles to Mr. S. Walker's, Jas. Lough., and John
              Ramsay's."

  " 11, 12 "rode 12 miles home John Maeben's, Widow Collins—
              rain—aguish."

      "   16 "Sabbath—preached 19–L and lectured Malachi 3:1–6
              —cold rain—Mr. McFadden with me." (At home.)

      June 19 "rode 16 miles Martha Robi., Jas. Ramsay's, home—
               all well—praise God."

      "   25 "Sabbath—preached 15–L. Lectured Nahum 1:1–8—
              preached Luke 24:17 and baptized James, son to Jos.
              Rob. g.a. praise God. Mr. McFadden present." (At
              home.)

  " 28, 29 "rode 12 miles to Jas. Lough. Rams. burial—H. Coul-
              ter." (From home.)

      July 27 "rode 6 miles to Wm. Steel's—gave John Clark 30, Dob.
               26." (From home.)

Middle Octoraro Society— *Continued*

1780 Aug. 29   "rode 6 miles to and from Widow Ramsay's and Jean Bigham's, etc." (From home.)

"   30, 31   "rode 12 miles to John Patterson's, Mary Collins; preached 79: 8 and preached Romans 16: 25, 26, and baptized Jean to Robert Kilpatric."

Sept. 4, 5   "rode 22 miles to Mr. S. and John Moor's (on way home), married Sam Cachy and Eleanor Moor—came by Ramsay; borrowed 4 bushels of rye."

"   15   "rode 8 miles to and from James Rosses—rs 75 lbs. by —— McKt. the 18th." (From home.)

"   24   "Sabbath—preached 7: 1–61 lectured 3–L and baptized Mary to James Richy—rain." (At home.)

Oct.   17   "rode and walked 11 miles home (from James Walker's); married Newport Walker and Jean Broadly negroes, mulatto at Gilb. married Sam Little and Elizabeth Spencer rs from S. 40 dollars talked Mr. M."

1781 Jan.   18   "rode 19 miles, rode 10 miles to and from James and W. Loughheads, visited." (From home.)

"   30   "rode 7 miles to Mr. Millars and Wm. Anderson's." (From home.)

"   31   "rode 10 miles to James Galbreath's, Robert's Mills, home."

Feb.   19   "rode 9. 20th—rode 4 miles to Wal. Buchanan's and to and from J. Stoner."

"   26   "rode 10 miles to H. Coulters, John Andrews." (From home.)

"   27   "rode 4 miles to Thomas Ewings; preached 81: lectured Jeremiah 31: 31 and baptized Wm. son to John Ewing." (From John Andrew's.)

Mar.   2   "rode 11 miles from R. Laws home."

"   26   "rode 7 miles Ewing's, Alisons, Wm. Dunlop, preached 108, preached verse 12 and baptized Joseph to James Glen, and James to W. D." (At Mid. Octoraro—Wm. Dunlop's.)

Apr.   30   "rode 4 miles to W. T. Eleanor sick, to James Loughhead's." (From home.)

May   9   "rode 6 miles, visited Eleanor Thomsons, James Richie; ½ bushel corn."

"   20   "Sabbath—preached 17–23; lectured 17–L; preached same concerning Hypocrisy, etc. and baptized John son to John Tod." (At home.)

June 29   "rode 10 miles to and from W. Anderson's—sick child." (From home.)

Middle Octoraro Society— *Continued*

1781 Aug. 9 "rode 9 miles D. McReady's, Wahob, Joseph Walkers."
(From home.)

" 12 "Sabbath—preached 5–9; lectured 9–14. Preached
from same and baptized Eliz. to Dan McReady."

Sept. 16 "Sabbath—preached 15–2–L; lectured Romans 8: 14–
16–23 preached Galatians 3: 19 and baptized Margaret
to Wm. Ewing, o.a." (At home.)

" 20 "rode 7 miles to Hanna's, Walker's, Mrs. Moor's,
home."

" 23 "Sabbath—preached 21–26; lectured 23–28 and preached
Galatians 3: 19 and baptized Thomas son to Newport
give all praise to God."

1782 Jan. 21 "rode 8 miles to Poequea's, conversed widow and Jean."
(From home.)

" 22 "rode 5 miles to James Loughhead's. Married Alexander White and Jean Fulerton."

May 12 "Sabbath—Mr. S. preached Job 5: 4. I discoursed
Isaiah 52: 7, 8 and baptized Samuel to James Patterson, little Britian song." (At home.)

" 21 "preached 46: 8–L. Lectured Romans 6: 1–5 and baptized Elizabeth to John Ramsay, and Margaret to
Arch McCready." (At home.)

" 27 "rode 15 miles to and from R. R's Field; conversed
widow Ramsay." (From home.)

" 28 "preached 51: 4; lectured 1 Corinthians 10: 1–6 and baptized John Murray to Rev. John Smith and Ann to
John Caldwell." (At home.)

June 2 "Sabbath—preached 32: 1; lectured 7–13 preached same
and baptized Hew to Wm. Carson and Wm. to James
Craig, g.a."

" 4 "rode 20 miles to and from Dan Brooks; preached 76:
4–L; lectured Romans 11: 13–18 and baptized Mary
Newberry to James Graham o.a." (From home.)

July 4 "rode 12 miles, visited sick Widow Colins and Esq.
Millars." (From home.)

Middle Octoraro Society—*Continued*

1782 July 17   "rode 9 miles Mr. S. Rocky's Ram. bought Ruckly's cow 4-19-9."

Sept. 22   "Sabbath—preached 25–L; lectured Revelation 3: 19–L preached same and baptized Elizabeth daughter to Wm. Law." (At home.)

"   30   "rode 12 miles Mr. S. Luig. R. James Law home." (From home.)

Oct.   6   "Sabbath. Mr. S. preached 100; lectured Luke 11: 20. I preached Habakkuk 2: 4 and baptized Wm. son to Sam McDowel o.a. praise God." (At home.)

"   16   "rode 8 miles and to Robert and James Paterson's now widow." (From home.)

"   24   "rode 12 miles, married John Reed and Agnes Motherel." (From home.)

Nov. 26, 27, 28   "rode 15 miles James Wilson's, Paters. D. Hess's, J. Bra." (From home.)

———

1783 Jan.   8   "rode 5 miles Captain Walker's, W. T. and James Loughhead's." (From home.)

"   9   "rode 2 miles—snow to John Ramsay's cold, cold."

"   10   "rode 2 miles home, very sick in my field, Mr. Smith."

———

"   20   "rode 10 miles to Mr. S. to James Colvils, to Wm. Robs." (From home.)

"   21   "rode 3 miles; preached 51: 1—catechized and baptized Sam to James Robs."

"   22   "rode 3 miles to Rob. Calbreath's, to John Caldwel's, G. Book."

"   23   "rode 1 mile, preached 51 close. Catechized 28 went to John Ker's." (Rode 4 miles home on 24th.)

———

Feb. 24   "rode 7 miles to Mr. Millar's, to Dan McConel's, cold."

"   25   "Preached 46: 7—and catechized 36 concerning death and resurrection."

"   26   "rode 5 miles from widow McCon. Sen., to J. And. Mr. M."

———

Mar. 10, 11   "rode 9 miles to widow Col., moth. R. Paterson's, preached 46: 1—catechized 32: 2 and baptized Thomas to R. Pat. and Peter to Robert Kilpatrick." (From home.)

"   12   "rode 7 miles by W. S. and James Wilson's, home, family all well."

———

Middle Octoraro Society— *Continued*

1783 Mar. 18, 19, 20   "Held Presbytery, Mr. S. to be installed in Oxford and me liberati from Octorara, etc."   (At home.)

Apr. 28, 29   "rode 15 miles to M. Mc widow F. Alexander Whites. J. R. 27 baptized Wm. son to James Gilmor, o.a. praise God. S. preached Ephesians 1: 22–3."   (From home.)

June 22   "Sabbath—Mr. S. lectured Revelation 7: 13—preached last verse and baptized Francis, James Th(orn?)."   (At home.)

Nov. 10, 11   "rode 9 miles visited Sam Caughy's, and John Ker's, lodged H. Cou."   (From home.)

1784 Apr. 1   "preached 44: 17—catechized 12 persons and baptized James Rea, born June 16, 1759 and Wm. his son born Oct. 17th last."   (At home.)

———

" 19, 20, 21   "rode 25 miles to John And., Ewins, W. & James Glens then to widow McConel's, Gab., Morrisons, Paisleys, K. Co., home."

" 22   "rode 5 miles to and from Hen Rocky's, H. sick, P. in a rage."   (From home.)

" 25   "Sabbath—preached 6: 2, lectured 10—preached Philippians 3: 10 and baptized Alexander son to John Ritchard, and Martha born March 5th, 1784."   (At home.)

May 1   "rode 5 miles to and from Hen. R. and Perrigrew's."   (From home.)

"   2   "Sabbath—preached 53: 1–6, lectured Colossians 3: 15–17 and preached Philippians 3: 10 g.a. praise God."

"   3   "Tramped 3 miles to James Wilson's, R. Ramsay's and home."

———

"   9   "Sabbath—preached 5–L. Lectured 16–L—preached from same and baptized John son to Jas. Wal.—b. Jan. 27—held session concerning Clan marr."   (At John Walker's.)

" 10   "rode 9 miles home—sold Snip to Gilb. Bu. —— 14-0-0."

———

" 24, 25   "rode 7 miles Hugh Coulte—married Nathaniel and Isobel (Park)."   (At home.)

July 18   "Sabbath—preached 7–L; lectured 30: 10–18. Preached 3: 17 and baptized John son to John Berry, B. May 28th, 1784 o.a. praise God—hot."

" 26   "rode 7 miles to Slaymakers and to Widow Fulerton's— McFadde(n)."   (From home.)

———

" 28   "rode 10 miles—preached 92: 12—lectured Genesis 18: 23–L and baptized John Woods, etc.—exhausted— trouble."   (From home.)

" 29   "rode 8 miles Widow Bigham's—Moore sick."

Aug. 1   "Sabbath—preached 60: 1–6. Lectured Genesis 22: 1—

Middle Octoraro Society— *Continued*

preached Galatians 6: 15 and baptized Josiah, son to Joseph Rob., born June 24th." (At home.)

1784 Aug. 8   "Sabbath—Mr. S. lectured John 20: 19–23—I preached Galatians 6: 15 and baptized Mary daughter to Jas. Glover, born July 1 o.a."

" 16   "preached 65: 1—preached Job 13: 15 burying Rob. Orr, J. Rich." (At home.)

" 29   "Sabbath—rode 7 miles—preached 61: 1–5; lectured Jeremiah etc.—preached Isaiah 50—last verse—(baptized?) John and Rachel, son, daughter to Jas. Hood born." (3 miles from Mordecai Persals.)

Nov. 16   "rode 9 miles to James Glens broke rib at Hums J. 8, 31 sore." (From home.)

" 21   "Sabbath—preached 65: 5–9; lectured Colossians 1: 18— and baptized Mary and Ann C. March 28, 1782 and Feb. 8, 1784, to Elijah Forsyth, and Martha and John C. August 28, 1782, and March 2, 1784, to John McCamon." (At home?)

1785 Oct. 17   "Married John Hanna and Dorathy Harris, pub. Mr. Semples, kept all night."

1786 July 22   "rode 8 miles to Mr. Millar's, preached 14: 20, lectured 2 Timothy 1: 6–10, preached verse 10, and baptized Elizabeth to John Barg. born June 23, o.a. praise God." (From home.)

Dec. 3   "Sabbath—preached 76: 7–L and preached Isaiah 32: 2 g.a. baptized Wm. son to Robert Templeton born July 28, 1785, Amelia daughter to Matthew Calhoun born Dec. 2d, '84, and Robert S and (or to) Alexander born July 10, '85 and James born Dec. 22, '84, and Agnes born Aug. 12th, 1786 to Sam Stewart, and to Thomas Smilie, 3 viz., John born Feb. 5, 1783, Ann - - - born Dec. 31st, 1784, and David born Sept. 29th, 1786." (From Hugh Stewart's and Mr. Cluney's, James.)

1787 Jan. 15, 16   "rode 18 miles, preached 32: 5–9, lectured Romans 5: 12 and baptized Thomas son to Henry Hanna, born Dec. 2d, '85 and Elizabeth Hamilton (alias Lefarty)— married James Purdy and Mary Farmers." (From home.)

Feb. 27   "rode 1½ miles, 6 McTeers, preached 25: 15 and preached Isaiah 55: 6, 7." (From Alexander McCulloch's—then 4 miles home on Mar. 1.)

Apr. 5   "A. McCuloch's, preached psalm 12: 1—lectured 1 Peter 4: 1–9 and baptized Agnes to Will Reid, born Feb. 16, 1787, o.a., praise God." (9 miles from home Robert Reid's.)

May 2   "rode 10 miles home, family all well, sister gone.

Middle Octoraro Society— *Continued*

Preached 6: 10, lectured preached from same and baptized Margaret to Arch McReady born."

1787 May 29   "rode 13 miles, 7 E. W., married Hew Sutherland and Sara Mehowl, (nothing) received Wals went off on the 27." (From home.)

Aug. 1   "rode 9 miles to widow Cachy's, Pais." (From home.)

Nov. (?)   "x x baptized James Purdy born 1747 (1787?)." (In page summary.)

Dec. 3   "rode 5 miles to Mr. Moors, John Bain, Jas. Lough." (From home.)

" 4   "rode 5 miles to Thomas and widow Fulerton's."

" 5   "rode 8 miles to Mr. F., Thomas Johnson's, Mary M., McGr."

1788 Jan. 20   "Sabbath—rode 4 miles A, Moor's, preached 48—lectured, visited Wha." (From home.)

Feb. 21   "Married James Teenan and Jean Brown nothing." (At home.)

Mar. 3   "rode 10 miles, Mr. F. A. Whites, home, all well."

" 4   "rode 2 miles, married Nathaniel Coulter and Margaret Moor, rs D. bad wedding."

" 13, 14   "rode 12 miles Wm. and James Loughhead's, etc., etc." (From home.)

" 22   "Tramped to and from Thomas Legates, exhorted, etc." (From home.)

May 11   "Preached 9: 1-8, lectured 23: 1-9 and baptized Hew, son to Dan McCready born." (At home.)

" 19   "rode 8 miles from Robert Patterson's, home."

1789 Jan. 20   "rode 7 miles, preached (at Wm. Downie's) 42: 1—lectured Matthew 28: 11-L and baptized Wm. McGown and Moses, about 20 and 18 years, and David son to Wm. Downie, born June 26, 1787—the (3) youths, sons to Malcolm Deliri." (Then rode 7 miles to Esther's, the Coulter's and home on 21st and 22nd.)

Mar. 2   "rode 3 miles by Helen Brown's—sick to John Ramsay's." (From home.)

" 3   "rode 1 mile; preached 107: 1-8, Exc. 1 Peter L: 6, 7 and baptized John to John Ramsay, born Mar., Sarah to Hugh McCuchon, born Dec. 18, 1788, came to James Loughhead's."

May 19, 20   "rode 14 miles to and from W. Down's—3 bushels corn." (From home.)

" 27, 28   "rode 10 miles to and from Talbot's, and Lough, etc."

Middle Octoraro Society— *Continued*

1789 July   6   "rode 17 miles home and Mrs. Tals dying—Tuesday 1
o'clock died, Elizabeth Talbot, etc."

Sept. 20   "Sabbath—rode 3 miles to R. P.—preached 117: 25–29
—D. 11 D.D. and baptized Andrew son to Jas. Purdie,
born." (Then rode 8 miles home on 21st.)

"   23   "rode 12 miles to R. P's and Henry Hanna's." (From
home.)

Oct. 22   "rode —— miles to Widow Collins, R. Kil., and Widow
Paterson." (From home.)

Nov. 9   "x x x rode 9 miles home—visited W. Steel—w. sick—."

"   11   "—— Walter begged to pray with and for."

"   12   "—— conversed with W.—told he hoped had seen the
folly of past life, etc., etc. had no view of recovery—
thus 3 til 7th day when he breathed his last, I would
hope in the Lord. On the 12th was decently buried
by his aunt." *

1790 Aug. 15   "Sabbath—preached 14th part, Lectured Genesis 45:
1—baptized Jean to Jos. Rob. xx." (At home.)

"   22   "Sabbath—preached 15 part—visited—25, etc."

"   29   "Sabbath—preached 16th part and lectured Genesis 18:
16–L."

Muddy Run Society and Meeting-house

About 4 miles from McCall's Ferry on the Susquehanna a log church
was built in 1750.

1751 Oct.   2   "Rode 2 miles to and from Muddy Run Meeting-house
where preached Psa. 43: 3–1 and preached Isaiah 28: 16
and baptized Agnes, daughter to Jo. Reid and John
and Margaret S. and daughter to Jo. McMillan, and
Agnes, daughter to Peter Paterson for these in good
health, praise to my gracious God." (From John Duncan's.)

Dec. 17   "Rode 4 miles to and from Muddy Run meeting,
preached Psa. . . . Preached Psalm 8 and . . . Baptized Mary, John and Helen: to Jo Brownlies. . . .
(From Jo. Brownlie's). . . . Baptized Janet and James
to Jo (John?) Paterson. . . . 2 miles to Jo. Robiesons
in good health praise the Lord. Conversed and
preached Psa. 129 L. Zechariah 12: 1–4 and baptized
Elizabeth daughter to Joseph Wishart, William and
John, sons to Thomas Paterson and John and Mary

* Dr. Cuthbertson is referring to his son, Walter.

Muddy Run Society and Meeting-house— *Continued*

S. and D. to William Robieson.   Then rode 6 miles to
Dan McClellan's."

1752 Apr. 23   "Rode 3 miles to Muddy Run meeting-house preached
Ps. 115: 1–6, preach. Ps. 5: 19 and bap. Mary daugh.
to Wm. Mitchel. . . ."   (From Joseph Ker's.)

1753 Jan. 3   "Preached Psalm 60: 1–5, and lectured Romans 19: 4—
and baptized Jean, daughter to The. Ker."   (At John
McMillan's—then rode 7 miles to John Duncan's on
4th.)

"   30   "Fa. Day—Rode 5 miles, preached Psalm 74: 1–8,
preached Psalm 74: 1–8, preached Jeremiah 14: 7.—
Rode 7 miles to Ja. Paterson's, William Mitch. and
John Duncan."   (From John Walker's.)

Feb. bet. 13 & 17   "Travelled 3 miles to and from Jo. Marshal's.
preached Psalm 119: 9–15, preached Luke 12: 1—etc.
baptized Alexander son to William Robieson . . An.
D. s. . . ."   (From John Duncan's.)

Nov. 8   "Rode 3 miles to J. Rob.   Married Robert Scot and
Mary McMuray."   (From John Duncan's.)

1754 Jan. 1   "Rode 6 miles to John Duncan's, good health, praise
to my good God."   (From Daniel McClellan's.)

"   2   "Rode 5 miles after marrying William Reynolds and
Mt. Paterson."

"   8   "rode 2 miles to W. R. and John Brownlie's—received,
invited, etc."   (From John Duncan's.)

"   9   "Rode 6 miles to lit.   Preached psalm preached Galatians 5: 24 and baptized Isobel daughter to John Brownlie and Jean daughter to William Mitchel.   Then went
to William Clark's—conversed etc. during the night."

Nov. 12   "Preached psalm 112: 1–5.   Preached Zechariah 8: 8.
Baptized Sarah, daughter to William Ker."   (From
John McMillan's.)

1756 Feb. 5   "Rode 6 miles to Mud. Meeting, preached psalm 93:
preached psalm 55: 22 and baptized John son to Robert
Duncan and Thomas and Charles adopted sons to Jo
Paterson and Wm. Smith; and James son to Elizabeth
Ayers, then rode to J. D. and John Robies."   (From
John Brownlie's.)

Dec. 30   "Rode 6 miles to and from Wm. Neilie's; married Hew
Reynolds and Mary K."   (From John Duncan's.)

1757 Jan. 3   "Rode 9 miles to J. Brownlies, married John Gebie and
Janet Brown."

Muddy Run Society and Meeting-house— *Continued*

1758 Apr. 11   "Rode 7 miles to John McMillan's—conversed Brownlie about ——." (From John Robieson's.)

"   12   "Rode 6 miles over Susquehanna to Hugh Rosses—in good health, praise God."

1759 Aug. 15   "rode 16 miles to Muddy Run—held session, etc. Preached psalm 119: 123 and preached Corinthians 11: 31; and baptized Jean, daughter to John Reid and Joseph to Hew Reynolds; then came home—family—unwell." (From John Duncan's.)

1760 Jan. 10   "Rode 10 miles after preaching psalm 86: 1—preaching Joshua 1: 15 and baptized Janet to John Gabby and Josphel daughter to John Robs." (From John Duncan's.)

1761 June 11   "Rode 28 miles to and from J. McMillan's; married John McConel and Mary Dougherty; also Wm. Gebby and Ann McMillan rs. 24 and 35, exhaust; swamp; Cutt 10, 11th." (From Carrol's Tract?.)

1762 Sept. 3   "Rode 6 miles to John Duncan's, W. Brown's." (From A. Stewart's.)

"   5   "Sabbath preached psalm 38: 12–17; lectured Philippians 3: 12–L; preached John 6: 24 and baptized Agnes daughter to Peter Paterson and Elizabeth and Susannah daughters to John Thomson, give all praise to God."

1767 Feb. 1   "Sabbath preached psalm 105: 24–32; preached Micah last chapter and baptized James son to Thomas Finey, give all praise to God." (At John Duncan's.)

1770 Jan. 19   "rode 3 miles to and from Finey's. Wrote his will." (From Wm. Brown's.)

"   23, 25   "rode 13 miles to John Dun. Hew Stewart's preached psalm 69: 1–6 lectured Mark 16: 15, 16 and baptized Joseph son to him."

1771 Jan. 31   "rode 6 miles; preached psalm 30: 1—lectured Deuteronomy 33: 26—and baptized John son to Elijah Stewart and Agnes, daughter to James McGlauchlin; visited And. Cal. a dying in Christ." (From Jean Sloan's and John Duncan's.)

Feb. 3   "Sabbath preached psalm 7–13; preached John 3: 18 and baptized Helen to Bartholomew Hains; read Edict. W.B.; T.M.; H.M."

1772 Jan. 15   "rode 5 miles to J. D., after preaching (at James Cal.)

Muddy Run Society and Meeting-house—*Continued*

and lecturing Psalm 42 and baptized William son to J. C." (Then rode 3 miles to W. B's.)

1772 May 13 "rode 3 miles to W(illiam) Brown's." (From John Duncan's.)

1773 Feb. 1 "rode 3 miles to Matt. Smith's, John Dunc.—cold." (From Wm. Brown's.)

Nov. 22 "7 miles to John Park's—married John Paterson and Janet Paterson o.a.—received 10 and 20." (From Jos. Ker's.)

1783 June 28 "rode 6 miles to and from J. Duncan's, burying ground, g.ga. Dr. Richy." (From Wm. Brown's.)

"   29 "Sabbath—preached 44: 5–11; lectured P. 4: 5–9 preached Prov. 11: 2 and baptized James and Susanna to Elijah Stewart give all praise to my gracious God."

1787 Oct. 11 "rode and walked 9 miles to Ruther., John Duncan's." (From Mr. Boyd's.)

"   12 "rode 3 miles to widow Browns W. died the 8th month."

"   14 "Sabbath—preached 87; lectured Jeremiah 11: 6–12 and preached Matthew 11: 28—G.a."

"   15 "rode 3 miles to T. Smily's, James Calhoun's, cold, etc."

"   16 "rode 10 to Sam S., to Hain's, John Ker's, etc."

1788 Oct. 5 "Sabbath rode 10 miles, preached 7: 13, lectured 10–12 preached 30: 17 and baptized S." (son John McMillan or J. Branon.) (From J. McMillan's.)

New Holland

1763 Mar. 4 "rode 22 miles home by Mr. Proudfoot's, H. Fulerton's." (From Robert Gilmore's.)

1779 Apr. 20 "rode 3 miles to Robert Pro., preached 129 and exercised Hebrews 9: 13, 14 g.a." (From John McCleary's.)

1783 May 12 "rode 12 miles to Mr. Proudfoot's, New Holland." (From Alexander McCleary's.)

1784 Dec. 1 "rode 3 miles to And. Proudfoot's, J. McCleary's." (From Rob. Dixon's.)

"   3 "rode 1 mile to Wm. Smith Esq. Slept Mr. Slemons."

"   5 "Sabbath—rode 2 miles, preached 66: 7–15, and lectured 11: 20, Robert Proudfoot's."

Octoraro Creek

1753 Bet. Feb. 19–24 "Rode 12 miles to Robert Andrew's, preached Psalm 86: 1–6, lectured Ephesians 6: 11–13, baptized

Octoraro Creek— *Continued*

Mary daughter to him, and Sarah, daughter to James Duncan." (From Humphrey Fulerton's.)

1755 May 27   "Rode 5 miles to Robert Andrews, the Creek Octoraro." (From Robert Lochhead's.)

1759 Jan. 4   "Rode 4 miles to R. Andrews—preached psalm 17: 4–7. Explained John 4: 39–48 and baptized Moses son to John Walker and Hanna daughter to J. Dunlap." (From Robert Loughhead's; then 8 miles home on 5th.)

1762 Mar. 16   "Rode 9 miles to R. Andrews, appears consumptive." (From home.)

May 7   "Rode 16 miles to and from Robert Andrews; preached psalm 84: 7—lectured Hebrews 4: 9–12 and baptized Rebecca to Isaac Walker, Jean to Peter Wilson, and Agnes daughter to John Park." (From home.)

June 28   "Rode 18 miles to my friend R. Andrews burial."

July 22   "Rode 18 miles with widow Andrews; married Andrew McCleary and Margaret Mitchel."

Nov. 4   "rode 6 miles to widow And. preached psalm 68: 9–13; lectured Solomon 2: 8–14 baptized Martha daughter to James Wilson o.a. praise to my gracious God." (From J. McCleary's.)

1770 Apr. 25   "rode 8 miles to Widow Andrews—preached 34: 17 catechized 20 persons concerning baptism and baptized Sidney to Francis McKnaught.—went to James ——."

Peach Bottom

1755 June 3   "Rode 13 miles to Peach Bottom 2 miles water to Andrew Ro(wan's.) "

"   4   "Rode 5 miles W. Nicols after preaching psalm 48: 10–L, preached 2 Corinthians 3: 20 and baptized Agnes and James daughter and son to Andrew Ro(wan.) "

1770 June 18   "rode 22 miles to Rowan's; then preached psalm 51: preaching 7th verse and baptized David son to Wm. Thomson, very tired." (From Hummel Spring—W. B's.)

1772 May 19   "rode 9 miles to Mr. Rowan's; married Jesse Mitchel and Ruth Mitchel Wm. Thom. and Jean Johnston." (From David Mitchel's.)

1782 Feb. 22   "rode 5 miles to John Reahs; bad roads, John Dyes." (From Walker's.)

"   23   "rode and sailed 10 miles to C. Semples, And. Rowans."

"   24   "Sabbath—preached psalm 28: 1–5 and preached Zechariah 13: 1–9 g.a. praise God." (At Rowan's.)

"   25, 26   "rode 5 miles to J. Mitch. Laird's, W. Reid's, etc."

Pequea Society

In the Pequea Valley, about fifteen miles from the mouth of Pequea Creek, which enters the Susquehanna River, a Society was formed in 1750; services were held at Humphrey Fulerton's. Rev. John Cuthbertson preached not only at Mr. Fulerton's but at the homes of different members of this Society.

1751 Aug. 13   "Rode 8 miles to Humphrey Fulerton's, exhausted, etc. Fell to study." (From Craighead's.)

"   14   "Preached 84: 4–10. Lectured Matthew 11: 25–30 and preached Genesis 49: 18."

bet.
Sept. 16 & 19   "Preached psalm 138: 1–4 and preached Luke 12: 32 and baptized Marjory, daughter to Neal McKnaught g.a. Discourse with Robert Andrew, tired, etc." (At Humphrey Fulerton's.)

1752 Jan.   5   "x x Rode 3 miles to and from the Coupers, married Phinehas Whiteside and Anna Couper. Give all the praise to my God." (From Humphrey Fulerton's.)

"   16   "Preached Psa. 84: 10–L and preached Zechariah 13: 1 and baptized Samuel son to Thomas Montgomery with g.a. but obliv." (At Pequea.)

May   5   "Preach. Ps. 27: 1–5 preach. Ephesians 5: 8 and bap. Charles son to McMeling (McClung?), Ann daugh. to Humphrey Fulerton, Jean daugh. to Robert McCurdy, and George son to John Boyd. good health praise God." (At Pequea.)

"   11   "Rode 6 miles to Neal McK.—fire—went to Sam Nickleduff's, tired, etc." (From Humphrey Fulerton's.)

Aug. 28   "Married Thoas. Paxton and Janet Estin, Poequey."

Dec. 21   "preach. Ps. 27: 5–L. lectured Act. 13: 38–42 and baptized John son to Phinehas Whiteside o.a. praise to my gracious God."

1753 June 1   "Rode 2 miles to John Robieson's lectured Ps. 43 baptized Mary daugh. to Jas. Ramsay, and examined 50 persons egi——."

"   11   "Rode 16 mi. at Thomas Johnston's preach. Ps. 60: 1–5 preach. Hebrews 4: 11 examined 14 persons and baptized Margaret daugh. to Neal McK. went to R. Gilm."

1754 Feb. 24   "Sabbath. Rode 5 miles preached psalm 51: 6–11. Lectured Joel 2: 15–18. Preached Romans 14: 1 and baptized Agnes, daughter to Corn. Collins and Isobel, daughter to Esther Paxton, g.a. praise to my God." (From John Walker's.)

Mar.   4   "Rode 8 miles to John Elliot and Humphrey Fulerton. Cold, etc." (From John Walker's.)

Pequea Society— *Continued*

1754 Mar. 5 "Preached 103: 1–5, preached Hosea 2–19 and baptized Margaret daughter to ——."

May 26 "Sabbath. Rode 12 miles. Preached psalm 56: 7–L. Lectured and baptized Sarah daughter to Isaac Walker —went to Poeq." (From Dan. McClellan's.)

" 30 "Rode 16 miles to and from Wm. Calbreath—preached psalm 126, examined 50 persons, and baptized James adopted son to William Calbreath—give all praise to God." (From Robert Lochhead's.)

June 2 "Sabbath—Rode 12 miles preached psalm 57: 1—Lectured Amos 2: 6–L and preached Heb. 10: 23 and baptized John and John, sons to George McGown and Magt. Fulerton, Martha, daughter to John Walker and Mt. daughter to Robert Ramsay—went to Humphrey Fulerton's—good health."

" (3) "10 miles B. after preaching psalm 43: 1–L—late. baptized Wm. son to Phinehas Whiteside and Mary, daughter to Mary Laieder."

Oct. 20 (At Robert Loughhead's, Middle Octoraro Society, Phineas Whiteside admitted to Office of Ruling Elder with others.)

Dec. (5) "Rode 12 miles to Humphrey Fulerton's, asked Russel's 3 questions etc." (Then rode 8 miles to John Walker's on 6th.)

1755 July 13 "Sabbath rode 11 miles to Humphrey Fulerton's after preaching psalm 14: 20–L. Lectured Amos 9: 8–L preached Micah 5: 5 rebuked Jas. Pat. and J. Y. baptized Thomas son to —— Brown and James son to James Duncan g.a." (From Wm. Thomson's.)

Sept. 21 "Sabbath. Rode 6 miles after preaching psalm 18: 6–12, lectured Matthew 6: 1–9. Preached Hosea 2: 19 and baptized Mary daughter to James Innes went to Neal McKts." (From David Dinwoody's.)

Oct. 14 "Rode 14 miles married James Hill and Helen Buchanan, went to Humphrey Fulerton's." (From John Duncan's.)

1756 Feb. 9 "Rode 11 miles to Greg. Dew.—held session, rebuked P. Bug. etc.—went to Humphrey Fulerton's." (From Joseph Ker's.)

Mar. 30 "Rode 6 miles to Humphrey Fulerton's after preaching psalm 129 (at Phinehas Whiteside's), preached Jeremiah 30: 22 and baptized Peter son to Phinehas Whitesides, give all praise to God."

Pequea Society— *Continued*

1756 June 13 "Sabbath. Rode 11 miles to Humphrey Fulerton's;
preached psalm 89: 5–10, lectured Matthew 10: —16;
preached Isaiah 26: 16—and baptized John son to Alex
Lackey and Eliza daughter to Cornelius Colins; the
sec.—their sacrament this day." (From John Walker's.)

July 26 " Rode 6 miles to Neal McKnaughts good health praise
God. Preached psalm 37: 1–5 and examined 27 persons concerning Repentance." (From David Dunwoody's.)

Aug. 22 "Sabbath. Rode 14 miles to P. W's, after preaching
psalm 90: 1–L (at Robert Lochhead's) lectured Mat-
thew 12: 1–8 and preached Hebrews 10: 1; baptized
James son to Peter Paterson and Agnes daughter to
Wm. Paterson. Rode and walked 16 miles to Wm.
Moores; family all well ——."

bet.

(Oct. 4 & 8) "rode 5 miles to Phinehas Whiteside's; very tender."
" Rode 4 miles to and from Robert McCurdys and widow
Caruthers."

1757 Jan. 10 "Rode 12 miles to Humphrey Fulerton's; married John
Rob. and Barb. McKn." (From Robert Lochhead's.)

"   24 " Rode 14 miles to Humphrey Fulerton's; and married
Alexander Rodger and Margaret S. bought Josias
Kers plantation at 350 lib. paid 93 lib. lodged there."
(From Humphrey Fulerton's.)

Mar. 1 "Preached psalm 112: 5–9 and preached Proverbs 23:
26 and baptized Martha daughter to Andrew Giffan
and married Charles Kilgore and Jean McClure; also
Alexander Young and Elizabeth Cany." (At James
McKnaughtan's.)

"   2 "Rode 8 miles to George Brandons; good health, praise
God. to p. at G. Cunninghams."

"   5 "Rode 7 miles to N. McKnaughtans after preaching
psalm 110 and preaching Solomon 7: 10 g.a."

"   27 "Sabbath. Rode 10 miles to Humphrey Fulerton's
after preaching psalm 102: 19–23; lectured Matthew
17: 1–9; preached 2 Chronicles 20: 12 and baptized
Thomas son to James Ramsay." (From Joseph Ker's.)

June 12 "Sab.—Rode 10 miles to Humphrey Fulerton's, after
preaching psalm 104, lectured Matthew 19: 13—
preached Zephaniah 2: 1 and baptized Ann daughter to
Robert Duncan."

Pequea Society— *Continued*

1758 May 18 "rode 5 miles to Phinehas Whitesides, after preaching
psalm 18: 27–31 (at Humphrey Fulerton's) and
preaching Job 17–9 explained Matthew 28: 18, 19.
Baptized Thomas to P. W."

"   19 "rode 6 miles to Robert Gilmors. Aguish both n. day."

"   21 "Sabbath—preached psalm 117. Lectured Matthew 28:
1–10. Preached Romans 5: 1 and baptized Ann to
Hugh Gib.—give all praise to God—a great gust."
(At Robert Gilmore's.)

Oct. 24 "rode 9 miles to Humphrey Fulerton's—preached psalm
27: 1. Explained Acts 5: 29 etc. Baptized Mathew,
son to Mathew McClung o.a. praise to my gracious
God."

Dec. 17 "Sabbath—rode 3 miles to Robert Gilmor's, after
preaching psalm 119—last part, and preaching Jeremiah 5: 1–2 and baptizing Martha, daughter to T.
Paxton; and Eliz. daughter to William Robieson."
(From Thomas Kennedy's, Brandywine.)

1760 Feb. 12 "Held session x x. Preached psalm 61: 1—lectured
Romans 13: 14–L baptized Rachel daughter to H.
Gib. and James son to T. Black." (At Humphrey
Fulerton's.)

bet.
Mar. 5 & 7 "rode 7 miles to Phinehas Whiteside's v(endue.) "
(From home.)

1761 Apr. 2 "rode 10 miles to Phinehas Whitesides; married Jos.
McCord and E. . . ." (From Lancaster.)

Oct. 28 "walked 3 miles to Phinehas Whitesides after preaching
psalm 61 and lectured 2 Corinthians 6: 16–L and baptized Ann daughter to him and Mary to Robert." (At
Humphrey Fulerton's.)

1763 Dec. 22 "rode 5 miles to P. Whiteside's—preached psalm 85.
Explained Mark 16: 15, 16 and baptized Edward, son
to him—give all praise to God." (From Humphrey
Fulerton's.)

1764 Jan. 24 "rode 8 miles to P. W. and Math. McClung's—preached
psalm 106. Explained Revelations 3: 18 and baptized
Hew son to him (McClung?)—great snow." (From
home.)

June 5 "rode 24 miles Widow Calbreath's—preached psalm 91:
5 catechized 43 and baptized James, son to John Park
and Agnes, daughter to Peter Wilson." (From home.)

Oct. 14 "Sabbath—preached psalm 73: 21–25. Lectured Colossians 2: 10–13—preached Hebrews 12: 29 and baptized
son to James Speir o.a."

Pequea Society— *Continued*

1764 Oct. 22 "rode 10 miles to Neal McKts. Married John Redduc and Mary Reid—received 10 shillings—x x."

1765 Feb. 28 "rode 12 miles—preached psalm 37: — lectured John 15: 9–15—baptized James, son to John Rob., and Sarah, daughter to John Walker." (From Alexander Robieson's, etc.)

Mar. 3 "Sabbath—preached psalm 78: 9–14—preached Hebrews 6: 12 and baptized Elizabeth and Arthur to Thomas Scott."

Mar. 11 "rode 7 miles to Neal McKts. (from David Dunwoody's) held session—sacrament."

" 12 "rode 2 miles—preached psalm 34: 19. Lectured Acts 8: 35—baptized James son to Mathew Richie."

Apr. 25 "rode 9 miles—married Arthur Scott and Jean Ross; and William Loughhead and Sarah Thomson—Peq.— preached psalm 23; Exc. Hebrews 9: 14. Baptized William son to H. Fu." (From home.)

1767 Apr. 19 "Sabbath preached psalm 106: 44—lectured Hebrews 13 etc. preached Micah L.L. and baptized Elizabeth daughter to James Spier o.a. praise to my gracious God." (At Humphrey Fullerton's.)

Oct. 4 (See Middle Octoraro for ordination of Humphrey Fulerton, James Ramsay, Cornelius Collins, and John Robb.)

1768 May 24 "rode 12 miles—preached psalm 73: 25—preached 2 Sam. 23: 9, 10 and baptized James son to John Crawfurd—went to McClung's." (From James Reid's.)

1769 Feb. 7 "rode 5 miles; married Humphrey Fulerton and Martha Mi(tchel?)." (From James Campbell's.)

May 12 "rode 8 miles from N. McK. after catechizing 26 and baptizing Wm. son to Mat. Richie."

Aug. 28 "preached 15 part; preached Jude and baptized John to T. Paxton, rode 8 miles N. McKts."

Sept. 26 "rode 16 miles to and from Humphrey Fulerton's; preached psalm 120; lectured Isaiah 1: 16–21 and baptized John son to James Loughhead; presented by the mother." (From home.)

Nov. 29 "rode 8 miles to Mat. McClung's—preached psalm 23–1 —exercised Zech. 13: 1 and baptized John son to M. Mc. got cold." (From home.)

1770 Feb. 21, 22 "rode 12 miles preached psalm 61: 5–L—catechized 36 and baptized And. son to John Rob; and Elijah, son to Sam Rob." (From James Paterson's.)

1770 Apr. 19   "rode 14 miles preached Jude 5—catechized, baptized James son to And. McKt. x x." (Then 5 miles to Hugh Coulter's on 20th.)

May 24   "rode 9 miles to H. Fulerton's after preaching 94: 15–18; lectured Romans 8: 26–29 and baptized Mary Cotter, adult, g.a."

"   27   "Sabbath—preached 8: 4–L, lectured 65: 9–17 preached 41: 10 and baptized Margaret daughter to David Mitchel, presented by the mother—rode 12 miles." (At Humphrey Fulerton's.)

"   28   "rode 3 miles to T. Wade's after preaching psalm 119: 15th part—catechized 36 and baptized William, son to John McConel—g.a.l. (give all praise.)"

Sept. 19, 20   "rode 8 miles to D. M. H. Rankin's; preached psalm 126; lectured Acts 10: 34–44 and (baptized) John and Humphrey to James Brownlie and Humphrey Fulerton, o.a." (From John Gebby's in Maryland.)—

Sept. 23   "Sabbath preached 5–10; lectured John 8: 20–28; preached Isaiah 63: 8 and baptized Margaret daughter to Sam Wilson and Martha to Agnes McConel." (At Humphrey Fulerton's.)

1771 Aug. 5   "rode 8 miles to S. Bells and McGrews, Neal McKnaughtans." (From David Dunwoody's.)

Dec. 30   "rode 10 miles to Humphrey Fulerton's; at M. McCl. married John Graham and Martha Miller, tired."

"   31   "rode 1 mile; held session; preached 90: 11–4; lectured 1 Corinthians 10: 1—and baptized Samuel son to Hew Pattison—x x."

1772 Apr. 14, 15   "Walked 5 miles—preached 51: 5—preached 1 John 3: 23 and baptized John son to Thomas McKnaughtan to M. R. and J. W." (From Neal McKnaughtan's.)

May 27, 28   "rode 17 miles Matt. McCl., Humphrey Fulerton's: preached psalm 89: 15–19; catechized 23 persons and baptized Joseph to Eleanor Loughhead; dull and aguish all day." (From Hugh Coulter's.)

Dec. 2   "rode 12 miles to John Robs; preached 23: 1—lectured Acts 2: 37–41 and baptized Sam son to Sam Rob g.a." (From Wm. Robs.)

1774 Mar. 30, 31   "rode 16 miles (from home); catechized 30 and baptized Sarah daughter to James Ramsay at R. Patterson's."

Aug. 12, 13   "rode 18 miles to Humphrey Fulerton's and R McCalyrs, sore." (From home.)

Pequea Society—*Continued*

1774 Nov. 22 "rode 8 miles to Humphrey Fulerton's with Mes. Lin. Dob. and W. Bro." (From home.)

" 23, 24 "held Pres. concerning prayer, praise, thanksgiving and G. Gra."

1775 Mar. 20, 21 "rode 17 miles to R. Bailey's and H. F.—preached 96: 1–5. Lectured Acts 8: 25–L and baptized Sarah daughter to Hugh Pattison, etc." (From home.)

1776 Mar. 11, 12 "rode 11 miles to Humphrey Fulerton's—married Ann to John Woods." (From home.)

June 5 "rode 18 miles to and from H. F's.—preached 121. Preached 2 Corinthians 6: 17. x x and baptized William x x x." (To Alexander McCleary.)

1780 May 9 "rode 10 miles to Widow Fulerton's, Mat. McC.—married John McFadden and Margaret Fulerton—came home."

1781 Mar. 20, 21, 22 "rode 30 miles with W. Brown to Mat. McClung's, Poequey, to preached—joined with N. Seceders, Mr. L wronged - - - step—shamefully - - -"

Apr. 24 "rode 8 miles married Matthew McClung and Elizabeth Jones." (From home.)

1782 Apr. 12 "rode 10 miles; baptized Charles son to Math. McClung." (From Widow Fullerton's.)

1784 Feb. 29 "Sabbath—preached 51: 1–7, lectured Collosians 3–1— baptized Martha to Mr. McClung, cold very." (At Pequea.)

1787 July 29 "Sabbath—preached 82, lectured Jeremiah 7: 1–7, preached John 4: 42 and baptized Janet daughter to Robert Wylie born March 11, 1786." (At Matthew McClung's.)

1788 Aug. 10 "Sabbath—preached 102: 20–25—lectured 29: 1–15; preached Malachi 4: 2 and baptized Adam, son to Rebekah Livingston, born Sept. 17, 1787, and Wm. son to Wm. Thomson, born Feb. 13, 1785, and Sarah, to Charles McClung, born Dec. 9, '87." (At Matthew McClung's?)

"Turbet Township etc. connected 8 leaves before (baptized) Mary, daughter to John Ferguson, born April 30, 1788, Sarah daughter to Matthew McClung, born May 6, '87, and Rob. son to John McGown, born Mar. 17, 1788."

" 11 "rode 8 miles Hays—canoe Eleanor Browns, S.S."

" 24 "Sabbath—rode 12 miles from James Espy's to Matthew McC. and preached 103: 1—lectured Jeremiah 30: 1–12 and rode to Dav. Ireland."

Pequea Society— *Continued*

1788 Oct. 12   "Sabbath—baptized Sarah to Alexander McCullogh, born Aug. 9 last. preached 104: 13–19, lectured 16–27 and baptized David son to Matthew McClung born Aug. 10 last." (At Mat. McClung's.)

" Poedleh "

1781 Nov. 3   "rode 12 miles to and from Poedleh with Mr. Annan, good news." (From home.)

"   14   "rode 23 miles to Poedleh to James Paterson's, Donegl." (From home.)

Seceder Meeting House

1778 Oct. 28   " 3 (miles) to and (from) Sec. meeting-house (from home); conv. Seced. Mas. Clark, P.R., son Rodg. Clarkson, Marshal, Logan, and Murray, etc., etc."

Sign of The Plow

1765 Mar. 5   "rode 35 miles to Ph. W. and the Sign Plow—Sus. great."

1768 Nov. 14   "rode 23 miles to Bairs, sign of the Plow—good health, praise God." (From David Dunwoody's.)

" Rocky Valley "

1771 Mar. 28   "rode and walked 10 miles to Rocky Valey; Susquehanna high J. McM." (On 29th 10 miles home.)

Silver Mine

1788 July 24   "rode 2 miles to and from Wm. Robs, silver mine." (From Robert Marlin's.)

Sneider's Tavern

1767 Dec. 9   "rode 32 miles over Susquehanna to Sneidar's Tavern." (From Seth Duncan's, and on 10th rode 21 miles home.)

Stoner's Dam

1769 Aug. 30   "rode 18 miles home; was in Stoner's Dam praise God. B." (From Dutch Tavern, Lancaster.)

Susquehanna River

(Crossed many times between Lancaster and York Counties.)

Tavern Third

1767 Sept. 2   "rode 42 miles to Lo. No's, Tavern 3rd rode 20 miles home." (From Wm. Walker's.)

LEHIGH COUNTY

Allentown

1780 Oct. 25 "rode 43 miles to Allens T. Beth., Eastown, Matz's."
(From Weidenhammer's Tavern.)

MONTGOMERY COUNTY

Abington

1758 Aug. 28 "at 4 P.M. my —— died, x x."
" 29 "rode 12 miles in great pain to and from Abington bury —."

Blue Ball (Hotel?)

1761 Nov. 23 "Rode 37 miles to the Blew-Ball-Weatherlys; good health etc." (24th 20 miles to Philadelphia.)
1762 Dec. 2 "Rode 20 (miles) Blue Ball; after sealing letter preached." (From Philadelphia.)
1769 Dec. 25–28 "rode 20 miles Blew Ball paid the hungry s. 100." (From Philadelphia.)

Goldsmith's Tavern

1754 Jan. 16 (See Swedesford.)

Hickorytown

1755 June 10 "Rode 33 miles to Hickory Town Sam Vernon's tired." (From Thomas Kennedy's.)
" 11 "Rode 15 miles to W. Moore's after preaching psalm 97: 5–11 and preached 2 Corinthians 5: 20."

bet.
1756 Oct. 16 & 31 "Rode 3 miles with Y's sister in company to A. Lyals Hick."
1758 June 5 "rode 12 (mi.) to Hickory Town—A Lyle's—Pony strayed." (On 6th rode 12 miles to John Christie's.)

1759 Oct. 2 "rode 14 miles to Hickory Town—paid 6 doll to —— Fulton —." (From Philadelphia.)
" 3 "preached psalm 68—preached 1 Corinthians 15: 33 and married John Kane and Mary Dunlap—conversed with Wilson and Speer about Scott."

1766 Apr. 29 "Rode 63 miles to N. Wales, Bartholomews, W. Doyles, and to Andrew Deniston's." (From Swedesford.)
1779 Nov. 22 "rode x x 16 to Barthol. Weaver's." (From Swedesford.)

Plymouth (Meeting)

1754 Dec. 2 (See Seven Stars.)

Merion

1782 May 1 "rode 7½ miles Merion visited Ship Washington." (From John Paedens, etc.)

1774 Sept. 5 "rode 28 miles Pots-g. widow Sneidars, Mich. Greer." (From Thomas Kennedy's.)

Oct. 20 "rode 40 miles to Jac. Millars, Cunich's, Potts.-G. and Dr. Valneer's." (From Bethlehem and Rodney Smith's.)

1775 Nov. 3 "rode 38 miles to Potts-Grove—Park's." (From Sewitz's Tavern.)

"Potts Grove"

1769 Oct. 3 "rode 36 miles, 18 to Potts Grove, then to Peter Hili'gs." (From Thomas Kennedy's.)

Pottstown

1769 Nov. 2 "rode 40 miles Swamp, M. Drumbower's, Potts T., Den. to Shyfly's 9 miles—5 shillings." (From Jacob Couker's.)

"Seven Stars"

1754 Jan. 19 "Rode 26 miles—10 to Ercus's—7 Stars—16 to W. Moor's." (From Conrade's Tavern.)

" 28 "rode 2 miles to White Marsh Church—preached here—7 Stars—to Widow Parry."

Dec. 2 "Walked and rode 18 miles to Seven Stars, by Sa. Morice Mil. Plymouth." (From Mr. Moore's.)

Swamp

1769 Nov. 2 (See Pottstown.)

"Swedesford"

bet.
1754 Jan. 16 & 18 "Rode 26 miles to Warwick's Fur. Carrol Brownback's Ta. Moor's, Goldsmith's T. Swedesford, Conrade's Tav." (From Thomas Kennedy's.)

June 5 "Rode 50 miles—15 Red-Ly; 5, White Horse; 15 Swedes Ford; 15 Sa. White Horse.)

Upper Merion

1755 June 24 "Rode 18 miles to Upper Merion, Henderson's—2—etc." (From Walter Moore's.)

"Welsh Tr(act)"

1752 Sept. 1 & 2 (See New Castle Co., Delaware.)

White Marsh Church

1754 Jan. 28 (See Seven Stars.)

NORTHAMPTON COUNTY

Bethlehem

1753 June 20   "Rode 32 miles to Twimmins Mills Bethl. Family and George Gray's." (From Tohicken.)

1754 July   1   "Rode 30 miles—8 to Beth., 15 to McCunzie 5 to Jost. Henricks." (From George Gray's.)

Easton

1759 Sept. 26   "rode 40 miles to Downy's—16 to Balls, 10 to Easton, 8 to Crookers." (From Woolverton's.)

1760 Sept. 30   "rode 44 miles to Bischop's, 8 to Waggonier's, 15 to East. 13 to McK." (On way to New York.)

Oct. 15   "rode 13 miles to Easttown, after preaching psalm 9: 7–11 and preaching Malachi 4: 2—Lowrys."

1764 Aug.   8   "rode 44 miles to George Glein's (9) Bischops (4) Wagg (8), Easton (13) and (8) to Finestt's." (From White Horse—Stoffield's.)

1766 Apr. 30   "rode 44 miles to Easttown; 21 Smeisars, 7 to old Goal, Moors, weary." (On way to New York.)

1780 Oct. 25   (See Allentown.)

" Twimmins Mills "

1753 June 20   (See Bethlehem.)

NORTHUMBERLAND COUNTY

Chillisquaque

1788 July 21   "rode 6 miles to Thomas Fulerton's, Chilesquagnas." (From Sunbury.)

(Indian Wigwam) Near Milton

1751 Oct. 21   "Travelled 3 miles to and from John Wigwam's conversed with Joseph concerning equality of the F. and S. deadness . . . at night conversed with Lawrence concerning the covenant of Cr. . . . this Med. and . . . its conditional, viz. F. etc. with . . ." (From George Gray's.)

"   27   "Sabbath. Preached psalm 14. Lectured Gal. 2: 11–17 and preached Jer. 3: 12 and baptized George, son to James Gray and Jean daughter to Mich. Clyde. . . ." (At George Gray's—Milton.)

1753 Mar.
(bet. 5 & 11)   "Rode 15 miles to William Clark's, after visiting and marrying Finlay Gray and ——."

Northumberland

1788 Aug. 30   "sailed 2 miles to Northum. Dan. Montgomery." (From Sunbury.)

"   31   "Sabbath—preached psalm 103: 3–13, lectured 30: 10–16 and preached 17, o.a. praise God."

Sept. 3   "preached 15, lectured Titus 2: 11–L and baptized Elizabeth to Hugh Beaty, born May 8, 1787, and Agnes to Alexander Beaty, born July 12, 1788, and Agnes to James Beaty, born July 13—wrote Wm. McAdams 500." (At Hugh Beaty's pens C.)

Rutherford

1787 Oct. 11   "rode and walked 9 miles to Ruther. John Duncan's.' (From Loneb. Mr. Boyd's, then 3 miles to widow Brown's on 12th W. died the 8th month.)

Sunbury

1788 July 16   "rode 37 miles to Sunberry, Wm. McAdams, Mr. Byar's." (From Rev. Peter's.)

Aug. 26   "rode and sailed 7 miles to Sunberry, Wm. McAdam's." (From Da. and James and J. Fulerton's.)

Warrior Run

1788 Aug. 3   "Sabbath—walked and sailed 2 miles to and from Wariours Run preached 102: 17—lectured 28, preached Malachi 4: 2 and baptized Mary, daughter to Nathaniel Coulter, born April 14, 1786." (Then rode 6 miles to Widow Smith's Mills.)

"   18   "rode 15 miles crossed Susquehanna in Weisner's canoe, led 2 horses, Wariours Run, preached 4: 1—lectured Hosea 14: 1–4—offer of Christ and baptized John son to John Mason, born Mar. 8th, 1788, and Andrew, son to John Lyttle born June 8, 1788 and Elizabeth McKee presented by Mary, sister, born Oct. 1779."

White Deer Hole

1788 Aug. 4   "rode 6 miles to widow Smith's Mills, preached psalm 57: and 6, and baptized George son to Wm. Orr, born Feb. 9, 1778, and Wm. and Margaret, born March 21, 1780, and Katharine, born Sept. 18, 1782, John born May 26, 1785, and Martha, born July 1, 1787—White Deer Hole."

PHILADELPHIA COUNTY

Cather's School

1764 Dec. 9 "Sabbath—preached psalm 75: 5–L. Lectured Colossians 3: 5–L and preached psalm 119: 37 and expounded Titus 2: 11–15 g.a.—Cather's School." (At Philadelphia.)
"   10 "rode 10 miles to the Buck. with John Jamieson."

Delaware River

1752 Oct. 3 "Rode 30 miles over Delaware past McCunzie went to Jack Trivelbest's." (From David McClean's.)

Frankford

1757 June 25 "Rode 5 miles to Widow McVagh's, Frankfort; am to lodge Bro." (From Philadelphia.)
1758 Aug. 14 "rode 20 miles to and from Frankford with Brother Leech's child dead." (From father-in-law's.)

Sept. 6 "rode 16 miles to A. Barclays, G. Graham agreed and— E. Smith."
"   7 "rode 5 miles Frankford—borrowed 40 pounds of —— Murray 25-19-2 ——."

1769 Dec. 21 "rode 16 miles to Philadelphia by Frankf. Aunt's, etc." (From Walter Moore's.)
1783 June 5 "rode — to J. Millar, preached 57: 1–6; lectured Corinthians 5: 17–20 and 9, baptized Thomas, Janet and Eleanor to Ezekial Alexander." (From McVagh's.)

Germantown

1753 June 14 "Rode 16 mi. to Germantown 6 mi. long to—Walter Moore's." (From John Reed's in Phil'a.)

Holton's Tavern

1761 Oct. 13 "Rode 47 miles to Holtons with H. McDowell, in safety." (From home.)
Nov. 27 "Rode 10 miles to Holtons Tavern; parted with Bartram etc." (From Ephraim Smith's in Philadelphia.)
1762 Nov. 23 "Rode 42 miles to Holton's. (From Pequea)." (Then 10 miles to Philadelphia on 24th.)
1765 June 20, 21 "rode 56 miles home from Holtons—borrowed 4-0-0 of G. G."

Moreland

1757 Nov. 16   "Rode 31 miles to Moreland, family all well, praise to my gracious God." (From White Horse.)

"   20   "Sabbath preached psalm 107: 9–19 and lectured 1 Peter 5: 5–8 o.a. praise God etc."

Pennypack Creek

1753 June 17   "Sab. preach. Ps. 76: 7–L, lectured 1 Peter 3: 17–21 preach. 2 Cor. 11: 2 g.a. and baptized Martha and Elizabeth daughters to John Purdie.—Talked." (At Walter Moore's.)

1754 Jan. 20   "Sabbath. Preached palms 50: 1–7 lectured Mark 10: 46–L. Preached 2 Corinthians 11: 2 and baptized Sarah, Elizabeth Leech and Mary, daughters to Walter Moor—23: 1–9." (At Walter Moore's.)

"   27   "Sabbath. Preached psalm 50: 7–14. Lectured Hosea 2: 14—Preached Hosea 3: 3 and baptized And. son to John Scot and Robert and James, sons to And. Lowrie, g.d. and a. although Lo. disatisfied with his wife (uxor)." (At Walter Moore's—then rode 2 miles to White Marsh Church on 28th.)

June 6   "Rode 12 miles to Walter Moore's at Pennypack Creek tired but." (From White Horse.)

1755 June 22   "Sabbath. Preached psalm 74: 5–12 lectured Hosea 11: 8–L and preached John 8: 36 and baptized Elizabeth daughter to Andrew Lowry, give all praise to God." (At Walter Moore's.)

1758 May 28   "Sabbath—preached psalm 118: 1–7. Lectured Matthew 28: 9–16. Preached Isaiah 33: 10 and baptized Mary daughter to And. Lowrie." (At Walter Moore's.)

Dec. 12   "tramped 2 miles—married John Moore and Margaret Ayres o.a." (Near Walter Moore's.)

1760 Feb. 28   "Married James Fulton and Mary Moore." (Probably at Walter Moore's.)

Philadelphia

The first Covenanter here, it is believed, was a Mr. Boyd, who, with his family, emigrated from Ireland in 1740. Mr. Boyd died soon after he arrived in America. His family roomed in the house of James Rainey from Ireland, who became a Covenanter, and removed to the Wallkill, Orange County, N. Y., in 1748. Mr. John Agnew and his wife emigrated from Ireland to Philadelphia in 1784, where they lived for three years, after which they moved to New York City. Rev. John Cuthbertson

Philadelphia— *Continued*

made many visits to Philadelphia, being drawn there often, no doubt, because of his wife's family, residing some fifteen miles away.

1753 June 13 "Rode 23 miles to John Reed's—in Philadelphia." (From Thomas Kennedy's.)

1754 Nov. 26 "Rode 15 miles to Philadelphia. Preached psalm 84: 4–10. Preached Acts 2: 39 g.a. and baptized Janet, daughter to George Grahams, etc., etc." (Then 17 miles to Walter Moore's on 27th.)

1759 June 28 "rode 31 miles to Chester, Darby, Philadelphia—left B. Leech." (From Wilmington.)

" 29 "preached psalm 56: 1–7. Lectured Hosea 14: 4–9 and baptized Isobel, daughter to George Graham; and Ann, daughter to John Wallace; give all praise to God."

Oct. 1 "rode 15 miles P. at Eph. Smith's—preached psalm 95: 6–L. Lectured Hebrews 3: 12, 13 and baptized Jean, daughter to Andrew Lowry g.a. etc."

" 16 "rode 51 miles—good health, praise God—baptized William son to Jos. Ker." (Then rode 9 miles to Philadelphia, Eph. Smith's, on 17th.)

1761 Oct. 14 "Rode 9 miles to Philadelphia; preached psalm 131 and baptized George son to G. Graham presented by the mother; Mr. M. preached Philippians 1: 27 de." (From Holton's with H. McDowell.)

1762 Nov. 24 "Rode 10 miles to Philadelphia." (From Holton's.)

" 28 "Sabbath preached psalm 95: 6–L and preached 2 o'clock Galatians, 5: 1; baptized John son to John Kain and Eleanor to widow Lowry."

1763 Aug. 15 "Rode 45 miles to Philadelphia with W. Crawford—family all well." (From Thomas Kennedy's.)

Nov. 29 "rode 26 miles to Philadelphia—W. Paden's—good health."

Dec. 2 "Preached psalm 86: 1–6. Exer. Phil. 4 and baptized Edward son to George Graham, presented by mother."

1764 Mar. 13 "rode 33 miles to Philadelphia—, frost, snow, rain, wet, well." (From John Down's with Watty.)

" 14 "tramped 4 miles—preached psalm 91. Explained Luke 24: 17 and baptized William son to George Kennety

Philadelphia— *Continued*

and John, son to R. Stewart." (Then on the 15th rode
13 miles to The Plow, T. Wilson's.)

1765 Dec. 9, 10   "rode 56 miles Philadelphia from J. Downing's—bad
road."
"   15   "Sabbath—preached psalm 89: 5–9. Lectured Hebrews
7: 23–L. Preached Ecclesiastes 1: 2 and baptized Alexander, son to George Kennety—o.a.—rs Seceder."

1769 Dec. 22, 23   "—— tramped —— P.—could not find books, letters,
etc."
"   24   "Sabbath—preached 6: 14. Lectured Isaiah 63: 1—
preached 54–L and baptized Thomas, son to John Dunbar; and David to Mr. Graham. Exercised 2 Kings
5: 13."

1772 Dec. 14, 15   "rode 50 miles to Yellow Spring, Warren, Philadelphia." (From Thomas Kennedy's.)
"   20   "Sabbath; preached 16: L; lectured same; preached
Isaiah 63: 8; exercised Galatians 3: 26–L and baptized
James son to John Dunbar and Alexander to John
Graham (gave 40 Lbs. Curr. for 26: 13–4 Irish to Carson etc.) "
"   23   "rode with W. Peden 6 miles to the Black Horse."

1774   (In this year Thomas Thomson came from County
Down, Ireland, to Philadelphia with his family and
religious services were held at his home for many years.)

Nov. 25, 26   "rode 54 miles to Philadelphia; held committee x x."
"   27   "Sabbath I preached and lectured 75: 1–5; Isaiah 7–L·
Mr. Dob(bin) preached Isaiah 55: 4."
"   29   "Mr. Dob. exercised psalm 89: 1–5; baptized Agnes to
J. Dun and Mary to ——."
Dec. 1   "rode 6 miles to the Black Horse with Sally."

1780 Nov. 17   "Rode 30 miles (from F. Elliot's) to Philadelphia John
McFadden well, praise gracious God."
"   19   "Sabbath—rode 2 miles Mr. T. lectured Galatians 3:
I preached Hebrews 7: 25 rs. paper."

Philadelphia— *Continued*

1780 Nov. 20 "walked 3 miles visiting Mr. Marshal,[a] Jan. etc. D.——."

1782 Oct. 29 "rode 16 miles to Philadelphia, W. Millars, Mr. Telfairs." (From Spread Eagle.)
" 30 "Convention met, W. Ritchards, did our business."
Nov. 1 "Constituted the A. R. Synod etc. Act. to a Fast."
" 3 "Sabbath Mr. Annan and Proudfoot preached; lodged Mr. Pat."
" 4, 5 "Finished Synod, bought hat, etc. was unwell."

1783 Oct. 17 "Rode 7 miles to Philadelphia." (From Rising Sun.)
" 19 "Sabbath—Mr. Mason preached and Mr. Clark after."
" 21 "Synod met Mr. Thomas Clark chosen moderator, etc."
" 26 "Sabbath. Mr. Dobbin preached and Dr. Theo. Clark lectured Revelations 11: 6, etc., etc."
" 28 "Conv. Gen. Mifflin and Fench Coxe concerning plantation."

Sorrel Horse Tavern

1774 Apr. 11 "rode 26 miles to the Sorrel Horse Tavern, in health." (From Thomas Kennedy's—on 12th rode 16 miles to Philadelphia.)

" Spread Eagle "

1767 Nov. 19 "rode 16 miles to the Spread Eagle—got buck and ate." (From Philadelphia.)
1779 Nov. 29 "rode 16 miles Inkle's—Spread Eagle—from J. McFads. 80 d." (From Philadelphia.)

1782 Oct. 28 "rode 34 miles Spread Eagle, recovering from James Welbs."
" 29 "rode 16 miles to Philadelphia, W. Millars, Mr. Telfairs."

Schuylkill County

Schuylkill

1751 Oct. 17 "Rode 35 miles—7 to James Gilmors and to Schoulkill— 21 to mo. pleas." (From Thomas Kennedy's.)
1760 Sept. 29 (See Pine Forge, Berks Co.)

[a] Rev. Mr. Marshall, of Associate Reformed Church.

SNYDER COUNTY

McClure's Gap

1752 June 26   "Rode 22 miles over McClure's Gap, marked on a beech tree 'J. C. 1752.' " (From Jø. Kilogh.)
"A plantation of 1000 acres—came to Fran. McNicols— tired."

Mt. Pleasant

1752 Sept. 20   "Rode 36 miles to Potts furnace, Mount pleasant furnace and pet phaedras."

SOMERSET COUNTY

Fort Hills

1779 Sept. 15   "rode 30 miles Cumberl., Fort Hills, Cr. Alegheny, Tomlinson." (From Old Town.)

Laurel Hill

"   17   "rode 37 miles Laurel-hill Mr. Greer's Forks of Yough Mr. Simson's."

Oct. 13   "rode 30 over Laurel-hill, Glades, lay on straw at Mr. Spiegers." (On way to Bedford from Allegheny County.)

WASHINGTON COUNTY

Chartiers

1779 Sept. 28   "rode 23 miles from J. Reid's to Shirtee, Al. McConel's, James Scot's."

Miller's Run (Venice)

"   29   "rode 9 miles Miller's Run; Cross George Marquers, S.W."

"   30   "rode 10 miles preached 25: 6–L and preached Titus 3: 6, James Mcgl. received 50."

Oct. 1   "rode 20 miles after preaching psalm 44: 1–9; exercised 6: 9; baptized James to James McGlaughlin; Francis and John to Matthew McConel and Sarah and Mary to Robert Walker."

"   3, 4 (See Allegheny Co.)

YORK COUNTY

" Burkholder " (Burnholder's Bridge?)

1754 May 20 "Rode 16 miles over Burkh.—Wm. Clarke, W. P. Jo.
Bro. and John Dunca(n)." (From Hugh Ross's.)

Chamber's Tavern

1751 Dec. 9 "Rode 32 miles to Chambers Tavern in York—exhausted
etc. but well." (From Marsh Creek.)
"   10 "Preached psa. 68: 18-21 and preached Acts 16: 31 then
rode 18 miles; to William Wil. . . ."

Chanceford

1752 Apr. 14 "Rode 18 miles to William Wilson's Chancefoord T.
near Muddy Creek Ch."

Cold Spring Mtn.

1786 Aug. 28 "rode 20 miles to Sis. over Moun. cold spring, John
Bourn's, wet." From Lower Chanceford, York Co.,
Pa.?

Deadman's Road

1773 Mar. 17 "rode 30 miles home and all well; praise God—saw Dead
man's road." (From Mr. Anderson's.)

Dutch Shoe

1762 July 26, 27 "Rode 44 miles to Dutch Shoe and to White Horse,
York."

Dutch Tavern

1752 July 27 "Rode 33 miles to Dutch Tavern in York, tired but
safe." (From David Dunwoody's.)
1774 June 1 "rode 44 miles to York, Andersons, Dutch Tavern."
(Then 18 miles home on 2nd.)

Latta's School, Mr.

1775 June 15 "rode 5 miles to and from Mr. Latta's School—conversed
with Walker, etc." (From Daniel Sinclair's.)
July 21 "rode 16 miles to S. D. with Johnny to Mr. Lata's—
entered him school." (From home.)
1779 Nov. 12 "rode 8 miles to Mr. S.—with him to and from Robert
Latta's burial."
1780 Jan. 31 "rode 10 miles to Mr. Lat., W. Ritchie's, to James Paterson's." (From John McMillan's.)
1783 Apr. 14 "rode 13 miles to Mr. Latta's, W. B., and James Walkers." (Then 3 miles to Widow Ewings and to David
Wats on 15th.)

Lower Chanceford (Society)

Including Muddy Run and Muddy Creek Societies. Lower Chanceford is known as " The Barrens." The Society here was organized in 1751. After the organization of the Reformed Presbytery in 1774, Rev. John Cuthbertson ministered to it, together with that of Middle Octoraro, being released from the latter in March, 1783. At the house of William Maughlin in Lower Chanceford, he preached his last recorded sermon on September 20, 1790, dying the following March.

1751 Dec. 14 "Rode 4 miles to Joseph Rosses in Maryland, Conn(ococheague)." (From William Wilson's.)

"   15 "Sabbath. Rode 2 miles; Whittleseys house, preached Psa. 18: 1–6, Galatians 3: 24–1 and preached Hebrews 14: 12 . . . then rode 8 miles to Neils ferry. . . ."

1752 Apr. 14 "Rode 18 miles to Wm. Wilson's Chancefoord T. near Muddy Creek Ch." (From York.)

"   16 "Preach. Ps. 75: 1–7, lect. Jer. 45 and bap. George son to Jo. Buchanan etc. rode 4 miles to Hugh Rosses."

Sept. 4 "Rode 18 miles to Jo. Rosses preach. Ps. 132: 1–9 lectured Mark 6, 45–51 bap. Joseph son to Jas. Dunlop presented by mother. . . ." (From James Wilson's— Middle Octoraro.)

"   17 "Sab. Rode 8 miles, preach. Ps. 28: 16–L. lect. So. 5: 10–13 and preach. 2 Pet. . . . and baptized John and Susanna son and daughter to George Mar." (From Lochhead's.)

Oct. 1 "Sab. Trav. 2 miles to and from meeting preach. Ps. 29 etc. lectured S. 5: 1 and preach. Jer. 5: 19 and baptized Mary daugh. to David McClean praise to God." (From David McClean.)

Nov. 7 "Rode 14 miles to William Wilson's Chanceford T. exhausted but well." (From York.)

"   8 "Rode 4 miles to H. Rosses after preach. Ps. 79: 20–L. preach. Isa. 45: 22 and bap. Martha daugh. to Jas. Anderson, presented by her mother."

"   9 "Rode 14 miles to Neilson's, Samuel Dicsons and Jo. Brownlies." (From Hugh Ross's.)

"   10 "Rode 3 miles to Jo. Dun., Jo. Robieson's and Dan McClellan's."

bet.
1753 Feb. 26 & 28 "Rode 7 miles, A. M. James Paterson, visiting . .

Lower Chanceford (Society)— *Continued*

to Jo. Duncan's got fog, married George Buch. and Jean Paterson ——." (From Dan McClellan's.)

1753 Mar. (4) "Sabbath—travelled 2 miles, preached Psalm 35: 7–23, lectured 1 Peter 1: 10–13, preached Hebrews 3–1, then baptized Esther daughter to Martin Mahaffy dull day." (From Henry Ross's.)

June 10 "Sab. Rode 12 mi. preach. Ps. 38: 17–L. lectured 1 Peter 3: 13–17 preach. Hebrews 4: 11 and baptized Jas. son to Wm. Nicol concerning the right mode Fi."

July 25 "Rode 17 miles to H. Ross Neilsons Fer. Jo. McM. and Jos. Brownlie." (From Wm. Wilson's.)

" 26 "Rode 2 miles to John Duncans all well tired God favors me."

Aug. 17 "Rode 10 miles to Wm. Wilson's preach. Ps. 9: 7–12 examined 15 persons." (From John McMillan s.)

" 18 "Rode 5 miles back to John Buchanans good health praise God—."

" 19 "Sab. Rode 6 mi. to Da. McKinleys after preach. Ps. 42: 1–9 and lectured 1 Peter 5: 1–5 and preached Hebrews 3: 12 and baptized Elizabeth daugh. to Wm. Buchanan."

Dec. 14 "Rode 12 miles to John Walker's after marrying Benjamin McCormick and Ann Brown in Widow Dickies - - - etc. compassionate God." (From John Ross's.)

1754 Feb. 11 "Rode 9 miles after buying Mar. McHaffy's plan. to Sa. Dicks."

" 12 "Rode 3 miles to Thomas McCamon's, John Marshal's and John Duncan's."

May 19 "Sabbath. Preached psalm 56: 1–7. Lectured Amos 1: 12–L. Preached Hebrews 10: 23 and baptized John son to George Buchanan—v. pub. all day—Fer." (At Hugh Ross's.)

23 "Rode 6 miles Rob. after preaching psalm 2: 1–L. Preached Amos 5: 4 and baptized John son to John Reid—give all praise to God—went to Joe. Rob." (From John Duncan's.)

Sept. 19 "Rode 9 miles to Sam. Dickson's, W. pat., Jo. Br. received 4 letters—went to Jo. Dunlop's." (From Wm. Wilson's.)

bet.

Dec. 23–28 "Rode —— miles to Jo. Marshals. Married William

Lower Chanceford (Society)— *Continued*

Ayres and Elizabeth Buchanan. Rode to Nath. Coulters—good health." (From Dan. McClellan's.)

1755 May 15   "Rode 7 miles to Sam. Dickson's after preaching psalm 61: 1–6 and lectured Isaiah 10: 1–5. Paid Hu. Ross 10-16-0 and to Jo. Finey 2-7-0." (From Wm. Wilson's.)

Dec. 28   "Sabbath—preached psalm 80: 1–6. Preached Isaiah 32–2—paper. Baptized Mar——— and Mary son and daughter to Mar. Mahafey; Jean to David Sloan and Margaret daughter to William Buchanan. give all praise to God." (At Hugh Ross's.)

"   29   "Tramped 7 miles to and round mountain—difficult and to Ma. Ma(hafey)."

"   30   "Rode and tramped 6 miles to Jo. McKinley's, after preached psalm 46 and examined 20 persons."

"   31   "Rode and tramped 9 miles to Jo. McMillan's after marrying William Wilson and Esther Thorn—received 5 shillings. Traveled on the ice—good health, etc."

1756 Jan. 28   "Rode 6 miles to widow Calbreath's, preached psalm 30: 4–10 and preached Job 13: 16 and baptized Samuel son to James Swan g.a." (From John Ross's.)

Sept. 19   "Sabbath, preached psalm 91: 1–7; lectured Matthew 31: 3, preached psalm 146: 7 g.a. and baptized Wm. and Sarah son and daughter to Wm. Nicol."

"   20   "Rode 8 miles to John McClellans; preached psalm 79: 5–9; preached Acts 2: — and baptized James son to J. McM. and Samuel son to Joseph —." (Then rode 10 miles to Dan McClellan's on 21st.)

bet.
Nov. 17 & 21   "Rode 6 miles to John McWilliams; wrote ——— next day etc." (From John Duncan's.)

1757 Mar. 18   "Rode and tramped 5 miles to and from m. Difficult—John Finey 7-6-." (From John Marlin's.)

"   19   "Rode 2 miles to John Buchanans; sore breast and throat."

"   20   "Sabbath. Preached psalm 102: 16. Lectured Matthew 16: 24–L and preached 2 Chronicles 20: 12."

June 1   "Rode 4 miles to Hew Rosses; hot, hot; very tired." (From Wm. Wilson's.)

Lower Chanceford (Society)— *Continued*

1757 June 2 "Rode 7 miles to John McM. after preaching psalm 138:
6–L; preached Philippians 4: 19 and baptized Mary
daughter to George Buchanan rs s Finleys."

July 27 "Rode 19 miles over Susquehanna 2 o'clock preached
psalm 112: 1—preached Matthew 11: 28—held session
and baptized Ebenezer son to John Buchanan and
James son to Wm. Buchanan; had my horse shod, rs.
by S. Dick." (From John Dun.)

"   28 "Rode 6 miles to John Robiesons; married Thomas
Dougherty and Mary Robieson rs 13-6; went to John
Duncans."

1758 Apr. 14 "Rode 7 miles to and from D. Sloan's." (From Hugh
Ross's.)

"   16 "Sabbath—preached psalm 115: 1–10. Lectured Mat-
thew 27: 11–24. Preached psalm 59: 5. Baptized
Hugh son to William Nicol; And., son to Da. Sloan; and
Jean, daughter to Sam Leiper—great gust."

"   17 "Rode 6 miles to John Marlins—gave H. Ross 1-0-0."

May 2 "Rode 22 miles to and from J. Dun. Married J. Brownlie and Jean Ker. rs a Dol. W. Spedie told of sister."
(From home.)

Oct. 11 "rode 8 miles to John McMillan's—preached psalm 39: 7
last. Lectured Hebrews 8: 6 and baptized Ebenezer
son to John McMillan o.a. praise to God."

"   12 "rode 7 miles to J. Marlin's—his son Thomas Boney—
went to Rosses."

Nov. 21 "rode 32 miles to W. W.—married John Crawford and
Margaret Wilson." (From W. Cooper's.)

1759 Feb. 21 "rode 6 miles to J. Rosses—preached psalm 37: 3.
Lectured June 1: 3 and baptized John son to James
Ross—caviled with ——." (From Robert Lochhead's.)

Mar. 1 "rode 10 miles—at Ferry preached psalm 25. Lectured
Ephesians 2: 11–14 and baptized Robert, Elizabeth and
Moses to Robert Gree(r) and at John Duncan's
preached psalm 9: 7. Explained Romans 1: 16 and
baptized son to Hanna Loekey o.a.—tired." (From
John Marlin's.)

Lower Chanceford (Society)— *Continued*

1759 May 1 "rode 14 miles over Susquehanna—at John Buchanan's —preached psalm 34: 19 and Exer. Hebrews 10: 23–26 and baptized William son to Geo. Buc——."

1760 Apr. 20 "Sabbath—preached psalm 148: 7–L. Lectured Habakkuk 1: 12, 13. Preached Romans 8: 30 and baptized Sam. son to William Nicol; Eliz., daughter to George Marlin and Esther, daughter to John Crawford o.a." (At Wm. Nicol's or Hugh Ross's.)

Nov. 13 "rode 4 miles to S. Dixon's after preaching psalm 9: 1–5 and preaching 1 Samuel 3: 6 and baptized William son to John Girvan (presented by A. Swan) and Sarah, daughter to James Paterson." (From John Marshal's and Widow Smith's.)

" 14 "rode 12 miles to S. Leiper's, Hugh Rosses, etc."

" 16 "Sabbath—tramped 2 miles to meeting. Preached psalm 19: 9–14. Preached 1 Samuel 12: 30, o.a."

" 17 "rode 12 miles to J. Duncan's, after preaching psalm 23. Lectured Titus 3: 8, 9 and baptized John son to And. Ferrier and Martha, daughter to Isobel Sloan." (Then 10 miles home on 18th.)

1761 Jan. 21 "rode 12 miles back (to W. Robieson's in Manadie)— preached psalm 105: 6–10. Lectured Ephesians 6: 1–9. Baptized David, son to him."

Feb. 24 "Rode 10 miles to John Duncan's. Paid W. Gebby 8-19-9." (From home.)

" 25 "Preached psalm 40: 1 and examined 62 persons ——."

1762 Mar. 24 "Rode 5 miles to Sam. D's. after preaching psalm 67; and lecturing Matthew 38 and baptized Wm. son to A. Baldridge, g.a. etc." (From Alexander Baldridge's.)

" 25 "Rode 4 miles preaching psalm 10: 15–L and lectured Zephaniah 2: 1–4 and married Wm. Young and Margaret Sconler (Scouler?) rs 15th."

" 26 "Rode 6 miles to J. and Marlins, lodged A. Fullton."

" 27 "Rode 3 miles H. Rosses."

" 28 "Sabbath preached psalm 33: 10; lectured Ephesians 5: 10–14 and baptized Sam son to Thomas Ramsay, Thomas–And. Ferrier and Mary daughter to Robert Grier. o.a."

Lower Chanceford (Society)— *Continued*

1762 Nov. 12 "Rode 22 miles to John McMillan's and to Wm. Gebby's." (From home.)

" 13 "Rode 5 miles to John Red's and Hugh Rosses."

" 14 "Sabbath preached psalm 40: 14–L; preached Hebrews 10–L and baptized Elizabeth daughter to George Buchanan and Sam to John Mc." (Then rode to J. Walker's, R. Thomson's and home.)

1763 Mar. 25 "rode 6 miles to J. McM.—at S. Dixon's preached psalm 63: 5–L. Explained Isaiah 44: 3. Baptized And., son to William Fulerton." (From James Paterson's.)

" 26 "rode 4 miles over Susquehanna to J. Marlin's."

" 27 "Sabbath—rode 4 miles—preached psalm 46: 1–6. Lectured Zechariah 7: 4–8. Preached Hebrews 4: 14 and baptized Archibald son to Sam Lieper."

" 28 "rode 9 miles to Geb. Henry's, Ross, and W. Nicols."

May 1 "Sabbath—preached psalm 48: 1–6. Lectured Zechariah 8: 20–L. Preached Hebrews 10: 23 and baptized John son to Henry McCormick." (At John Duncan's.)

July 6, 7 "rode 50 miles to Hawthorn's, Wilson's and Warnock's." (From home.)

Aug. 10 "rode 9 miles to and from Sam Hawthorn's—got 20 Bus. . . ." (From home.)

Sept. 9 "rode 14 miles to John McMillan's. Mason's and Carp. g.a." (From home.)

" 10 "rode, etc. 3 miles to John Marlin's etc."

" 11 "Sabbath—rode 3 miles—preached psalm 55: 9–15. Lectured Zechariah 14: 16–20 preached Isaiah 27: 9 and baptized John son to And. McCleary and Jean to William Geb."

Nov. 23, 24 "rode 17 miles—married George Henry and Margaret Young." (From home.)

1764 Feb. 22 "rode 9 miles to W. Nickols after preaching psalm 62: 5 lectured Songs 3: 3–6 and baptized George son to James Mitchel—tired." (From John McCleary's.)

" 23 "rode 7 miles to Money's Ross and T. Ramsay's."

" 24 "rode and walked 8 miles to Sinc., Wms. and John Marlins."

" 26 "Sabbath—rode 5 miles—preached psalm 65: 1—lectured Phil. 3: 10–15 preached 1 Corinthians 16: 13 and baptized Margaret and James daughter and son to John Mony." (Then 15 miles home on 27th.)

Lower Chanceford (Society)—*Continued*

1764 Mar. 20   "rode 7 miles to D. Sinclair's wife's burial—an invalid up to this time." (From Daniel Sinclair's or home.)

July 1   "Sabbath—preached psalm 69: 22-27. Lectured Malachi 3: 16–L. Preached Hebrews 13: 13, 14 and baptized Thomas, son to Thomas Ramsay; Joseph, son to James Mitchel; and Mary Buchanan, for John Marlin." (Then 20 miles home on 2nd.)

Sept. 15   "rode 4 miles over Susquehanna to John Marlin's." (From John McMillan's.)

" 16   "Sabbath—rode 5 miles—preached psalm 72: 15–L. Lectured Colossians 1: 21–24 and preached Hebrews 12: 29."

" 17   "rode 8 miles—at S. Buchanan's, exer. 2 hours psalm 84: 14–L and married John McCleary and Elizabeth Jamiesons—went to McW." (Then 18 miles home on 18th.)

Oct. 29   "rode 26 miles to W. B.—married Sam Biggar and Abig. Wil."

" 30   "married John Thomson and Mary Sloan; and Alexander Sloan and Elizabeth Sloan—received 30."

Dec. 13   "rode 18 miles to J. McMns. S. Dixon's, married William Marlin and Mary McMillan—received Dol."

1765 Apr. 19   "rode 18 miles over Susquehanna to R. Greer's, Ramsay's." (From James McKnaughtan's.)

" 21   "Sabbath—rode 6 miles—preached psalm 78: 40–46. Lectured Acts 13: 25–32—preached Hebrews 8: 6 and baptized Agnes to And. Ferrier; Margaret to John McCulloch; Mary to William Fulerton and Sara to Sam Leiper." (Then rode 9 miles to Alexander Robieson's on 22nd.)

July 5   "rode 15 miles to Isaia McBride's, Works, Rob., and McMilan's." (From home.)

" 6   "rode 4 miles over Susquehanna to John Marlin's—tired."

" 7   "Sabbath—rode 4 miles—preached psalm 80: 5–11. Lectured Hebrews 7: 12–18—preached psalm 17: 15 and baptized Mary, daughter to William Gebby—give all praise to my gracious God."

Lower Chanceford (Society)— *Continued*

1765 Sept. 30 "rode and walked 13 miles to S. Hawthorn's burial."
(From home.)
Oct. 1 "rode 10 miles to and from Robert Burney's burial."
" 3 "rode 36 miles to and from J. White's, married John
Buch. and Jean ——."

" 11 "rode 20 miles over Susquehanna to John Marlin's, etc."
(From home.)
" 13 "Sabbath—preached psalm 86: 1-6, lectured Hebrews
9: 11-15 preached Hebrews 9: 16, and baptized Jean
daughter to Robert Greer—Give all praise to my gracious God."
" 14 "rode 20 miles after marrying Dan. Sinclair and Mary
Marlin."
" 15 "rode 6 miles to and from Dan Sinclair's and Mary Marlin's."

1766 Feb. 14 "rode 9 miles to Nicols, Rosses—preached psalm 68:
1-5. Lectured Ephesians 8—baptized Rose-Ann, to
D. Sloan; Wm., son to James Mitchel; Martha, daughter to Andrew McCleary; and John, to David Robieson
—o.a. praise God." (From Peechbottom.)
" 15 "rode 5 miles to John Marlin's—conversed, etc."
" 16 "Sabbath—rode 4 miles—preached psalm 90: 1—
preached John 17: 24. Baptized Elizabeth to Wm.
Young o.a. praise my gracious God."
" 17 "rode 12 miles over Susquehanna, McMns. and Mc-
Murdy's Robert." (Then 5 miles home on 18th.)

June 18 "rode 25 miles to Wm. Nicols; with Jos. Walker."
(From home.)
" 19 "rode 20 miles to and from G. Buchanan's over Maryland line."
" 20 "rode 10 miles to H. Ross, T. Grier's, Sinclair's and J.
Marlin's."
" 22 "Sabbath—rode 2 miles—preached psalm 99: 4-L. Lectured John 15: 15—preached John 2: 28 and baptized
Sam to T. Ramsy; George, son George Buchanan; and
Wm. son to Alexander McCalister, g.a.—lodged in Wm.
Wilso(n's)."

Lower Chanceford (Society)—*Continued*

1766 June 23   "rode 7 miles to Sam Dixons with Jo. Walker good health, etc." (On 24th rode 12 miles home.)

"   30   "rode 12 miles to Sam Dixon's—very tired." (From home.)

July 1   "rode and walked 20 miles—married John Marlin and Susanna Mar ——." (Then rode 12 miles home on 2nd.)

Aug. 29, 30   "Rode 19 miles to John McMn's by McKt's to John Marlin's." (From home.)

"   31   "Sabbath—preached psalm 102: 25–L; lectured Hebrews 11: 32–36; preached Jude; baptized Andrew son to John Buchanan." (Then rode 20 miles home on Sept. 1.)

1767 Mar. 1   "Sabbath—preached 106: 6–9; lectured 13: 1–4; preached Micah L, L—rode 3 miles (J. Mc) and baptized Mary daughter to Wm. Marlin." (At Wilson's.)

Aug. 7   "rode 17 miles to John McMns; and Marlin's with Lr. (Fr.?) Sal(ly) praise God."

"   9   "Sabbath—rode 6 miles, preached psalm 110: lectured Proverbs 1: 20–25 preached Habakkuk 3: 2 and baptized Rachel daughter to John Marlin o.a. praise God."

"   10   "rode 13 miles to R. Greer's, Ross, and W. Nicol's, left R——."

Nov. 24   "rode 18 miles to Reid's Ferry—back to W. Clark's." (From home.)

"   25   "Rode 4 miles over Susquehanna, John Reid's,—married Wm. Mauchlin and Martha Reid—tired 2 sh.—10."

1768 Jan. 31   "Sabbath—tramped 4 miles—preached psalm 119: 9–13 —preached Philip. 4: 6 and baptized Rachel daughter to Dan Sinclair g.a." (From John Marlin's.)

Apr. 29, 30   "rode 20 miles to J. McM and J. Marlin's—invalid." (From home.)

May 1   "Sabbath—preached 52–57. Lectured 1 Peter 4: 12–17 —preached Isaiah 57: 6 and baptized Janet to Wm. Gebby; James to Wm. Young; George, to And. Mc-

Lower Chanceford (Society)— *Continued*

Cleary; Eliz. daughter to John McCleary and Rachel to James Mi(tchel) rode 5 miles—exercised psalm 4 and baptized Jean to Wm. Mar."

1768 May 10 "rode 16 miles—married Sam Nelson and Reb. Loughhead." (From home.)

June 21, 22 "rode 12 miles—preached psalm 19: 7—catechized 28 persons and baptized John, son to James Ross—give all praise to my gracious God." (From Middle Octoraro.)

Aug. 31 "rode 10 miles—preached 89: 29—exercised Revelations 3: 11 and baptized John and Jean to Janet M—ray (Murray); James to J. Buchan.: John Marlin; Jean, to T. Ramsay." (Then on Sept. 1 rode 19 miles home.)

1769 Jan. 2 "rode 20 miles to John Marlin's, Susquehanna extremely high." (From home.)

" 3 "rode 10 miles; Bott, Sold J. Moor 80 lbs. in Wm. Maughlin's, exercised psalm 68; and baptized Jean daughter to Wm. Maughlin."

" 4 "rode 16 miles to S. Nelson, Dixon, and James Paterson." (Then 7 miles home on 5th.)

Apr. 10 "rode 16 miles to walk over Susquehanna; Stew, married J. Dun." (From home.)

" 11 "rode 3 miles to W. Brown's; invalid but recovering."

May 2 "rode 20 miles with J. Moore to W. Wilson's, wet." (From home.)

" 3 "rode 1 mile to G. Henry's; preached psalm 31: 19— preached Galatians 4: 6."

1770 Mar. 5 "G. M. 6th—rode 7 miles to James Calhoun's—preached 34: 8—preached Ruth 1: 16 and baptized Isobel, daughter to James Calhoun—went to John Duncan's." (From Paxton.)

Apr. 5, 6, 7 "rode 6 miles to Wilson's, Gebby's and Reid's, etc., wet." (From George Henry's.)

" 8 "Sabbath—rode 6 miles preached 5: 9–L.; lectured Isaiah 27: 1–7 preached Jude and baptized John, John, John, sons to John Marlin, William Gebby and William Mar-

Lower Chanceford (Society)— *Continued*

lin and Mary, to Dan Sinclair. Exercised psalm 30: 5."

1770 Apr. 9 "rode 9 miles—preached psalm 102: 13–17 examined 46 persons and baptized Margaret to John Stewart and Martha to John Buchanan and came to John McMillan's—tired." (Then rode 14 miles home on 10th.)

July 6 "rode 24 miles to Dan Sinclair's—milan irritated." (From home.)

" 7 "rode 10 miles to and from Wm. Nicol's to George Henry's."

" 8 "Sabbath rode 5 miles; preached 6: 11; lectured 15–L; preached Jeremiah 30: 11 and baptized And. son to Wm. Young; Janet daughter to James Mitchel and John son to John McCleary—went to John Mar——." (Then rode 22 miles home on 9th.)

Sept. 4 "rode 15 miles John McM's after sowing 2 bushels rye paid 2-10- to Borland." (From home.)

" 5 "rode 9 miles to W. G's after preaching psalm 34: 11— and lectured Luke 8: 4 etc."

1771 Jan. 10 "rode 4 miles to W. W.'s; then preached 13; lectured Hosea 14: 1–4 and baptized Mary daughter to Thomas Ramsay; agreed J. M. etc."

" 11, 12 "rode 19 miles to John Buch., G. Henry's and W. M's and W. Geb."

" 13 "Sabbath; preached 21: 1–6; lectured Deuteronomy 33: 26–L and baptized Mary daughter to Alexander Ewing o.a."

" 14 "rode 10 miles to J. Marlin's, Mark's and John McMillan's." (Rode 18 miles home by J. Marshal's on 15th.)

Mar. 21 "rode 12 miles to John Marlin." (From A. Robieson's.)

" 22, 23 "Held session day and night—agreed all etc. etc."

" 24 "Sabbath rode 3 miles; preached 6–L; preached 2 Corinthians 4: 3 and baptized Margaret daughter to Wm. Maughlin; give all praise to my gracious God."

" 25, 26 "rode 3 miles; visited G. H. held session at D. Sinclairs."

Lower Chanceford (Society)— *Continued*

1771 Mar. 27 "rode 9 miles; held session—preached 132; lectured
Ephesians 4: 7—ordained W. G. (Wm. Greer) and Dan
Sin., baptized Margaret to Hew McFadzean and Grizzel
to Sam Pollogh; married Wm. McWilliams and Sarah
Nickle, H. R."

June 17 "rode 18 miles widow Swan's; married And. Nicol and
Mary Hilton at John Duncans." (From Joseph Junken's.)

July 30, 31 "rode 13 miles S. Duncan's, preached Galatians 2: 16
and baptized Jean daughter to Wm. Smith, give all
praise to my gracious God."

Nov. 11 "rode 4 miles to C. S. W. W's and J. Marlin's; preached
psalm 22: 23–26; exercised Ecclesiastes 9: 10 and baptized George son to And. McCleary and Rachel daughter to W. Marlin." (From George Henry's.)

1772 Apr. 3 "Birth-day; entering 55; rode 4 miles; river big, etc."

" 5 "Sabbath; rode 8 miles to W. Nickles; preached 39—etc.,
lectured Isaiah 7: 11 preached Luke L29 and baptized
William son to John Marlin; Hannah to Dan Sinclar;
Rebecca daughter to John Stewart and Hannah to
James Mitchel."

" 6 "rode 3 miles to H. Ross'; preached 76: 8–L; lectured
Luke last."

" 7 "rode 28 miles Smeizar's; married W. Hen. and Marjory
Sconler (or Scouler) at W. Young's g.a. snow, etc."

May 12 "rode 16 miles to An. Stewart's, John Duncan's." (From
Joseph Junken's.)

" 13 "rode 3 miles to W. Brown's."

" 17 "Sabbath; preached 41: 1—lectured 10: 12–20; preached
Luke L32 and baptized Walter, son to James Robieson
and Sar. to Sam Taylor."

June 14 "Sabbath; preached 5: 9; lectured Isaiah 12: preached
Jude and baptized Agnes daughter to John Buchanan,
give all praise to God." (At G. Henry's.)

July 3 "x x x; sailed to John Marlin's." (From J. Red.)

" 5 "Sabbath; rode 4 miles; preached 4–L; lectured 14: 1–16
and preached Acts 20, 21 and baptized Helen daughter
to Isobel Sloan, g.a. hot."

Sept. 21 "rode 5 miles to John Hilton's, Jean Sloan's; dying; and
J. Duncan's." (From W. Brown's.)

Lower Chanceford (Society)— *Continued*

1773 May 1 "rode 2 miles to John Marlin's—sick, etc." (From W.
Gebby's.)

"   2 "Sabbath—rode 6 miles—preached 55: 7–12. Lectured
22–L. Preached Isaiah 30: 15 etc. and baptized Martha's to Alexander Ewing and Wm. Muchlin."
"at night exercised psalm 50: 5—baptized Wm. son to
T. Ramsy, etc."

1774 May 12 "rode 11 miles (from Walter Buchanan's) to J, Whiteside's, after preaching 34: 8–12 catechized x x James
Walker—baptized Jean, his daughter—give all praise
to God."

"   13 "rode 5 miles to Dan Sinclare—held session, etc., etc.,
paid Reed."

"   15 "Sabbath—preached psalm 69: 29–33. Lectured Isaiah
5: 1–9. Preached Galatians 3, 26, 27—2 miles to and
from G. Henry, exercised psalm 61: 1–6 and baptized
Agnes to John Stewart and Margaret to William
Henry."

June 13 "rode 9 miles to G. Henrys; mare shod; Mary Nicols,
H. Ross." (From McMillan's.)

July 30 "rode 7 miles to John Reids, Mauchlin's, Gebbys, Wils."
(From Wm. Gebby's.)

"   31 "Sabbath. Rode 8 miles; preached 7–11; lectured 55:
1–6; preached Genesis 41: 55 and baptized Andrew and
Margaret to John Dougherty and Mary to John Buchanan, o.a. praise God."

Nov. 4 "rode 9 miles to S. Dixon's; preached psalm 23; exc.;
baptized David." (Then rode 8 miles to Wm. Wilson's
on 5th.)

"   10 "rode 8 miles to H. Ross'; preached and exercized psalm
23; baptized Robert son to H. M." (From H. McFad-
den's.)

Dec. 18 "Sabbath; rode 4 miles; preached 7–L; lectured 6–L baptized James son to James Maglaughlin; give all praise
to God. Came to T. Ramsay's." (From Wm. Wilson's.)

"   20 "rode 7 miles to W. Geb. preached psalm 110: 1—and
catechized persons concerning pr."

" 21, 22 "rode 4 miles to John Reid's; John Mar. preached 110;
catechized 30."

Lower Chanceford (Society)— *Continued*

1774 Dec. 23, 24 "rode 8 miles G. Hen., H. Ross'; McM., D. Sin."

1775 Feb. 13, 14 "rode 9 miles—married George Clark and Margaret Sinclair." (From John Marlin's.)

Mar. 24, 25 "rode 23 miles to S. Dixons, W. Wilson's."
" 26 "Sabbath—preached 68–L. Lectured 8–14 and baptized John, son to Hugh Davies."

Apr. 1 "rode and walked 4 miles W. Gebby's James Duncan's." (From D. Sinclair's.)
" 2 "Sabbath rode 8 miles to J. M.—preached 79: 1–5. Lectured 14–20—preached Zechariah 13: 7 and baptized James, son to Alexander Ewin; and Margaret to W. Young."
" 3 "Birth-day—56 years—rode 17 miles home."

May 14 "Sabbath—preached 9–14. Lectured 15 and preached Zechariah 13: 7 g.a. Baptized Alexander and Hannah son and daughter to Alexander McCalister." (At Dan Sinclair's.)
June 11 "Sabbath—preached 81: 6–11. Lectured Hosea 13: 9– 15. Preached Jeremiah 3: 7 and baptized Thomas, son to William Maughlin g.a. praise my gracious God." (At William Wilson's.)
July 23 "Sabbath—preached 4–10. Lectured 5–12. Preached James 4: 1 o.a. and baptized Martha, daughter to John McCleary—great rain—God be merciful."

Nov. 17 "rode 16 miles to Wm. Steel's—saw 8 comp. Exer. J. McMns."
" 18 "rode 6 miles D. Sinclair's—saw Comp. Exer. at Doug."
" 19 "Sabbath—rode 3 miles to W. G's after preaching 89: 1–5 and lecturing Jeremiah 4: 10–19. S. nothing."
" 21 "rode 1 mile J. Reed's after preaching 35: 17—and catechizing persons."
" 22 "rode 5 miles—visited Maugh., G. Henry and Wm. Young's—cold."
" 24 "rode 4 miles—visited Jas. Duncan's, Hew Davison, J. Marlin."
" 25 "rode 3 miles to Dan. Sinclar's—great rain and wind."

Dec. 1, 2 "rode 3 miles to Wm. Henry's, W. W. and D. Sincl." (From And. McCleary's.)

1776 Mar. 17 "rode (Sabbath) 6 miles W. W.—preached 91: 5–9, Lectured Zechariah 9: 1–9—dull—and baptized Agnes.

Lower Chanceford (Society)— *Continued*

daughter to John Dougharty—sick." (From John McMillan's.)

1776 Mar. 18, 19 "rode 4 miles to Mr. Rosses, Buchanan's, Alexander Ewins."

" 21 "rode 5 miles to McCal., Robiesons, Nicols, H. Rosses—sick."

" 22 "rode 8 miles to Henry's, Maugh., Reid's, W. Gebby's."

" 24 "Sabbath—preached 9–14. Lectured Zechariah 9: 9–13 and preached Ezekial 34: 16, 17."

" 26 "Fastday—prayed, rs. the causes, etc.—preached 74: 5–12—preached Micah 7: 9 R. W. H.—rode 7 miles Thomas Ramsay's—very tired o.a. praise God."

" 29 "rode 4 miles to J. Mar.—preached 51: 6–11. Lectured Micah 7: 16–L and baptized Robert, son to T. Ramsay; Sarah to John Duncan; and Jean to John Buchanan, g.a. praise my God."

" 31 "Sabbath—rode 7 miles—preached 14–L. Lectured 12–L—preached Ezekial 34: 16, 17 and baptized George, son to Wm. Henry—went to John McMillans." (Then rode 15 miles home April 1st.)

June 9 "Sabbath—13 miles W. W.—rode 3 miles Ann. G.—preached 20–L. Lectured 5–9 and preached 2 Cor. 6: 17, 18 g.a."

" 10 "rode 8 miles R. Smith's, Review, Thomas Ramsay's—7–6."

" 11 "rode 8 miles Sam. Dix.—married Wm. Cross and Margaret Ramsay." (Then rode 13 miles home on 12th.)

Aug. 15, 16 "Rode 17 miles to Robert Paterson's—preached and lectured psalm 73: 21–L and baptized Ann, daughter to Robert Kirkpatrick."

" 17 "rode 4 miles to D. Sinclair."

" 18 "Sabbath—rode 3 miles to and from Frame-meet. H. R. preached 99: 1–6. Lectured Phil. 4: 5–10 and preached Jeremiah 30: 21, 22 g.a. praise God."

Sept. 1 "Sabbath—rode 7 miles McM. (from Hugh Ross's)—preached psalm 99: 6–L. Lectured 10–15. Preached Amos 5: 14 and baptized Wm. McMn., son to Ann Gebby, Janet, daughter to James McGlaughlin; Margaret to Wm. Young, and John, son to John Stewart." (Then rode 17 miles home on 2nd.)

Oct. 6 "Sabbath—preached 102: 6–11. Lectured Colossians 1: 18–23 preached from same and baptized Thomas son

Lower Chanceford (Society)— *Continued*

to Jas. Robieson went 5 miles to J. McMn's." (From W. W's.—then 16 miles home on 7th.)

1776 Nov. 14 "rode 4 miles to and from Mary Nickols, Hew Rosses, D. J." (From Wm. Wilson's.)

Dec. 5 "rode 3 miles J. A's.—preached 51: 5–9. Lectured Isaiah 26: 1–9 and baptized Jean to John Ewin." (At John Andrew's—then 13 miles home by Captain Ross's, Mr. Smith's.)

1777 Jan. 22 "rode 15 miles Al. Robieson's, S. D. and John McMillans."

" 25 "rode and —— 6 miles—ice, rain, to Dan Sinclair's."

" 26 "Sabbath—preached 105: 1–6. Lectured Colossians 3: 1–5 and baptized Martha to Wm. Buchanan."

" 27, 28, 29 "rode 10 miles J. Marlin's, A. G., Widow Reid's, and to Tho. Ramsay's."

Feb. 6 "rode 1 mile John Marlin's—preached psalm 91: 1–5— exer. Isaiah 26: 20, 21 and baptized Sarah Leffarty, adult, Eliz. Hen's. maid." (From Ann Gebby's.)

" 8 "rode 4 miles to Wm. Henry's, Hew Rosses—x x."

" 9 "Sabbath—rode 9 miles to meeting-house—preached 10—lectured 9: 10. Alexander McCulloch's preached psalm 51: 8—exc. Malachi 4: 2 and baptized Jean to him."

Apr. 10 "rode 16 miles to A. Rob., S. D., and John McM.— Jean dead, William sick." (From home.)

" 11, 12 "rode 8 miles to W. Wil., Hugh Rosses, and Dan. Sinclair's."

" 13 "Sabbath—rode 4 miles T. Ramsay's—preached 17: 23 and dis. Col. 4: 1 o.a."

" 15 "rode 2 miles John McCulloch's—x x."

" 16 "rode 5 miles McM's after preaching 54: 1—catechized 35 persons and baptized Rebec. to Alexander Ewing; and Jean to Sam Pollock."

" 17 "rode 5 miles Wm. McMns. burial—con. Mr. Latta, etc."

" 18 "rode 5 miles Dan Sinclair's—rs. 6-14-9."

" 20 "Sabbath—preached 24: 30. Lectured Colossians 4: 2–5. Preached psalm 106: 30 and baptized And., son to John McCleary—rode 5 miles J. Mns." (Then rode 17 miles home on 21st.)

Lower Chanceford (Society)— *Continued*

1777 May 23, 24   "rode 10 miles to Ann Gebby's, Wid. Reed's, etc."
(From Alexander McCulloch's.)
"   25   "Sabbath—rode 8 miles to J. Mc. after preaching 107: 1
lectured Jeremiah 2: 5–12, preached verse 13 and baptized James son to Alexander McCalister." (Then
rode 16 miles home on 26th.)

July 19   "rode and walked 15 miles to A. Rob., Milroy's, Rippy's,
Sam Dixon's." (From home.)
"   20   "Sabbath—rode 12 miles to and from Tent—preached
8–18. Lectured 11–15—preached from same and baptized Hugh, son to Hew McFadzean; and John to Wm.
Maughlin." (Then rode 17 miles home by Simpson's
on 21st.)

Aug. 13   "rode 1 mile W. Maughlin's—conversed Sam and Jean
Reed, etc." (From W. B. R.)

Nov. 5   "rode 8 miles to and from Widow Andrews, Buch. and
Ross's." (From Al. Ewins.)
"   6   "rode 4 miles to D. S.—preached 83: 11–L and lectured
Matt. 13: 24–31 at J. Marlin's. Excer. psalm 301:
1–6 and baptized Hew and Sam to Agnes Davison; and
Eleanor daughter to John Duncan—5 hours."
"   7, 8   "rode 6 miles Ann Gebby's and to W. W's—tired."
"   9   "rode 8 miles to meeting-house, McMn's.—preached
12–L and lectured 24–28 g.a."

Dec. 14   "Sabbath—rode 3 miles to T. Ramsay's—preached 118:
1–10. Lectured Joel 2: 12. Baptized John son to Wm.
Henry g.a. praise my gracious God."
"   15   "rode 6 miles—visited Sam Pol. and John Dougherty,
etc."

1778 Mar. 17   "rode 8 miles to T. Ram.—preached 68: 16–19—catechized 36 and baptized James to Francis Andrews—
went A. D."
"   18   "rode 6 miles Rippy's, Row. Hews.—gave Finley, etc. 8."
"   19, 20, 21   "rode 16 miles to John Buch. Robi., W. Wilson's."
"   22   "Sabbath—rode 3 miles to J. Mar.—preached 25: 29

Lower Chanceford (Society)— *Continued*

Lectured Jeremiah 17: 9–15.   Preached psalm 3: 5 and baptized Elizabeth to John Dougherty."

1778 Mar. 23   "rode 7 miles to Sam. Dix.—married John Branon and May ——."

Apr.   9   "rode 15 miles (from Mat. McClung's) to Jean Paton's, married to John McMillans—went to J. Wod."   (On 10th rode 11 miles home.)

"   18   "rode 8 miles (from home) to John McM. over Susquehanna—gt. to H. R. Dan."

"   19   "Sabbath—preached 37–41.   Lectured Isaiah 58: 3–10 and preached Ephesians 2: 13 o.a."

"   20   "rode 9 miles, 3 on Sabbath night to T. Ramsay's and 6 Josh Brown's."

"   21   "rode 7 miles to Mr. Sm., Rowl. Hews, J. Parks, Thomas Ram."

"   22   "Fastday—rode 8 miles—prayed, preached 74: 10–15. Discoursed Zechariah 12: 10 A. R. bur."

"   23   "rode 10 miles W. Y.—married John Reid and Susan Ramsay at Widow Reid's; married James Stewart to Jean Reid."

"   26   "Sabbath—rode 5 miles—preached 41: 44.   Lectured Proverbs 1: 24–32.   Preached Isaiah 58: 8—and baptized Jean, daughter to Moses McWhorter."   (From William Young.)

May 20   "rode 16 miles to Mr. S., S. Robs., W. Buch., and J. Jackson, John Patterson."

"   21   "rode 5 miles—preached 42: 8–11.   Lectured Isaiah 1: 16–20 and baptized Elijah and Thomas to Robert Patterson—went to Sam Dixon's by W. Metier's saw ——."

"   22   "rode 9 miles to Mr. McMn's, W. W. and H. Ross—tired."

"   23, 24   "Sabbath—rode 6 miles—preached 57–60.   Lectured Micah 4: 1–8.   Preached 1 Peter 1: 3—went to Jas. Robis."

"   25   "rode 12 miles T. Michle's (or Nickle), John Mitchel's."

"   26   "rode 4 miles W. Gemble's—preached 102: 13–17. Excer. 1 Corinthians 3: 3, 4, 5 and baptized Jean daughter to John Mitchel—pp kind—rs. 3."

"   27   "rode 10 miles Mr. Finlay's, Js. McGlaighlin's, Al. McCulloch's—rs. 2–10."

"   28   "rode 9 miles to Jo. Reid's, Esq., Stewart's, Widow Reid's, tired."

Lower Chanceford (Society)—*Continued*

1778 May 30 "rode 2 miles to Ann Gebby's."

" 31 "Sabbath—rode 13 miles—preached 60: 65. Lectured 8–L. Preached 1 Peter 1: 3 and baptized John to Jas. Robieson; and Agnes to John Taylor."

Oct. 3 "rode 2 miles to B.'s, W. Henry's, son dying—had Bess shoed." (From William Wilson's.)

" 4 "Sabbath—rode 4 miles to T. R. after preaching 124–29. Lectured Matt. 22: 1–8 and preached 6: 19–21 and baptized Thomas (son) to John Buchanan and William son to W. Fulerton o.a. praise God."

" 8 "rode 9 miles to Mr. McMns. preached x x and baptized Mary daughter to William Young x x." (From George Henry's.)

" 11 "preached 139: 33—lectured Mark 14: 22–29. x x John Mitchel x x and baptized Elizabeth, daughter to him o.a. praise God."

Nov. 25, 26 "rode 6 miles widow Reid's; married James Long and Ann Gebby, exc. at J. Marlin's—preached 69: 32 and exercised Acts 13: 44–49." (From Hugh Ross's.)

" 28 "rode 3 miles to James Long's, D. Sinclair's; sick."

Dec. (5) "rode 22; Baptized Jean daughter to Wm. Buchanan."

1779 Mar. 1 "rode 5 miles to the R. to Ful. bur. James Robies." (From Dan. Sinclair's.)

" 2 "rode 4 miles to the Ful., W. Y., and James Loganes Lex."

" 3, 4 "rode 3 miles to Widow Reed's; catechized 30; baptized Margaret daughter to Wm. Maughlin; went to John Marlin's, etc."

" 5 "rode 2 miles to Wm. Marlin's, Francis Andrew's."

" 6, 7 "Sabbath, rode 3 miles to W. W. preached 125; lectured Galatians 3: 1–9 o.a. praise God."

" 8, 9 "rode 7 miles H. Ross, J. Buch. T. Ramsay's; married Richard Easton and Elizabeth Buchanan; rs 8 D."

" 12, 13 "rode 8 miles James Robieson's, F. and D. Sinclar's."

" 14 "Sabbath—preached 126 lectured Galatians 3: 10–19 and baptized Jean, daughter to John Reed; went 4 miles to Thomas Ramsay's."

" 16 "rode 4 miles to A. Ewing's; preached; catechized 42 persons, etc."

Lower Chanceford (Society)— *Continued*

1779 Mar. 17, 18 "rode 8 miles to A. Meca (Alex. McCalister?), W. Ful., Wm. Maughlin's, exercised psalm 68: 18 and baptized George son to Wm. Henry, o.a."

" 19, 20 "rode 4 miles to W. Y's, Love's bur; Neil's W. W."

" 21 "Sabbath—rode 1 mile; preached 27; lectured 20–L and baptized John son to James McGlaughlin; give all praise to my gracious God."

" 22 "rode 10 miles to Branons, Latta's, Arch. Ancruons."

Apr. 21 "rode 11 miles to W. G. Ed. Manifolds, Al. Ewings." (From Robert Proudfoot's.)

" 22 "rode 3 miles to H. R. preached 125: lectured Acts 2: 37–41; baptized Henry son to A. Ewing and John to George Mitchel."

" 23, 24 "rode 6 miles to John Marlin's to D. Sinclair's."

June 20 "Sabbath—rode 5 miles; preached 8—lectured and preached Hebrews 10: 19–23 and baptized Ann daughter to John Mitchel; went to Thomas Ram." (From Hugh Ross's.)

" 21 "rode 7 miles to 4 fam. round John Mit. to Josh Br."

" 22 "rode 6 miles to T. R. preached 91: 1–5; lectured Matthew 11: 25–L and baptized Margaret daughter to Hugh McFadzean; give all praise to God."

" 23 "rode 8 miles Mr. Clarkson's; conversed and Mr. Fulton's, etc."

" 24 "rode 6 miles to J. Rob. H. Rosses D. and James Logues."

" 25, 26 "rode 5 miles to W. M. John Mar; S. N. W. W. and Daniels."

" 27 "Sabbath—rode 7 miles to Mr. McMillans; preached 15–L; lectured 25: 31 preached 31 and baptized James Henry to John Stewart and John to John McCulloch; give all praise to God."

" 28 "rode 15 miles to S. D., A. Rob., R. Kilpatrick and home."

Aug. 14 "rode 2 miles from James Logues to D. Sinclair's, rainy weather."

" 15 "Sabbath. Rode 7 miles to Al. McCulloch, after preaching 6–L; lectured Hebrews 11: 1–5, preached verse 6; at night preached 30: 3—and exercised Mat-

Lower Chanceford (Society)— *Continued*

thew last chapter 16–L, and baptized Margaret, daughter to Alexander McCulloch, give all praise to God."

1779 Aug. 25 "rode and walked 5 miles to John McCleary's wet and weary." (From Robert Proudfoot's.)
" 26 "rode 12 miles to A. McCulloch's; preached 31: 1–5; preached Solomon 6: 3 and baptized Sarah daughter to John McCleary, o.a. praise God, etc."
" 27 "rode and walked 9 miles to John Reid; married James Ridgeway and Agnes Pattison, paid 10 went to J. Logues."

1780 Jan. 5 "rode 6 miles S. L's and to A. Ewins—2nd child dead—great storm." (From Dan Sinclair's.)

" 17 "rode 5 miles to Ross's, J. Robieson, to and from Fulton's." (From Dan Sinclair's.)
" 18 "preached psalm 25: 7–11 and lectured 11–14—baptized Eliz. to J. Rob."
" 19 "rode 6 miles to F. Ross's—wrote letter to Crawfurd, to D. S."
" 20 "rode 3 miles to Wm. Maughlin's, James Logue's."
" 22 "rode 2 miles to John Marlin's—very cold, cold, cold!"
" 23 "Sabbath—preached 142: 1–5 and lectured 9–14 and baptized Elizab. to Francis Andrew; and Jean to John Duncan."

Feb. 16, 17, 18 "rode 5 miles to and from Latta's—17th preached 65: 1–5 catechized concerning law and baptized Mary, daughter to Dan McReady—g.a. praise God." (From H. Coulter's.)
Apr. 30 "Sabbath—rode 5 miles to J. McMns.—preached 7–L. Lectured Malachi 3: 13–L and baptized Jean to Alexander McCalister, and Robert, son to William Fulerton g.a."

May 31 "rode 5 miles to W. Ross—Tent preached 133. Lectured Zephaniah 2: 1–4—went to J. Mar." (From Alexander Ewing's.)
" " "—catechized at Alexander Ewings 19 persons—a great rain."
June 1 "rode 3 miles Jas. Dun. W. Marlin's, And., J. Logue's."

" 5 "rode 48 miles—married David Sloan and Jean Stewart —J. Parks." (Then rode 20 miles to Mr. Dobbin's and Francis Meredith's on the 6th.)
Aug. 20 "Sabbath—rode 7 miles, S. Dixon's; preached 4th psalm

Lower Chanceford (Society)— *Continued*

6–L; lectured Ephesians 4: 8–18 and ordained elders— Wm. Fulerton and Alexander Ewin—preached Jeremiah."

1780 Sept. 3 "Sabbath—preached 5: 8–L and lectured 6–L and preached verse 12 and baptized John to John Porter." (At Bileston's and 22 miles from home.)

Oct. 5 "rode 6 miles to Coll. Rosses, Tent; preached 7th psalm 13–L. Mr. Dobin preached Luke 16: 29, 30, 31. Mr. Telfair came that morning." (From Alexander Ewing's.)

" 6 "rode 2 miles to Dan Sinclair's, sick, 5 to Wm. Maughlin."

" 11, 12 "rode 10 miles to and from And. Finley's paid Bess 100 lbs. to Michal Morris for roan mare 7 old; preached and preached Zechariah 13: 9 g.a." (From John McCleary's.)

Dec. 12 "rode 4 miles J. L. preached 92: 13–L; lectured Galatians 3: 11–15 and baptized Andrews son to Alexander McCleary."

1781 Jan. 1 "rode 2 miles to W. Mar. James Dun. J. Ma." (From James Logue's.)

" 2 "rode 1 and preached 72: 15—catechized 32 and baptized Letitia daughter to W. S."

" 3 "rode 4 miles from J. Logue's to W. Maugh. Elizabeth Henry's—and to John Reid's; rs Rollins Bess L. 3 vol. wet."

" 9 "rode 5 miles to Fulton's, Pederis. G. Henry's, Wm. Pollock." (Then 2 miles to James Logue's on 10th.)

Apr. 1 "Sabbath—rode 2 miles, preached 17: 1—lectured Jeremiah 17: 1–9 preached 108: 12." (From Dan Sinclair's.)

" 2, 3 "rode 2 miles J. Marlin's, married Wm. Balantine and Susanah Marlin. nil received, came to James Logue's."

" 4, 5 "rode 8 miles W. Mau., Ful. R. Fulton's, Rob. Ross."

" 6 "Rode 2 miles to John Fulerton's, T. Matthews."

" 8 "Sabbath—rode 5 miles; preached 4–L; lectured 9–15 and preached 14th verse great wind, exercised psalm 23 and baptized James to James Ramsay."

May 27 "Sabbath—rode 3 miles (from D. Sinclair's), preached 23–29; lectured Romans 6: 1–10 and preached Romans 8: 13; (24th married Elijah Forsyth and Jean Ewing)." (At Walter Buchanan's and Esq. Ewing's on 24th.)

" 28 "rode 14 miles to G. H. J. Mar. S. N. Jos. Brown's."

" 29 "rode 4 miles to Hew McFadzean preached 143: 5–10;

Lower Chanceford (Society)— *Continued*

preached 10th verse and baptized John son to Hew McFadzean o.a. praise God."

1781 Aug. 26   "Sabbath—rode 2 miles; preached 22: 1–6; lectured Romans 7: 1–7 preached Galatians 3–19 and baptized George son to James Robison and Agnes daughter to Wm. Maughlin." (From Dan. Sinclair's.)

"   27   "rode 6 miles from Ross's, Fulton's, Fulerton's, Maughlin's, to Logue's."

"   28, 29   "rode 4 miles to Wm. Pollock's, John Reid's, ague; Logues."

Sept.   2   "Sabbath—rode 4 miles; preached 6: 11; lectured 7–15 and preached Galatians 3: 19 give all praise to God." (From Dan Sinclair's.)

"   3, 4   "rode 16 miles A. Proudfoot's, A. Finley's, W. Ayrs, married John McClintock and Agnes Ayres, etc. preached 103: 1–5 and lectured Romans 8: 1–5."

"   5   "rode 11 miles to widow Andrews, H. Dixon's, W. Gembles, W. Robinson."

"   6   "rode 8 miles to Fulton's Col. W. W. dying, Loughhead's, W. Maughlin's."

"   7   "rode 4 miles to James Logues, J. M. married James Ayres and Eleanor Davidson, wrote to Cap. McBride Walkil. went to D. Sin."

"   9   "rode 8 miles, preached 11: 15; lectured 14–L and preached Galatians 3: 22 W. W. Bury's." (William Wilson's burying.)

1782 Feb. 28   "rode 10 miles to Mos. McWhort., to Mr. Finley's dying."

Mar.   1   "rode 7 miles to W. Maugh. James Logues—."

"   2   "rode 4 miles burying James Duncan, to D. Sinclair's, cold."

"   5   "rode 4 miles to Dan. at J. Lo. preached 13, catechized and baptized James son to Jean Marlin widow; received dollar from Bety."

"   6   "rode 4 miles to Mary W. G., Ors and T. Ramy's."as

Lower Chanceford (Society)— *Continued*

1782 Mar. 7 "rode 1 mile, preached 17: 4—catechized 35 and baptized Sam to Wm. Valentine."

" 8 "rode 3 miles from And. McCleary's to Col. Ross', bad roads."

" 13 "rode 9 miles back, preached 60: 1—lectured 1 Peter 2: 19–L and baptized George son to John Mitchel o.a. praise God."

" 15 "rode 1 mile John Buchanans, constant fog."

" 17 "Sabbath—rode 3 miles James Robertson's, preached 5–L and lectured 22–27 o.a. praise."

" 18, 19 "rode 4 miles to and from Fulton's and to D. Sinclair's. lectured."

" 20 "rode 2 miles W. Maugh. preached 102: 1–17–22 and lectured Acts 10: 34–44."

" 21, 22 "rode 6 miles to John Reid's, Mr. Pollock's, G. Henry's, James Logue's."

" 23 "rode 3 miles to D. S., Sam Neilson's, Mary Wilson's."

" 24 "Sabbath—preached 30–6; lectured Romans 9: 27–L give all praise to God, weary."

" 25 "rode 2 miles to W. and John Fulerton's, cold weather."

" 27 "rode 3 miles to John Marl. exc. 6 psalm 1—o.a."

" 28 "rode 7 miles, married Robert Clark and Jean Gebby."

" 29 "rode 17 miles home from J. McMns. paid M. R. 16 dollars."

July 24 "rode 4 miles to J. Robi. preached 19: 5 lectured 1 Corinthians 10: 1–5 and (baptized) Thomas son to Alexander Ewing o.a. praise God." (From Alexander Ewing's.)

" 25 "rode 6 miles Ful., Ross, Fuler. W. Maughlins."

Aug. 25 "Sabbath—rode 10 miles; preached 35: 1—lectured John 19: 8–1, preached same and baptized Adam son to Wm. Fulerton o.a. went Al. McCuloc." (From Wm. Maughlin's.)

Dec. 7 "rode 3 miles to Mary Wilson's, rs. news." (From Thomas Ramsay's.)

" 8 "Sabbath—rode 2 miles—preached 6–10 and preached Prov. 18: 24 give all praise to God."

" 9 "rode 4 miles G. Henry's, burying, James Robieson."

Lower Chanceford (Society)— *Continued*

1782 Dec. 23 "rode 2 miles from Wm. Reed's to Thomas Ramsay's J. K."

"   24 "rode 3 miles, preached 9: 7–11. Catechized 26 and baptized Wm. to W. Red."

"   25 "rode 2 miles to George Mitchels from Al. Ewings."

"   26, 27 "rode 5 miles to and from Milor, A. McCleary's, Mary Wilson's."

"   29 "Sabbath—rode 2 miles, preached 20—lectured James 4: 10–L and baptized Mary Rowan to Margaret Clark, o.a."

"   30, 31 "preached 57: 1—catechized 20. Rode 5 miles John McMns."

1783 Apr. 3 "rode 5 miles to Ro. Marlin's burial went to S. Neilson's." (From Thomas Ramsay's.)

"   6 "Sabbath—rode 4 miles, preached 41: 1–5; lectured 3: 1–8, discoursed same. Excer. 1 Corinthians 10: 1–5, baptized George to John Buchanan." (From Maughlin's.)

"   7 "rode 11 miles from Alexander Ewing's to John McCleary's."

"   9 "rode 4 miles to Wm. G. preached 73 and lectured Revelations 3: 14–21 o.a."

May 11 "Sabbath—preached 42: 6–L. Lectured Philippians 2: 5–12 and baptized Robert son to Alexander McCleary, preached Isaiah 55: 10, 11 o.a. praise God." (At Alex. McCleary's.)

Nov. 17 "rode 3 miles, married James Kennedy and Margaret Clark, saw furnace rolling and slitting Qt. Dol., Mr. McMillan." (At J. Clark's.)

"   18 "rode 5 miles over Susquehanna Jean Ross, went to John Stewart's, tired."

"   19 "rode 4 miles Eliz. Henry, W. Fulerton's, Da. Sinclair's."

"   20 "rode 2 miles to Wm. Maughlin's, James Logue's."

"   22 "rode 1 mile John Marlin's, sick, slept, cold very."

"   23 "Sabbath—rode 6 miles, preached 7: 13, lectured 7–18 and baptized Wm. son to W. Maughlin, James to James Logue and James to John Duncan, went to Th. Payns."

Lower Chanceford (Society)— *Continued*

1784 May 29 "Sabbath—rode 3 miles—preached 55: 1–9. Lectured 18–23 and preached Philippians 3: 10, etc." (From Dan. Sinclair's.)

" 30 "rode 9 miles—got mare shod—Stew Reeds, Haw., L. Marlin's."

June 6 "Sabbath—rode 4 miles—preached 12–20. Lectured 23–L—preached from same and baptized Mary daughter to Alexander Ewing, uncle b. December 20, 1783. went to W. Reed's."

" 24 "rode 7 miles Widow Shuttles—preached ex., baptized Agnes." (From John Smeizar's, Alexander McKitterik's.)

" 28 "rode 12 miles—married John Marlin and Rachel—received do. and shirt ——." (From Sam Neilson's—then 10 miles home on 29th.)

Oct. 5, 6 "rode 5 miles, preached 63: 1–6; lectured Haggai 1: 1–12 and baptized John son to David Mauson C. Jan. 1, 1784, o.a. went to W. Smith Esq." (From Robert Proudfoot's.)

" 10 "Sabbath—rode 5 miles, preached 6–L, lectured 10–L and baptized Mary to W. Valentine." (From Wm. Maughlin's.)

" 11 "rode 3 miles, held session, etc., preached 70: 7–9, discoursed Romans 3: 32 and baptized An. to Hugh McFadzean born April 3, '83, Margaret and Elizabeth, daughters to John Harbison born Sept. 16th, '82 and July 22nd, 1784, and Alexander to Alexander Ewing born Sept. 6, '84, went to T. Ra."

" 13, 14 "rode 8 miles W. Reid's, D. S., held session, preached Psalm 40: 6 discoursed Galatians 2: 20 and baptized Samuel son to —. Fulerton born Sept. 21."

" 17 "Sabbath—rode 3 miles, preached 64: 1—preached Samuel 12: 20–23, baptized John, son to James Ayrs, born Sept. 28 Elizabeth to Wm. Reid born 21, x x."

Nov. 28 "Sabbath—rode 5 miles, preached 66: 1–6, lectured John 4: 1–11 and baptized Thomas to John Reid C. Oct. 18, 1784, o.a. res." (From James Logue's.)

" 30 "rode 8 miles to Rob Dixon's."

Dec. 1 "rode 3 miles to An. Proudfoot's, J. McCleary's."

" 3 "rode 1 mile to Wm. Smith Esq., slept Mr. Slemons."

Lower Chanceford (Society)— *Continued*

1784 Dec. 12 "Sabbath rode 3 miles, preached 15–L, lectured 4: 19–31 and baptized Alexander son to James Robinson, o.a. sick with cold." (From Dan Sinclair's.)

1786 Apr. 9 "Sabbath rode, preached 24–31, lectured John 4: 19–34 held session, rode i.o. 16 miles John Marlins, preached psalm 32: 1–5 Exc. 5 and baptized John to John Duncan born Dec. 1785, Thomas to James Ramsay born April 3, 1785, and John to John Marlin born Dec. 19th, '85, give all praise to my God, came James Logue's."

" 16 "Sabbath—rode 3 miles, James Ram. preached 31–L and preached verse 42, give all praise God."

June 21, 24 "rode 9 miles to Young's, F. Maugh., Logue's." (From Thomas Ramsay's.)

" 25 "Sabbath—rode 7 miles, preached 69: 10–L, lectured John 16: 23–31, preached 32–3 and baptized Sar. daughter to John Marlin born June 4th and John son to Alexander McCulloch born May 29th, '86."

Aug. 20 "Sabbath—preached 13–16 and lectured 10–17 and preached Hebrews 2: 16 and baptized Mary to Antony Nicols born June 7, ult., and Agnes to John Reid, born July 8 give all praise to benign God."

Sept. 10 "Sabbath preached 79: 10–15, lectured 1 Peter 2: 1–6, preached Titus 2: 14, etc. discoursed Romans 5: 12 and baptized Jeany daughter to Sam McCulloch, child dying." (At Sam McCulloch's.)

Nov. 6 "rode 5 miles to S. Dixon's, country-side, J. Bran." (From W. McReary's.)

" 7 "Preached 32: 1–5, lectured Hosea 1: 4–L and baptized Hugh son to James Black born March 31st, '85 and Margaret to Gregory Farmer born July 1st, 178–." (Then rode 11 miles home on 2nd.)

1787 Jan. 21 "Sabbath—rode 6 miles T. R., preached Romans 12: 12 lectured 8–15 - - - - widow." (From Dan Sinclair's.)

" 25 "Married James Oliver and Martha Brown—14." (At Thomas Ramsay's?)

" 28 "Sabbath—rode 10 miles, preached 17–L, lectured 16–L, and baptized Margaret to Dr. Sam McCulloch, rode 8 miles to W. F., W. Mau., G. H. and John Ram."

Feb. 4 "Sabbath—preached 78: 1–6 and preached Isaiah 32: 2,

Lower Chanceford (Society)— *Continued*

o.a. baptized Margaret daughter to S. McCul. born July 7."

1787 Feb. 11 "Sabbath—preached 6–12, lectured 2 Peter 2: 1–11 and baptized Margaret to W. Ful. born Jan. 13th, 1787, g.a. 5–10 rode 12 miles."

" 12 "rode 4 miles to Jos. Glens, sick, hoarse."

" 14 "rode 2 miles James Hills rs 1 dollar and Thomas Ramsay's; rain."

Apr. 29 "Sabbath—rode 3 miles, preached 79: 1–6, lectured 9: 19 preached Luke 19: 10 and baptized Agnes to James Ayres born Mar 13 8–."

" 30 "Married Sam Morrison and Mary Gebby."

July 8 "Sabbath—rode 7 miles, preached 8—lectured 96: 18 and preached same and baptized Hanna to Gregory Farmer born June 1st, 1787, sick at night." (From Sam Dixon's.)

Sept. 1 "wnd. Sabbath—rode 6 miles preached 8–L, lectured 13–L and preached James 10–16 and baptized Agnes Loughhead to Robert McCullough born Oct. 14, 1786— read review paper, etc." (Then rode 6 miles to Muddy meeting-house on 3rd.)

" 16 "Sabbath—rode 4 miles preached 8–L, lectured 14–L and preached John 10: 16, etc." (From Wm. Maughlin's.)

" 17 "rode 11 miles, preached 51, preached Titus 2: 14 and baptized Kathrine to Alexander McKitterick in John McCleary's. C. Jan. 26, 1786."

1788 Mar. 30 "Sabbath—rode 5 miles, preached 94: 1–9 and lectured Jeremiah 19 and baptized Robert son to Henry Hanna; born Nov. 19th, 1787." (From Robert McCulloch's.)

" 31 "rode 5 miles 1 yr. landing to D. Sinclairs, sick, cold."

Apr. 1 "rode 2 miles to James Logue's, to D. Sinclair's, sick, cold."

" 2 "rode 2 miles John Reid, widow Pol., John Stewart's."

" 3 "rode 1 mile to Wm. Maugh., wrote James Ben."

" 6 "Sabbath—preached 9–16, lectured 20 and preached Hebrews 8: 10 and baptized Agnes to James Ramsay, born Jan. 18, 1788 (or 1768)."

" 7 "rode 4 miles to J. Mit. and widow Browns from Jos. Glens, etc. Agnes rode 3 miles to ———."

Lower Chanceford (Society)— *Continued*

1788 Apr. 8 "rode 5 miles T. R., preached and lectured psalm 23 and baptized John to James Oliva."

" 10 "rode 5 miles And. McCl., John Buch., Ross', James Robinson (baptized) born March 26, 1788, give all praise to God."

" 11 "rode 5 miles to Fult., F. Maugh., Ramsay, J. Logue's."

" 15 "rode, visited, 4 miles to D. H., etc., widow married J. Dun."

June 8 "Sabbath—rode 3 miles—preached 97: 8–L, lectured Jeremiah 25: 1–15, preached same, held session, baptized George to Wm. Valentine born 5th, last and Elizabeth to Antony Nicol, born Dec. 13th." (From Wm. Maughlin's.)

" 9, 10 "rode 9 miles to widow J. Dun. preached, Exc. psalm 40: 1–6 and baptized James son to John Marlin, born Ma 2nd, went to J. McMns."

" 11 "rode 16 miles to S. D., A. McC., Mr. McIn., R. P. and Porter's, home."

July 29 "From Wm. Master's rode 8 miles to John Muligan's, preached 89: 26—discoursed Matthew 28: 15—and baptized James son to Wm. Anderson, born Aug. 28, 1778, and John born Sept. 22nd, 1780, and Andrew born Sept. 16, '84, and Wm. born Mar. 20, last And to John Mulligan, James born April 30, 1777, and John born Oct. 4, '79, and Janet born Feb. 24th, '81 and Grizel born March 25, '83, and Samuel born June 25th, 1786—F., Jacob Mills."

Sept. 7 "Sabbath—preached 103: 13–18; lectured Hosea 14: 4– L, preached Jeremiah 30–17 x x baptized Jean (to James Black and Mary, his wife) born Aug. 19, '87 and Mary to James Buchanan, born July 9, 1788, and Barbara to George Taylor, born July 20, 1788." (At J. Taylor's—then rode 6 miles to Robert McCord's on 8th.)

Oct. 22 "came 6 miles J. Rip., married Robert Wilson and Jean Maughlin, rs 2 dollars, visited Fulerton's and Stewart's." (From James Robieson's.)

" 23 "rode 3 miles Squire Reid's and went to John Reid's salem."

" 24 "rode 4 miles to L., widow Marlin's, Dun., J. M., Sam Neilson."

" 25 "1 mile, 26th. —— rode 4 miles, preached 25–31, lectured 31–35, went to T. Ramsay's."

Lower Chanceford (Society)— *Continued*

1788 Oct. 27 "rode 1 mile G. Orson's."

"   28 "rode 6 miles Dan., married James Spier and Hanna Lyttle, rs 3 dollars went to J. McMns. Toltha."

Dec. 1 "rode 3 miles Sp. mau. D. preached John 7: 45–46 and baptized John son to W. Maugh., born 3rd—87." (From James Logue's.)

1789 Feb. 9, 10 "rode 2 miles, married James Gebby and Janet Gebby, son and daughter to John and Wm. Gebby, received 0 dollars—a gun." (From James Logue's.)

June 6 "rode 3 miles to J. Branons, J. McMil., Barn. Rosses." (From Jas. Rogers.)

"   7 "Sabbath—rode 5 miles—preached 111: 1–5; lectured 44: 1–15—discoursed from same and baptized Sarah, daughter to Robert McCulloch, born February 7th."

"   28 "Sabbath—rode 1 mile—preached 5–L; lectured 45: 1–15 —preached from same and baptized Lititia daughter to Sam. McCulloch (born) April 25 '89, Esther daughter to George Smith, born March 29, 1789; and Agnes, daughter to Stewart Kennedy, born December 18, 1788; and Sarah, daughter to Hugh McFadzean, born July 2, 1788." (From Wm. Maughlin's.)

Nov. 1 "Sabbath—rode 5 miles—preached 118: 17–24; lectured 1 Corinthians 3: 18–24 x x and baptized Elizabeth to Alexander Gerry—born May 9th." (From Wm. Maughlin's.)

"   2 "rode 1 mile from Jos. Glens to Jas. Hills etc. T. Ramsays."

"   3 "rode 14 miles to Sam Neilson's—received mittens from Js. Hill and married Jas. Quin and Agnes Weaver— 2 D."

1790 Mar. 1, 2 "rode 5 miles—preached 46: 8–L. Discoursed Philip 3: 7–10 and baptized John, son to John Reid, born Jan. 29th last and Ann to Jean Maughlin (or Wilson) born Jan. 11th, '89." (From James Logue's.)

"   3 "rode 5 miles to S. Neilson, G. Orson's, and T. Ramsay's."

"   4 "rode 2 miles—married Joseph Glen and Jean Ramsay."

Lower Chanceford (Society)— *Continued*

1790 Mar. 7 "Sabbath—rode 1 mile—preached 3rd. part Romans 5: 1—etc." (From Wm. Maughlin's.)

"   8 "5 miles to J. McMns.—weary—John Phyliss—great cold."

"   9 "rode 5 miles to W. McIntires—came in great snow that night."

June 5, 6 "rode 10 miles to McMns.—6th—preached 11th part. lectured Titus 3: 4–8 preached from same and baptized William son to Hen. Hana, born Feb. 6: 1 o'c. praise God."

"   7 "rode 5 miles—visited, went to T. Black (8) John Caldw. widow (9), W. Mc."   ,

Sept. 26 "Sabbath—preached 19." (At Wm. Maughlin's—last recorded sermon.)

Mount Difficult

bet.

1756 Sept. 16 & 18 (See "The Island.")

1757 Mar. 18 & 19 (See Lower Chanceford.)

1758 Apr. 13 "Rode 8 miles to and from Mount Difficult settled with Sin." (From Hugh Ross's.)

Aug. 11 "Rode 9 miles—visit to Mount Difficult, etc. alarmed at F. C." (From Hugh Ross's.)

1759 Jan. 10 "sold Mount Difficult to W. Marlin for 110 pounds 6 Gales 19 and 20."

Muddy Creek

1752 Apr. 14 (See Lower Chanceford.)

1754 May 16 "Rode 22 miles to William Wilsons, then to William N. Muddy Creek." (From David Hunter's.)

1761 Apr. 13 "Rode 19 miles to Thomas Ramsay's, Muddy Creek." (From home.)

"   14 "Held session; preached psalm 119: 105–111; preached Lamentations 3: 40. g.a. and baptized John son to John Buchanan; Mary daughter to George Buchanan and Margaret and Mary to John Roan (Rowan)." (Then rode 6 miles to Hugh Ross's on 15th.)

1762 May 29 "Rode 20 miles to Hew Rosses in Muddy Creek with W. B." (From home.)

1763 Nov. 1, 2 "rode 20 miles Muddy Creek—Ten, preached psalm 80: 1. Lectured Philip 4: 4–8 and baptized Thomas to

Muddy Creek—*Continued*

Robert Greer; R... to William Fulerton; John, to William Young; Isobel, daughter to Isobel Sloan; and Elizabeth to And. Ferrier." (Then rode 20 miles home.)

Muddy Run Meeting-house, etc.

(See Lancaster County.)

Neilson's Ferry

1753 July 25   "Rode 17 mi. to H. Ross Neilsons Fer. Jo. McM. and Jos. Brownlie." (From Wm. Wilson's—then 2 miles to John Duncan's on 26th.)

Price's Ferry

1754 Aug. 13   "Rode 20 miles—5 to Price's Ferry,—6 J. McH. and 9 Wm. Brown's." (From James Dill's—James McC—.)

Ramsay's Tent, Thomas

1782 June 14   "rode 4 miles to T. R. Tent, rs. Agreement, printed pro . . .—praise." (Then rode 5 miles and lodged John Ful. on 16th.)

Ross's Tent, Colonel

1780 Oct.   5   "rode 6 miles to Coll. Rosses, Tent; preached 7th psalm 13–L. Mr. Dobin preached Luke 16: 29, 30, 31. Mr. Telfair came that morning." (From Alexander Ewing's—then rode 2 miles on 6th to Dan Sinclair's, sick, 5 to William Maughlin's.)

Somerville

1779 Oct. 12   "rode 18 miles to Somerville, York, McCairnahans, Jacob's, Ewing, Capt. McClelan's, a waste house 3 miles; from Williams 50 miles." (On way to Bedford.)

Susquehanna River

(Crossed many times.)

The Island

1756 Sept. bet.
   16 and 18   "Rode and tramped 12 miles 10 miles Dif.—the Island and to Hen."

Twelve Tavern

1770 Nov. 20   "rode 27 miles to 12 Tavern with Qua. Chamberlan." (From Wm. Steel's—then rode 34 miles home on 21st.)

White Horse, The

1762 July 26, 27   (See Dutch Shoe.)

York

There are 22 visits to York specifically mentioned by Mr. Cuthbertson in his Diary.

1751 Dec. 9 & 10   (See Chamber's Tavern.)

1752 July 27   "Rode 33 miles to Dutch Tavern in York—tired but safe." (From Marsh Creek.)

    Nov. 6   "Rode 32 miles to Jo. Crooks, York, to a field lay 11 hours in the rain and snow." (From Three Springs.)

1754 May 15   "Rode 20 miles to York—killed a viper—then to David Hunter's." (From Wm. Couper's.)

1762 Oct. 25   "Rode 30 miles York; married And. McMiens and Ann Wilson." (From David Dunwoody's.)

1771 Sept. 19   "rode 29 miles to York Mr. Fulton's; paid 10 shillings to mend my watch." (From John McMillan's.)

1774 June 1   "rode 44 miles to York, Anderson's, Dutch Tavern." (From T. Cross's;—then on 2nd rode 18 miles home.)

1778 Aug. 17   "rode 28 miles Smeizar's—married Wm. Neaton and Margaret Buchanan." (From D. S's.) (Then rode 22 miles with Sheriff and Peggy Fulerton to Jos. Kerr's.)

1779 Oct. 12   (See Somerville.)

1780 June 14   "rode 33 miles to York—Mr. Alexander's—conversed, etc. Alexander McKittrick." (From John Murphy's.)

    "   15   "rode 22 miles after preaching 61—Lectured Titus 2: 11 and baptized Katharin, daughter to Al. McKit." (Then rode 3 miles to Col. Ross's and Dan Sinclair's on 16th.)

1781 Oct. 25   "rode 26 miles by John Parks to York, Mr. Alexander Wm." (From T. Girvan's.)

DELAWARE

Kent County

Dover *

1758 Nov. 20   "rode 11 miles from J. C. to W. Cooper's—preached and lectured psalm 32: 5-L and baptized Katharine, daughter to Hew Hail o.a. praise to my gracious God."

1777 Oct. 7   "rode 30 miles to H. Hail's, McNick., Gregory's, John Lamb's, Longstaff, etc." (From York.)

* A Dover in York Co., Pa.

Dover— *Continued*

1779 Aug. 16   "Rode 34 miles to Y(ork), Mr. Rowans and with him to Dover, Hew Hails."

"   17   "rode 18 miles to B. McNic., Hamil., Lambs, Silvers, Longstaffs, and widow Junkens, Wm. Walkers, W. Junkens, good health, praise God."

NEW CASTLE COUNTY
New Castle

1751 Aug.   5   "After being forty-six days, twenty and six-tenth hours at sea from London Derry Loch, landed safely at Newcastle August 5th, 1751, about eight in the forenoon; lodged with Griffins, in good health, praise to God. . . ."

Newport

1759 June 26, 27   "rode 20 miles to Cochran's, Caldwell's, Youngs, Newport, Wilming., Marshal's." (From home.)

Pencader

1752 Sept.   1   "Rode 18 miles over Elk to Benkadar 100 Welsh Tr. Da. Bar."

"   2   "Preached Ps. 89: 15–19, preach. Micah 7.7 and baptized May and Elizabeth, daughters to Hugh Stewart, then rode 15 miles to Moses And. and James Wilson's."

Red Lion

1754 June   5   "Rode 50 miles—15 Red Ly; x x. (From Thomas Kennedy's.)

1783 Oct. 29, 30   "rode 43 miles McFoss, Red Lion, James Millars, J. Ken." (On way home from Philadelphia.)

St. Georges

1759 Apr.   5   (See Whiteclay Creek.)

Whiteclay Creek

1759 Apr.   4   "rode 28 miles to Hew McHorter's, Whiteclay creek— rs. 10, wife." (From home.)

"   5   "rode 18 miles to John Farie's—St. George's—dam's broke."

Wilmington

1759 June 27   (See Newport.)

MARYLAND

ALLEGANY COUNTY

Cumberland

1779 Sept. 15   "rode 30 miles Cumberl., Fort. Hills, Cr. Alegheny, Tomlinson."

Baltimore

Covenanters were in Baltimore, probably as early as 1752; namely, John Anderson, Mrs. James Black, Samuel Moody, John Mortimer, from Ireland; Robert Carothers, James Fletcher, James McCauseland, John McLean, from Scotland.

1752 Feb.   5   "Rode 8 miles to Hew Rosses, Baltim. on the ice 15 f. thick and 9 f. where it diged, etc." (From Jo. McMillan's.)

Old Town

1779 Sept. 14   "rode 40 miles to Rednour's, to Old-town lodged in Mr. Blacs." (From Widow Linn's.)

FREDERICK COUNTY

Cedar Creek Meeting-house

1751 Nov. 24   "Sabbath.—Rode 6 miles to and from Cedar Creek Meeting-house; preached psalm 17: 1–6. Lectured Gal. 3: 10–15 and preached Heb. 4: 12 g.a. and G. concern etc." (From David Logan's.)

Frederick

1751 Nov. 21   "Rode 30 miles to Fred. Town, Opicken, Jos. Colvil's, g.a." (From Lemmon's.)

Opicken

Nov. 21   (See Frederick.)
"   23   "Rode 8 miles to David Logan's—tired and God saved me."

"   26   "Married Jo. Blackburn and Ann Logan. Rode 8 miles."

Opicken Meeting-house

1751 Nov. 27   "Rode 2 miles to Oppicken meeting-house. Preached psalm 23 and preached Heb. 4: 7 o.a.   Then rode 6 miles to Ben Blackburn's. Slept a little."

HARTFORD COUNTY
Crossroads, Bush, Joppa, Trap

1774 Nov. 8 "Rode 28 miles to Trap; 10 Cross Roads, 4 Bush 6 Joppa."

MONTGOMERY COUNTY
Morgan's Mill

1751 Nov. 28 "Rode 41 miles to Morgan's Mill." (From Ben Blackburn's.)

NEW JERSEY

In the middle of December, 1685, on the "Henry and Francis" of New Castle, charted by George Scott of Scotland, and with Richard Hutton as Master, there landed at Perth Amboy, N. J., 95 Covenenters, who, with few exceptions, were banished from Scotland. Thirty others died on the voyage. These persecuted people were scattered at intervals throughout New Jersey, Eastern Pennsylvania, New York, Connecticut, Delaware and South Carolina. Their names are listed in Doctor Wm. M. Glasgow's History of the Reformed Presbyterian Church in America, as taken by him from Woodrow's list. Rev. John Cuthbertson made trips into New Jersey, usually on his way to and from New York.

BERGEN COUNTY
Dekaes Mills

1769 Oct. 6 "rode 35 miles to Dekaes Mills, Florida, Goshen, McBride." (From John Stun ——.)

Hackensack

1759 Oct. 23 "rode and walked 18 miles to Hacken-seck (6) and to Abra. Oakerman's." (On way to New York.)
      Nov. 30 " Rode 50 miles, 8 Heckensack, Newark, Baskenridge." (From Oakerman's—on return trip from New York.)

ESSEX COUNTY
Newark

1759 Oct. 22 " Rode 37 miles—25 to Newark—12 to Barbadoes Neck." (From A. Paterson's.)
      Nov. 30 (See Hackensack.)

GLOUCESTER COUNTY

Rambo's Ferry

1770 Dec. 14 "rode and walked 26 miles Howel's 7 Rambo's Ferry."
(From Walter Moore's, Pennsylvania.)

HUNTERDON COUNTY

Amwell

1754 June 11 "Rode 40 miles after 1 o'clock to Wale's Fer.—Amwell
M. Lamington M. A." (From Robert Henderson's.)

"   12 "Rode 4 miles—in a barn preached psalm 132: 5–L and
preached Jeremiah 3: 7 g.a. people attentive."

"   13 "Rode 38 miles—7 to Galston's; 5 and 9 to Drake's,
Black River, 4 and 6 to Coo's and to Byram's—3 to
Long Meadow and 5 to Rich-Master's lay on the floor
unstript."

1759 Sept. 11 "Rode 27 miles to Wells Ferry and to Amwell—lodged
Ringoe —."

MORRIS COUNTY

Dutch Tavern

1759 Sept. 13 (See Morristown.)

Morristown

1759 Sept. 13 "rode 43 miles to Morristown, Dutch T(avern) lodged at
Post's—3— —ssies." (From Lakes Mill—Eph. Mc-
Dowell's.)

PASSAIC COUNTY

Ringwood's Furnace

1759 Sept. 14 (See Sterling, Orange Co., N. Y.)

SOMERSET COUNTY

Basking Ridge

1759 Nov. 30 (See Hackensack.)
Dec. 1 "Rode and tramped 13 miles to Eph. McDowel's and
McKown's." (From Baskingridge.)

Lakes Miln

1759 Sept. 12 "rode 35 miles to Dumonts on Raritan, Lakes Miln—
Eph. Mc(Dowel)." (From Amwell.)

Lakes Miln— *Continued*

1759 Oct. 20 "rode 33 miles to Seaborns, Dutch Church, Lakes Miln, —A— —." (From Ringoe's.)

" 21 "Sabbath—preached psalm 96: 1-6. Lectured Hosea 14: 1-L at A. Patterson's ——."

Raritan

1759 Sept. 12 (See Lakes Miln.)

Wells Ferry

1759 Sept. 11 (See Amwell.)

Dec. 4 "Rode 26 miles; 6 Well's Ferry; 20 to father's—well, etc." (From Seaborn's.)

SUSSEX COUNTY

Andover

1769 Oct. 31 "Rode 41 miles to Andover, Hacket's T. and T. Lecken's." (From Sterling, N. Y.)

WARREN COUNTY

Hackettstown

1769 Oct. 31 (See Andover.)

1774 Sept. 7 "rode 46 miles to Hacket's Town, 30 miles to Petits, 16 miles." (From Muskingoe.)

1775 Sept. 27 "rode 32 miles to Hacket's Town (9), to Ware's, Quak. Tav." (From Durham Furnace and Jones.)

Nov. 1 "rode and walked 39 miles to Hackets-Town, W. Reynold. (From Widow Simpson's.)

Lewistown

1780 Nov. 16 "rode 40 miles Lewis T. Pitts. T. Qua. Robis. F. Elliots." (From Hackettstown on return trip from New York.)

Moravian Mills

1780 Oct. 26 "rode 31 miles by Marav. Mills, Gershon Goble's; tired." (From Easton, Matz's.)

Muskingoe

1774 Sept. 6 "rode 36 miles to Shyfelts Trumbours, Croukers, Potts' Muskingoe." (From Pottsgrove.)

Sewitz's Tavern

1775 Nov. 2 "42 miles to Sewitz's Tavern." (From Hackettstown.)

Quaker Tavern

1775 Sept. 27 (See Hackettstown.)

NEW YORK

ALBANY COUNTY

Albany

1764 Aug. 15   "rode 13 miles—4 to Albany, 9 to Ferry, 4 to Capn. Lauson's—weary." (From Quiem's.)

"   21   "rode 34 miles to Major Mathies, Albany—very tired." (From W. Clark's.)

1766 May 7   "rode 50 miles to Cocksaeky, Caenans,[1] Albany, C. Lausons." (From Brandoe's.)

"   26   "rode 46 miles to Garret Vanderberghs; 4 miles Albany." (From Colerain.)

1769 Oct. 12   "rode and walked 42 miles to Albany Lauson's and to Backer's." (From Philip Kaenan's.)

"   23   "rode 40 miles to Albany K's Arms widow Vernon's." (From W. Cooper's.)

1774 Sept. 15   "rode 50 miles to Albany, Mr. Boyd's, Ogden's." (Then 30 miles to Eph. Cowan's on 16th.)

1775 Oct. 4   "rode 51 miles to Folecker's, Cockseky, Quiems, Alb. Lau." (From Brandoe's.)

"   16   "rode 30 miles Todd's, etc., lodged in John Boyd's, Albany." (From Phinehas Whiteside's.)

(Dumback's) Ferry

1764 Aug. 15   (See Albany.)

GREENE COUNTY

Coxsackie

1764 Aug. 22   (See Kaaterskill.)

1766 May 7   (See Albany.)

"   27   "rode 48 miles—Cocksacky, Brandoes, old Jok; folks."[2] (From Albany.)

1775 Oct. 4   (See Albany.)

Esopus (" Sopoze ")

1764 Aug. 13   "rode 48 miles over Rosindale, Sopoze, to Johanes Folch's."[2] (From Wallkill.)

1766 May 28   "rode 50 miles Sopoze, Paltz, Browns, J. Raeneys." (From Brandoes.)

1769 Oct. 10   "rode 40 miles to Paltz, Sopoz, Masters and Corn. Byring." (From James Rainey's.)

[1] Coeymans.
[2] Falconer's.

Esopus (" Sopoze ")— *Continued*

1775 Oct. 3 "rode 50 miles to Sopoz, Foalk's,[1] Widow at Brandoe's."
(From Shamgam, Widow DuBois's.)

" 18 "40 miles to Sopoz to the Widow Dubois's."[2] (From
Coatskill.)

Kaaterskill

1764 Aug. 22 "rode 52 miles Cocksekky, Cater's-kill, to Johanes
Folch's." (From Albany.)

New Paltz

1766 May 28 (See Esopus.)

Orange County

Most of the Covenanters in this County belonged to the Wallkill
Society.

Florida

1754 June 14 "Rode 44 miles—12 to H. Simpson's, McCamb. Flo.
Goshen and A. McBride's." (From Richmaster's.)

" 24 "Rode 11 miles to George Ker's,—Florida—spoke about
3 o'clock to the people."

" 25 "Rode 19 miles to Mr. Elmore's, talked to Armstrongs,
McCam. Simson's."

" 26 "Rode 18 miles to Hull's after preaching psalm 23 and
preaching Zechariah 14: 7.——."

1760 Oct. 2 "rode and walked 23 miles to John Simson's (10),
Florida, Goshen, Arch. McBride's." (From Gracehill's.)

1769 Oct. 6 (See Dekaes Mills, Bergen Co., N. J.)

1780 Oct. 27 (See Goshen.)

Goshen

1754 June 14 (See Florida.)

1760 Oct. 2 (See Florida.)

1769 Oct. 6 (See Dekaes Mills, Bergen Co., N. J.)

1775 Oct. 1 "Sabbath—preached 11–14. Lectured 9–L. Preached
Haggai 2: 4 and baptized James, son to Wm. Oliver,
o.a. praise God—very tired." (At Goshen—Widow
McBride's.)

[1] Falconer's.

[2] Widow DuBois was located near the present Village of New Paltz. It was
a favorite meeting place for officers during the War of the Revolution.

J. Erskine Ward.

Goshen— *Continued*

1780 Oct. 27   "rode 53 miles to Walin's, Florida, Goshen, W. Wilkin's." (From Gershon Goble's, N. J.)

"   28   "rode 3 miles to James and widow McBrides con. Mr. Anan."

"   29   "Sabbath—rode 3 miles to Mr. An. meeting-house; preached Micah 4: 10 o.a."

"   30   "rode 3 miles to W. W. James, J. Gilchrist's and back, etc."

Gracehill's Tavern

1760 Oct. 1   "rode 44 miles to Stevenson's (5) Petits (7), Wolv. (6), Gracehill's [1] (16) and —." (From McK.)

"   13   "rode 36 miles to Gracehill's T.—6 miles beyond H. Simson's." (From McDowell's meeting-house.)

Hudson River

1753 June 28   (See Wallkill.)

Little Britain

1780 Nov. 2   "Fast-day. Rode 18 miles to Math. McDowel's—L Br —Mr. Annan preached 2d psalm. 11th verse." [2]

"   4   "rode 2 miles; I preached 43: 1—and preached Hebrews 7: 25 o.a. distributed tokens."

Sterling (Furnace)

1759 Sept. 14   "rode 42 miles to Ringwood's Fur Sterling, Heedy's, to D. Swansie's." (From Morristown, N. J.)

"   16   "Sabbath—preached psalm 140: 9–L. Lectured Phil. 3: 15–17 and preached Luke 24: 17—McCirm's."

Valley of the Wallkill

The first Covenanters, called "Wallkillians" by Rev. John Cuthbertson, settled in northern Orange and southern Ulster Counties, in the State of New York, in 1748, in the Valley of the Wallkill. They were visited by Rev. John Cuthbertson in 1753, 1754, 1759, 1760, 1764, 1766, 1769, 1774, 1775, 1780 and 1783, during which time he preached, lectured, catechized, baptized and performed marriage ceremonies. James

[1] Grace Hill's Tavern was located near the Goodwill Church, 2 miles southeast of Montgomery.   *J. Erskine Ward.*

[2] Rev. Robert Annan was in charge of the Little Britain Church, located in the Town of New Windsor. It was also known as McDowell's Church. Mr. McDowell was one of its founders.   *J. Erskine Ward.*

Valley of the Wallkill— *Continued*

Rainey, prominent in this Society, moved here from Philadelphia Co., Pa., probably in 1748.

1753 June 28   "Rode 8 mi. to James Rainey's [1]—on H. River 200 from York—130 from Alb."

"   29   "Rode 9 mi. back after preaching Ps. 132: 11–L and preaching Luke 12: 32 and baptized Sam Christain Ruth and Esther children to Jas. Rainey."

July 1   "Sab. preached Ps. 39: 6–L and lectured 1 Peter 4: 1–6 preached Jer. 3: 9 praise to God and baptized Jas. and Patrick sons to Ach McBride and Wm. to Wm. Wil."

1754 June 17   "Rode 10 miles—received 5 s. Jo. Neilie; 7 —— James Nunnel's, went to James Rainey's." (From Archibald McBride's.)

"   19   "Rode 12 miles to Wm. Wilkins after preaching psalm 130 and preaching Luke 12: 32 g.a."

"   20   "Rode 3 miles over the Walkill, by Js. Rogers to A. McCl. stayed all night."

"   21   "Transcribed society rules, talked John Neilie and Smith about Frazer."

"   23   "Sabbath.—preached psalm 58: 6–L. Lectured Hosea 2: 19–L. Preached Jeremiah 3: 7 and baptized Katharine, daughter to John Gilchrist—give all praise to my God." (Then on 24th rode 11 miles to George Ker's, Florida."

1759 Sept. 17   "rode 2 miles over Wokil in a canoe to William Wilkins— fleas—." (From McCirm's.)

"   18   "rode and walked 16 miles to John Archibald's, Gilchrist's and James Rainey's—good health."

"   19, 20   "held session, etc.—preached psalm 96: 1—preached Luke 24: 17 and baptized Susanna and David, to James Rainey o.a. praise my God."

"   21   "rode 9 miles to Arch. McBride's."

"   23   "Sabbath—preached psalm 141: 1–5. Lectured Phil. 3: 17–20 preached Malachi 4: 2—sick—baptized Mary and Arch., daughter and son to Arch McBride; Daniel

[1] James Rainey's farm was located four miles west of the Wallkill, on what is now known as the Walden-Pine Bush Road, and is called the Brick House Farm. When erected it was the first brick house west of the Wallkill. The brick was manufactured on the farm.   *J. Erskine Ward.*

Valley of the Wallkill— *Continued*

and Jean, son and daughter to William Wilkins; John, Helen, and Agnes, son and daughters to John Gilchrist—a burning fever."

1760 Oct. 8 "rode 12 miles to Pat. McGee's—then to James Rainey's." (From Goshen, Arch. McBride's.)

" 9 "rode 12 miles to W. W.'s after preaching psalm 119: 129 and preaching Ephesians 6: 13."

" 10 "rode 5 miles to Arch. McBride's—o.h.—of McDowel."

" 12 "Sabbath—preached psalm 9: 7–12. Lectured Ephesians 2: 7–11. Preached Hosea 2: 14 and baptized James son to Kaesy (Henry?) Trap; Jean, daughter to James Thomson; George son to W. Wilkin; and Joseph, son to John Archibald."

1764 Aug. 10 "rode 34 miles with Phinehas Whiteside, to Warwick meeting-house, etc." (From Henry Simpson's.)

" 12 "Sabbath—rode 10 miles—preached psalm 71: 14—Lectured Matthew 11: 26–L—preached 1 John 5: 11, 12 and baptized John and Rosanna, son and daughter to James Thomson; James, son to Wm. Wilkin; Eleanor, daughter to John Gilchrist; and Abigail, daughter to John Archbald."

" 24 "rode and walked 30 miles to J. Rainey's—preached psalm 55: 20. Lectured Isaiah 45: 20." (From Henrie Debuois's.)

" 25 "tramped 2 miles from Widow McBride's to Al. Paterson's and back."

" 26 "Sabbath—preached psalm 72: 1–7 and lectured Hebrews 10: 26–32—preached Titus 2: 14 and baptized Sarah and Eliz., daughters to Kaesy Trap—give all praise to my gracious God." (Then rode 32 miles on 26th to Henry Simpson's with Mr. Whiteside.)

1766 May 2 "rode 12 miles to Goshen, widow McBride's, More's."

" 4 "Sabbath—preached psalm 96: 6–10; lectured John 15: 1–7; preached Revelations 3: 20 and baptized Robert son to Wm. Wilkings; Archibald son to John Gilchrist

Valley of the Wallkill— *Continued*

and Jean daughter to John Archibald, give all praise to my gracious God, sick."

1766 May 29   "rode 12 miles to W. W's.; preached psalm 85:6— preached 1 Timothy 1:15 baptized Esther, daughter to Joseph Crawfurd." (From J. Rainey's.)

"   30   "rode 4 miles to widows."

June 1   "Sabbath—preached psalm 98: L; preached John 15:8; preached Revelation 3:20; and baptized John and Lydia son and daughter to Robert Lowdon (or London) give all praise to God."

1769 Oct. 8   "Sabbath preached Jude; lectured Acts 16:9–14; preached Matthew 20:32–33, and baptized Joseph son to Wm. Wilkin's, Margaret, John Archibald." (At McBride's, Goshen.)

"   9   "rode 10 miles to James Rainey's, wet day."

" 26, 27   "rode 16 miles to J. Rainneys; preached 119:113; preached 1 Corinthians 10:2; rode 12 miles W. W. Baptized Martha and Susanna to Kaesy Trapp."

"   29   "Sabbath—preached 145:1–7. Lectured Ephesians 4: 8–17—ordained James Rainey and William Wilkins elders—preached 1 Corinthians 15–L o.a. praise God."

"   30   "rode 30 miles to Capn. Dekaes to Henry Simpson's." (On return trip to Pennsylvania.)

1774 Sept. 9   "rode 7 miles to widow McBride's; family all well— praise my gracious God." (From "Dek Ga's.")

"   11   "Sabbath; preached psalm 73:7–12; lectured 67:1–11; preached Philippians 3:3 and baptized Elizabeth, daughter to W. Wilkins; Charles to John Gilchrist, James, son to Sam Rainey and Janet, daughter to Francis McBride, o.a. praise God, etc."

"   12   "rode 10 miles to James Raineys, weary, etc."

"   13   "rode 22 miles to Col. Hardenberg's,[1] wet, etc."

"   14   "rode 42 miles to Brandoes, Moore's, Mr. Cuming." (Then 50 miles to Albany on 15th.)

[1] Colonel Hardenberg resided at Rosendale. The old house is still standing.

J. Erskine Ward.

Valley of the Wallkill—*Continued*

1774 Oct. 4 "rode and walked 48 miles to Brandoes." (From John Boyd's, Albany.)

"   5 "rode 40 miles to Low's (Law's?), blacksm. 2 miles from Paltz."

"   6 "rode 22 miles to DeBuois, Grahams and Js. Rainey."

"   9 "Sabbath; preached 25–L; lectured Isaiah 58: 12–L and preached Hosea 6: 3 and baptized Ruth daughter to Kaesy Trap o.a. praise my gracious God."

"   10 "rode 12 miles W. Wilk. etc."

"   11, 12 "rode 6 miles; visited John Gilchrists, Falconers,[1] W. McBrides."

"   13 "held session x x; preached 96; lectured Acts 2 x x x and baptized James and Elizabeth son and daughter (to Jean Rea.)—."

"   16 "Sabbath; preached 74: 1–4; lectured 59: 1–8 and preached Hosea 6: 3 and baptized John and Jesse sons to John Archibald presented by the mother and Bess McBride Negroe o.a. praise God." (Then rode 26 miles to Warwick to Dr. Hinchman's, a sick man, on 17th.)

1775 Oct. 18 "rode 40 miles to Sopoz to the Widow Debuois's." (From Coatskill.)

"   19 "rode 16 miles to Mr. Graham's etc., Gilespy's,[2] Widow Rainey's." [3]

"   20 "preached 30–1. Lectured 1 Thessalonians 4: 13–L conversed Thomas Millar."

"   21 "rode 12 miles to Mr. Annan's, Widow McBride's,—tired."

"   22 "Sabbath— 88: 1 lectured Isaiah 59: 16—and preached Micah 5: 5 g.a. praise God."

"   24, 25 "rode 12 miles to W. W.—preached 37 and catechized 22 persons."

"   29 "Sabbath—preached 8–13. Lectured Zechariah 13: 7–L. Preached from same and baptized Jas. son to Fran. McBride, etc."

"   30 "rode 24 miles—married Gavin Millar and Susana Rainey."

[1] Capt. William Falconer resided near what is now known as Stony Ford.
                                                                J. Erskine Ward.

[2] Lieut. Samuel Gilespy married Esther, daughter of James Rainey. His farm adjoined the farm of James Rainey.   *J. Erskine Ward.*

[3] Widow Rainey was the wife of James Rainey, who died in February, 1775.
                                                                J. Erskine Ward.

Valley of the Wallkill—*Continued*

1775 Oct. 31   "rode 33 miles to Widow Simson's." (On return trip to Pennsylvania.)

1780 Oct. 27   "rode 53 miles to Walin's,[1] Florida, Goshen, W. Wilkins."[2] (From Gershon Goble's.)

"   28   "rode 3 miles to James and widow McBrides, con. Mr. Anan."

"   29   "Sabbath—rode 3 miles Mr. An. meeting-house; preached Micah 4: 10 o.a."

"   30   "rode 3 miles to W. W. James, J. Gilchrist's and back, etc."

"   31   "rode 11 miles to W. Douglas', Sam Rainey's;[3] preached 4: 6—preached Zechariah 13: 9; baptized Wm. to W. Trap, Archibald to James McBride, Wm. and Elizabeth to Sam Raney and Hugh Melvin to Gavin Millar, o.a."

Nov. 2   "Fast-day. Rode 18 miles to Math. McDowel's—L Br—. Mr. Annan preached 2d psalm 11th verse."

"   4   "rode 2 miles; I preached 43: 1—and preached Hebrews 7: 25 o.a. distributed tokens."

"   5   "Sabbath—walked 2 miles; Mr. Annan preached Matthew 22: 11; I served 6 tables; Mr. Annan discoursed from Matthew 28: 18; good day."

"   6   "rode 12 miles; preached 65: 1–6; preached Hebrews 7: 25; give all praise to my gracious God."

"   7   "rode 1 mile from Mr. Ann. to James McBride's; elephants—."

"   12   "Sabbath—rode 3 miles; preached 66: 8–15; preached 2 Chronicles 20: 12; exercised same at night and baptized John and Jean to Francis Burns, and John son to Wm. Wilkin's Junior, give all praise to God."

"   13   "rode 12 miles to Florida Kennedy's; received 7 dollars; snow, etc."

"   14   "rode and walked 28 miles to Yeat's; lost 4 miles; lodged poorly, but well." (On return trip to Pennsylvania.)

---

[1] Wallkill refers to what is now known as the Goodwill Church, 2 miles southeast of Montgomery.   *J. Erskine Ward.*

[2] William Wilkin's home was located on the road running north from Goshen to the Village of Montgomery, about 5 miles north of Goshen, and near the home of James and Widow McBride.   *J. Erskine Ward.*

[3] Samuel Rainey resided on what is now known as the Walden-Pine Bush State Road, first house west of the Dwaarkill.   *J. Erskine Ward.*

Valley of the Wallkill— *Continued*

1783 Aug. 4 "rode 41 miles Petets, Loughhead, Mr. Baird's, Wallin's was." (From McCulloch's.)

"   5 "rode 32 miles to widow Simsons, Kennedys, Neks, McC."

"   7 "rode 5 miles to G. Peck's, married Henry Rich and Magda Peck."

"   8 "rode 6 miles, preached 18: 20 lectured Romans 5: 12— and baptized John to John Munell (or Nunnel), rs. F. Crown from Rich. very weary."

"   10 "Sabbath—rode 3 miles Mr. Mas. preached John 3: 3. I preached Hebrews 9: 2 last verse, a fall etc."

"   11 "rode 12 miles to widow Rainey's by Wm. Dalg-lies, his head sore."

"   13 "preached 40: 6—lectured Hebrews 10: 1–9 and baptized Robert and John to Jonathan Jordan, John to David Rainey and Sarah and Janet to Sam Rainey Mr. Finesse D. minister."

"   14, 15 "rode 12 miles to W. Dalg. Mr. Ann. and James Mc-Brides."

"   16 "rode 3 miles to and from Annan's burying, wrote R. Sm. and self."

"   17 "preached (Sabbath) 45: 1—lectured Philippians 1: 1–8 and preached Hebrews 9–L."

"   18 "rode 4 miles Cap. B. Falconers, Mr. Hall's, W. Wilkins."

"   20 "rode 12 miles—preached 42: 1—lectured Titus 2: 11–15, and baptized Win. Thomas, James, Mary and John to Thomas Turner, g.a."

"   21 "rode 8 miles, preached 42: 8–L, exc. Hebrews 9–L and baptized Hanna to James McCord, came to J. McCord and Wm. Edgar's."

"   22 "rode 9 miles to Captain Telfair's, Matt. McDowel's, a mason."

"   24 "Sabbath—rode 3 miles, preached 5–9; lectured 8: 15 and preached Habakkuk 2: 4, hot, great sweat."

"   26 "rode 10 miles to the Camps, Windsor, Nesbets, Maj. Robert Boyd's."

"   27 "Preached 119: 172–L. exc. Acts 2: 37–41 and baptized Elias to R. Boyd."

"   28 "rode 12 miles to Matt. McD. meeting-house, preached 26: 1 examined 40."

"   30 "rode 3 miles from Nathaniel Baoyd's to Wm. Scot's, good health, praise God."

"   31 "Sabbath—rode 7 miles, preached 45: 9–14; lectured 15–23 and preached Habakkuk 2: 4 g.a."

Sept.   1 "rode 12 miles to Wm. Gilespy's from John Finley's, tired."

Valley of the Wallkill—*Continued*

1783 Sept. 2, 3 "rode 7 miles to widow Rainey's, to and from Sam Gilespy's, preached psalm 26: 6–L Catechized 38 and baptized Nathaniel son to Sam Gilespy."

" 4 "rode 11 miles to Robert Graham's, Coulter's, Mr. Annans, widow McBrides."

" 7 "Sabbath—rode 3 miles, preached 14–L; lectured 23–L and preached John 3: 36 g.a. Wm. Young's."

" 9 "rode 5 miles to Wm. Edgars and Francis Burns, mare shod, 5-6."

" 10, 13 "rode 11 miles preached 15 catechized 40 persons—got saddle mended 3-9 coze."

" 14 "Sabbath—rode 7 miles, preached 46: 1–6; lectured 2: 1–9, and preached same."

" 15 "rode 4 miles to W. Gillespy's, gone to York—x x."

" 17, 18 "rode 8 miles R. Robert Graham, Sam Gil., R. Jackson."

" 19 "Preached 76: 5—preached Genesis 24: 58 and B(ap.) Benj. Jacob and Joseph to Robert Jackson, very sick shaked much ag."

" 21 "Sabbath—preached 6: 9 and lectured 9–12 in a great fever, discord in — R."

" 22 "rode 8 miles Wards Bridge, John Coulter's and Wm. Dalgliesh—3."

" 25 "rode 3 miles to Captain McBride's, very sick, from Sa. Wil."

" 28 "Sabbath—preached 9–L and lectured 12–19 g.a. weak, shake stopped, bark."

Oct. 2 "rode 9 miles to Mr. Telfair's, Col. McCarthy's, W. Scots."

" 5 "Sabbath—rode 4 miles, preached 47: 1–7; lectured Philippians 3: 1–8; preached John 3–L and baptized David, son to Wm. Telfair, Bap., Janet, daughter to Alexander Lowry and David, son to David Parshal."

" 6 "rode 9 miles to Mr. Annans to Cap. McBride's, sick."

" 8 "rode 4 miles by Jos. Wilkins, wet, to W. Wilkins."

" 12 "Sabbath—rode 2 miles, preached 7–L and lectured 8—Mr. Morrison preached and Mr. Ann. baptized 3."

" 13, 14 "rode 42 miles to widow Coulters and Dr. The Clark, sick."

" 15 "rode 27 miles to McCul., Buskirk's, Quaker Town, Buchanan's." (On return trip to Pennsylvania.)

RENSSELAER COUNTY

Hoosick (Falls)

1764 Aug. 16 "rode 26 miles—4 to Smith's, 5 to Dutch, 14 to Sanhoit, Houseck, 4 to Cambridge." (From Capt. Lauson's.)

Sanhoit

1764 Aug. 16   (See Hoosick Falls.)
"   20   "rode 10 miles—at W. Clark's—preached psalm 46: 1–6
and preached Hosea 2: 14—then at Sanhoit, Corn.
Finest's, preached psalm 18: 19–24 Lectured Matthew
16: 24." (From Ephraim Cowan's.)

SARATOGA COUNTY

Halfmoon

1775 Oct. 17   "rode 42 miles to Halfmoon, Coats Kill with Jas. Robieson." (From Albany.)

ULSTER COUNTY

Rosendale

1764 Aug. 23   "rode 34 miles—10 to Sopos., 10 to Rosindal, Palts,
Henrie Debuois."

Shawangunk (" Shamgam ")

1775 Oct. 3   (See Esopus, Greene County.)

WASHINGTON COUNTY

Buskirks Bridge

1783 Oct. 15   (See Wallkill Society.)

Cambridge Society

Covenanters settled here probably as early as 1755. Rev. John
Cuthbertson visited them in 1764, 1766, 1769, 1774, 1775.

1764 Aug. 16   (See Hoosick Falls.)
"   17   "tramped 10 miles from the Settlement to Selfriges,
Morison's, Clark."
"   18   "tramped 2 miles from old Eph. Cowan's place—killed a
rattlesnake."
"   19   "Sabbath preached psalm 71: 21–L. Lectured Hebrews
10: 19–26. Preached Hosea 2: 14 and baptized Edward, son to William Selfrige; and Martha, daughter to
Oliver Self."
"   20   (See Sanhoit.)

1766 May 8, 9   "rode 31 miles to Russels j Cowans and Ephraim Cowans." (From Albany.)

Cambridge Society— *Continued*

1766 May 11   "Sabbath—preached psalm 96: 110–L; lectured John 15: 7–13; preached Romans 3: 12; baptized Sarah C(owan.)

1769 Oct. 13   "rode 20 miles Mathies, St. Coit and Cambridge W. C." (From Albany, Lauson's, Backer's.)

" 14   "Tramped 3 miles; visited T. Morton, R. Cowan ¹ and Eph. Cowan."

" 15   "Sabbath rode 3 miles; preached psalm 144: 9–13; lectured Isaiah 4; and preached 2 Kings 5: 12."

" 16   "rode 8 miles bad road to Maloperd, Phinehas Whitesides." ²

" 18   "rode 9 miles preached psalm 119: 49 and lectured Matthew 18: 15–21 E. Cowan."

" 19, 20   "rode 10 miles to W. S. and W. Edgar; then to W. Cooper's."

" 21, 22   "Sabbath tramped 3 miles; preached 13–L; lectured Ephesians 4: 8–16 and baptized Agnes to W. S. (Wm. Selfridge) and Wm. son to Sam Clark, and James son to John McClung g.a." (Then 40 miles to Albany on 23d.)

1774 Sept. 16   "rode 30 miles to Eph. Cowans; 17th—rode 2 miles T. M."

" 18   "Sabbath; preached 12: 16; lectured 12–L and preached Isaiah 49: 9 rode 8 miles to and from ——."

" 19   "rode 10 miles to Phinehas Whitesides."

" 21   "Preached psalm 15 and lectured Isaiah 56: 3–9, very particular."

" 22   "rode 10 miles to T. Morton's after catechizing 8 or 10."

" 25   "Sabbath; rode 8 miles; preached 16: 21; lectured Isaiah 58: 1–8 and preached verse 22."

" 26   "rode 4 miles to Sam Clarks, conversed, etc., Jos. Stewart."

" 27, 28   "rode 16 miles to John Blair's, etc. visited and catechized."

Oct. 1   "rode 4 miles; preached; catechized 21 persons J. McC. etc. held session."

" 2   "Sabbath; rode 4 miles; preached 21: 25; rebuked W.

¹ R. Cowan lived near Buskirks Bridge.   *J. Erskine Ward.*

² Phineas Whiteside, formerly of Pequea, Lancaster County, Pa., settled 8 miles west of Colerain Colony in 1766. William Whiteside, his son, acquired the title to 1200 acres of the finest land in the valley and settled his sons, John, Peter, Thomas, William and James, upon large farms near him. These estates were all owned (in 1860) by his descendants.   *J. Erskine Ward.*

Cambridge Society— *Continued*

and Oliv. Selfridge, baptized Ann to John Mony, Wm.
and Martha to W. Selfridge, Neal to Oliver, Mary and
John to Sam Clark." (Then 40 miles to Albany on
3rd.)

1775 Oct. 5 "rode 30 miles to Cambridge, Sam Clark's, tired."
(From Law's.)

"   8 "Sabbath—preached 14–L. Lectured from same—
preached Haggai 2: 4 and baptized Robert son to Oliver
Selfridge—was very pub.—many Torys there, etc."

"   9 "rode 9 miles to P. Whiteside's after preaching 85: 6–11
and catechizing 21 persons."

"   12 "preached psalm 2: 1–7 and lectured Isaiah 16: 59–L
o.a."

"   13 "rode 6 miles from J. Blair's—married Robert McKee
and Mary Thomson."

"   15 "Sabbath—rode 9 miles to Phinehas Whiteside's—
preached 87. Lectured Malachi L. and preached Haggai 2."

"   16 "rode 30 miles Todd's, etc., lodged John Boyd's, Albany."

Melopard

1769 Oct. 16 (See Cambridge.)

Settlement, The

1764 Aug. 17 (See Cambridge.)

WESTCHESTER COUNTY

Dobbs Ferry

1759 Oct. 24 "rode 22 miles (5) Dobbs ferry (2) W. B's plains (7),
to Es. Golden's (8)." (From Abraham Oakerman's.)

Bedford

1759 Oct. 25 "rode 40 miles to Bedford, Ridgefield, Danbury, Newton, Bot." (From Es. Golden's.)

(White) Plains

1759 Oct. 24 (See Dobbs Ferry.)

MASSACHUSETTS

BERKSHIRE COUNTY

" Coliver's Bridge "

1766 May 12 "rode 26 miles to Williams-town, Simons, Coliver's Bridge." (From Ephraim Cowan's.)

Sheffield

1759 Oct. 27 "rode 62 miles to Simsbury, Sheffield, Westfield, Northam. Pelham." (From Farmingham.)

Nov. 27 "Rode 36 miles; 8 to Col. Whitney's, Canan. Shef; bridge Baldin." (From Taylor's.)

Williamstown

1766 May 12 (See Coliver's Bridge.)

Windsor

1783 Aug. 26 "rode 10 miles to the Camps, Windsor, Nesbets, Maj. Robert Boyd's." (From Matt. McDowel's.)

FRANKLIN COUNTY

Colerain

1759 Nov. 7 "rode 30 miles with him (A. McDowel) to Sunderland, Dearfield, Colerain, John Cochran."

"   8 "Rode 2 miles to Mr. McDowels. Conversed concerning various things to satisfaction."

"   11 "Sabbath. Preached psalm 78: 5–12; lectured Luke 12: 31–37 and preached Galatians 5: 1 o.a."

"   12 "Rode 2 miles; visited Wilson; conversed etc.; lodged Deacon McGees."

"   13 "Rode 2 miles to Cochran's; preached psalm 60: 1— and preached Jeremiah 24: 7 g.a."

1766 May 14 "rode 37 miles C. Stewarts over Connecticut River Colein Taylor."

"   15 "rode 6 miles James McConel; preached psalm 109: 21–27 and lectured Ephesians 2: 1–7."

"   16 "rode 30 miles; preached psalm 102: 12–17; preached John 17: 14 and baptized Robert and Wm. sons to John Blair; went to Charles Stewart's Cole."

"   18 "Sabbath—preached psalm 97: 1–8; lectured Hebrews

259

Colerain— *Continued*

10: 19–26; preached 13: 12, 13 and baptized Jonathan, and Solomon sons to Joseph Stewart, David son to Nathaniel Carswel, Sarah and Jonathan daughter and son to Wm. Stewart, and Martha, Ben and Cynthia to Sam Stewart."

HAMPTON COUNTY
Blandford

1759 Nov. 20 "Rode 11 miles to Blanford, John McKinstries; Morton raged." (From Westfield.)
"   21 "Rode 1 mile to Robert Henry's, was unwell and disbelieving, etc."
"   23 "Preached psalm 84: 4–10 and preached Malachi 4: 2 Give all praise to God—pp distressed."
"   24 "Rode 3 miles; visited Robert Wilson's and Dea. Hamilton, trou."
"   25 "Sabbath—preached psalm 60: 1; lectured Zephaniah 3: 8–14 and preached Galatians 5: 1 g.a."
"   26 "Rode 26 miles, 4 to —— Stewart's, 15 to Brewers, 7 to Taylor's —."

Westfield

1759 Oct. 27 (See Sheffield.)
Nov. 19 "Rode 30 miles—Hadley, Northampton, to Westfield, Clap's." (From Pelham.)

HAMPSHIRE COUNTY
Hadley

1759 Oct. 27 (See Sheffield, Berkshire Co.)
Nov. 19 (See Westfield, Hampton Co.)

Northampton

Oct. 27 (See Sheffield, Berkshire Co.)
"   28 "walked 3 miles to and from Meeting-house—preached psalm 48: 7–L—preached Hosea 2: 19—g.a." (From Pelham.)
"   30, etc. "rode and tramped 6 miles—visited Blair, Morton, McCulloch's, Clark, etc."
Nov. 4 "Sabbath—rode 4 miles—preached psalm 137: 1–7. Lectured Hosea 6: 4–8 and preached Galatians ——."

Pelham

1759 Oct. 27 (See Berkshire Co., Mass.)
Nov. 14 "Rode 30 miles; parted McDowel; went over Connecticut River to Pelh." (From Cochran's.)

CONNECTICUT

In the fall of 1759 Rev. John Cuthbertson visited Connecticut on one of his New York trips, giving little in the nature of definite information:

FAIRFIELD COUNTY

Botsford, Danbury, Newtown, Ridgefield

1759 Oct. 25   "rode 40 miles to Bedford, Ridgefield, Danbury, Newton, Bot."

HARTFORD COUNTY

Farmington, Painthorn

1759 Oct. 26   "rode 40 miles to Woodbury, Waterbury, Painthorn, Farmington."

Simsbury

1759 Oct. 27   (See Sheffield, Mass.)

LITCHFIELD COUNTY

Canaan

1759 Nov. 27   (See Sheffield, Mass.)

Woodbury

1759 Oct. 26   (See Hartford County.)

NEW HAVEN COUNTY

Waterbury

1759 Oct. 26   (See Hartford County.)

OTHER PERSONS VISITED

PERSONS IN PREVIOUS QUOTATIONS OTHER THAN THOSE MARRIED AND BAPTIZED.

Names below often appear more than once on page cited.   Persons of the same Christian and surname are listed here but once and may be, and often are, different people.

Agnew
—, 100
John, 90, 100, 104, 202
Alexander
Sm., 127
William, 240
Allan
William, 132
Allison; Alison; Alieson
—, 178
A., 124
John, 92
Ancruon (or Ancrum)
Archibald, 227
And.
—, 228
Moses, 241
Anderson
—, 122, 207, 240
David, 156
James, 122
John, 242
Mr., 207
Thomas, 75, 98, 121, 128
William, 178
Andrew; Andrews
Francis, 226
John, 167, 169, 174, 176, 177, 178, 181, 223
Robert, 137, 138, 140, 141, 143, 150, 152, 153, 187, 188, 189
W., 132
Widow, 155, 160, 165, 188, 224, 230
Annan
Mr., 196, 205, 248, 252, 253, 254, 255
Rev. Robert, 248
Archibald
John, 249

Armstrong
—, 247
Ash.
Joseph, 133
Ayres; Ayrs
W., 230

Backer
—, 246, 257
Bailey
—, 133
R., 195
Bain
John, 183
Baird
—, 130
Moses, 164
Mr., 254
Baldridge
Alexander, 212
Ball
—, 199
Barclay
Adam, 173, 201
Bartholomew
—, 197
David, 241
Bartram
—, 201
Bates
John, 85
Bay
—, 74
Beatty; Betty
C., 130
Hugh, 200

Bell
  James, 94
  Margaret, 146
  S. and Sam, 97, 194
Bileston
  —, 229
Bischop
  —, 199
Black
  Ag., 167
  Mr., 242
  Mrs. James, 242
  T., 238
Blackburn
  Ben, 242, 243
Blaflum
  Mar., 100
Blair
  —, 260
  John, 257, 258
Blane
  —, 91
Boles
  —, 86
Bonar
  Robert, 82
Boyd; Baoyd
  John, 131, 246, 252, 258
  Mr., 99, 187, 200, 202, 246
  Nathaniel, 254
  Robert (Major), 254, 259
Brandoe
  —, 246, 251, 252
  Widow, 247
Brandon; Branon
  —, 227
  George, 191
  J., 180, 234, 237
Brewer
  —, 152, 260
Brigham; Bigham; Bicam
  J., 92, 150
  Jean, 178
  Mr., 133
  Widow, 181
Brison
  Widow, 104
Bro., Br.
  Jo., 207, 209
    * See p. 284.

Brooks
  Dan, 179
Broomfield
  John, 70, 72
Brown
  —, 246
  Alex., 101, 104, 109, 111, 113, 114,
    123
  Ben., 84, 97, 104, 108, 109
  Colin, 153, 163
  Eleanor, 115, 195
  Helen, 183
  J., 100, 108
  James, 107, 109
  Jean, 2nd, 99
  John, 176
  John, Jun., 171
  Josh, 227
  Matthew, 110, 137, 143, 144, 145
  Widow, 105, 187
  William, 69, 91, 95, 96, 98, 100, 101,
    102, 103, 105, 106, 107, 108, 109,
    110, 111, 112, 113, 114, 115, 131,
    133, 141, 186, 187, 195, 217, 219,
    239
Brownback
  Carrol, 198
Brownlie
  —, 101, 186
  John, 184, 185, 208
  Joseph, 209, 239
Buchanan
  —, 222, 224, 255
  G. 215
  *Gilbert, 98, 181
  J., 226
  John, 209, 210, 212, 218, 224, 231,
    236
  S., 214
  *Walter, 89, 91, 92, 93, 94, 98, 105,
    118, 139, 163, 170, 178, 220, 225,
    229
  Widow, 168
Burd.
  —, 101
Burg., Bug.
  P., 79, 190
Burney
  Robert, 215

Burns; Bourns
—, 70
Archibald & Brother, 70, 72, 73, 120
Francis, 255
John, 118, 207
Buskirk
—, 255
By.
W., 94
Byar
Mr., 200
Byram
—, 244
Byring
Corn., 246

Cachy; Caughy,
Nath., 170
Sam, 143, 170, 175, 176, 181
Widow, 183
Cairn
—, 165
W., 94, 97, 100
Cal.
—, 162
Calbreath;* Galbreath
—, 115, 122, 137, 160, 162
And., 186
James, 178, 186
Jo., 134, 135
Robert, 139, 166, 176, 180
Thos., 151
W., 100, 121
Widow, 126, 141, 151, 154, 163, 192, 210
William, 100, 121, 139, 143, 190
Caldwell
—, 241
John, 180
Joseph, 84
Widow John, 238
Caleb
—, 175
Calfman
—, 101
Calhoun
James, 99, 187, 217
Sam, 92

* Dr. Glasgow.

Camp
—, 125, 127, 254, 259
Alex., 150
Mr., 125
Campbell
James, 109, 193
Carson
—, 204
Carp.
—, 213
Carr
John, 73
Caruther; Carother
Robert, 242
Widow, 191
William, 87
Cather
—, 201
Chamberlan
Quaker, 239
Chambers
—, 118, 207
Chi(cky?)
—, 172
Christie
—, 170
John, 197
Clark; Clarke
—, 196, 256, 260
G., 117
J., 232
John, 177
Mr., 205
Sam, 257, 258
Theo. (Dr.), 205, 255
Thomas, 205
William, 185, 199, 207, 216, 246, 256
Clarkson
—, 196
Mr., 227
Clayton
Mr. (Wid.), 162
Cluney
James, 182
Mr. James, 114
Cochran
—, 82, 241, 259, 260
John, 80, 82, 117, 124, 126, 127. 128, 129, 259

Collins
  Charles, 167
  Cornelius, 160, 193
  Mary, 178
  Molly, 170
  Widow, 172, 177, 179, 180, 184
Colvil
  James, 180
  Joseph, 242
Conrade (Weiser?)
  —, 198
Cook
  A., 73
  Col., 83
Coo's
  —, 244
Cooper; Couper
  —, 189
  W., 83, 155, 157, 211, 246, 257
  Widow, 164
  William, 73, 74, 130, 131, 240
Corkle; Corckle (See McCorkle)
  Mr., 175
  Will. 175
Couker
  Jacob, 86, 198
Coulter
  —, 162, 183, 255
  Hew; Hugh, 143, 148, 152, 153, 156,
    158, 159, 161, 162, 167, 168, 171,
    173, 175, 177, 178, 181, 194, 228
  Janet, 176
  John, 86, 255
  Nathaniel, 136, 161, 162, 170, 171,
    175, 210
  R., 143, 167
  Samy; S., 157, 166
  Widow, 171, 255
Cowan
  Ephraim, 246, 256, 257, 259
  J., 256
  R., 257
Coxe
  Fench, 205
Craighead
  —, 134, 189

Crawford; Crawfurd
  —, 118, 228
  John, 169
  W., 203
Crook
  —, 71, 81
  J., 117
  James, 82
  Jo., 240
  John, 73, 117, 129, 130, 240
Cross
  Jean, 122
  Thomas, 123, 133, 240
Crouker; Croocker
  —, 199, 245
Crunkleton; Crunckleton
  Robert, 78, 82, 117, 121, 128, 129
Culbert
  John, 88
Cuming; Cumin; Comin
  —, 172
  Jonathan, 136
  Mr., 251
Cunich
  —, 198
Cunningham
  G., 99, 191
  John, 160
Cuthbertson (Refers to)
  John, 168, 207
  Rev. John, 134, 181, 189, 202, 208
    240, 243, 248, 256, 261
  Sally, 204
  Walter, 184

Dalgliesh; Dalg-lie
  William, 86, 254, 255
Davidson
  J., 102, 128
  James, 128, 129
Davison
  Hew, 221
Dekaes; Dek Ga's
  Captain, 251
Deniston
  —, 198
  Andrew, 197

Denny
  W., 152, 162
Dew.
  Gregory, 190
Dickies . . .
  Widow, 209
Dill
  James, 82, 93, 239
Dining
  George, 135, 165
Dixon; Dickson
  —, 217
  H., 230
  Robert, 187, 233
  Samuel, 155, 207, 208, 209, 210, 212,
    213, 214, 216, 220, 221, 222, 224,
    225, 227, 228, 234, 235, 236
Dobbin
  —, 177, 195
  James, 81
  Mr., 81, 82, 171, 204, 205, 228. 229.
    239
Dorby
  —, 155
Dougherty; Docherty
  John, 224
  Thomas, 127
Douglas; Douglass; Dowglas
  —, 221
  Charles (?), 139
  James (?), 139
  Jo., 139
  Thomas, 139
  W., 253
  Walter (?), 139
Dow.
  —, 155
Down (Downey?)
  John, 203
  W., 166, 183
Downey; Downie; Downy
  —, 131, 172, 199
  James, 129
  William, 129, 153, 159, 183
Downing
  J., 204

Doyle
  W., 197
Drake
  —, 244
Drenan
  John, 84
Drumbower
  M., 198
Drumond
  John, 95
DuBois; Debuois &c.
  —, 252
  Henrie, 250, 256
  Widow, 247, 252
Duff (Nickleduff?)
  N., 74
Dumont
  —, 244
Dun.
  —, 149, 236
  J., 112, 236
Duncan
  Betty, 147
  J., 102, 114, 141, 219, 236
  James, 221, 228, 229, 230
  John, 98, 113, 132, 133, 138, 139,
    143, 146, 150, 184, 185, 186, 187,
    190, 200, 207, 208, 209, 210, 211,
    212, 213, 217, 219, 239
  Seth, 69, 196, 219
  (Widow), 236
Dunlap; Dunlop
  —, 89, 119
  John, 132, 146, 155, 175, 177, 209
  Wm., 90, 178
Dunwoody, Dinwoody; Dinwithier, &c.
  David, 70, 71, 72, 73, 74, 75, 76, 77,
    78, 79, 80, 81, 82, 83, 97, 116, 119,
    122, 123, 128, 130, 157, 161, 190,
    191, 193, 194, 196, 207, 240
"Dutch Doctor." 144
Dye
  John, 188

Edem
  James, 86
Edgar
  William, 254, 255, 257

Edwards (?)
—, 151
Elliot; Eliot
—, 153
F., 204, 245
John, 144, 147, 189
Elmore
Mr., 247
Ercus
—, 198
Ervin
H., 167
Espy; Espie
George, 108
James, 195
Esteman
Hugh, 103, 104
Evans
—, 149
Ewing; Ewin
—, 178, 181
Alexander, 222, 224, 226, 227, 228,
229, 231, 232, 239
Esquire, 229
Hen., 123, 161
Thomas, 178
Widow, 123, 207

Falconer; Folecker; Foalk
—, 246, 247, 252
Capt. B., 254
Capt. Wm., 252
Johanes, 246, 247
Farie
John, 241
Felix (?)
—, 156
Fin.
—, 122
Finesse; Finest
—, 199
Corn., 256
Mr., 254
Finey
—, 186
James, 83, 84
John, 210

Finley
—, 211, 224
And., 117, 229, 230
Bess, 229
John, 254
Mr., 225, 230
Wm., 129
Fleming
Jo., 88
Fletcher
James, 242
Frazer
—, 249
Fregan
Sam, 171
Frunk
And., 162
Ful.
—, 172, 226, 231
John, 239
Fulerton
—, 100, 118, 166, 230, 231, 236
Da., 200
Humphrey, 72, 75, 86, 87, 88, 111,
131, 132, 133, 135, 136, 137, 140,
144, 147, 148, 150, 153, 157, 160,
161, 164, 169, 172, 187, 188, 189,
190, 191, 192, 193, 194, 195
J., 200
James, 200
John, 229, 231, 239
Mr., 183, 189
Peggy, 240
Sheriff, 240
Thomas, 183, 199
W., 227, 231, 232, 234
Widow, 177, 181, 183, 195
William, 229
Fulton; Fullton
—, 197, 228, 229, 230, 231, 236
A., 212
Brother, 152
Mr., 227, 240
R., 92, 159, 229
Galbreath
(See Calbreath)

Galston
—, 244
Gardner; Garner
Ja., 87
John, 100, 103, 104
Joseph, 95
Wm., 92
Gay
Robert, 174
Gebby; Gabby
—, 82, 181, 213, 217, 220
Ann, 223, 224, 226
John, 194
Wm., 150, 212, 213, 218, 220, 221, 222
Gemble; Gembel; Gemie; Gemmil
—, 93, 166
Lv., 96
Wm., 121, 225, 230
Gibson
—, 73
Widow, 74
Giffen
And., 94
Gilchrist
—, 113, 249
J., 248, 253
John, 252
Gilgour
(See Kilgour)
Gillespy; Gilespy
—, 252
Lieut. Samuel, 252
Samuel, 255
William, 254, 255
Gilmore
James, 89, 205
Jat., 77
Robert, 85, 86, 87, 111, 128, 142, 187, 189, 192
Girvan; Givan
John, 161
Thomas, 135, 148, 149, 160, 161, 164
Glasgow
Dr., 243

Glen; Glein
George, 199
Jacob, 85
James, 171, 175, 177, 181, 182
Joseph, 235, 237
W., 181
Glendining
John, 94, 118
Goble
Gershon, 245, 248, 253
Golden
Es., 258
Goldsmith
—, 198
Gracehill
—, 247, 248
Graham
—, 252
George, 195, 201
Mr., 252
Mrs., 173
Robert, 255
Gray
George, 199
Greer; Grier
—, 158
Mich. (?), 198
Mr., 83, 115, 206
R., 214, 216
T., 215
W., 132, 143, 149, 153, 219
Wm., 158
Gregory
—, 240
Griffin; Griffen
—, 172, 241
Gushwa
Isaac, 101, 104

Hail
Hugh; Hew, 94, 240, 241
Hain
—, 166, 187
Bartholomew, 115
Hall
Mr., 254
Widow, 109

Hamilton
—, 241
Deacon, 260
Hans, 74
Hammond
—, 121
Hanna
—, 166, 172, 179
D., 143, 167
Henry, 184
Hardenberg
Colonel, 251
Harris
—, 110
Havisha
Dan, 119
Hawthorn
—, 213, 233
Sam, 154, 177, 213, 215
Hays
—, 195
Heedy
—, 248
Helm
Mr., 133
Henderson
—, 198
Mr., 162
Robert, 86, 244
Henrick
Jost, 85, 199
Henry
—, 213, 222
Elizabeth, 223, 229, 232
George, 93, 217, 218, 219, 220, 221,
226, 229, 231, 234
Robert, 260
William, 221, 223, 226
Hess
D., 180
Hews
Bar., 108
Rowland, 224, 225
Hickman (Kickman?)
—, 156, 172
Hills
James, 235, 237
Hilliges
Peter, 198

Hilton
John, 114, 219
Hinchman
Doctor, 252
Hodges
S., 76
Hog . . .
W., 96
Holland
—, 132
Holton
—, 201, 203
Howel
—, 244
Howston
—, 166
Hull
—, 247
Hummel
David, 103, 104
Hunter
David, 238, 240
Hutton
Richard, 243

Ingle; Inkle
—, 205
Mrs., 133
Ireland
David, 195
James, 100
Irvine
Widow, 165

Jackson
J., 225
R., 255
Sam, 135, 138
Jacob
—, 87, 239
Jamieson; Jamison
John, 201
Matthew, 83
Robert, 83
Johnson
Thomas, 183, 189
Jones
—, 86, 245

Junken
Joseph, 90, 94, 95, 96, 97, 114, 219
W., 241
Widow, 99, 241

Kaenan
Philip, 246
Kain; Kean
John, 89
Kennedy; Kenety; Keneats
—, 253, 254
An., 88
John, 71, 241
Thomas, 85, 86, 87, 88, 89, 111, 133,
192, 197, 198, 203, 204, 205, 241
Kerr; Ker
And., 158
George, 247, 249
Jo., 137
John, 87, 121, 180, 181, 187
Joseph, 75, 77, 79, 81, 132, 133, 137,
138, 140, 141, 142, 150, 162, 185,
187, 190, 191, 240
Josias, 135, 136, 142, 161, 191
Wm., 135
Kerson
G., 69
Kickman (Hickman?)
Kron, 172
Kil.
R., 184
Kilgore; Kilgour; Gilgour
Charles, 89, 90, 91, 93, 94, 99, 100,
106, 114
Kilogh
Jo., 118, 206
Kilpatrick
R., 227
Kinkead
E., 171
Kirkpatrick
Gavin, 153
Kisack
—, 174
Kyle
—, 147
J., 147
Sam, 128

Laird
—, 188
Lamb's
—, 240, 241
Lamington
M., 244
Latta
—, 91, 227, 228
Mr., 207, 223
Robert, 207
Lauchlin; Lachlin; Laughlin
Robert, 136
Widow, 132, 164, 166
William, 135
Lauson
—, 246, 257
C., 246
Captain, 246, 255
Law
—, 252, 258
James, 180
Martha, 143
Robert, 123, 165, 169, 178
Lecken; Leckin
T., 86, 245
Lecky; Lackey; Lockey
Alexander, 128
Leech
—, 87
B., 115, 203
Brother, 201
Legate
Thomas, 183
Leiper
James, 82
Jo., 119, 127
Sam, 127, 212
Lemmon
—, 242
Lind; Linn; Lynd
—, 81
Mr., 81, 91, 118, 195
Widow, 242
Lindsay
John, 87
Little
Andrew, 138
Martha, 138
Widow, 131

Logan; Logane; Logue
—, 196
D., 227
David, 116, 127, 242
—, 230, 234
James, 226, 227, 228, 229, 230, 231,
232, 233, 234, 235, 236, 237
Long
James, 226
Longstaff
—, 240, 241
Loughhead; Lochhead
—, 183, 208, 230, 254
James, 88, 161, 172, 174, 177, 178,
179, 180, 183
Janet, 134
Robert, 126, 131, 132, 134, 135, 136,
137, 138, 139, 140, 141, 142, 143,
144, 145, 147, 149, 150, 151, 152,
153, 190, 191, 211
W., 178
Widow, 155
Wm., 183
Love
—, 227
Lowry; Lowrie
—, 119, 199
J., 147
John, 119, 126, 127
Robert, 168
Lyal
A., 197
Lynch
—, 133, 157

McAdams
William, 200
McBride
—, 243, 251
Archibald, 247, 249, 250
Captain, 230, 255
Isaia, 214
James, 248, 253, 254
W., 252
Widow, 247, 248, 250, 251, 252, 253,
255

McBryar
David, 116, 127
McCain
—, 153
McCairnachan
—, 239
McCal.
—, 222
McCall., McCalyrs
Robert, 104, 194
McCamblin; McCirm.
—, 247, 248, 249
McCamon
Thomas, 209
McCarter
—, 144, 151
McCarthy
Colonel, 255
McCauseland
James, 242
McClean
David, 201, 208
McCleary
A., 232
Alexander, 187, 232
And., 221, 231
John, 121, 187, 188, 213, 228, 229,
232, 233, 235
McClellan
—, 159
Captain, 239
Daniel, 74, 95, 131, 134, 136, 138,
139, 140, 141, 142, 143, 145, 155,
157, 185, 190, 208, 209, 210
James, 125
John, 210
Mr., 159
Sam, 88
McClenachan
—, 127
J., 82, 128, 129
James, 82, 116, 117, 126, 128
John, 129, 130
Joseph, 126
W., 129
Widow, 117, 122, 128

McClung
—, 122, 193
John, 90
Matthew, 130, 131, 133, 164, 165,
  166, 192, 193, 194, 195, 196, 225
McClure
W., 143, 158, 161
Widow, 124
William, 137, 138
McConnell; McConel
Adam, 125
Alexander, 100, 206
Dan, 180
James, 259
Robert, 83, 118
Widow, 181
Widow, Senior, 180
McCorachan (McClenachan?)
James, 116
McCord
J., 254
James, 109, 110, 113
Robert, 236
McCorkle
—, 80
James, 175
Mr., 174, 175
Will, 175
McCormick
Hew, 94
T., 107
Widow, 146
McCoubray
Widow, 177
McCready
D., 124
McCulloch
—, 254, 255, 260
Alexander, 124, 182, 224, 225, 227,
  228, 231, 236
John, 223
Robert, 78, 235
Sam, 234
McCurdy
D., 81, 117, 129
Robert, 191
McCumpry
—, 169

McDowell; McDowel; McDowal
—, 126, 134, 159, 248, 250, 260
A., 259
Ephraim, 244
H., 201, 203
Math., 248, 253, 254
Mr., 259
S., 171
McEld.
James, 124
McElheron
Ch., 156
McFadden; McFadian; McFadzean
Hew, 229
J., 205
Jeremiah, 138
John, 204
Mr., 177
McFoss
—, 241
McGee
Deacon, 259
Jo., 87
Patrick, 250
McGahy
David, 70
McGill
Mr., 168
McGlaighlin
Js., 225
McGown; McKown
—, 244
George, 143
McGra.
John, 172
McGrew
—, 194
McGuffey
—, 164
McHaffy (See baps. Mahaffey)
Mar., 209
McHenry
Mr., 85
McH.
J., 239
McIntire
Mr., 236
W., 238

McIrvine
—, 133
McKinley
David, 209
Jo., 210
McKinstrie
John, 260
McKitterick; McKittrick
Alexander, 233, 240
McKnaughtan; McKnaught; Mc-
Knaighta n; McKnaight; Mc-
Knight; McNight
—, 78, 83
James, 72, 92, 93, 99, 100, 130, 132,
145, 147, 149, 153, 155, 156, 157,
164, 166, 177, 191, 214
Neil, 73, 78, 79, 80, 93, 94, 163, 189,
190, 191, 193, 194
McLean
John, 242
McLung
—, 177
McMeans
Andrew, 83
McMichan; McMeehan
—, 127
James, 119, 125, 126, 127
Mary, 127
McMillan
—, 214, 215, 220, 221, 223, 224, 238
J., 186, 187, 196, 214, 216, 223, 224,
228, 231, 236, 237, 238
Jean, 223
John, 75, 98, 139, 145, 164, 185, 186,
187, 207, 209, 210, 211, 213, 214,
216, 218, 222, 223, 225, 232, 239,
240. 242
Mr., 225, 226, 227, 232
William, 223, 238
McMurdy
Robert, 158, 215
McNair
David, 103
McNicol; McNickle
—, 94, 240
B., 241
Francis, 89, 90, 93, 94, 99, 111, 206
T., 96
Widow, 94

McReady
D., 179
McReary
W., 234
Mc'shel
Leonard, 79
McVagh
—, 201
Widow, 201
McWhorter; McHorter
Hew, 241
Moses, 230
McWilliams
—, 214
John, 210
Maeben
John, 173, 175. 177
Manifold
Ed., 227
Marlin
—, 164, 212, 216
J., 167, 213, 215, 216, 219, 221, 229
John, 210, 211, 213, 214, 215, 216,
217, 218, 219, 220, 221, 223, 224,
226, 227, 228, 231, 232, 234
L., 233
Mary, 215
Ralph, 94
Robert, 196, 232
Thomas (?), 211
Widow, 236
William, 226, 228, 229, 238
Marquer
George, 206
Marsh (Marshall?)
Da., 146
Mr. S., 170
Marshall; Marshal
—, 115, 196, 241
J., 218
John, 152, 170, 185. 209, 212
Mr., 176, 205
Martin
—, 91
Sam. 94, 104, 105, 112

Mason
—, 196, 213
Mr., 205, 254
Master
—, 246
William, 236
Mathies
—, 257
Major, 246
Matthew
T., 229
Matz
—, 197, 245
Maughlin; Mauchlin
—, 220, 221, 222, 230, 232
F., 234, 236
William, 173, 208, 217, 224, 227, 228,
229, 230, 231, 232, 233, 235, 236,
237, 238, 239
Maxwell
—, 126
Meredith
Francis, 80, 83, 228
Metier; M'Teer; McTeer
—, 182
W., 225
Michan
(See McMichan)
Mickleroy; Milroy
—, 224
Alexander, 85
Mifflin
General, 205
Miller; Millar; Milor
—, 132, 133, 152, 171, 175, 232
Esquire, 179
J., 162, 166, 201
Jac., 198
James, 171, 172, 241
Joseph, 148, 151, 173
Mr., 178, 180, 182
Thomas, 252
W., 205,
Widow, 162
Mills
Jacob, 236

Mitchel; Michel; Michael
—, 81, 198
Alexander, 119
David, 94, 95, 96, 97, 98, 100, 101,
103, 104, 106, 109, 110, 111, 112,
114, 115, 121, 122, 133, 188, 194
George, 118, 119, 120, 123, 126, 167,
232
J., 188
James, 97, 115, 118, 119, 120, 121,
122, 123, 124, 126
John, 91, 96, 120, 225, 226, 227
Joseph, 119
Matthew, 83
Thomas, 124, 225
William, 185
Money; Mooney
—, 213
Montgomery
—, 160, 161, 162
Dan., 200
Moody
Samuel, 242
Moore; Moor; More
—, 181, 198, 199, 250, 251
A., 183
J., 217
John, 178
Mr., 168, 183, 198
Mrs., 179
W., 122, 197, 198
Walter, 86, 89, 169, 198, 201, 202,
203, 244
Widow (Grandmother), 174, 177
William, 86, 122, 126, 191
Morgan
—, 125, 243
Morice (Moore's?)
Sam, 198
Morris
Michal, 229
Morrison; Morison
—, 181, 256
Jean, 129
Joan, 98
Mr., 255
Widow, 98
William, 128, 129

Mortimer
    John, 242
Morton
    —, 260
    T., 84, 257
Moth.
    —, 180
Mulligan
    John, 236
Murghat
    J., 163
Murphy
    John, 80, 81, 240
Murray
    —, 196, 201
    Jeremiah, 71, 72, 119
    John, 79, 83
    Widow, 74

Neal; Neil; Niel
    Letitia, 117
Neilie; Neallie; Neily
    J., 142
    John, 89, 249
    Wm., 185
Neilson; Nilson; Nelson
    —, 208, 209, 239
    Sam, 217, 231, 232, 233, 236, 237
Neks
    —, 254
Nesbit; Nisbit; Nisby
    —, 254, 259
    Hen., 84
    James, 88, 124
Nickleduff
    —, 88
    Sam, 189
Nicol; Nickle; Nickol
    —, 215, 222
    Mary, 220
    William. 188, 212, 213, 215, 216, 218,
        219, 238
Noble
    J., 169
    Wm., 136
Noll
    —, 148, 152, 162, 172, 176
    Doc., 156
Nunnel
    James, 249

Oakerman
    Abraham, 243, 258
Ogden
    —, 246
Orson; Orr's (Orison?)
    —, 230
    G., 237
    Rob., 182
Owen
    Widow, 166

Paden; Peden; Paeden
    John, 198
    W., 203, 204
Padlehouser
    —, 133
Paisley
    —, 162, 181, 183
    J., 162
Park; Parks
    —, 198
    John, 81, 131, 187, 225, 228, 240
Parkieson; Parkeson
    —, 99
    William, 90, 91, 93, 94, 95, 96, 97,
        122
Parry
    Widow, 198
Paterson; Patterson
    —, 86, 122, 180
    A. & Al., 243, 245, 250
    James, 75, 84, 131, 152, 155, 164,
        165, 168, 169, 171, 180, 185, 190,
        193, 196, 207, 208, 213, 217
    John, 93, 171, 173, 177, 178, 225
    Mr., 205
    Peter, 84
    Robert, 171, 172, 180, 183, 184, 194,
        222, 236
    Sally, 176
    Sam, 158, 170
    Thomas, 76, 96, 157
    Widow, 180, 184
    William, 84
Paton
    —, 124
    Jean, 225

Paxton
—, 147
Captain, 173
J., 131, 163, 172
Na., 74, 147
S., 147
Payne
Th., 232
Peck
G., 254
Pederis (Peden's?)
—, 229
Perrigrew
—, 181
Persal
Mordecai, 88, 182
Peter
—, 175
Rev., 200
Petit; Petet
—, 245, 248, 254
Phyliss
John, 238
Pickering
—, 86, 89
Plum
David, 94, 105
Dr., 91
Poa
Alexander, 75, 116
Poak
—, 151, 170
Mr., 94
Sam, 92
Sam's wife, 171
Poequea; Poequey
—, 179
Jean, 179
Widow, 179
Polloch
Mr., 231
Sam, 224
Widow, 235
William, 229, 230
Porter
—, 236
David, 72
James, 174
Joan, 158

Post
—, 244
Prey
W., 164
Price
—, 239
Priest
—, 85
Pringlered
John, 99
Proudfoot
And., 187, 230, 233
Mr., 187, 205
Robert, 187, 227, 228, 233

Quiem
—, 246

Rainey; Raeney; Rainney
Esther, 252
James, 202, 246, 249, 250, 251, 252
Samuel, 253
Widow, 252, 254, 255
Ralston
—, 168
Andrew, 89
Ramsay
—, 156, 169, 177, 178, 180, 214, 236
James, 152, 160, 167, 177, 193, 234
John, 165, 170, 176, 177, 180, 183, 234
Joseph, 133
Robert, 146, 160, 162, 165, 168, 171, 177, 179, 181
Robert's wife, 167
Sus., 175
Thomas, 139, 143, 144, 152, 213, 220, 222, 223, 224, 225, 226, 227, 230, 231, 232, 233, 234, 235, 236, 237, 238
Widow, 172, 176, 178, 179
Rankin
—, 82
H., 194
Ready
Robert, 70
Reagh; Rea
James, 175
John, 91, 188
Reddick
Robert, 71, 75, 116, 117

Rednour
—, 242
Reid; Reed
—, 216, 222, 233
Ad., 101
Esquire, 100, 225, 236
J., 170, 206, 219, 221
James, 75, 118, 120, 193
Jean, 224
Jo. & Jo. Esq., 120, 225
John, 77, 84, 100, 201, 203, 213, 216, 220, 228, 229, 230, 231, 235, 236
Robert, 182
Sam, 224
W., 188
Widow, 84, 223, 224, 225, 226
William, 232, 233
Reynolds; Reynold
George, 116, 126
W., 245
Rich
Henry, 254
Rich.
J., 182
Richard; Ritchard
Mr., 86
W., 205
Richmaster
—, 244, 247
Ringoe
—, 244, 245
Ringwood
—, 248
Rippy
—, 224
J., 236
Ritchie; Ritchy; Richy
Dr., 187
James, 178
John, 171, 172
Matthew, 135, 136, 139, 140
W., 92, 98, 207
Riter
James, 100
Robb
John, 193
Robertson
James, 231

Robieson; Robinson; Robeson
—, 214, 222, 224, 245
Alexander, 157, 160, 161, 166, 167, 169, 193, 214, 218, 223, 224, 227
David, 84
J., 175, 185, 227, 228, 231
James, 133, 136, 225, 226, 231, 236, 256
Jo, 140
Joe., 209
John, 84, 145, 160, 167, 172, 184, 185, 186, 189, 194, 208, 211
Martha, 177
Quaker, 245
R., 85, 102
Sam, 166, 171, 225
Widow, 118
William, 102, 118, 166, 180, 194, 196, 212, 230
Rocky
—, 180
Henry, 151, 176, 181
Roger; Rogers
James, 237, 249
Mr., 123
Rollins
Bess (?), 229
S., 150
Ross
—, 211, 213, 215, 216, 224, 228, 229 230, 231, 236
Barn. (?), 237
Capt. & Colonel, 172, 223, 229, 231, 239, 240
F., 228
Henry, 209
Hugh; Hew, 69, 131, 186, 207, 208, 209, 210, 211, 212, 213, 215, 219, 220, 221, 222, 223, 225, 226, 227, 238, 239, 242
J., 211
James, 146, 178
Jean, 232
Jo., 88, 134
John, 126, 208, 209, 210
Joseph, 208
Mr., 222
W., 228

Rowan; Roan
—, 103, 188
Andrew, 188
Mr., 188, 241
Ruckly (Rocky?)
—, 180
Russel
—, 190, 256
A., 166
Hew, 169
Ryburn
—, 151
David, 139, 151
Rynford
—, 85

St. Coit (?)
—, 257
Sayres
Ben, 124
Schever
Peter, 162
Scott; Scot
—, 197
Ar., 136
George, 243
James, 206
John, 150
Polson, 132
William, 254, 255
Seaborn
—, 245
Selfridge
—, 256
Semple
C., 188
Mr., 182
Sewitz
—, 198, 245
Sharp
—, 96, 116
Mr., 169
Shearer
—, 133
Sherman, 118

Shel. (?)
Ch., 89
Shirt
John, 158
Shuttle
Widow, 233
Shyfelt; Shyfly
—, 198, 245
Side
—, 162
Benjamin, 155
Silver
—, 241
Simpson; Simson; Simon
—, 224, 247, 259
H., 247, 248
Henry, 250, 251
John, 247
Mr., 83, 115, 206
S , 173
Widow, 245, 253, 254
Sinclair; Sinclare
—, 213
Daniel, 155, 207, 214, 215, 218, 219,
    220, 221, 222, 223, 226, 227, 228.
    229, 230, 231, 232, 233, 234, 235,
    239, 240
F (?), 226
Slaymaker
—, 181
Slemon
Mr., 187, 233
Sloan
—, 118
D. & Da., 211
Jean, 114, 186, 219
Jo, 141
John, 95, 101
Sam, 101, 103
Small
Henry, 165
Smeizar; Smizart; Smizar
—, 78, 81, 199, 219, 240
John, 233
Smiley; Smielie; Smily
T., 187

Smith
- —, 249, 255
- Ephraim, 201, 203
- Gus, 93
- Jus., 124, 125, 126
- Matt., 187
- Mr., 91, 134, 169, 170, 172, 175, 176, 178, 179, 180, 181, 182, 207, 223, 225
- R., 222
- Rodney, 198
- Widow, 151, 152, 200, 212
- William & Wm. Esquire, 86, 187, 233

Sneider; Sneidar
- —, 196
- Widow, 198

Spedie
- W., 211

Spieger
- Mr., 115, 206

Spier; Speer
- —, 122, 197
- James, 80, 163
- N., 171

Steel
- Wm., 170, 172, 177, 184, 221, 239

Stevenson
- —, 248
- Mary, 138
- R., 75

Stewart
- —, 69, 100, 225, 233, 236, 260
- Andrew, 91, 103, 105, 106, 145, 186, 219
- Charles, 259
- Hugh, 104, 114, 182
- John, 84, 232, 235
- Jos., 257
- Mary (?), 138
- Sam, 107, 187
- W., 153

Stigle
- —, 133

Stiller
- —, 156

Stoffield
- —, 85, 199

Stoner
- John, 173, 178

Strehorn
- D., 102
- William, 102, 109

Sug.
- Wat., 133

Super.
- Andrew, 101

Swan
- Ag., 158
- Alexander, 101, 102, 103, 104, 105, 106, 115, 130, 133, 212
- Widow, 219

Swansie
- D., 248

Taeff
- —, 101

Tait
- —, 115

Talbot
- —, 172, 183
- Elizabeth, 184
- James, 100

Taylor
- —, 259, 260
- Colein, 259
- J., 236
- Mat., 111

Telfair
- Captain, 254
- Mr., 205, 229, 239, 255

Thievley
- —, 86

Thomson
- —, 102, 149, 152, 159, 166, 169, 172
- A., 152
- Eleanor, 178
- Mr., 172
- Robert, 131, 152, 159, 163, 165, 168, 175, 213
- Thomas, 204
- Widow, 176
- William, 110, 190

Thorn
- James, 100
- John, 119, 126

Todd; Tod
- —, 172, 246, 258
- John, 88

Tomlinson
—, 83, 242
Trivelbest
Jack, 201
Trumbour
—, 86, 245
Tsennedy (Kennedy)
Thomas, 89
Tweed
R., 160

Valneer
Doctor, 198
Vanderbergh
Garret, 246
Vernon
Sam, 197
Widow, 144, 246
Vogan
W., 163

Wade
—, 122
John, 96. 121
T., 194
Waggonier
—, 199
Wahob; Wahub
—, 179
Edw., 131
Walace
Ben, 113
Walker
—, 98, 101, 148, 151, 177, 179, 207
Captain, 180
F., 144
Gab., 156, 157
Hanna, 147
J., 149, 153, 158, 213
J. (Doc.), 155
James, 98, 173, 177, 178, 207
Jo., 135, 151
John, 92, 123, 136, 138, 139, 151,
    156, 163, 164, 167, 170, 171, 175,
    176, 177, 181, 185, 189, 190, 191,
    209, 216
Joseph, 80, 88, 134, 135, 139, 140,
    142, 144, 149, 150, 153, 160, 176,
    179, 215
William, 95, 96, 99, 158, 196, 241

Ware
—, 245
Warnock
—, 213
Watt; Watts
David, 207
John, 70, 71, 74, 97, 117, 128
Weatherly
—, 197
Weaver
Bartholomew, 85, 197
Weidenhamer; Widenhammer
Mr., 85, 197
Weisner; Wiser; Woeser
—, 200
Conrad; Conrade, 85, 101
Welb
James, 205
Welsh
John, 140, 144
Wha.
—, 183
White
—, 170
Alexander, 181, 183
J., 159, 215
Whiteside
J. & James, 220, 257
John, 257
Mr., 250
Peter, 257
Phinehas; Phineas, 139, 190, 191,
    192, 196, 246, 250, 257. 258
Thomas, 257
William, 257
Whitney
Colonel, 259
Whittlesey
—, 208
Wiggin
—, 113
Wigwam
John, 199
Joseph, 199
Lawrence (?), 199
Wilkin
Joseph, 255
William, 248, 249, 251, 252, 253, 254.
    255

Williams
—, 213, 239
George, 105
Wilson
—, 124, 197, 213, 216, 217, 220, 237, 259
Aaron, 83
J., 155, 158
James, 83, 119, 121, 123, 124, 125, 126, 127, 132, 138, 141, 148, 174, 180, 181, 208, 241
John, 102, 125, 126, 128, 149, 167
Joseph, 119, 126
Mary, 231, 232
P., 168
Robert, 260
Sam, 84, 114, 255
Thomas, 71, 74, 75, 76, 79, 80, 119, 122, 137, 155, 204
Widow, 74, 117, 128
William, 207, 208, 209, 210, 215, 217, 218, 220, 221, 223, 224, 226, 238, 239
Zaccheus, 83

Withrow
—, 128
John, 70, 73
W. (or J.), 73
Wolverton; Woolverton
—, 199, 248
Woodhul
Mr., 172
Woods; Wod
J., 118, 124, 225
Work
—, 153, 156, 169, 214
Andrew, 136, 144, 147, 163, 171, 172
Mr., 152
R., 163
W., 177
Wylie
Jo., 92, 118, 120
John, 120

Yeat
—, 253
Young
—, 176, 234, 241
William, 219, 221, 225, 227, 255

*BUCHANANS

Information has recently been received from Miss Emma M. Campbell of La Jolla, Calif., a relative of President James Buchanan, on the Buchanans, (some of whom are mentioned by Doctor Cuthbertson) as follows:

* Gilbert Buchanan of East Nottingham, Chester County, Pa., died in 1771; his children were Walter,** Sarah, Agness, Margaret and Jannet, and from Family Bible, the following:
** Walter (of Little Britain, Lancaster County, Pa.) married Jean McLaughlin. His children were Gilbert,*** b. Mar. 12, 1750; Janet,**** b. Jan. 23, 1752; Mary, b. Oct. 14, 1754; James, b. May 23, 1761; John, b. Aug. 12, 1763; Sarah, b. Dec. 24, 1765; Margaret, b. Sept. 10, 1768; Agnes, b. Oct. 11, 1772.
*** Gilbert married Sarah Walker—children, Walter, Isaac, James, Sarah, Rebecca.
**** Janet married James Glenn—children, Walter, Agnes, Joseph, Jean.

The Walter Buchanan of East Pennsboro Township married Mary Roney. He died in 1788. The children were Andrew, James, William, Robert, Walter; Elizabeth, who married Walter Smith; Jannet, who married David McClelland; Mary, who married William Herron; Margaret, who married Hercules Roney, and Ann Davidson. (From one of his descendants to Miss Campbell.)

PERSONS VISITED—ADDITIONAL QUOTATIONS

The quotations given below from the Diary of Rev. John Cuthbertson are for the purpose of bringing out each name which may not have appeared in the previous citations, thus covering all names recorded in Diary. The reader should have no difficulty in placing these families where they belong by association with those heretofore given, aided by explanations in parenthesis by the writer. As previously stated, only entries are quoted bringing out the names sought. Complete copy of Fields' Index to Diary in D. A. R. Library, etc., would have to be consulted for additional information bearing on these and other names.

Adams:
James 1759 Sept. 28 "rode 8 miles by James Adams—bought Lexic., Justin and Salust at 18-9." (From Neshaminy.)

Archer:
Dr. R. and J. 1789 Sept. 13 "Sabbath—nothing—wife, Dr. R. and J. Archers, sick—Bilow F." (At home.)
Th. 1787 Sept. 6 "rode 5 miles to widow Brown's, gave letters to Th. Archer." (Then rode 8 miles to James Logue's on the 7th.)

Armstrong:
Francis 1758 Aug. 4 "Rode 12 miles to Francis Armstrong's by Walter Buchanan's with J. D." (From Junken Tent on way home.)

Arson:
G. 1780 July 29 "Rode 5 miles to G. Arson's. W. Rosses—a fine rain." (From Thomas Ramsay's.)

Beggs:
Robert 1768 Apr. 4 "rode 8 miles to J. G. to sisters bargaining with Robt. Beggs 4½ years." (From David Dunwoody's.)

Bigham:
James 1783 Jan. 1 "rode 5 miles by Mr. Sutters to James Bigham." (From John McMillan's.)
Widow 1782 July 31 "rode 4 miles to H. Rocky's, widow Bigham's, etc. visited." (From home.)

Blyth:
—— 1788 July 30 "rode 16 miles back to Tityre le Varts, Blyth's, N. C."

Boag:
Mr. 1786 Dec. 11 "rode 13 miles to Mr. Boag's, the bears by the mill, tired." (From Mr. James Cluney's.)

Bogle:
Joseph 1753 Aug. 20 "Rode 12 mi. to Joseph Bogles preach. Ps. 76: 10—and preach. Luke 24: 29." (From Da. McKinley's.)

Boyd:

William 1753 Dec. 18 "Rode 4 miles to William Boyd's in the valey—conversed variously." (Then rode 10 miles to Pequea on 19th—Humphrey Fullerton's.)

Brandon:

John 1767 July 12 "Sabbath preached psalm 109; lectured 1 John 2: 1—preached Jude; rebuked John Bran." (At Middle Octoraro.)

Breeden:

Widow 1760 Mar. 20 "tramped. visited 5 miles to Widow Breedens, W. Col——." (Paxton?)

Brown:

L. 1766 Jan. 15, 16 "rode 45 miles to L. and B. Brown's—16 ex. cold." (From home—then 10 miles to John Duncan's, W. Brown's on 17th.)

Buchanan:

James 1764 Feb. 1 "rode 12 miles over Susquehanna, James to Wal. Buchanan's." (Then rode 2 miles to W. Walker's on 2nd.)

—— 1778 Mar. 9, 10 "rode 14 miles to Jas. Glen's, Gilb. Buch., Jas., W. & John." (Then rode 5 miles to Walter Buchanan's on 11th.)

Burney:

Robert 1765 Oct. 1 "rode 10 miles to and from Robert Burney's burial." (From home?)

Cain:

—— 1763 Feb. 25 "went to W. Pedens—visited Walace, Johnston, Cain, etc." (From Gavin Kirkpatrick's.)

Calbreath:

Mary 1779 Apr. 16 "rode 22 miles to Mary Calb. S. D. W. Wilson's." (From home?)

Caldwel:

Captain 1779 Dec. 22, 23 "rode 13 miles to J. McCulloch's, Cap. Caldwel's, Society and John Dolaps, Gs. preached 18–28 —and lectured Romans 3: 27 g.a." (From Walter Buchanan's.)

Campbel:

Rosa 1787 June 13 "rode 6 miles to Rosa Campbels, Hamil., James Chineys." (From Widow McCormick's.)

Rose 1772 May 18 "rode 15 miles to David Mitchels; preached; Rose Campbel." (Then rode 9 miles to Mr. Rowan's on 19th.)

Carson:

John 1790 (bet. Aug. 8–14) "rode 16 miles to John Carson— received doll—rode 2 miles to Ro. Kil. and 7 home."

Widow 1751 (bet. Sept. 16–18) "Rode 33 miles to Donegal Widow Carsons very weary." (Then 2 miles to Derry.)

Case:

1766 May 1 "rode 52 miles to petits, wallon's, Wilking's, cases." (Then 12 miles to Goshen on May 2.)

Chever:
—— 1760 Oct. 16 "rode 50 miles x x Dor. Chever's (18), W. horse 5." (Then 40 miles home on 17th.)

Chicky:
—— 1771 Feb. 28 "rode 26 miles; was in Chickys; went Humphrey Fulerton's past 10." (Then 8 miles home Mar. 1.)

Cline:
Mr. 1784 Oct. 31 "Sabbath—rode 12 miles, preached 65:1— and discoursed 18:23 Hum. Mr. Cline." (Near James Calhoun's.)

Cochran:
Margaret 1772 Aug. 31 (Wife of T. Cochran—see pages 80–81.)

Cooper:
James 1784 Feb. 24 &c "12–m to Matt. McCl., Fulerton's, James Cooper." (From home?)

Crooks:
Joseph 1753 Aug. 23 "Rode 12 mi. to Joseph Crooks after preaching Ps. 78:7-12 and preach 1 John 2:15—." (From William Cooper's.)

Crutchlow:
—— 1752 July 1 "Rode 4 miles to Crutchl. Sos. no peace etc. went to James McKnaught's." (From James Dill's.)

Cummin:
John 1758 July 26 "rode 30 miles to Sam Henry's pund—39. Got John Cummin's horse etc. x x."
Old 1758 July 27 "rode 8 miles home—borrowed 30 shillings from old Cumins—x x."

Dawson:
—— 1766 June 3 "rode 60 miles, 20 Petits, 10 Dawsons, 20 Johnstons, O. Forge and Ferry." (From "Walloons.")

Dean:
—— 1759 Nov. 28 "Rode 35 miles to Rosses; then Cap. Dickenson's and to Deans." (On way home from Col. Whitney's.)

Delf:
Mr. 1780 Aug. 12 "Held Presbytery; rs. Mr. Telfair, Mr. Delf; preached 2 Corinthians 9:15—came to B." (At Widow Junken's or Alex. Brown's.)

Dick: (Dickson?)
Wm. 1787 Aug. 31 "rode 13 miles to Wm. Dick rs and to Al. McCulloch's and Wm. Mc." (From home.)

Dickenson:
Captain 1759 Nov. 28 (See Dean's.)

Dougherty:
G. 1757 Jan. 4 "Rode 12 miles to Robert Lochheads; conversed G. Dougherty, etc."

Dowglas:
Esquire 1775 Sept. 25 "rode 28 miles to Burd's Fur. from Esq. Dowglas,—Pine Forge 6–4 to Mr. Richard's."

Duncan:
   T. 1787 Apr. 17, 18   "rode 14 miles from T. Duncan's to widow
      Marl. L. Reed's, and Logs."
Elmor:
   —— 1753 July 2   "Rode 32 mi. to Henry Simsons conversed
      Gelston Elmor etc. pp efectio."
Evans (Ervin's?):
   John 1776 Jan. 11   "rode 8 miles to John Evans, Robs. Millars,
      H. Coulter's."   (From John and James Petterson's.)
Ewing:
   Mr. 1782 June 6   "rode 18 miles to J. McM., Mr. Ewing's,
      Stoner's, Barg. Carmickl, Mc."   (Then 5 miles to Dan Sin-
      clair's on the 7th.)
Finey:
   A. 1771 Sept. 23   "rode 9 miles to Jos. Kers, 24th—rode 10 miles
      after preached 44: 14 and catechizing 27 persons; to A. Finey
      and T. Wilson."   (From David Dunwoody's.)
Finlay:
   Richard 1784 Oct. 28   "rode 2 miles to Mr. Woods, Richard Fin-
      lays, etc. etc."   (From Wm. Tom's.)
Forbes:
   General 1759 Jan. 12   "rode 40 miles to D. Mitchel's—saw g.
      Forbes and the Army, etc."
Fraeland:
   —— 1788 Aug. 7   "rode 7 miles Fraeland's, James McClung's,
      etc. etc."   (Turbit Tp.?)
Frazer:
   Mr. M. 1790 Aug. 4, 5, 6, 7   "rode 19 miles to Mr. M. Frazers,
      Kip. McMillan's."
Fulerton:
   Alex. 1752 May 25   "Rode 15 miles. Preached psalm 121. Lec-
      tured Philip 1: 27-30. Rode pat. Alex. and Humphrey Fuler-
      tons."   (Then rode 12 miles to Lancaster on the 26th.)
Fulton; Fullton:
   Alex. 1762 Oct. 26   "Rode 30 miles to Alex Fulton's, John Mc-
      Millan's."   (From York.)
   Sally 1780 Dec. 20   "rode 6 miles with Sally Fullton to Widow
      Collins—well."   (Then rode 2 miles back to Colonel Ross's.)
Gellatly:
   Mr. 1761 Apr. 9   "etc. Mr. Gellatly's * vendue; indebted Octo-
      ber 10, 3-4-3."   (Middle Octoraro.)
Gemble:
   —— 1765 Apr. 2   "rode 5 miles to William Parkieson's—E - -
      Gemble cleaned W."   (From Hew McCormick's.)
Gemmel; Gemmil:
   Mr. 1787 July 5   "rode 9 miles to W. Mc. and got spectacles

* Alexander Gellaty buried in Neshaminy Cemetery, Bucks Co., Pa.

from Mr. Gemmel." (Then 2 miles Alex, McCulloch's on the 7th.)

William 1764 Apr. 30 "rode 12 miles to William Gemmil's." (From J. Marlin's.)

Gibson:

W. 1758 Aug. 23 "had blood let. 9 or 10 (ounces) by old W. Gib.—very sick 3rd ——." (At Frankford.)

Giffen:

Widow 1770 May 30 "rode 12 miles to Widow Giffen's." (Then rode 6 miles to C. Kilgore's on 31st.)

Gillilan:

—— 1762 Dec. 23 "rode 15 miles—visited Gillilan and Thomson to W. Brown." (From Sloan's.)

Gilmor:

Janet 1767 Dec. 3 "rode 8 miles Jat. Gilm. to D. D. got 3½ from sister." (To David Dunwoody's.) (Possibly with Janet and Gilmor.)

Glaygh:

G. 1781 Sept. 10 "rode 17 miles to G. Glaygh, about boys." (From Col. W. W.'s burying—Lower Chanceford.)

Green:

Sam 1753 June 25 "Rode 32 miles to Joseph McWhirtries 12 to Sam Greens moravian etc." (From Phil'a. on way to New York.)

Griffith:

—— 1775 June 19 "rode 15 miles—family all well—paid Griffith 13 s. for 3 bushels co——." (From Latta's School.)

Guthrey:

Esther 1765 May 20 "rode 22 miles to Sis's—conversed Esther Guth., R. Reddick."

Hanna:

Ad. 1775 Aug. 29, 30 "rode 9 miles to Hu. Coulter's, etc. and to Ad. Hanna's, home."

Dav. 1753 June 7 "Rode 8 mi. to and from the meeting, held session 2—etc. preach. Ps. 20: 1—examined 50 session 8 hours visited W. N. and Dav. Han. conversed 3 hours held infallible assurance concerning Christ." (From Robert Lochhead's.)

Harold:

—— 1788 Sept. 4 "rode and sailed 30 miles to Harold's, to Peter's, Weaver's." (From Hugh Beaty's.)

Haslet:

—— 1780 Nov. 15 "rode 32 miles to Petits, Hackets—Y. and lodged Haslets."

Hayes; Hays:

—— 1765 Oct. 18 "rode 38 miles to and from Haye's, Connawag.—o.h. Praise God."

Widow 1767 Mar. 13 & 14 "rode 48 miles to Hays widow and to W. Brown's."

Hart:
> Roger   1787 Sept. 24   "rode 12 miles to sis. and to Roger Harts."
> (Then 9 miles to John Burn's on 25th and 16 to Greencastle,
> etc., on 26th.)

Herin:
> T.   1754 June 28   "Rode 24 miles to A. Hunter's, T. Herin's,
> George Gray's, good health, praise." (From Robert McMur-
> tries.)

Hilton:
> Widow   1787 June 11   "rode 6 miles to J. D., widow Hilton, and
> to Elijah Stewart's." (From Paxton.)

Hinchman:
> Widow   1775 Sept. 28   "rode 44 miles to Pet. Mart., Suns.,
> Widow Hinchman's, H. Ken." (Then rode 12 miles to Goshen
> on 28th.)

How. (Howel or Howston):
> Christopher   1755 Jan.   "Rode 10 miles over Susquehanna; then
> to Christopher How."

Howston:
> D.   1782 Apr. 14   "S. 2 miles; Mr. S. preached and lectured Acts
> 1:5–10; I preached Zechariah 15:1 o.a. rode 12 miles to D.
> Howston's, Mr. Proudfoot C rain." (From Mat. McClung's.)
> John   1753 Oct. 31   "Rode 13 miles to John Howston's, John Wal.
> and Robert Lochhead's." (Then 10 miles to Dan McClellan's
> and John Duncan's, Nov. 1.)

Hunter:
> Alex.   1753 July 4   "Traveled 7 mi. to Alex. Hunters x x." (From
> Robert McWhirtrie's.)
> Sam   1755 Dec. 15   "Rode 15 miles to and from Sam Hunter's
> Garson, exhorted prayed, saw the —." (From home?)

Inglis:
> Mrs.   1772 Sept. 1   "rode 48 miles to Lancaster with Mrs. Inglis.
> fv." (From Thomas Cross's.)

Ireland:
> John   1788 June 2   "rode 2 miles to R. R. and Al. McCl., con-
> versed John Ireland." (From Robert McCulloch's.)

Irwine:
> G.   1783 May 13   "rode 10 miles to G. Irwines, J. Kenety's and
> catechized law 12." (From New Holland.)

James Sr. (?):
> P.   1783 Dec. 22, 23, 24   "rode 19 miles to W. F's, P. James Sr.
> Widow McClung's, home."

Jamieson:
> Mr.   1783 Dec. 7   "Sabbath Mr. S. lectured Genesis 22:1–7, Mr.
> Jamieson preached Isaiah 65:1." (At home.)

Jenks:
> ——   1775 Mar. 22   "rode 5 miles to Mr. Sm.—Jos. Walker's—
> bor. Jenks, etc." (From Humphrey Fullerton's.)

Kennedy:
> Mr. 1777 Oct. 6 "rode 26 miles to York, Mr. Kennedy's—saw Mr. Annan, Dobin, George Syfo——." (From H. Ross's.)
> Old 1775 Apr. 10 "rode 22 miles by the Compass, old Kennedy's." (From Brandywine?)
> W. 1756 Nov. 1 "Rode 32 miles W. Kennedy's; tired but safe." (Then 15 miles to Humphrey Fullerton's.)

Ker:
> Thomas 1779 Sept. 10 "rode 38 miles to Thomas Kers with John Richard, etc." (From Peter Peter's—then 30 miles to Alexander Millars on 11th.)

Kisack:
> —— 1777 Oct. 22, 23 "rode 10 miles seeking hay—bought bushels beans from Kisack." (From home.)

Knox: (Place?)
> —— 1755 Apr. 23 "Rode 9 miles to Knox, Th. Docharty's and Jo Lowries." (Then 2 miles to George Mitchel's on 24th.)

Khun:
> —— 1774 May 31 "rode 23 miles to Mr. Dob., D. D's., to Khuns, T. Cross'." (From sister's—Carrolls Tract.)
> —— 1774 May 17 "rode 29 miles to Smeizars Khun's, Parks, Jos. Kers."

Kyle:
> John 1753 Jan. 23 "Rode 3 miles to Jo. Kyles And. Works, in good health etc." (Then rode 5 miles to Dan McClellan's on 24th.)

Langlan:
> William 1752 Jan. 5 "Sabbath. Rode 6 miles to the meeting. preached psalm 18: 17–23, lectured Galatians 4: 12–19 and preached Hebrews 4: 12 o.a. at William Langlans explained psalm 90, give all praise to God. x x." (From Joseph Walker's.)

Launder:
> —— 1762 Aug. 20 "rode 21 miles to Launders, McConel's and Thomas Anderson's." (From John Wilson's.)

Leech:
> Watty 1763 Dec. 9 "rode 22 miles home—great rain—brought Watty Leech." (From Dun. or Dan. Leech's.)
> Widow 1756 Sept. 1 "Rode 12 miles with —— to and from widow Leech's visiting." (From Wm. Moore's.)

Little; Lyttle:
> William 1753 July 7 "Rode 44 mi. to Tobias pickle etc. wand this and former day Wm. Little." (And on the 8th preached at Paxton.)

Long:
> T. 1772 Aug. 15 "rode and walked 7 miles to T. Longs, James Downy's and widow." (From Robert Crunkleton's.)
> Herman 1758 Oct. 25 "rode 19 miles to Herman Long's—bought shoes from Helm 7-6 rain." (From Matthew McClung's.)

Lopez: (Place?)

—— 1769 Oct. 25 "rode 43 miles, 15 to Lopez, 28 to Shangam, Graham." (Then 16 miles to James Rainey's on 26th and 27th.)

Lorimer:

Joseph 1780 Apr. 20 "rode 16 miles to Mr. S.—pet. p. Jos. Lorimer's so - - to S. Dixon's—cold." (From home.)

McAgil:

W. 1761 Dec. "Letters to W. McAgil 1 to Presbytery 2 McM. Dan. 1 Brother 1 - - x x." (In page summary.)

McCarter:

John 1761 Nov. 6 "Rode 5 miles to and from John McCarters— x x." (From home.)

McClellan; McClelan:

David 1752 Jan. 25 "Rode 4 miles to Kyles (where I am to preach) and to David McClelands." (From James Paterson's.)

" 1755 July 9 "Rode 8 miles to David McClellan's, Thomas Ramsay's—r bad." (From R. L.—then 10 miles to Humphrey Fulerton's on 10th.)

Mary 1757 Mar. 10 "Rode 7 miles to Mary McClelans and to brother Burns; all well, and preached psalm 23: 1—and lectured Zephaniah 2: 1–4; give all praise to my gracious God." (From Jeremiah Murray's.)

McCreery:

W. 1770 May 14 "rode and walked 10 miles to W. McCreery's and T. Wilson's etc." (From David Dunwoody's.)

McCulloch:

W. 1787 Nov. 22, 23, 24 "A. McCul. 1 dollar, W. McCul. and R. Reid's etc." (At Sam Dixon's.)

McCurdy:

Da. 1768 Nov. 11 "rode 10 miles sister's—received 5-10-0 from Da. McCurdy—5 m—." (Then rode 8 miles to David Dunwoody's on 12th.)

Widow 1769 Nov. 18 "rode 8 miles to Bottom, by Widow McCurdy's etc. to T. Ram. (From home.)

McDowel:

John 1765 July 8 "rode 21 miles home by John McDowel's, McGlachlin's, etc." (From John Marlin's.)

McElvain:

George 1788 Feb. 29 "rode 7 miles to George McElvain's and Mr. McClung's." (From home.)

McGlaughlin:

George 1777 May 8 "rode 16 miles to Mr. S., Widow Collins, George McGl., John McMns." (From home.)

McGown; McKown:

John 1782 Apr. 19 "rode 8 miles to John McGown's, Mr. P. and to John Todd's, etc." (From Mr. D. Howston's and Mr. Proudfoot's.)

McGrue; McGrew:
>   F. 1754 July 9 "Rode 20 miles to R. Bon; John Richmond's,
>   Popes, Dunlops, F. McGrue's, D. Din."

McIntire:
>   Robert 1788 Nov. 21 "rode 9 miles to R. Pat. and W. McIntire's
>   his B—Robert." (From home.)

McKigley; McKinley:
>   —— 1787 Apr. 16 "rode 4 miles to J. Marl. etc. 6 McKigley's—
>   tore coat 246 acres."

McKnight:
>   T. 1781 Oct. 24 "rode 15 miles by Mr. Dobins to T. McKnight's,
>   T. Girvan's." (From T. Cross's.)

McLeary: (McCleary?)
>   A. 1784 July 27 "rode 14 miles to widow F. to Math. McClung's
>   Woods, A. McLeary."

McLure
>   Mr. 1779 Nov. 25 "met Mr. M. all 3 nothing—rode 40 miles to
>   Philadelphia—Mr. McLure's."

McMichan; McMeehan:
>   Widow 1761 May 4 "rode 17 miles widow McMichan's, Lauder's
>   to John Wade's." (2 miles from J. Mitchel's.)

McMurdy:
>   Mr. 1765 Apr. 29, 30 "rode 12 miles to Mr. McMurdy's, Green-
>   lie's, etc., W. Thoms. Smart." (From Paxton.)

McMurtrie; McWhirtrie:
>   Steve 1760 Oct. 14 "rode 36 miles to Wolverton's, Downy's,
>   Stev. McMurtries." (Then 15 miles to Easton on 15th.)
>   Robert 1753 July 3 "Rode 50 miles to Robert McWhirtries
>   grived because I did not preach among em." (Then 7 miles to
>   Alex. Hunter's on 4th.)

McNiely:
>   W. 1780 Sept. 1 "rode 10 miles to W. McNiely's, Oatmans,
>   Bilestons." (From Mary Collin's.)

McTeer:
>   W. 1787 Feb. 27 "rode 1½ miles, 6 W. McTeers preached 25; —
>   15 and preached Isaiah 55: 6, 7." (Then 4 miles home on
>   Mar. 1.)

McUre:
>   —— 1781 Aug. 24 "rode 13 miles to McUres, Dix, Latta's,
>   McM., D. Sinclair's." (Lower Chanceford.)

Maglaughlin:
>   G. 1790 Feb. 22 "rode 4 miles to G. Magl., J. B., John McM.—
>   bad r."

Marshal:
>   James 1773 Oct. 14 "rode 12 miles to and from James Marshal's
>   W. Steel's." (From home.)

Martin:
>   Eph. 1774 Sept. 8 "rode 50 miles to Eph. Martins, to Srimp,
>   to Dek Ga's." (Then rode 7 miles to widow McBrides.)

Martin:
> Widow 1757 May 14 "Rode 3 miles to Samuel Stewarts etc. widow Martin carried off etc." (From Wm. Brown's, Paxton.)

Maxwel:
> John 1777 Nov. 1 "rode 4 miles to and from Susquehanna—impassible—John Maxwel." (From John McMillan's.)

Mearns:
> Hew 1758 Dec. 9 "tramped 1 mile to Hew Mearn's—his house—good health." (From Neshaminy.)

Meem:
> Dr. 1756 July 14 "Rode 32 miles to Wm. Coopers; conversed Dr. Meem x x." (From Hew Ross's.)

Melie (Nelie?):
> John 1756 Oct. "x x to John Melies; x x." (From Robert Gilmore's—then rode 8 miles to Philadelphia.)

Mercer:
> Colonel 1789 Jan. 12, 13 "rode 7 miles Col. Mercer's, A. W., Js. L., J. R., etc. home." (From Matthew McClung.)

Miller:
> Jus. 1767 Dec. 28, 29—"rode 23 miles to Jus. Millers, W. & J. Loughhead, etc." (From T. Kennedy's.)

Mitchel:
> Gen. (Geo.?) 1767 Aug. 11 "rode 26 miles to Gen. Mitchel's. York and Wolfe."

Montgomery:
> Mr. 1784 Oct. 26, 27 "rode 10 miles Mr. Montgomery, J. D., E. Hil., W. R. Wm. Tom's." (From Wm. Brown's, Paxton, then 2 miles to Mr. Woods, etc.)

Morison:
> Evander 1753 Aug. 6 "Rode 6 mi. 4 - - met Evander Morison cavilled 4 hours etc. holds only 1 Bible 6 Testament terms etc.—cited 4 charged etc." (From Dan McClellan's.)

Morris (Moore's?):
> Wm. 1753 June 18 "Received 30 letters from S.—rode 28 miles to Shamony Toehicken Wm. Morris." (From Walter Moore's.)

Moses (Mores?):
> Wm. 1783 June 25 "rode 18 miles to James Walker's, Sterret's, etc., Wm. Moses." (From Lancaster—then 2 miles to Wm. Brown's on 27th.)

Neilie:
> Jos. 1757 June 29 "Rode 30 miles to Jos. Neilie's with Sally;—all in tears." (From Father-in-law's—15 mi. from Philadelphia.)

Neilson:
> Mr. 1787 Nov. 13 "2 miles 14th.—5-D. 15th.—6 to Elizabeth, Mr. Neilson's." (From G. Orson's and Jos. Glen's.)

Newberry: (Place?)
> —— 1787 May 1 "rode 8 miles Mr. Smith, Newberry." (Then rode 10 miles home on 2nd.)

Nicol:
> James 1778 Aug. 25 "rode 36 miles—hot, hot—to Mr. Finley's, Jas. Nicol, H. F's, Begs." (From John Park's.)

Niely:
> Mr. 1773 Mar. 5 "rode 9 miles to Mr. Niely's, D. D.—roads very bad." (From sister's.)

Nillson:
> Wm. 1771 July 27 "rode 4 miles to Dan Sinclair's; Wm. Nillson's, tired." (From John Marlin's, etc.)

Noble:
> James 1780 Nov. 22 "rode 23 miles to James Nobles; bad roads —Wal. 3 finger hurt." (Then 7 miles by Widow Walker's—home.)

Norris:
> —— 1757 Apr. 5, 6 "Rode 30 miles to and from Philadelphia; paid 34-11-9 to Norris bor. 16-3." (From father-in-law's.)

Oatman:
> —— 1780 Sept. 1 "rode 10 miles to W. McNiely's. Oatmans, Bilestons." (From Mary Collin's or John Patterson's.)

Overtakes: (Place?)
> —— 1778 June 2 "rode from Jos. Reid's to Ormostogg, overtakes, Lane, (Lanc?) over Cannowago to Michael—Shanks—tired etc.—40 miles."

Paden; Paeden; Peden:
> John 1782 Apr. 30 "lodged John Paedens etc."
> " May 1 "rode 7½ miles Merian visited the Ship Washington."
> Mr. 1782 June 17 "rode 9 miles to Mr. Paedens, ended with Stoner, Kenet Hi." (From John Ful.)
> Sarah 1774 Apr. 15 "Paid 5 to Sarah Peden. Rode 33 miles down." (Phil'a. or Frankfort.)

Park:
> A. 1760 Jan. 19 "Paid 3 s. to John Ker Coll. and allowed 12 in A. Park." (From sister Burns'.)

Parry:
> Widow 1754 Jan. 28 "Rode 2 miles to White Marsh Church—preached here—7 stars—to Widow Parry."

Patterson:
> Molly 1790 Mar. 14 "Sabbath—preached 4th part and preached from same, 1 mile road 13 to Molly Patt." (Then 3 miles home on 14th.)

Paxton:
> Widow 1760 July 8 "Rode 15 miles to widow Paxtons; preached psalm 28: 5-L: preached Mark 9: 24—." (Then rode 8 miles to Thomas Wilson's to Murphys and McClellen's on 9th and 2 miles to David Dunwoody's on 10th.)

Perry (see also Parry):
> —— 1768 Dec. 2 "extra cold—rode 23 miles (from Philadelphia)

to the Waren, Perry's Tavern." (Then 18 miles to Thomas
Kennedy's on 3rd.)

Peters:

Peter 1779 Sept. 9 "rode 35 miles to Peter Peters by James
Reid's, good health, etc. praise God." (From home.)

Rev. 1788 July 15 "rode 15 miles (from Taylor's) to Thomas
Black's, Clark's, Rev. Peter's, sick." (Then 27 miles to Sunbury on the 16th.)

Peters(on?):

James 1782 July 18, 19 "rode 24 miles to James Peters., McCul.
T. S. and D. Sinclair's." (From home.)

Pickle:

Tobias 1753 July 7 "Rode 44 mi. to Tobias pickle etc. wand
this and former day Wm. Little." (Then preached at Paxton
on 8th.)

Poak:

Sam 1771 Oct. 29 "rode 10 miles to And. Mts. S. Poak's, Walter
Buchanan's." (From home.)

Pricerly:

Mr. 1788 Sept. 28 "rode 32 miles to Mr. Pricerly's, Matthew
McC., home." (From Hummelstown, 17 miles.)

Proupehaz:

John 1786 Dec. 18, 19 "Rode 28 miles to John Proupehaz, 5
miles home, praise God." (From James Paterson's.)

Quigley:

Mr. 1780 Aug. 22, 23, 24 "rode 20 miles to Quigley's, McCl.,
Ful., Lough., Moors and home, Y." (From home.)

Ralston:

W. and Widow 1755 Sept. 3 "Rode 6 miles to Widow Ralston's
after preaching psalm 44: 4–11 (at Charles Kilgore's) and
preaching Isaiah 31–1 g.a. received from Sm. and Bel McNickel
and W. Ral. 11-3 and 1-2-6 d."

Ramsay:

D. 1775 Mar. 27 "rode 20 miles—visited Dough., Poll., Row.,
Browns and D. Ramsay's." (From W. Wilson's.)

Reed:

Robert 1779 Aug. 30 "rode 18 miles by Robert Reed's, Al. Ro.,
Mr. Smith's, home."

Reid:

David 1752 Jan. 20 "Rode 4 miles to David Reid's, Jo. Duncans
—Wrote a letter to Joseph Colwis." (From Jo Ross's.)

Richard:

John 1782 Jan. 24 "rode 5 miles John Richard, preached 19: 23,
catechized, home."

Richardson:

Esq. 1755 June 25 "Rode 12 miles to Esq. Richardson's after
preaching psalm 4 and preaching Jeremiah 3: 12." (At or near
Upper Merion—Mr. Henderson's.)

Richmond:
> John 1754 July 9 "Rode 20 miles to R. Bon; John Richmond's, Popes, Dunlops, F. McGrues, D. Din." (From James Dill's, Redland.)

Rippy; Ripey:
> Matthew 1781 Sept. 25–29 "rode 36 miles to Mr. Latta's, Mr. Sin., W. Buch., James Wa. home, entered boys Mat. Ripey's, wife with me, praise gracious God."
> " 1788 Dec. 12, 13 "rode 5 miles Matthew Rip., S. Dixon's cold." (From W. McIntire's.)

Robieson:
> E. 1782 Aug. 29 "rode 22 miles, 10 with Mr. Paterson, E. Robi., R. Ross, Calbreath." (From H. Rocky's.)
> T. 1779 Aug. 10 "rode 4 miles to A. Ewins, McCalesters Society T. Robieson." (From George Mitchel's.)
> Widow 1773 Apr. 29 "rode 12 miles to Widow Robies. etc. Sam Dixon's." (From home.)

Rocky:
> John 1781 Oct. 3, 4 "rode 10 miles to and from Widow Ram., John Rocky's." (From home.)

Rodes:
> —— 1754 July 18 "Rode 28 miles by Finley's old plan. Rodes, Bay's s.- - - to James Ma. . . ." (From Brother's—Carroll's Tract.)

Rodgers; Rogers:
> Jas. 1789 June 5 "rode 3 miles (from Robert Patterson's) to W. Mc., A. Mc., S. D., and Jas. Rogers." (Then 3 miles to J. Brannon's on 6th.)
> —— 1773 Feb. 16 "rode 8 miles W. C's—preached 34: 19—exercised Deuteronomy 7: 22—went to Roger's." (From Charles Kilgore's.)

Ronalds (Reynolds):
> George 1751 Dec. 3 "Rode 18 miles to Geo. Ronalds, Antrim T. con. praise to God."

Roney:
> Mr. 1782 May 2 "rode 30 miles James Millars, Mr. Roney, best pair shoes." (Then 6 miles to J. Todd's on Sabbath, the 6th, where preached.)

Ross:
> Henry 1753 bet. Mar. 1–3 "Rode 6 miles over the Susquehanna to Henry Rosses, good health, praise to my gracious God." (From John McMillan's.)
> Robert 1777 Sept. 15 "rode 15 miles Robert Ross, R. Calbreath's—received 3 dollars from him, to Shan.—Mr. Sm."

Rowe:
> L. 1790 Apr. 26 "rode 16 miles to Port. Widow, F. G., R. R. L. Rowe." (From Wm. Maughlin's.)

Russel:

And.   1777 June 17   "rode 7 miles H. Coul., J. Millar's, paid And. Russel." (From home or Thomas Paxton's.)

John   1754 Sept. 17   "Rode 32 miles to York to Wm. Wilson's— met John Russel, Scot. etc. W. Ca. . . . ." (Then 9 miles to Sam Dickson's on 19th.)

Scot:

Widow   1757 July 20   "Tramped 4 miles to and from widow Scots x x." (From home.)

Semple:

Widow   1762 Dec. 16   "rode 40 miles to Widow Semple's—at plow." (From home.)

Shanon:

——   1777 Sept. 10   "Shanon's, sick, buryings, etc. Rode 20 miles, frail, etc. got confusions." (From home.)

Sharp:

F.   1781 Aug. 20, 21   "rode 18 miles to M. M's, F. Sharp's, McCa. Loughhead's, etc. with Z." (From home or Joseph Walker's.)

Shearer:

D.   1772 Sept. 15   "rode 7 miles to and from D. Shearer's wife's burial." (From home.)

Sides:

P.   1782 May 14   "rode 12 miles to P. sides, ½ Joe, then to Robieson's and old John Reagh." (From home.)

Smart:

——   1765 Apr. 29, 30   "rode 12 miles to Mr. McMurdy's, Greenlie's, etc., W. Thoms. Smart." (From Paxton.)

Smeizar; Smizart:

——   1768 Mar. 23   "rode 30 miles to Cub. Tavern at Smizart's Michal."

Widow   1774 Oct. 18   "rode and walked 52 miles to Mart. Sussex, Log, Jail Widow Smeizars."

Smith:

Ezekial   1758 Nov. 3   "rode 7 miles to Ezek. Smith's and to Francis McKnicols." (From Joseph Junken's.)

Gener. P.   1778 Jan. 24   "paid Gener. P. Smith 3-10-8."

James   1752 Apr. 6   "Rode 8 miles to Jas. (or Jus.) Smith's, Ind. of Cum. studies etc." (Then rode 7 miles to and from Ja. McClellan's on 7th.)

T.   1763 May 31   "rode 16 miles to S. D. T. Smith's, A. Baldridge, W's, Ram." (Then 5 miles home on June 3.)

"   1764 Dec. 14   "rode 19 miles to T. Smith's Furnace and home." (From Sam Dixon's.)

Somers:

Stoffald (?)   1752 Oct. 5   "Rode 24 miles near Stoffald Somers etc. to Da. Mitchel's Cataphelce." (From Conrad Wiser's and Reeit's Mills etc.)

Spreager; Spieger:
—— 1782 Apr. 22 "rode 31 miles from James Millar's to Spreagers, tired; 9 sh. 24."

Stedman:
—— 1788 Aug. 25 "rode 7 miles to Stedman's, Da. and James and J. Fulerton's." (Then rode and sailed 7 miles to "Sunberry" on the 26th.)

Sterrat; Sterret:
Elij. 1788 Sept. 12 "rode 3 miles to widow Brown's by Elij. Ster. x x." (From Widow Hilton's.)
James 1783 July 7 "rode 10 miles to James Sterrat's." (Then rode 3 miles to and from James Patterson's on 8th.)
Robert 1774 Mar. 7, 8 "rode 48 miles to Lan. to Robert Sterrat's —great floods, etc." (From home.)

Sturgeon:
—— 1770 July 31 "rode 20 miles to Sturgeon's, Youland's, Taylor's Peter's M." (From Wm. Brown's.)

Stun.:
John 1769 Oct. 5 (See New York trip.)

Sunwell:
Mr. 1782 Feb. 17 "Sabbath—preached 9–L and lectured 14: 22. Mr. Sunwell, o.a. rode 9 miles to and from Mr. S. to Maeb. Collins, James Patterson's." (Then 5 miles to Walter Buchanan's on the 19th.)

Sutter:
Mr. 1783 Jan. 1 "rode 5 miles by Mr. Sutters to James Bigham." (Then rode 13 miles to John Walker's and home on 2nd and 3rd.)

Swan:
Mary 1765 Aug. 5 (See baptisms—Mary Owens.)

Syfo.:
George 1777 Oct. 6 "rode 26 miles to York, Mr. Kennedy's— saw Mr. Annan, Dobin, George Syfo—." (From Hugh Ross's.)

Talbot:
Sister 1782 Aug. 26 "rode 14 miles James Pat., R. K., Mr. S. sis. Talbot 22 Mr. Pat." (From Alexander McCulloch.)

Taylor:
Mr. 1766 May 13 "rode 30 miles Old Fort Housac mount Deerf. R. Mr. Taylors." (From Coliver's Bridge.)

Thomson:
Al. 1752 Oct. 10 "x x rebuked Al. Thomson." (At Wm. Brown's.)

Tom:
Wm. 1783 July 2, 3 "rode 8 miles to Mr. Lind's, to Wm. Toms, etc." (From Wm. Brown's.)

Trawer:
Colonel 1774 Apr. 14 "Paid Col. Trawer's 150 lbs. in part to 447." (At Fulton's.)

Trexler:
    Jo. 1751 Oct. 28   "Rode 15 miles to a Du. Batch at McCunzie
        miler. Good health praise . . . Jo. Trexler." (From Mich.
        Clyde's.)
Uncan:
    James 1756 Feb. 13   "Rode 10 miles to Joseph Kers, James uncan
        —plush Broc—vexed." (From Jo Duncan's.)
Walace:
    Ben 1770 Aug. 2, 3   "rode 8 miles to Wiggin's, Sus; Ben Wal-
        ace's, W. Brown's."
    "   1774 Oct. 21   "rode and walked 35 miles to T. Ken. Ben
        Walaces and home, family well." (From Potts Grove and Dr.
        Valneer's.)
Walker:
    Hanna 1759 June 6   "rode and walked 8 miles to Hanna Walker's,
        T. and home." (From home.)
    Widow 1773 Dec. 16   "rode 6 miles to Widow Walker's, etc."
        (From McClung's, etc.)
Warnock:
    J. 1762 Nov. 2, 3   "Rode 28 miles; 4 to Robert Lochheads, J.
        Warnock's, and J. McCleary." (From home.)
    "   1777 Feb. 27, 28   "rode 18 miles J. Warn., Walkers, Glens,
        Mr. Sm., home."
White:
    Math. 1753 June 2   "Rode 5 mi. to Math. Whites and Dan
        McClellan's good health praise to God." (From John Robie-
        son's.)
Wig,:
    Edw. 1756 Jan. 22   "Rode 30 miles to Phin. Whiteside, Edw.
        wig. 17 s. and Humphrey Fulerton's."
Wilson:
    Matthew 1775 Aug. 8   "rode 40 miles with Mr. Lind to Matthew
        Wilson's tired but well." (From Alexander Brown's.)
Winters:
    Joseph 1789 Apr. 28, 29, 30   "rode 16 miles R. P., W. McM.,
        Jos. Winters, etc." (From Woods'.)
Wiser; Woeser:
    Conrad 1752 Oct. 4   "Rode 34 miles over Maiden C. by Stairs,
        Con. Wisers, Reeits Mills, etc."
    "   1754 July 2   "Rode 40 miles—25 Reading Town, 15 Con.
        Wiser, with Lynford ——."
    "   1753 July 6   "Rode 50 mi. to Tavern at Conrad Woesers no
        good rest cards played." (From McCunzie Mill.)
Wolfe:
    —— 1754 Sept. 28   "Rode 8 miles to Jo. Walker's—U's Wolfe
        and McM. angry —."

Woods:
  John   1776 Oct. 23, 24, 25 "rode 23 miles to John Woods's,
    H. F's, home." (From Lancaster.)
  Mr.   1786 Sept. 9   "rode 4 miles to John Wood's and G. Ch. (or
    Cl.) aguish, Sam McCulloch, sick."
Work:
  John   1772 Apr. 28   "rode 5 miles to John Works Dav. Humph.
    J. Da." (Then rode 8 miles to David Mitchel's.)
Wright:
  A.   1754 Nov. 5, 6   "Wrote letters to A. Wright and Hall."
Wylie:
  Als.   1757 Feb. 22   "Rode 27 miles to Als. Wylies etc. and to A.
    Burns; all well." (Then rode 2 miles to and from J. Wood's.)
Youland:
  (See Sturgeon.)